Library of New Testament Studies

429

Formerly the Journal for the Study of the New Testament Supplement series

Editor
Chris Keith

Editorial Board
Dale C. Allison, Lynn H. Cohick, R. Alan Culpepper,
Craig A. Evans, Jennifer Eyl, Robert Fowler, Simon J. Gathercole,
Juan Hernández Jr., John S. Kloppenborg, Michael Labahn,
Matthew V. Novenson, Love L. Sechrest, Robert Wall,
Catrin H. Williams, Brittany E. Wilson

Paul's Use of the Old Testament in Romans 9:19-24

An Intertextual and Theological Exegesis

Brian J. Abasciano

LONDON • NEW YORK • OXFORD • NEW DELHI • SYDNEY

T&T CLARK
Bloomsbury Publishing Plc
50 Bedford Square, London, WC1B 3DP, UK
1385 Broadway, New York, NY 10018, USA
29 Earlsfort Terrace, Dublin 2, Ireland

BLOOMSBURY, T&T CLARK and the T&T Clark logo are
trademarks of Bloomsbury Publishing Plc

First published in Great Britain 2022
Paperback edition published 2024

Copyright © Brian J. Abasciano, 2022

Brian J. Abasciano has asserted his right under the Copyright, Designs and
Patents Act, 1988, to be identified as Author of this work.

For legal purposes the Acknowledgments on pp. ix–x constitute an
extension of this copyright page.

All rights reserved. No part of this publication may be reproduced or transmitted in any
form or by any means, electronic or mechanical, including photocopying, recording, or any
information storage or retrieval system, without prior permission
in writing from the publishers.

Bloomsbury Publishing Plc does not have any control over, or responsibility for, any
third-party websites referred to or in this book. All internet addresses given in this
book were correct at the time of going to press. The author and publisher regret any
inconvenience caused if addresses have changed or sites have ceased to exist, but
can accept no responsibility for any such changes.

A catalogue record for this book is available from the British Library.

Library of Congress Cataloging-in-Publication Data
Names: Abasciano, Brian J., author.
Title: Paul's use of the Old Testament in Romans 9.19-24 : an intertextual and theological
exegesis / by Brian J. Abasciano. Description: London ; New York :
T&T CLARK, 2022. | Series: Library of New Testament studies, 2513–8790 ; 429 |
Includes bibliographical references and index. |
Summary: "In this third volume Brian Abasciano continues
his acclaimed intertextual and exegetical reading of Paul's use of the
Old Testament in Romans 9"– Provided by publisher.
Identifiers: LCCN 2022009921 (print) | LCCN 2022009922 (ebook) |
ISBN 9780567536518 (hardback) | ISBN 9780567708021 (paperback) |
ISBN 9780567528322 (pdf) Subjects: LCSH: Bible.
Romans, IX, 19–24–Criticism, interpretation, etc. |
Bible. Old Testament–Relation to Romans. | Bible. Romans–Relation to the Old Testament.
Classification: LCC BS2665.52 .A2325 2022 (print) | LCC BS2665.52 (ebook) |
DDC 227/.106–dc23/eng/20220503
LC record available at https://lccn.loc.gov/2022009921
LC ebook record available at https://lccn.loc.gov/2022009922

ISBN: HB: 978-0-5675-3651-8
PB: 978-0-5677-0802-1
ePDF: 978-0-5675-2832-2

Series: Library of New Testament Studies, volume 429
ISSN 2513-8790

Typeset by Newgen KnowledgeWorks Pvt. Ltd., Chennai, India

To find out more about our authors and books visit www.bloomsbury.com
and sign up for our newsletters.

To Paul Ellingworth (1931–2018), Doctorvater
And to my precious children, Noah, Jacynth, Benaiah, and Hannah

Contents

Acknowledgments		ix
List of Abbreviations		xi
1	Introduction	1
2	The Potter and Clay Texts in Their Old Testament Contexts	23
3	Interpretive Traditions Relating to the Old Testament Potter and Clay Texts	51
4	Intertextual Exegesis of Romans 9:19-24	69
5	Conclusion	171
Bibliography		191
Index of References		203
Index of Modern Authors		215

Acknowledgments

I wish to thank the many people who have helped to make this book possible in one way or another. I am grateful to T&T Clark for accepting this work for publication, and to senior editor Dominic Mattos and assistant editor Sarah Blake for their great patience in waiting for me to submit the manuscript, which I am submitting years past the original due date. My second volume was published about ten years ago. The idea was that I would write this volume over the next few years and that it would cover the rest of Romans 9, treating Rom. 9:19-33. But with pastoring full time, teaching seminary part time, and a bustling family, my life proved too busy to finish the book in a timely manner, and here I and the book are after multiple due dates passed. The material also proved too rich for me to cover all of Rom. 9:19-33. And so I am thankful to Dominic for his understanding and flexibility with the scope of the work. I am also grateful to those who have read portions of the manuscript and provided helpful comments: Paul Ellingworth, B. J. Oropeza, Chad Thornhill, A. Philip Brown II, Michael Brown, Ron Fay, Paul Eddy, Luke Gowdy, Ben Henshaw, and David Pallman. As it is standard to mention, I alone am responsible for any defects in the content of the monograph. I would also like to thank some of the librarians that have been helpful to me from Andover-Harvard Theological Library: Laura Whitney, Michelle Gauthier, and Ryan Miniot.

Many of the acknowledgments from my first two books remain the same all these years later. I continue to experience God's blessing in the privilege of pastoring at Faith Community Church (FCC) in Hampton, New Hampshire, which has remained a wonderful situation in which to research and write while also providing for my family, serving my Lord, and fulfilling his call on my life. I thank and praise God for our church family, which has loved and cared for us in so many ways and is the type of godly community the New Testament calls the Church to be. Their prayers for us are precious in the sight of God and of us, and to them we owe a continuing debt. Indeed, the many prayers that have gone up before the throne of God for this book from members of FCC are partly responsible for its completion and any articulation of truth its pages may hold.

This book is dedicated to my main doctoral supervisor, the late Paul Ellingworth, a humble, erudite, devout Christian scholar and churchman. He was always willing to read over my work and give me feedback after his supervisory duties toward me ended, and I was amazed at how responsive he was to my requests. This book is also dedicated to my children, Noah, Jacynth, Benaiah, and Hannah. I am proud of them and tremendously thankful for them. They are invaluable gifts. My first book was dedicated to my wife, Valerie. I remain overflowing with thankfulness for her, who is, as I often say, the best woman in the world. Her constant friendship, help, and support are invaluable gifts. I thank and praise God for my family. It is a wonderful, enormous blessing to which words cannot do justice. I wish to thank them for their patience and sacrifice for any time we may have missed as a family because of my work on this book.

Above all, I remain thankful to and for God, who is the source of every good and perfect gift (Jas 1:17), has given me his Holy Spirit (Tit. 3:5-6), and blessed me with every spiritual blessing in Christ (Eph. 1:3), "who loved me and gave himself for me" (Gal. 2:20) and in comparison to whom everything is a loss (Phil. 3:8). To the triune God "be the glory forever! Amen" (Rom. 11:36).

Scripture quotations marked ESV are from The Holy Bible, English Standard Version®, Copyright © 2001, by Crossway Bibles, a publishing ministry of Good News Publishers. Used by permission. All rights reserved.

Scripture quotations marked NRSV are from the New Revised Standard Version Bible. Copyright © 1989, Division of Christian Education of the National Council of the Churches of Christ in the United States of America. Used by permission. All rights reserved.

Quotations marked NETS are taken from A New English Translation of the Septuagint, © 2007 by the International Organization for Septuagint and Cognate Studies, Inc. Used by permission of Oxford University Press. All rights reserved.

Scripture quotations marked NASB are from the New American Standard Bible®, Copyright © 1960, 1962, 1963, 1968, 1971, 1972, 1973, 1975, 1977, 1995, The Lockman Foundation. Used by permission. www.lockman.org.

Abbreviations

AB	Anchor Bible
ACCSNT	Ancient Christian Commentary on Scripture: New Testament
ALGNT	T. Friberg, B. Friberg, and N. F. Miller, *Analytical Lexicon to the Greek New Testament* (BGNTL; Grand Rapids, MI: Baker, 2000, BibleWorks, v. 8)
AnBib	Analecta Biblica
ANRW	Aufstieg und Niedergang der römischen Welt
ANTC	Abingdon New Testament Commentaries
AOTC	Apollos Old Testament Commentary
ATJ	*Ashland Theological Journal*
BBC	Broadman Bible Commentary
BCOTWP	Baker Commentary on the Old Testament Wisdom and Psalms
BDAG	W. Bauer, F. W. Danker, W. F. Arndt, and F. W. Gingrich, *A Greek–English Lexicon of the New Testament and Other Early Christian Literature*, 3rd ed. (Chicago: University of Chicago Press, 2000)
BDB	F. Brown, S. R. Driver, and C. A. Briggs, *A Hebrew and English Lexicon of the Old Testament* (Oxford: Clarendon, 1907)
BDF	F. Blass, A. Debrunner, and R. W. Funk, *A Greek Grammar of the New Testament and Other Early Christian Literature* (Cambridge: Cambridge University Press, 1961)
BECNT	Baker Exegetical Commentary on the New Testament
BGNTL	Baker's Greek New Testament Library
BHT	Beiträge zur historischen Theologie
Bib	*Biblica*
BIS	Biblical Interpretation Series
Bsac	*Bibliotheca Sacra*
BST	The Bible Speaks Today
BTB	*Biblical Theology Bulletin: Journal of Bible and Culture*
CBCNEB	Cambridge Bible Commentary on the New English Bible
CBOT	Coniectanea Biblica Old Testament Series
CBQ	*Catholic Biblical Quarterly*
CCC	Crossway Classic Commentaries
CHALOT	W. L. Holladay (ed.), *A Concise Hebrew and Aramaic Lexicon of the Old Testament*, 12th corrected impression (Leiden: Brill, 1988)
ConBNT	Coniectanea Biblica New Testament Series
ConNT	*Coniectanea neotestamentica*
CPNIVC	College Press NIV Commentary
DNTB	C. A. Evans and S. E. Porter (eds.), *Dictionary of New Testament Background* (Downers Grove, IL: IVP, 2000)

DOTP	M. J. Boda and J. G. McConville (eds.), *Dictionary of the Old Testament Prophets* (Downers Grove, IL: IVP, 2012)
DOTWPW	T. Longman III and P. Enns (eds.), *Dictionary of the Old Testament: Wisdom, Poetry, and Writings* (Downers Grove, IL: IVP, 2008)
ECC	Eerdmans Critical Commentary
EDNT	H. Balz and G. Schneider (eds.), *Exegetical Dictionary of the New Testament* (3 vols.; Grand Rapids, MI: Eerdmans, 1992)
EQ	*Evangelical Quarterly*
ErFor	Erträge der Forschung
ETR	*Etudes théologiques et religieuses*
EvBC	Everyman's Bible Commentary
Expos	*Expositor*
FOTL	The Forms of the Old Testament Literature
FRLANT	Forschungen zur Religion und Literatur des Alten und Neuen Testaments
FWB	Fundamental Wesleyan Publishers
GKC	E. Kautzsch (ed.), *Gesenius' Hebrew Grammar* (rev. and trans. A. E. Cowley; Oxford: Clarendon, 1910)
HALOT	L. Koehler and W. Baumgartner et al. (eds.), *The Hebrew and Aramaic Lexicon of the Old Testament Study Edition* (ed. and trans. M. E. J. Richardson; 2 vols.; Leiden: Brill, 2001)
HAR	*Hebrew Annual Review*
HBD	T. C. Butler (ed.), *Holman Bible Dictionary* (Nashville, TN: Broadman & Holman, 1991), http://www.studylight.org/dic/hbd/
HCOT	Historical Commentary on the Old Testament
HCSB	Holman Christian Standard Bible
HTKNT	Herders theologischer Kommentar zum Neuen Testament
IBC	Interpretation: A Bible Commentary for Teaching and Preaching
IBS	*Irish Biblical Studies*
ICC	International Critical Commentary
ISBL	Indiana Studies in Biblical Literature
IVP	InterVarsity Press
IVPNYC	InterVarsity Press New Testament Commentary Series
JETS	*Journal of the Evangelical Theological Society*
JSJSup	*Journal for the Study of Judaism*, Supplement Series
JSNTSup	*Journal for the Study of the New Testament*, Supplement Series
JSOT	*Journal for the Study of the Old Testament*
JTS	*Journal of Theological Studies*
LN	J. E. Louw and E. A. Nida, *Greek–English Lexicon of the New Testament: Based on Semantic Domains*, 2nd ed. (2 vols.; New York: United Bible Societies, 1989, BibleWorks, v.8)
LNTS	Library of New Testament Studies
LSJ	H. G. Liddell, R. Scott, and H. S. Jones, *Greek–English Lexicon*, 9th ed. (Oxford: Clarendon, 1968)
NAC	The New American Commentary

NASB	New American Standard Bible
NBBC	New Beacon Bible Commentary
NCBC	New Century Bible Commentary
NCBCOT	New Collegeville Bible Commentary on the Old Testament
NCCS	New Covenant Commentary Series
Neot	*Neotestamentica*
NET	New English Translation
NETS	A New English Translation of the Septuagint
NIB	New Interpreter's Bible
NIBCNT	New International Biblical Commentary on the New Testament
NIBCOT	New International Biblical Commentary on the Old Testament
NICNT	New International Commentary on the New Testament
NICOT	New International Commentary on the Old Testament
NIDNTT	C. Brown (ed.), *The New International Dictionary of New Testament Theology* (4 vols.; Grand Rapids, MI: Zondervan, 1975–8)
NIDNTTE	M. Silva (ed.), *New International Dictionary of New Testament Theology and Exegesis* (5 vols.; Grand Rapids, MI: Zondervan, 2014)
NIV	New International Version
NovT	*Novum Testamentum*
NovTSup	*Novum Testamentum*, Supplements
NRSV	New Revised Standard Version Bible
NRT	*La nouvelle revue théologique*
NTS	*New Testament Studies*
OTL	Old Testament Library
OTP	J. H. Charlesworth (ed.), *The Old Testament Pseudepigrapha* (2 vols.; New York: Doubleday, 1983–5)
OUP	Oxford University Press
PBTM	Paternoster Biblical and Theological Monographs
PNTC	Pillar New Testament Commentary
RBL	*Review of Biblical Literature*
SAP	Sheffield Academic Press
SB	*Subsidia Biblica*
SBET	*Scottish Bulletin of Evangelical Theology*
SBG	Studies in Biblical Greek
SBL	Society of Biblical Literature
SBLDS	Society of Biblical Literature Dissertation Series
SBLSymS	Society of Biblical Literature Symposium Series
SBT	The Bible Speaks Today
SCDS	Studies in Christian Doctrine and Scripture
SHBC	Smyth & Helwys Bible Commentary
SSBL	Studies in Scripture and Biblical Theology
SSEJC	Studies in Scripture in Early Judaism and Christianity
STDJ	Studies on the Texts of the Desert of Judah
STR	*Southeastern Theological Review*
SVTP	*Studia in Veteris Testamenti Pseudepigrapha*

TAB	The Aramaic Bible
TDNT	G. Kittel and G. Friedrich (eds.), *Theological Dictionary of the New Testament* (trans. G. W. Bromiley; 10 vols.; Grand Rapids, MI: Eerdmans, 1964–76)
TDOT	G. J. Botterweck and H. Ringgren (eds.), *Theological Dictionary of the Old Testament* (Grand Rapids, MI: Eerdmans, 1974–)
THKNT	Theologischer Handkommentar zum Neuen Testament
TOTC	Tyndale New Testament Commentaries
TPI	Trinity Press International
TPINTC	Trinity Press International New Testament Commentaries
TTCS	Teach the Text Commentary Series
TTJ	*Trinity Theological Journal*
TWOT	R. L. Harris, G. L. Archer Jr, and B. K. Waltke (eds.), *Theological Wordbook of the Old Testament* (2 vols.; Chicago: Moody, 1980)
TynBul	*Tyndale Bulletin*
UBSHS	United Bible Societies Handbook Series
VT	*Vetus Testamentum*
WBC	Word Biblical Commentary
WBCo	Westminster Bible Companion
WPH	Wesleyan Publishing House
WUNT	Wissenschaftliche Untersuchungen zum Neuen Testament
ZAW	*Zeitschrift für die alttestamentliche Wissenschaft*
ZECNT	Zondervan Exegetical Commentary on the New Testament

1

Introduction

This investigation continues the intertextual exegesis of Romans 9 begun in my previous volumes on the chapter,[1] picking up where the previous study left off. The first volume covered the first nine verses of Romans 9 (9:1-9) and the second volume the next nine (9:10-18). The present volume covers the next six verses (9:19-24). The reasons, goals, and approach of this investigation are covered in the introduction to the first volume, so there is no need to address those matters here; the reader should consult that discussion for insight into those matters in the present investigation.

This investigation was originally meant to extend to the end of Romans 9, but the material proved too rich. Ideally, I would like to finish treating the rest of the chapter in one more volume. However, I currently have no plans to do so. Romans 9 is notorious for its controversial theological subject matter, but happily, this volume brings us through the thick of that. Indeed, it covers what is probably the most intense, theologically controversial section of the chapter. When John Piper sought to address the most theologically pressing part of Romans 9 in his well-known monograph *The Justification of God*, he only treated through v. 23.[2] I can now boast that I have done him one better in my exegesis of the chapter by getting through v. 24! Before previewing the investigation, I will give consideration to some criticisms of my previous volumes on Romans 9.

1.1. Replying to Some Criticisms of My Previous Volumes on Romans 9

1.1.a. Steve Moyise's Review of Volume 2 (on Rom. 9:10-18)

In his review of my monograph on Rom. 9:10-18, Steve Moyise offers what I regard to be unfair criticism based on misrepresentation of what I actually say and argue in the

---

[1] B. J. Abasciano, *Paul's Use of the Old Testament in Romans 9.1-9: An Intertextual and Theological Exegesis* (JSNTSup/LNTS, 301; London: T&T Clark, 2005); *Paul's Use of the Old Testament in Romans 9.10-18: An Intertextual and Theological Exegesis* (JSNTSup/LNTS, 317; London: T&T Clark, 2011).
[2] J. Piper, *The Justification of God: An Exegetical and Theological Study of Romans 9:1-23*, 2nd ed. (Grand Rapids, MI: Baker, 1993).

book.³ I will not address all of the criticisms Moyise leveled at the book but will try to remain brief and take up those that are based on misrepresentation rather than simple difference of perspective or approach.

In Moyise's first main criticism, he gives the impression that I argue that Paul largely derived his view that ethnic Israel's hardening is temporary from what is said about Edom and Pharaoh, and that everything can be deduced from the local context of Paul's Old Testament quotations. But that is simply false. My contention is far more nuanced, arguing that one of those texts contributed to Paul's view of the hardening as temporary (not that it is the main text contributing to Paul's conception or even one of the main texts) and that the other gives some subtle support for the idea in our assessment of Paul's intention. With regard to the former, I wrote, "It would appear that Mal. 1.2-3 provides *some* of the scriptural basis for Paul's conviction that God's judgment of unbelieving ethnic Israel would bring Gentiles to faith and that his merciful treatment of the Gentiles would bring Jews to faith, summed up in 11:30-31."⁴ With regard to the Pharaoh text, I said that it "gives *some support* to the reversibility of the hardening of 9.18,"⁵ and then later, on the same page, I specify the nature of this support as hinting and subtle. Nowhere do I say that everything can be deduced about Paul's argument from the local context of his Old Testament quotations.

However, if Paul was drawing his arguments from the Old Testament texts, as he seems to claim and I believe I have shown, then we should expect a great deal of his argumentation to be elucidated by examination of the Old Testament texts he quotes or alludes to. Moreover, I do examine the original contexts of Paul's Old Testament quotations and compare them to his argument. If that yields many striking correspondences, then it behooves us to acknowledge that. Indeed, we should follow the evidence wherever it leads. Moyise himself concedes that I "provide a significant challenge to those who think that Paul had little interest in the original context of his quotations."⁶

Moyise's other major criticism is that I assume Paul's readers would be able to follow Paul's exegetical moves. But he again misrepresents what I actually say (unintentionally, I am sure). Moyise claims that I argue that Paul's readers would take ἐξήγειρά σε in the sense of "I have spared you" because they would know that the Hebrew uses the hiphil of עמד (to stand), which was rendered by the LXX with διετηρήθης (you were spared). I neither say nor imply any such thing. I do point out that both the Hebrew and the LXX (i.e., the original context of Paul's quotation in both language versions) carry the sense of "I have spared you" and that this accords with Paul's only other usage of the verb ἐξεγείρω as well as with his dominant usage of the cognate verb ἐγείρω. These are standard types of exegetical observations for scholarly biblical literature, and it is surprising if Moyise would find it objectionable for them to be cited as support for construing Paul's intention. But even if he does, they do not make the sort of claim that Moyise claims I make. He has simply misrepresented me here.

---

³ S. Moyise, "Review of B.J. Abasciano, *Paul's Use of the Old Testament in Romans 9:10-18: An Intertextual and Theological Exegesis*," *RBL* (April 2012), https://www.sblcentral.org/home/bookDetails/8334.
⁴ Abasciano, *Romans 9:10-18*, 72-3; emphasis added.
⁵ Ibid., 212; emphasis added.
⁶ Moyise, "Review."

Moyise also misrepresents me when he claims that I "would not countenance the possibility that Paul changed" the text of an Old Testament quotation "for rhetorical reasons."[7] I think that Paul may well have changed the text of a biblical quotation in order to most effectively communicate his point. Indeed, I think that he did so in his quotation of Ps. 68:18 in Eph. 4:8, for example.[8] But I do not think that Paul would have intentionally misrepresented what he regarded as the word of God. It was acceptable literary practice in antiquity to give interpretive quotations,[9] and it appears that Paul did sometimes alter the text of his quotations in such a way as to best fit into his rhetoric while accurately representing what he thought to be the meaning of the Old Testament text.

I believe that Moyise and I have sharp differences in our approaches to Paul's use of the Old Testament, differences that reflect major debates in the field of Old Testament in the New studies. These differences come out in his review, and I have intentionally not addressed them much here because that is beyond the scope of the present volume; I have addressed such well-worn issues in my first volume on Romans 9 (which Moyise reviewed), especially in the introduction (in the methodology section) and in the concluding chapter, and elsewhere,[10] and I pointed to responses to Moyise's approach and his criticisms of my type of approach.[11] However, Moyise's two main criticisms of my book are grounded in misrepresentation of what I actually say and argue. That calls for correction. We should represent others' views rightly when we criticize them.

Excursus 1.1: Response to Christopher Stanley on Paul's Use of Ps. 115:1 LXX (116:10, Heb./Eng.) in 2 Cor. 4:13

Christopher Stanley has replied very briefly to my criticism of his appeal to Paul's use of Ps. 115:1 LXX (116:10, Heb./Eng.) in 2 Cor. 4:13 as a prime example of Paul quoting Scripture out of context.[12] Stanley contended that "what the psalmist 'spoke' was not 'good news' as in Paul's case but rather a word for which he was 'humbled' by God."[13]

---

[7] Ibid.
[8] Cf. F. S. Thielman, "Ephesians," in G. K. Beale and D. A. Carson (eds.), *Commentary on the New Testament Use of the Old Testament* (Grand Rapids, MI: Baker Academic, 2007), 813–33 (819–26).
[9] See C. D. Stanley, "The Social Environment of 'Free' Biblical Quotations in the New Testament," in C. A. Evans and J. A. Sanders (eds.), *Early Christian Interpretation of the Scriptures of Israel: Investigations and Proposals* (JSNTSup, 148; SSEJC, 5; Sheffield: SAP, 1997), 18–27.
[10] See the corresponding sections of B. J. Abasciano, "Paul's Use of the Old Testament in Romans 9:1-9: An Intertextual and Theological Exegesis" (PhD thesis; University of Aberdeen, 2004), upon which my first volume on Romans 9 is based, for a more extensive treatment of these issues than contained in the published version. See also my article "Diamonds in the Rough: A Reply to Christopher Stanley Concerning the Reader Competency of Paul's Original Audiences," *NovT* 49 (2007), 153–83; see further Excursus 1.1.
[11] See Abasciano, *Romans 9.1-9*, 21 n. 82, 233 n. 41; G. K. Beale, "Questions of Authorial Intent, Epistemology, and Presuppositions and Their Bearing on the Study of the Old Testament in the New: A Rejoinder to Steve Moyise," *IBS* 21 (November 1999), 151–80 (esp. 167–72), and my comments in support of Beale in Abasciano, *Romans 9:1-9*, 372 n. 55.
[12] C. D. Stanley, "Paul's 'Use' of Scripture: Why the Audience Matters," in S. E. Porter and C. D. Stanley (eds.), *As It Is Written: Studying Paul's Use of Scripture* (SBLSymS, 50; Atlanta, GA: SBL, 2008), 125–55 (147–8 n. 62). Cf. Abasciano, "Diamonds," 173–7.
[13] Stanley, "Audience," 147 n. 62.

But in response I argued in detail that the psalmist's words are actually "an expression of faith in God despite suffering and opposition contained in a psalm of thanksgiving which does indeed breathe a spirit of praise and joy."[14]

Stanley pushes back on two points. First, he points out that negative speech can appear in a psalm of thanksgiving. That is true. But I did not indicate that the statement merely appearing in a psalm of thanksgiving refutes Stanley's interpretation. As an expression of faith, the statement fits into the psalm's context of thanksgiving, praise, and joy. This leaves Stanley's second point as crucial.

Stanley claims that my "interpretation of ἐπίστευσα in v. 1 as an expression of faith disconnects the word from v. 2, where the psalmist summarizes his speech in the words, 'Every man is a liar.'"[15] But that is a severe non sequitur; the very opposite is true. My interpretation posits a direct connection between the word and v. 2. That connection is a ground for the psalmist's prayer, explicitly indicated by the inferential conjunction διό (therefore) in the LXX, the version Paul quotes (the nuance is a little different in the Hebrew but still involves a direct connection, indication that the psalmist's prayer was accompanied by an attitude of trust).

Stanley has not offered any substantial counter to my detailed treatment of the verse itself, which is more extensive than his; I would urge the reader to compare the two. Rather than rehearsing the details of my interpretation and its substantiation, I will point out a simple fact that avoids even the question of whose interpretation of the psalm is more likely (though it also happens to support my exegesis as much more likely than Stanley's) but is definitive in negating Stanley's appeal to it as an obvious example of Paul taking Scripture out of context: the vast majority of modern scholarly commentators agree with my interpretation of the psalm or something similar to it; they see ἐπίστευσα in v. 1 (LXX) as an expression of faith.[16] But how can Paul's interpretation of the psalm be obviously out of context if even a substantial minority, let alone the vast majority(!), of modern Old Testament scholars who have commented on the passage take a similar view? This is fatal to Stanley's view of Paul's use of Scripture as non-contextual because his case for it relies on Paul's interpretation being totally

---

[14] Abasciano, "Diamonds," 174.
[15] Stanley, "Audience," 148 n. 62.
[16] In Abasciano, "Diamonds," 174 n. 91, I already cited L. C. Allen, *Psalms 101-150* (WBC 21; Waco, TX: Word Books, 1983), 112, 115; D. Kidner, *Psalms 73-150: A Commentary on Books III-V of the Psalms* (TOTC 14b; London: IVP, 1975), 409-10. I will add a few more for good measure here: see, e.g., J. Goldingay, *Volume 3, Psalms 90-150* (BCOTWP; Grand Rapids, MI: Baker Academic, 2008), 343-4; A. Weiser, *The Psalms: A Commentary* (trans. H. Hartwell; OTL; Philadelphia, PA: Westminster, 1962), 720; N. deClaissé-Walford, R. A. Jacobson, and B. L. Tanner, *The Book of Psalms* (NICOT; Grand Rapids, MI: Eerdmans, 2014), 658-9; T. Longman III, *Psalms: An Introduction and Commentary* (TOTC, 15-16; Downers Grove, IL: IVP Academic, 2014), 396. It seems like the main and perhaps the only exceptions are commentators who construe the Hebrew unusually; see, e.g., John Eaton, *The Psalms: A Historical and Spiritual Commentary with an Introduction and New Translation* (New York: Continuum, 2005), 400 (A. A. Anderson, *The Book of Psalms, Volume 2* [NCBC; London: Marshall, Morgan, and Scott, 1972], 793, mentions G. R. Driver as suggesting such an alternative view of the Hebrew, though Anderson does not indicate agreement with Driver). But for multiple reasons, the possibility of an alternative construal of the Hebrew on the part of a few modern scholars does not help Stanley's position. Paul quoted from the LXX, and the alternative way of reading the Hebrew is not possible in the Greek. Moreover, Stanley regards the issue to be the same in both Greek and Hebrew. See further below.

implausible. Ironically, in the judgment of modern Old Testament scholarship, Paul is a far more reliable interpreter than Stanley in this instance. Given that Stanley presents this as a prime example of Paul quoting Scripture out of context, it undermines his broader approach of considering attention to the original contexts of Paul's allusions to be unnecessary normally.

1.1.b. Thomas Schreiner's Review of Volume 2 (on Rom. 9:10-18)

In Thomas Schreiner's review of my monograph on Rom. 9:10-18, against my position on calling as effectual naming he asserts that "calling in Paul isn't merely an effectual naming based on faith, but is an effective action that creates faith (Rom 8:30). Faith is a consequence of calling, not a presupposition for it (cf. 1 Cor 1:23–31)."[17] But these are mere assertions that beg the question. The passages he cites are not particularly supportive of his assertions of a call that creates faith over against a call that is based on faith. These passages work just as well, and even better, with an effectual naming by faith. Romans 8:30 is best understood as meaning, "And those whom he predestined he also named as his own, and those whom he named as his own he also justified, and those whom he justified he also glorified" (adapting the ESV). 1 Cor. 1:26a is best understood as meaning, "For consider your naming as God's own children, brothers" (adapting the ESV), obviously referring to the Corinthians' conversion.

The strength of the doctrine of effectual calling, the view Schreiner espouses, has always been the instances when calling seems to clearly have reference to those who have already become Christians. Hence the idea of a call that is "effectual." But an effectual naming fits such instances just as well. In fact, it fits them better because it does not rely on assuming an extra, unstated element—positive response to the call— as part of the meaning of the term. One might argue that it does assume something extra, namely, faith. But the term itself does not. It refers to the act of naming people as God's children, which, in effect, makes them God's children. Pauline (and indeed, New Testament) theology is what informs us that such a calling can only come through faith, for in Paul's view, people become God's children through faith. The fact that "the called" in Paul's epistles = "believers" goes along much better with the fact that "God's children" and "those who belong to God" = believers than does the idea that "the summoned/invited ones" = believers. There is more to say, but I will be interacting further with Schreiner on Paul's conception of calling in my treatment of Rom. 9:24 in this investigation and so will move on to other aspects of his review.

Schreiner's objection that "it seems unlikely that the Roman Christians would question God's justice/righteousness/fairness if Paul's argument in 9:10-13 is that God elects based on faith instead of works or ancestry"[18] is rather surprising. He seems to confuse who Romans was written to with what it was written about. It is very odd that he cites other sections of Romans in which Paul argues against the assumption of unbelieving Jews that their works could commend them to God, including later in

---

[17] T. R. Schreiner, "Review of Brian J. Abasciano. *Paul's Use of the Old Testament in Romans 9.10–18: An Intertextual and Theological Exegesis*," *Themelios* 38.3 (November 2013), 450–3 (452).
[18] Ibid.

Romans 9 in the conclusion of the chapter's argument(!), yet claim that Paul could not be so arguing elsewhere in Romans 9. Moreover, he himself, along with the majority of scholars, believes that in Romans 9 Paul is picking up and continuing the argument of verses that Schreiner concedes are surrounded by passages that argue against the assumption of unbelieving Jews that their works could commend them to God (Rom. 3:1-8 surrounded by 2:1-29 and 3:9-20). Relatedly, Romans 9–11 defends Paul's gospel of justification by faith against its most potent objection—that it is unfaithful to God's promises to Israel.

Regarding Rom. 9:16's reference to willing and running, Schreiner argues that it is a general reference to human will and effort rather than specifically relating to the Law.[19] But several scholars regard it as a reference to works, including John Piper, with whom Schreiner normally agrees regarding exegesis of Romans 9.[20] Piper points out that there is a substantial parallel to Rom. 9:11's reference to works.[21] And there is good evidence to think that Paul more specifically has the works of the Law in mind. I lay that case out in the book Schreiner reviewed and will not go over it again here.

Instead of reviewing the evidence for my view delineated in my monograph, I will ask, why should we accept Schreiner's position that Paul speaks generally of human will and effort? He does not seem to have much positive evidence for it but seems mainly to rely on the fact that Paul does not explicitly qualify his terms. But it is a fundamental principle of exegesis that meaning is derived from context and background, and so it will not do to insist on only a general meaning based on only what is said explicitly when there are contextual and background factors that suggest a more specific meaning. Let me also point out that whether Paul refers specifically to works of the Law, he does refer to works more than once in Romans 9, including in parallel to Rom. 9:16. And faith can never be works in Paul. But finally, as I point out in the book, even if Paul referred not to works generally or to works of the Law specifically but to any human will or effort of any sort, it does not conflict with my basic reading of the verse that God is the Lord and source of mercy, which he bestows as he sees fit, and that no one can coerce God's mercy.

For more than one reason, I find it ironic that Schreiner contends that I smuggle faith into Rom. 9:6-18.[22] In his commentary on Romans, he implies that Paul's doctrine of justification is in view in the section.[23] But Paul does not explicitly mention justification in the section. It clearly is in view, and we can tell that because of context (cf. my point about context and background in the immediately preceding paragraph). Moreover, if he admits that justification is in view in the section, then it makes little sense to

---

[19] Ibid.
[20] Piper, *Justification*, 151–3, though Piper is careful to say that this specific reference to willing and running as works does not limit Paul's reference to only willing and running with regard to the Law but includes all human willing and running of any sort, including faith. However, this gets Piper into the problematic notion of regarding faith as a type of work in Paul's thought, but Paul is very clear that faith is not a work or works; see Abasciano, *Romans 9.10-18*, 190–1 n. 153, for an explanation and critique of Piper's position.
[21] Piper, *Justification*, 153.
[22] Schreiner, "Review," 452.
[23] See T. R. Schreiner, *Romans*, 2nd ed. (BECNT, 6; Grand Rapids, MI: Baker, 2018), 473, 481, ProQuest Ebook Central.

deny that faith is also in view, since Paul's doctrine of justification is justification by faith! This is not even to mention the implication of faith in Rom. 9:8[24] and that the conclusion of Paul's argument in which he seems to draw up the thrust of what he argues in Romans 9 explicitly mentions faith and refers to justification (though not using the exact word; see 9:30-33 and Section 5.2 in Chapter 5 of this volume).

This statement in Schreiner's review is inaccurate: "Even though Rom 9:6-18 does not mention faith, Abasciano thinks faith is implicit in these verses since justification is clearly by faith in Paul."[25] My reason for thinking faith to be implicit in the passage is not because justification is by faith in Paul. That would be an obvious non sequitur. I think faith is implicit for the same types of reasons many scholars, including Schreiner, think justification is implicit. Now perhaps he neglected to point out that justification is implicit in the section and really meant to say that I think faith is implicit in these verses because justification is implicit, and justification is clearly by faith in Paul and in Romans. That would be a more adequate description. But it is worth noting that it is not as if faith is merely derivative of justification. The two are so intertwined that the same sorts of textual elements that imply justification also imply faith. However, it is also true that justification in Paul involves faith.

Schreiner claims that I do not distinguish between corporate election in the OT and corporate election in the NT.[26] But I do. There is obvious difference even on the face of it since election is now in Christ and tied up in the New Covenant. But I discussed the difference he mentions here in both my first and second volumes.[27] It is true that election did not necessarily entail salvation in the OT. But it was ideally meant to issue in salvation as a result of participation in the blessings of the covenant and its conditional promises. As I mention elsewhere,

> In the Old Covenant, the covenant promises were conditional in that they could only be possessed by faith while the covenant generally included all Israelites, including the unbelieving. (Nevertheless, members of the covenant who demonstrated persistent unbelief by violating the covenant law without repentance were to be cut off.) But in the New Covenant, all in the covenant truly possess the promises because all in the New Covenant have faith since it is entered into by faith and believers only continue in the covenant by faith; if they forsake faith in Christ then they are cut off from the covenant.[28]

I do not think my view of corporate and individual election suffers from ambiguity as Schreiner charges. In line with so much of the Old Testament that finds its fulfillment in the New, New Covenant election is the fulfillment of Old Covenant election, with Christ now fulfilling the role of the covenant head and mediator and his people sharing in his election.

---

[24] See Abasciano, *Romans 9.1-9*, 196-8.
[25] Schreiner, "Review," 451.
[26] Ibid., 452.
[27] Abasciano, *Romans 9.1-9*, 98-9 including n. 181 on p. 99; *Romans 9.10-18*, 62.
[28] B. J. Abasciano, "Clearing Up Misconceptions about Corporate Election," *ATJ* 41 (2009), 59-90 (83 n. 18); henceforth, "Misconceptions."

Schreiner asserts that I take Exod. 33:19 to teach that God shows mercy to those who repent of their sin.[29] But while I do think the broader passage does communicate this, that is not what I say Exod. 33:19 itself means. The verse simply states that God will have mercy on whomever he chooses without itself stating whether God will make his choice conditionally or unconditionally. In principle, the verse could go along with either conditional or unconditional election. However, the language used virtually never refers to unconditional choice. But many interpreters treat it as though it is the most natural meaning of the language when the very opposite is the case. And when we look to the Old Testament context of the statement, there are indeed positive indications that God's choice is conditional. So the standard usage of the language supports conditional election and the context supports it as well. There is simply nothing whatsoever in the Exodus context that would even hint that God's choice would be, contrary to the standard usage of the language employed, unconditional.

Schreiner's description of the Old Testament context of Exod. 33:19 seems inaccurate and like a reading of his theology into the text. I present a full exegesis of the Old Testament context in my first book on Romans 9, which covers Rom. 9:1-9. Exodus 33:19 in context is essentially a response to Moses's request that God restore covenantal election and its blessings to Israel. God goes on to do just that in the following verses, choosing Israel in covenantal election, not only some from Israel. It is true that Exod. 34:5-7 expresses how God acts within the covenant, as I pointed out in the book. But Exod. 34:5-7 contains a fuller expression of 33:19 and is a direct development of it. As I state in the book, "Exodus 34.6-7 explain how the principle of 33.19 gets expressed within the covenant,"[30] which confirms that the principle of 33:19 is expressed naturally with conditional action/choice/election.

Finally, concerning the hardening of Pharaoh, Schreiner merely asserts positions opposite to mine without substantiation.[31] I understand that he did not have the space to get into the complex discussion required to provide a compelling critique. But his comments on the topic provide no substance to respond to. So I will take the opportunity to point out that a recent major commentary on Exodus agrees with me that God's hardening of Pharaoh's heart in Exodus is not irresistible/deterministic.[32] It is not as if it should be obvious that the divine hardening of Pharaoh was deterministic or irreversible.

1.1.c. Erik Waaler's Review of Volume 2 (on Rom. 9:10-18)

Erik Waaler's review of my monograph on Rom. 9:10-18 gets off to a bad start by getting the title wrong,[33] and this raises concern about how the quality of the rest of the review will be. That concern is confirmed when Waaler, despite noting that the

---

[29] Schreiner, "Review," 451–2.
[30] Abasciano, *Romans 9.10-18*, 180.
[31] Schreiner, "Review," 453.
[32] See T. D. Alexander, *Exodus* (AOTC, 2; Downers Grove, IL: IVP, 2017), 163–71.
[33] E. Waaler, "Book Review: *Paul's Use of the Old Testament in Romans 9.10-18: An Intertextual and Theological Analysis*," *BTB* 44.2 (2014), 115–16 (115). The mistake only involves one word of the title, but it is more than a typo; he uses the word "analysis" in place of the word "exegesis."

methodology of the work is implicit and connects to a former volume, and eventually recommending reading my first volume before reading the second, curiously complains that "there is no reference to intertextual literature and no reflection on the complicated nature of the concept," citing merely marginal usage of Richard Hays's seminal work on the phenomenon in Paul as an example.[34] This is curious because I explicitly state in the introduction to the investigation that such matters are dealt with in the first volume and need not be repeated in the second, implicitly directing readers to the first volume for that sort of referencing and reflection and for the methodology of the study. Moreover, I draw on and interact with Hays's work significantly in the first volume. The concern over the reliability of Waaler's review is strengthened by his also getting the title of Richard Hays's landmark book wrong, calling it *Seminal Echoes of Scripture* when the actual title is *Echoes of Scripture in the Letters of Paul*.[35]

Waaler charges that my treatment of Old Testament background texts is often cursory.[36] This is an astonishing assertion. No other review of my work has ever suggested such a notion. Quite to the contrary, my treatment of Old Testament background texts has regularly been described with descriptors such as thorough,[37] careful,[38] detailed,[39] and the like. James Leonard writes that my work

> is indeed a commentary in the sense that it provides a worthy exegesis of a preeminently important Pauline text (with copious notes, bibliography, indices of references and authors cited). However, it exceeds all expectations of a typical commentary in that it gives a thorough exegesis of all the Old Testament allusions contained in the text, of which there are many; as such, it is also an Old Testament commentary, one that Old Testament exegetes will be remiss if they do not avail themselves of it.[40]

Background texts are usually just one verse or part of a verse, and my treatment of those texts is usually far more extensive than what is given in Old Testament commentaries. In exegeting those texts, I normally extend my detailed exegesis to the passage in which the text is found, and that treatment also is often on par with or more extensive than typical Old Testament commentaries. I will give just one example from each major background text treated in my book on Rom. 9:10-18.

---

[34] Ibid., 116.
[35] Ibid. But this is probably a complicated typo. My best guess is that Waaler meant to use a shortened title (*Echoes of Scripture*) and to describe Hays's book as "seminal," but accidentally included the adjective in the title. Typos are not normally to be held against a piece unless they are excessive; we all commit them. However, it is strange that Waaler got both the title of the book he reviewed and the title of the most influential book in the field wrong.
[36] Ibid.
[37] J. M. Leonard, "Review of *Paul's Use of the Old Testament in Romans 9.10-18: An Intertextual and Theological Exegesis*," *JETS* 55.4 (December 2012), 869–71 (869).
[38] C. G. Kruse, "Review of Brian J. Abasciano, *Paul's Use of the Old Testament in Romans 9.10-18: An Intertextual and Theological Exegesis*," *CBQ* 76 (2014), 341–2 (342).
[39] Moyise, "Review," speaking of my treatment of Exod. 9:16.
[40] Leonard, "Review," 869.

I devote over eleven pages to detailed exegesis of Gen. 25:23 with significant attention to its context of Gen. 25:19-34. Gordon Wenham's commentary gives less than a page to commentary on Gen. 25:23 and about the same space as me to exegesis of Gen. 25:19-34.[41] I devote six pages to detailed exegesis of Mal. 1:2-3a with significant attention to its context of 1:2-5. Ralph Smith's commentary gives a little more than three pages to the whole passage of 1:2-5.[42] I devote a little more than sixty-five pages to detailed exegesis of Exod. 9:16 (Moyise calls my exegesis of this Old Testament text "long and detailed")[43] with significant attention to its context of Exodus 1-15. John Durham gives less than a page to the exegesis of Exod. 9:16.[44]

Waaler makes a similar complaint about my treatment of interpretive traditions concerning the Old Testament background texts, that is, that they are cursory.[45] Admittedly, my treatment of interpretive traditions is much less extensive than my treatment of the Old Testament background texts. But reviewers have tended to find my treatments helpful even if they do not typically impact my NT exegesis much. While more extensive treatment of interpretive traditions would be more ideal, there is only so much space available, and one has to make judgments about the best use of space for the various aspects of research.

Waaler also points out that focus on the text of Paul gets lost in the Old Testament exegesis of the investigation.[46] But it is surprising that he sees this as a problem; it is quite intentional and part of proper methodology. Exegesis of the Old Testament text apart from Paul's rhetoric is important for seeking to understand the Old Testament text on its own terms and not have Paul's view of it or our pre-understanding of Paul's view of it skew our own. Ironically, that puts us in the best position to assess how Paul understood and used the text. It allows the exegete to be open to new understandings of how Paul might have understood the text.

Finally, Waaler characterizes my monograph on Rom. 9:10-18 as having an apologetic agenda.[47] This strikes me as unfair. The passage is immensely controversial

---

[41] See G. J. Wenham, *Genesis 16-50* (WBC, 2; Dallas, TX: Word, 1994), 175-6 and 170-81, respectively; and cf. Abasciano, *Romans 9.10-18*, 3-15.

[42] See R. L. Smith, *Micah-Malachi* (WBC, 32; Waco, TX: Word Books, 1984), 303-7; and cf. with Abasciano, *Romans 9.10-18*, 16-21. To be fair, some Old Testament commentaries give more attention to the material than me, though that is not surprising given their focus is on the Old Testament and my monograph has the New Testament text as its ultimate focus. P. A. Verhoef, *The Books of Haggai and Malachi* (NICOT; Grand Rapids, MI: Eerdmans, 1987), gives about seven pages to Mal. 1:2-3 (195-202) and a little more than fourteen pages to the whole passage of 1:2-5 (193-207); and A. E. Hill, *Malachi: A New Translation with Introduction and Commentary* (AB, 25D; New York: Doubleday, 1998), whose commentary is known for its extensiveness, gives about twelve pages to Mal. 1:2-3a (146-52 and 163-8) and twenty-five pages to the whole passage (145-70).

[43] Moyise, "Review."

[44] See J. I. Durham, *Exodus* (WBC, 3; Waco, TX: Word, 1987), 127-8; and cf. Abasciano, *Romans 9.10-18*, 75-140. Now, it is true that Durham's treatment of Exodus 1-15 is far more extensive than mine, about 213 pages. However, my treatment of the passage explicitly focused attention on the theme of the hardening of Pharaoh's heart in addition to assessing it as the broader context of Exod. 9:16. It would have been infeasible for me to provide a full-scale exegesis of Exodus 1-15; Durham's commentary on that section is almost as long as my entire book on Rom. 9:10-18. Nevertheless, 65 pages on Exodus 1-15 is more than cursory.

[45] Waaler, "Review," 116.

[46] Ibid.

[47] Ibid.

theologically, and my work is framed as a theological exegesis, by which I mean an exegesis that attends to theology and the theological implications of the exegesis and that contributes to theology. Every scholar who exegetes the text takes a position on the meaning of the text, and in Romans 9, this involves taking a position on the text's view of certain theological claims. To take just one example, Paul clearly speaks of election in Romans 9. That election is either conditional or unconditional, or perhaps one could argue that Paul had no opinion on the conditionality of election as he conceived of it in Romans 9. But taking any one of these positions and arguing for it as the meaning of the text with implications for Pauline theology should not be considered an apologetic agenda. That would make the characterization practically meaningless, for it would apply to almost every interpreter.

So perhaps having an apologetic agenda for Waaler means something like holding a particular view that one brings to the text and reads into the text and seeks to conform the text to and make the text support. But that is not what is going on in my work, and if it is what Waaler means, it is an uncharitable characterization, and one might wonder if it is actually born of an apologetic agenda on Waaler's part. My work on Romans 9 has been first and foremost a work of exegesis. I am willing to go where the text leads for my conclusions about its meaning. Even scholars who disagree sharply with my conclusions have regarded my work as legitimate exegesis. Schreiner, for example, says of my book on Rom. 9:10-18, "The argument is tightly constructed and well-done, consisting of careful exegesis of the text in conversation with other scholars,"[48] and he later expresses thankfulness for my "careful exegesis."[49]

Despite disagreeing with it, Schreiner also expresses thankfulness for the book as what he calls "a fine defense of the Arminian reading."[50] Perhaps this is the sort of thing Waaler is getting at. Theologically speaking, my work does support an Arminian reading of Romans 9. However, that is the result of exegesis, not what determines the exegesis. Schreiner's and a number of other scholars' exegesis supports a Calvinistic reading of Romans 9. But that does not necessarily mean that their scholarly work on Romans 9 has an apologetic agenda even when they strongly advocate their view of the text and argue strongly against alternative views of the text.

1.1.d. SungJin Kim's Analysis of My Understanding of Rom. 9:1-13

1.1.d.1. Rom. 9:7-9's Use of Gen. 18:10, 14; 21:12

In his article critiquing my interpretation of Rom. 9:1-13, SungJin Kim describes my view of Gen. 21:12b (quoted in Rom. 9:7b) as holding to the singular noun "seed" "as indicating 'the elect covenant people,' a corporate identity, and considers Isaac as representing the corporate head, through whom individuals would join the covenant community by connecting themselves to Isaac."[51] That is partly correct. But primarily

---

[48] Schreiner, "Review," 451.
[49] Ibid., 453.
[50] Ibid.
[51] S. Kim, "Does Romans 9 Teach Corporate Election? Revisiting Brian Abasciano's Understanding of Romans 9:6-13," 「한국개혁신학」 67 (2020), 237–66 (241).

in the OT itself, this would be physical offspring. They were naturally connected to Isaac. But critically, nonphysical descendants could be added into the covenant people by connecting themselves to Isaac/the covenant head. And ethnic Israelites could be cut off from the covenant people for unfaithfulness to the covenant.

Kim points out that "the singular noun 'seed' (σπέρμα / זֶרַע) can denote either a singular seed (e.g., Gen 4:25, 15:3) or a collective seed (e.g., Gen 13:16, 15:5), and its precise meaning is contextually determined."[52] This is true, but the context of Gen. 21:12 clearly indicates a collective sense. However, Kim goes on to argue for a singular sense in an entirely implausible reading of the passage.

Kim begins his argument for a singular sense to the word "seed" in Gen. 21:12 with the observation that "the text is generally considered obscure and difficult."[53] This is also true, but Wenham also points out that "the general sense is clear."[54] And that sense happens to match my corporate approach to the passage rather than Kim's individualistic approach. In Wenham's words, "The elect line of Abraham's descendants will run through Isaac."[55] This is a fatal point to Kim's argument, for he himself ends up arriving at this very interpretation, but astonishingly, he does not seem to realize it is a corporate interpretation.[56]

Kim affirms Rolf Rendtorff's conclusion that "the primary purpose [of Gen. 21:12b] is to emphasize the legitimate line of the posterity through Isaac in contrast to Ishmael."[57] Kim also specifically identifies the theme of Gen. 17:19-21 as "'the legitimate line' of the covenant" and as reappearing in Gen. 21:12-13.[58] It is surprising that he brings up Gen. 17:19-21 as a parallel since the one occurrence of "seed" there is clearly corporate ("I will establish my covenant with him [Isaac] for a lasting covenant for his seed after him"; Gen. 17:19). He further approvingly cites paraphrases of Gen. 21:12 featuring the notion of Abraham's line and approvingly cites Wenham's conclusion that I quoted above about the clear meaning of the text as about the elect line.[59] The problem for Kim here is that the notion of an ancestral line is inherently corporate. It refers to multiple descendants. Kim appeals to the position of some scholars that the emphasis of the verse is on Isaac as "God's choice of Isaac over Ishmael as the heir of the covenant,"[60] but if that is the emphasis (I am not making a judgment either way here), it is wholly intertwined with Isaac's line inheriting the covenant. That is indeed an expression of corporate election. Isaac's line was chosen because Isaac was. The choice of him as the covenant heir is the choice of his descendants as the covenant people.[61]

---

[52] Ibid., 241–2.
[53] Ibid., 242.
[54] Wenham, *Genesis*, 83.
[55] Ibid.
[56] Kim, "Revisiting," 244–5.
[57] Ibid., 244. In context, Rendtorff sought to separate the promise of posterity from the promise of the posterity being numerous; see R. Rendtorff, *The Problem of the Process of Transmission in the Pentateuch* (trans. J. J. Scullion; Sheffield, UK: JSOT, 1977), 79–80. But that is irrelevant to the point being made; his statement is still corporate in its interpretation of Gen. 21:12.
[58] Kim, "Revisiting," 244–5.
[59] Ibid. N.b. that Wenham speaks of the line of Abraham's descendants (plural).
[60] Ibid., 244.
[61] Of course, this could be, and was, narrowed to a subset of Isaac's line/descendants by the choice of a new covenant head (Jacob) descended from Isaac, but that is only a further occurrence of the phenomenon of corporate election.

Kim's chief argument for his interpretation is a novel and exceedingly unlikely construal of the grammar. He identifies what he sees as four grammatical possibilities.[62] One or the other of the first two options he identifies is favored by the vast majority of scholars.[63] In fact, the last two options have no support among scholars as far as I can tell except for Kim's own lone support for the third option he identifies—"regarding לְ as the subject of a passive verb and זֶרַע as a direct object (e.g., Gen 17:5, 35:10): 'for through Isaac, you shall be called/named a seed.'"[64] Kim cites no scholar who interprets Gen. 21:12 as he does, and there is good reason for that. It simply does not make much sense.

First, the two main examples Kim gives of the usage he supports (Gen. 17:5; 35:10) are not valid; surprisingly, neither of them contains the Hebrew word זֶרַע or, more critically, a relevant use of the Hebrew word לְ.[65] In support of his interpretation, he points out that לְ + קָרָא is often used to indicate naming.[66] He further asserts that the construction in Gen. 21:12b (יִקָּרֵא + לְ) is used thirteen times elsewhere, eleven of which have לְ as the subject of the niphal verb[67] and that which is named as the direct object with no instances of any of the other three options he identified as possibilities.[68] But of the eleven instances he cites as examples of his position, two are invalid.[69] Moreover, he mentions two instances of (יִקָּרֵא + לְ) (Isa. 14:20; 56:7) that differ from the usage he favors but claims that they do not support either of the options supported by most scholars (his options 1 and 2).[70] However, Isa. 14:7 is significant as an example of זֶרַע as the subject of יִקָּרֵא without being marked as the subject by לְ, and Isa. 56:7 turns out in fact to be an example of what should be Kim's option 2.

---

[62] Ibid., 242. The second option Kim identifies (זֶרַע as the subject and לְ as a direct object) is erroneous. First, לְ would not be the direct object but indicate/mark it, though this is understandable as a shorthand manner of reference. Second, and much more substantially, לְ would indicate the indirect object rather than the direct object in the second option Kim identifies. Perhaps he meant to say, "indirect object." This is not a small mistake, for it seems to keep Kim from seeing an example of the second option he identifies; see further below. Kim's example for option 4 also seems to be mistaken. Leviticus 1:4 does not seem to have לְ marking a direct object. Nor does it seem to have an indirect object parallel to what Kim suggests for זֶרַע in Gen. 21:12.
[63] Presuming the correction to Kim's second option mentioned in the previous note.
[64] Ibid.
[65] לְ does not appear in Gen. 17:5 at all, and it appears once in Gen. 35:10 to indicate who is spoken to: "God said to [לְ] him."
[66] Ibid., 243.
[67] Again, this is a faulty way to describe the grammar; see note 62 above.
[68] Ibid.
[69] Deuteronomy 22:6 involves a different verb (II קָרָא rather than I קָרָא) and does not involve לְ as marking the subject of a passive verb but uses it in combination with the word פָּנֶה to form the common preposition לִפְנֵי (before). In Deut. 3:13, לְ does not mark the subject but is used in a rhetorical absolute/*casus pendens* with the function of specification and a resumptive pronoun as the actual subject: "concerning all Bashan, it is called the land of Rephaim" (all translations of Scripture in this investigation are mine unless otherwise noted). English translations that do not reflect this do so for smoothness rather than carrying over the Hebrew grammar precisely or construe the grammar differently yet without taking לְ as marking the subject. On the *casus pendens* and the לְ of specification in Hebrew, see, respectively, R. J. Williams, *Hebrew Syntax: An Outline*, 2nd ed. (Toronto: University of Toronto, 1976), § 35 and § 273. While marking the subject of a passive verb is a form of the לְ of specification, it is a distinct form of it from the form of mere specification translated "with respect to, concerning."
[70] Kim, "Revisiting," 243.

I say "should be Kim's option 2" because, as detailed in note 62 above, Kim's option 2 is mistaken and should be "viewing זֶרַע as a subject and לְ as marking an indirect object," which would yield a translation of the last clause of Gen. 21:12 such as "for in Isaac, seed shall be named for you." Perhaps getting option 2 wrong is what kept Kim from recognizing that the last clause of Isa. 56:7 is an instance of it (though with a different word than זֶרַע): "for my house will be called [יִקָּרֵא] a house of prayer for [לְ] all the peoples." It is worth noting that Kim's options 1 and 2 for translation of Gen. 21:12, which seem to be the only options supported by scholars besides Kim, end up amounting to roughly the same thing. Option 1 involves a possessive, referring to "your [Abraham's] seed." Option 2 involves a לְ of advantage, "seed will be named for you [Abraham]."[71] In context, seed named for Abraham would amount to Abraham's seed/offspring.

Perhaps the biggest problem with Kim's suggestion for construing the grammar of Gen. 21:12 is that it is practically nonsensical, which is why no one seems to have suggested it before him and scholars have taken the grammar more in line with what we see in Isa. 14:20 and 56:7. While Kim has shown that לְ typically marks the subject when used with יִקָּרֵא, he has not shown that it must or always does, and his interpretation has Abraham being told that he, Abraham, will be called/named a seed through Isaac. Abraham being named a seed does not make sense. Kim seems to try to make sense of it by arguing that the text focuses on the promised line of the covenant (we have already seen that this actually supports a corporate interpretation) and that its point is the "legitimacy of Isaac over Ishmael as a covenant heir."[72] All of this is accomplished as much if not more by the consensus construal of the grammar.[73] But it is hard to see how *Abraham* being a seed through Isaac conveys any of this clearly or reasonably.

The best attempt at bringing some coherence to Kim's approach is his quotation of John Skinner's paraphrase, "In the line of Isaac shall thy name be perpetuated."[74] But this still does not make sense of Kim's translation. First, it is still corporately oriented in speaking of the line of Isaac. And second, Abraham being called a seed in or through Isaac does not convey his name being perpetuated in the line of Isaac (it conveys he is a seed in the line of Isaac, which is incoherent). But the consensus construal does. For Abraham's offspring being named in or through Isaac indicates the continuation of Abraham's line through Isaac, which can be thought of as Abraham's name continuing on. Descendants have traditionally been thought of as continuing the name of the family line.

Another point that must be taken into consideration is that Paul quoted the LXX, which makes it clear that "seed" (σπέρμα in Gen. 21:12 LXX/Rom. 9:7) is the subject and "you" (σοι in Gen. 21:12 LXX/Rom. 9:7) is a possessive or indirect object. That tells us how the ancient Jews who knew Hebrew and translated the Hebrew text of Gen. 21:12 understood the grammar, and it is unlikely that Paul took it any differently.

---

[71] On the לְ of advantage, which is a form of the לְ of interest, see Williams, *Hebrew*, § 271.
[72] Kim, "Revisiting," 244–5 (quotation from 245).
[73] By consensus here, I mean זֶרַע as the subject and לְ as indicating either possession or advantage, not that there is no deviation over which of these senses the לְ carries.
[74] Cited in ibid., 245.

He certainly did not think it important to alter the Greek translation he quoted in conformity to the understanding of the text advocated by Kim. But that would be very surprising if he took the Hebrew as Kim does without altering the Greek of his quotation, since Kim seems to think that his position is critical to denying a corporate interpretation of Gen. 21:12b and Rom. 9:7b (at least he never gives any indication that my corporate interpretation of these verses is contradicted by anything other than his novel interpretation).

However, Kim claims that, "in Greek, when a pronoun is dative (e.g., σοι) and a verb is passive (e.g., κληθήσεταί), the dative pronoun *often* functions as the subject of a passive verb," appealing to Daniel Wallace's Greek grammar.[75] But Kim has severely misunderstood Wallace's grammar. Wallace states, "When the verb is in the *passive* voice, the indirect object receives the subject of the verb ('the ball was hit *to me*')."[76] It appears that Kim has taken Wallace's statement that the indirect object receives the subject of the verb to mean that the indirect object functions as the subject. But that is not what it means. It means that the subject itself or the action associated with the subject moves to or is directed at the indirect object, which is distinct from the subject. Wallace's own example demonstrates the principle. In the sentence "The ball was hit to me," "the ball" is the subject and it is sent to the indirect object, which in this case is "me."[77]

Kim's argument against a corporate understanding of Gen. 21:12 is so baffling that it serves to strengthen the corporate view. That such technical but straining arguments have been brought forth to try and refute it only shows how strong the view is.

1.1.d.2. Rom. 9:10-13's Use of Gen. 25:23

Kim's objection to my interpretation of Gen. 25:23 is curious. He acknowledges that the "oracle deals with the future of two nations" but quickly asserts that "this oracle clearly contains the individual component."[78] What is curious about this is that I also acknowledge both corporate and individual elements to the oracle. Indeed, Kim quotes me saying that the oracle's primarily corporate significance and emphasis "does not mean that the individuals to whom Rebekah will give birth (Jacob and Esau) are not in view at all. They are very much in view, but primarily as the corporate representatives of their descendants."[79] Kim argues against my position by pointing out individual motifs in the narrative. But that approach is without force since I already acknowledged a substantial individual aspect to the passage in my exegesis.

This problem with Kim's argument comes to further expression in his conclusion that "the oracle in Genesis 25:23 cannot be merely taken corporately"[80] as if that argues against my position. I do not argue that the oracle is to be merely taken corporately but that it has a substantial individual aspect yet is nevertheless primarily corporate. In this

---

[75] Ibid., 243 n. 17; cf. D. B. Wallace, *Greek Grammar beyond the Basics: An Exegetical Syntax of the New Testament* (Grand Rapids, MI: Zondervan, 1996), 140–1.
[76] Ibid.
[77] See further Wallace's additional explanation in ibid., 141 (including note 13).
[78] Kim, "Revisiting," 247.
[79] Ibid., 246 n. 27.
[80] Ibid., 248.

instance, that means that its focus is on the corporate aspect. It is hard to see how this can be denied when the bulk of the oracle talks about peoples and nations explicitly (see the quotation of the oracle below in the next paragraph).

Kim further argues that, at a "more profound level, the theme of individual election precedes the prophecy of nations. In other words, Jacob will be an eponymous ancestor that embodies a nation, but before that, he was first chosen by God over Esau."[81] The assertion that the theme of individual election precedes the prophecy of nations is an incredible claim, as it is demonstrably false. The oracle begins with the prophecy of nations: "Two nations are in your womb. And two peoples from your belly will be divided. And one people will be stronger than the other people. And the older will serve the younger" (Gen. 25:23). Indeed, the prophecy is explicitly and primarily about nations/peoples, a point Kim does not directly counter, a fatal failing in his case.

But perhaps Kim's point is that Jacob's election temporally and/or causally preceded the advent of the nation. If so, he did not express it well by speaking of the "*theme* of individual election" preceding the prophecy.[82] In any case, it is a more reasonable point, yet one that does not support Kim's argument against corporate election and for individual election. First, his description of the meaning of the passage almost amounts to corporate election! He states its meaning thus: "Jacob will be an eponymous ancestor that embodies a nation, but before that, he was first chosen by God over Esau."[83] Compare that to how I define the biblical concept of the corporate election of God's people: "the election of a group as a consequence of the choice of an individual who represents the group, the corporate head and representative. That is, the group is elected as a consequence of its identification with this corporate representative."[84] Now there is some difference between Kim's description of Gen. 25:23 and my description of corporate election. But notice the essential similarity. Corporate covenantal election starts with the choice of an individual who embodies a group that will be defined by connection to him.

The corporate election perspective agrees that the corporate head is chosen first, though neither the perspective of corporate election nor Gen. 25:23 would see this as a temporal precedence like Kim does in asserting that before Jacob would be an eponymous ancestor that embodied Israel, "He was first chosen by God over Esau."[85] Of course, it is correct that Jacob was chosen before he became an eponymous ancestor; he would not be an ancestor until he had offspring, and his eponymous status would come later still. But from a corporate election perspective, he embodied Israel from the moment of his election. In corporate election, there is a logical priority to the election of the corporate head, as the election of God's people is a consequence of his election and of the group's association with him. The chosen people's election is rooted in the election of the covenant head; they share in his election. Thus, the timing of the election of the people is coincident with the election of the covenant head, because his

---

[81] Ibid.
[82] Ibid.; emphasis added.
[83] Ibid.
[84] Abasciano, "Misconceptions," 61.
[85] Kim, "Revisiting," 248.

election is their election insofar as they share in his election. This is the perspective of Gen. 25:23, which identifies Jacob (the individual covenant head) with his people. Jacob is not specifically said to be in Rebekah's womb; the people/nation are. Of course, the reader is expected to know that the individual Jacob is referenced because of the context and because Jacob and his people are identified, an obvious manifestation of the concept of corporate solidarity and a deathblow to Kim's argument against corporate election in the passage.

1.1.d.3. Rom. 9:10-13's Use of Mal. 1:2-3

Kim argues that Mal. 1:2b-3a (and Rom. 9:13) focuses on the individuals Jacob and Esau,[86] but his argumentation is again baffling. He points out that, in Israel's questioning of God's love for them, they asked, "How have you loved us?"[87] He then argues that God's reply ("Is not Esau Jacob's brother?" and "I have loved Jacob, but Esau I have hated") points back to Gen. 25:23 and God's election of Jacob over Esau in answer to the question of how God had loved the nation Israel.[88] Though there is a good case to be made for the reference being to the nations Israel and Esau/Edom rather than the individuals Jacob and Esau,[89] I agree with Kim that the text alludes to Gen. 25:23 and that the patriarchs Jacob and Esau are referenced (though for me unlike Kim, not to the exclusion of the nations). But this is very problematic for Kim's position that holds that the text emphasizes individual rather than corporate election.

First, we have already seen that Gen. 25:23 is primarily corporate in its significance, which strongly supports corporate election in this text that alludes to it. Second, the text's indication that God loved the nation of Israel by choosing Jacob is inimical to Kim's position, especially as Kim himself rightly argues that the language of love in this context refers to covenantal election.[90] How did God love the nation of Israel, including choosing them? The text answers: by choosing Jacob. God chose the nation of Israel by choosing Jacob. That is corporate election. His election was their election.

Even Kim's own description of the significance of this response on God's part betrays his argumentation into unwitting support for the corporate election position: "God, by reminding [sic] his election of Jacob over Esau (Gen 25:23), assures the post-exilic Israelites that he will perpetuate the covenant that he first established with Jacob."[91] How would God's election of Jacob assure the postexilic Israelites that he would perpetuate the covenant that he first established with Jacob if it was merely the election

---

[86] Ibid., 248–50.
[87] Ibid., 249. The translation Kim uses, which employs the present tense concerning Jacob and Esau's brotherhood, actually pushes against his interpretation. For the present tense would suggest the reference is to the brotherhood between the nations identified by their patronymic ancestors Jacob and Esau, since these names were sometimes used of the nations. In my book on Rom. 9:10-18, I translated that portion of the text with the past tense in recognition of the reference to the individuals Jacob and Esau. I am using the translation Kim provides when describing his arguments.
[88] Ibid., 249–50.
[89] See Abasciano, *Romans 9.10-18*, 17–18 n. 12.
[90] Kim, "Revisiting," 249.
[91] Ibid., 250.

of Jacob without corporate significance? And what good would it do them for God to perpetuate that covenant? It could assure them and would do them good because God's choice of Jacob as his covenant partner was also his choice of Jacob's people, the nation bearing the name of Jacob/Israel. They were members of that very covenant. But Kim's own approach of taking the reference to be primarily to Jacob's individual election does not make sense of the text's indication that God's love/election of Jacob was how God loved/elected Israel in Malachi's time.

1.1.d.4. The Sociocultural Milieu of the Old Testament Period

Kim claims that my argument for the sociocultural milieu of the Old Testament as primarily corporate hinges on the work of Gary Burnett, who he claims "borrows the very idea from J. S. Kaminsky."[92] I dispute both claims. I did appeal to Burnett liberally in the article Kim addresses, but I cited other scholars as well and share my own perspective, which I found aptly articulated by Burnett on certain points. Moreover, I was describing well-known phenomena, and Burnett's study was an important, recent work that addressed the topic. Similarly, Burnett's work does not suggest that he got his idea that Old Testament culture was collectivist from Kaminsky. He appeals to various scholars and provides his own synthesis and conclusions as he traces the history of scholarly discussion of "The Collective and the Individual in Judaism."[93]

More substantially, Kim alleges that my quotation of Burnett, which includes quotation of Kaminsky, is misleading.[94] His reasoning is that Burnett quoted from a portion of Kaminsky's work that deals with divine retribution in analysis of Jer. 31:29-31 and Ezekiel 18, and that I mistakenly connected "the corporate dimension of divine retribution to the socio-cultural milieu of the OT, and even to the issue of attaining salvation."[95] This is another baffling contention from Kim.

While Kaminsky's monograph does focus on corporate responsibility, that does not mean his analysis does not have relevance for the sociocultural milieu of the Old Testament. Moreover, it is too simplistic to think that a society's view of responsibility and retribution vis-à-vis the relationship between the community and the individual would be so isolated from its broader worldview that it does not give insight into that society's view of the relationship between the community and the individual more generally. Indeed, Kaminsky gives indication that his investigation intersects with ancient Israelite thought beyond its view of retribution.[96] Furthermore, it is often the case that scholars make statements that concern broader realities that they relate to a

---

[92] Ibid. Kim's discussion concerns my argumentation in B. J. Abasciano, "Corporate Election in Romans 9: A Reply to Thomas Schreiner," *JETS* 49/2 (June 2006), 351–71 (357–8, 370–1).
[93] See G. W. Burnett, *Paul and the Salvation of the Individual* (BIS, 57; Leiden: Brill, 2001); the quotation is the title of chapter 5.
[94] Kim, "Revisiting," 251–4.
[95] Ibid., 251–2; quotation from 252.
[96] See J. S. Kaminsky, *Corporate Responsibility in the Hebrew Bible* (Sheffield: JSOT, 1995), and the way he frames his study in the introduction and conclusion to the book and how he interweaves discussion of broader Israelite thought and discussion of divine retribution in his survey of the history of scholarship in chapter 1.

more specific focus. Those are the sort of statements Burnett quotes from Kaminsky and the way Burnett reads Kaminsky.[97]

Kim also alleges that I "confuse readers," mistakenly linking "the notion of salvation derived from the first century AD Judaism to the entire OT period" by putting together quotations from Burnett concerning Old Testament thought and first-century Jewish thought.[98] Kim concedes that I specified the quotations as describing the scripturally shaped Jewish view.[99] So it seems unfair to charge me with confusing readers or making a mistake here. But even if I had given the impression that this was Burnett's description of the Old Testament view, that matches his description of the Old Testament view,[100] and if anything, he portrays the Old Testament view as even more strongly corporate than the first-century Jewish view in that he posits a growing sense of individualism beginning in the postexilic period.[101] In his view, any notion of salvation would be more temporal and more corporate in the preexilic Old Testament period and moving toward the type of view he attributes to the postexilic period. Moreover, his discussion intermingles treatment of Old Testament thought and extra-biblical Jewish thought because he portrays first-century Judaism as shaped by the Old Testament and tradition.

Kim also claims that Kaminsky "firmly espouses the doctrine of individual election."[102] I would dispute that as well in the way that Kim means it. Kim concedes that Kaminsky "holds to the corporate election of Israel (Deut 9:4-5)."[103] Indeed, Kaminsky asserts that "the Hebrew Bible's theology is fundamentally corporate in its outlook."[104] That is the very sort of point that I cited Burnett and Kaminsky to support, though my focus was more on first-century Judaism as it was shaped by Old Testament thought. The problem here is probably that Kim misunderstands corporate election. He seems to take Kaminsky's recognition of God's individual election of the patriarchs as an indication that election of God's people (i.e., the election at issue in my work, the election of God's people) is primarily individual. But corporate election does not deny that there are instances of individual election in the Old Testament. It also recognizes the individual election of the patriarchs yet regards their individual election to have corporate significance and the election of God's people to be corporate in that it is a consequence of the election of the patriarchs. Thus, Kaminsky's comments about instances of individual election seem to be consistent with Israel's election in the Old Testament as primarily corporate, which harmonizes with his views that Israel's election was corporate and that the Old Testament's theology is primarily corporate.

---

[97] See Burnett's (*Salvation*, 73–6) discussion of Kaminsky's monograph.
[98] Kim, "Revisiting," 253.
[99] Ibid., n. 45.
[100] Cf. the overall characterizations he gives of the OT and first-century Judaism, respectively, in Burnett, *Salvation*, 76–7 and 80. See pp. 84–5 for a holistic synthesis.
[101] Ibid., 77–80.
[102] Kim, "Revisiting," 253.
[103] Ibid.
[104] J. S. Kaminsky, "The Sins of the Fathers: A Theological Investigation of the Biblical Tension between Corporate and Individualized Retribution," *Judaism* 46.3 (1997), 319–32 (327).

1.1.d.5. The Concept of Corporate Solidarity/Representation

Kim critiques my appeal to the concept of corporate solidarity/representation.[105] But bafflingly, he actually critiques H. Wheeler Robinson's concept of corporate personality as if that were my view when I indicate that it is not.[106] Moreover, I indicate that corporate personality and corporate solidarity are distinct concepts and that Robinson's concept of corporate personality is inadequate.[107] Thus, Kim's entire critique of my appeal to corporate solidarity/representation is irrelevant and unwarranted. As we have looked at Kim's critique of my interpretation of Rom. 9:1-13, I have repeatedly characterized his arguments as baffling. At every turn he offers untenable or at least strained arguments. Thus, his article ultimately serves to strengthen my interpretation of Rom. 9:1-13. What I said of Kim's grammatical arguments concerning Gen. 21:12 is intensified by the rest of the article—that such technical but straining arguments have been brought forth to try and refute my interpretation only shows how strong it is.

1.1.e. Miscellaneous Criticisms

In his review of my book on Rom. 9:1-9, Moyise finds my conclusion troubling that "Exod. 32.32 meets every test for a scriptural allusion discussed in our introductory chapter"[108] despite there being no verbal or structural parallel to Rom. 9:3.[109] He comments, "If it 'meets every test' yet does not contain a single word in common or structural parallel, something has surely gone awry with the tests."[110] This is a fair criticism. The reason why I classified Paul's allusion to Exod. 32:32 that way despite no verbal or structural parallel is that the criterion of volume, which includes verbal and structural similarity, includes the precursor text's degree of distinctiveness or prominence in Scripture as part of the same criterion.[111] And Exod. 32:32 is distinctive and prominent in Scripture.[112] Therefore, it could be said that every test for a scriptural allusion had been met since the distinctiveness and prominence aspect of the volume test justified the volume test as having been met. But while technically true because of how my criteria for detecting allusions are set up, it would have been better to say that Exod. 32:32 met most of the tests for detecting allusions.

In his review of my book on Rom. 9:10-18, J. K. Goodrich comments, "Driving his interpretation (mistakenly in this reviewer's view) is the assumption that the true/spiritual Israel (Rom 9:6) is the entire multiethnic church, rather than merely those Jews who believe."[113] It is true that that position, established by exegesis in my earlier

---

[105] Kim, "Revisiting," 254–8.
[106] See Abasciano, "Corporate," 355 n. 17.
[107] Ibid.
[108] Abasciano, *Romans 9.1-9*, 73.
[109] S. Moyise, "Review of B.J. Abasciano, *Paul's Use of the Old Testament in Romans 9:1-9: An Intertextual and Theological Exegesis*," RBL, https://www.sblcentral.org/home/bookDetails/5248 (October 2006).
[110] Ibid.
[111] See Abasciano, *Romans 9.1-9*, 22–6, for delineation and discussion of the criteria for detecting allusions used in my books on Romans 9.
[112] See ibid., 73, for my explanation of the point.
[113] J. K. Goodrich, "Review of *Paul's Use of the Old Testament in Romans 9.10-18: An Intertextual and Theological Exegesis*," RSR 38.1 (March 2012), 21.

study on Rom. 9:1-9 and further buttressed by exegesis in the present volume (see especially the exegesis of 9:24), is something of a driving aspect of the interpretation. But I wanted to point out here that it is not an absolutely essential element of my interpretation of Romans 9. Much of the exegesis could remain the same on the assumption of the true/spiritual Israel in Rom. 9:6 being Jewish Christians. In that case, Paul's argument would have to do with defending his gospel of justification/election by faith among Jews and God's right to name whom he desires as his covenant people among ethnic Israel.

Finally, in his review of my book on Rom. 9:10-18, George Brooke comments,

> It is significant that A.'s own reading of the Genesis and Exodus passages that Paul uses keeps to the surface of the texts alone and their own literary contexts; there is no serious engagement with why the texts were written or when ... We may wonder whether this was how Paul read his Scriptures; perhaps it was—it is certainly how many people read them uncritically today.[114]

Brooke appears to be registering a concern that I did not engage in source criticism of Paul's Old Testament background texts as part of my exegesis. It is surprising that he wonders if Paul read his Scriptures apart from practicing source criticism. He certainly did not. Are we to think of Paul studying Scripture like a modern source critic, investigating the tradition-historical prehistory, literary sources, and redactional stages of biblical texts? The final form of the text is the most fitting focus of study for understanding Paul's use of Scripture. I have explained my rationale for this approach in my fist volume on Romans 9 and direct the reader there for explanation.[115]

But I do take exception to Brooke asserting that "there is no serious engagement with why the texts were written or when."[116] While there is no serious engagement with why the texts came to be what they are in terms of their source critical development, I do pay attention to why the texts were written in the sense of their respective purposes as reflected in their final, canonical form. I regard it as an important part of exegesis to determine the purpose of a passage in its context. As to when the texts were written, there is no need to investigate that beyond assessing the dating implied by the final form of the text. But that dating does play a role in the exegesis since the historical context implied by the final form of the text is important for exegesis.

1.2. Previewing the Investigation

We will proceed with the investigation as we have with the previous volumes in this series. We will conduct an intertextual exegesis, this time of Rom. 9:19-24. By "intertextual exegesis" I mean standard grammatical-historical exegesis of a New

---

[114] G. J. Brooke, "Review of Abasciano, Brian J., *Paul's Use of the Old Testament in Romans 9.10-18: An Intertextual and Theological Exegesis*," *JSOT* 37.5 (Book List 2013), 207.
[115] See Abasciano, *Romans 9.1-9*, 46.
[116] Brooke, "Review," 207.

Testament text that alludes to the Old Testament, informed by a detailed analysis of the author's use of Scripture. Such analysis involves exegeting the Old Testament text in its original context, surveying the history of its interpretation in Judaism and Christianity prior to and roughly contemporaneous with Paul, and comparing its extant relevant textual traditions to the form of Paul's allusion. Hence, we will subject the Old Testament background of Paul's discourse in Rom. 9:19-24 to this sort of analysis, specifically Isa. 29:16, 45:9, and Jer. 18.6. We will then bring the results of that research to bear on the exegesis of Rom. 9:19-24. Specifically, we will cover the intertextual background material for the passage in Chapters 2–3, culminating in our exegesis of the passage in Chapter 4. Chapter 2 provides exegesis of the relevant Old Testament potter/clay texts, and Chapter 3 surveys ancient interpretive tradition related to those passages. Finally, Chapter 5 will bring the investigation to a close with a detailed summary of the exegesis of Rom. 9:19-24, consideration of how the rest of Romans 9 after v. 24 impacts exegesis of 9:1-24, a sketch of the logical flow of Romans 9, and some brief concluding reflections.

As mentioned at the beginning of this chapter, Romans 9 is notorious for its controversial theological subject matter. That is one thing that makes the passage such an exciting one to study. Each volume of our exegesis of Romans 9 has brought us into greater focus and intensity vis-à-vis these weighty, theologically charged issues. Now we turn to tackling the most intense, theologically controversial section of the chapter as Paul's argument gets into the issues with greater precision and depth.

2

The Potter and Clay Texts in Their Old Testament Contexts

There are three Old Testament texts that appear to be particularly relevant to Paul's use of the potter/clay metaphor in Rom. 9:20-21; Isa. 29:16, 45:9; and Jer. 18:6.[1] This chapter will provide an exegesis of each of these passages in their Old Testament context in turn for the purpose of preparing to exegete Rom. 9:19-29.

2.1. Isa. 29:16 in Its Old Testament Context

Isa. 29:16 appears in the larger passage of Isa. 29:15-24,[2] which begins with the third of six woe oracles in the greater section of Isaiah 28–33 (28:1; 29:1, 15; 30:1; 31:1;

---

[1] Isaiah 64:8 uses the potter/clay metaphor but does not appear to be particularly relevant to Paul's use of it and is not typically regarded as such by scholars. E.g., neither J. R. Wagner, *Heralds of the Good News: Isaiah and Paul "in Concert" in the Letter to the Romans* (NovTSup, 101; Leiden: Brill, 2002), the bulk of which is given over to analysis of Paul's use of Isaiah in Romans 9–11, nor S.-L. Shum, *Paul's Use of Isaiah in Romans: A Comparative Study of Paul's Letter to the Romans and the Sybilline and Qumran Sectarian Texts* (WUNT, 2.156; Tübingen: Mohr Siebeck, 2002), gives substantial attention to the verse in relation to Rom. 9:20-21 (though Shum, 204–5, does mention Isa. 64:8 in a list of texts given as examples of the types of texts most scholars rightly think shaped Paul's thought in Rom. 9:20-21). The situation is similar with Job 10:8-9, which uses potter/clay imagery of the relationship between God and man. Interestingly, both of these passages appeal to God's role as potter/Creator as something expected to move God to have mercy on the clay (his creature). We do think there is a general allusion to Job in Rom. 9:20-21 but not to any particular text in the book (see Section 4.2.b.4 in Chapter 4 of this volume). Isa. 41:25 also uses potter/clay imagery but does not seem to be particularly relevant to Paul's use of the imagery except as part of the very broad conceptual background of the general meaning of the figure in the OT. In Isa. 41:25, the imagery conveys destructive power over others and is used in passing to portray a king's decisive victory over enemies. Hence, it testifies to the figure indicating sovereignty or power over others.

[2] B. S. Childs, *Isaiah* (OTL; Louisville, KY: Westminster John Knox, 2001), 219, notes, "Traditionally, vv. 15-16 were considered an independent oracle ... However, more recently a more convincing case has been made (e.g., Sweeney)" for the unity of the passage; cf. W. A. M. Beuken, "Isa 29,15-24: Perversion Reverted," in F. C. Martinez, A. Hilhorst, and C. J. Labuschagne (eds.), *The Scriptures and the Scrolls: Studies in Honour of A. S. van der Woude on the Occasion of His 65th Birthday* (Leiden: Brill, 1992), 43–64 (1); C. Balogh, "Blind People, Blind God: The Composition of Isaiah 29,15–24," *ZAW* 121 (2009), 48–69. In any case, we need not concern ourselves with the source criticism of this or any of the other Old Testament passages we consider in this volume since, inter alia, Paul and his contemporaries would have approached the text in its final form; see Abasciano, *Romans 9.1-9*, 46, for further explanation of my approach. Although favoring literary unity for the

33:1).[3] According to John Oswalt, "In chs. 28–33 Isaiah continues his treatment, begun in ch. 7, of the foolishness of trusting the nations instead of the Lord ... Here the focus is upon Judah's choice to trust him or not."[4] Similarly, Gary Smith observes, "In these chapters the prophet is attempting to persuade his audience ... not to foolishly put their trust in other nations or their own defensive fortifications. Instead, they need to trust in God's sovereign ability to save them and God's plan to establish his righteous kingdom."[5] As most commentators have concluded, the historical context for Isaiah 28–33 almost certainly and mostly relates to the period of time during the reign of Hezekiah when Assyria was attacking the land of Judah and there was temptation for the nation to look to Egypt for help (705–701 BCE).[6] The issue of trusting in YHWH versus trusting in other nations or anything else, which commentators have identified as part of the main thrust of these chapters, emerges in them from this concrete historical background of the choice Judah faced of what they would trust in for salvation from Assyria. Would they trust in the Lord and the means of salvation he provided, or would they rely on their own power or other nations to deliver them?

Thus, the purpose of Isaiah 28–33 is to urge trust in the Lord and in his chosen means of salvation rather than in some means of human making. Isaiah 29:15-24 fits into this purpose by issuing a warning to those who would try to escape YHWH's judgment by hiding from him plans of their own making for salvation. This warning is issued on the ground that God's blessing would fall upon the (righteous) needy and his judgment upon the wicked, leading to vindication of God's holiness and reverence for him among his erring people.

Reversal is the theme of this passage.[7] Those who try to hide from God and fail to trust him reverse the proper order of things (vv. 15-16). God himself will reverse the fortunes of the (righteous) lowly and the (godless) great, and he will bring the erring

---

passage, Balogh's article is filled with source critical conjecture and serves as an example of how speculative Old Testament source criticism tends to be.

[3] Childs, *Isaiah*, 199, notes that "it is commonly recognized that chapters 28–33 are characterized in a formal sense by a series of woe oracles." Some scholars, including Childs, would group Isaiah 34–35 with chs. 28–33. Nevertheless, as Childs's comments indicate, there is a special unity to the latter; cf. G. V. Smith, *Isaiah* (2 vols.; NAC, 15A-B; Nashville, TN: B&H, [2007] 2009), 1.471, who takes chs. 28–35 as a unit, but admits that chs. 34–35 are not as closely interconnected to its material. Some commentators group ch. 33 with chs. 34–35 instead of 28–32, but this lacks good reason; see J. N. Oswalt, *The Book of Isaiah* (2 vols.; NICOT; Grand Rapids, MI: Eerdmans, [1986] 1998), 1.505, on the question.

[4] Oswalt, *Isaiah*, 1.504.

[5] Smith, *Isaiah*, 1.468.

[6] See, e.g. (some of the following exclude ch. 33 from this background), ibid., 1.468-9; Childs, *Isaiah*, 199; Oswalt, *Isaiah*, 1.504; J. Goldingay, *Isaiah* (NIBCOT, 13; Peabody, MA: Hendrickson, 2001), 151; W. A. M. Beuken, *Isaiah II: Chapters 28–39* (trans. B. Doyle; HCOT; Leuven: Peeters, 2000), 2, 5-7; O. Kaiser, *Isaiah 13-39: A Commentary* (trans. R. A. Wilson; OTL; Philadelphia, PA: Westminster, 1974), 234. J. D. W. Watts, *Isaiah* (WBC, 24–25; Waco, TX: Word, [1985] 1987), 1.353-7, goes his own way, unconvincingly locating the historical background of Isaiah 28–33 in the period of 640–587 BCE; see Smith, 1.468 n.2, for critique.

[7] See Beuken, *Isaiah*, 104; Beuken, "Reverted," throughout, esp. 48-9. J. A. Motyer, *The Prophecy of Isaiah: An Introduction and Commentary* (Downers Grove, IL: IVP, 1993), 240-4, speaks in terms of transformation.

to correction (vv. 17-24). The theme runs through the various sections of the passage, the structure of which may be sketched as follows:[8]

1. 29:15-16 Woe to those who reverse the divine/human relationship by attempting to escape God's judgment, make him the object of their judgment, and rely on their own plan of salvation.
2. 29:17-21 God will reverse the spiritual blindness of his people and the fortunes of the (righteous) needy and the (wicked) oppressor.
3. 29:22-24 God will reverse his people's erring.

2.1.a. Isa. 29:15-16

The oracle begins with the cry of "Woe!" (הוֹי), a "grievous threatening cry of the prophets"[9] normally—as here—indicating lament and pointing toward impending judgment from the Lord that would bring grief upon the objects of his judgment.[10] As Willem Beuken states, "It colours the prophetic oracles with the suggestion of death as the inevitable consequence of immoral behaviour."[11] The rest of v. 15 identifies those who are in danger of the fatal judgment of the Lord while v. 16 explains why it will come upon them:

> Woe [to] those who deeply hide a plan from YHWH, whose deeds are in a dark place and who say, "Who sees us or who knows us?" [16] Your perversity! Should the potter be regarded as clay, that what is made should say about the one who made it, "He did not make me," or something shaped say about the potter, "He does not understand?"[12]

YHWH and Isaiah's rebuke is aimed at "those who deeply hide a plan from YHWH" (v. 15). The meaning of this identification is aptly captured by the rendering of the HCSB: "those who go to great lengths to hide their plans from the LORD" (cf. similarly, the NIV). Given the likely historical context of the oracle (see 2.1 above), this probably refers to Judean political leaders who secretly planned to ally with Egypt and rely on it to save Judah from Assyria.[13] Mention of their deeds done in a dark place undoubtedly refers to their hidden planning. And their question "Who sees us or who knows us?" implies the answer "no one" and reveals that they think they successfully hid their plans from everyone, including the Lord.

It is surprising that these Judean leaders would think they could hide from God. Such a thought runs against basic theology, and so in biblical thought, against basic

---

[8] For this type of tripartite structure, cf. Beuken, *Isaiah*, 113-14; Smith, *Isaiah*, 1.503; Motyer, *Isaiah*, 240-3. See esp. Beuken for a detailed defense of such a structure, which he observes is marked by three macrosyntactic words (הוֹי, v. 15; הֲלוֹא, v. 17; לָכֵן, v. 22). Balogh, "Blind," argues for five segments.
[9] *HALOT*, s.v. הוֹי.
[10] Cf. Beuken, *Isaiah*, 3; C. P. Weber, "הוֹי," *TWOT*, 1.212.
[11] Beuken, *Isaiah*, 3.
[12] All translations of Scripture in this study are mine unless otherwise noted.
[13] So most commentators, including Oswalt, *Isaiah*, 1.536; Smith, *Isaiah*, 1.503; Childs, *Isaiah*, 219; Kaiser, *Isaiah*, 276.

reality. It implies that God is not all-knowing and all-seeing, as if he were a man, a mere created being, indeed, one that the Judean leaders could outsmart![14] From Isaiah's vantage point, this only shows the depth of their apostasy and corruption. Given their limited view of God, hiding their plans from YHWH was probably largely equivalent in their eyes to hiding their plans from YHWH's prophet, Isaiah,[15] who presumably could pass the information on to YHWH and would do so.

But why would the Judean leaders want to hide their plans from YHWH? Clearly they knew of his opposition to his people relying on foreign nations rather than himself to save them, a position they would have heard from at least Isaiah.[16] Thus, it naturally follows that the Judean leaders went to such great lengths to hide their plans from YHWH in order to avoid his divine opposition and judgment for their disloyalty and rebellion.[17] This would almost certainly include Isaiah's public denunciation of their plans, which might have put a stop to them by influencing the king and/or public sentiment, not to mention possibly bringing the result of alerting Assyria to their rebellious plot. Their concern would likely also include fear of supernatural retribution. Though limited in their view, YHWH was still a god after all.

Verse 16 denounces the actions and mindset described in v. 15 and draws out their logical implications to reveal the perversity of the convictions underlying them. Indeed, Isaiah begins his assessment of the Judean leaders' actions with the cry, "Your perversity!" The term translated "perversity" (הֶפֶךְ) comes from a Hebrew root that has to do with overturning or changing something, "often changing it into its opposite."[18] Here it refers to turning the divine/human relationship into the opposite of what it is supposed to be.

Isaiah criticizes the Judean leaders' attempt to hide their plans from God and their assumption that they could do so by pointing out that their actions were tantamount to regarding God as though he were not the Creator but something created, on the same or lesser level than them. "Regarding the potter as the clay" denotes exactly this, as the text's elaboration on the phrase makes clear.[19] It is not necessarily that the Judean leaders actually said that YHWH did not make them or that he lacked understanding; it is that their actions implied these sentiments.

---

[14] Kaiser, *Isaiah*, 274–7, goes so far as to imply that this attitude is tantamount to atheism.

[15] Cf. F. Delitzsch, *Isaiah* (trans. J. Martin; Commentary on the Old Testament, 7; 2 vols. in 1; repr., Grand Rapids, MI: Eerdmans, 1973), 2.23; Oswalt, *Isaiah*, 1.536.

[16] On this position in Isaiah, see the introduction to chs. 28–33 in Oswalt, *Isaiah*, 1.501-6, and to chs. 28–35 in Smith, *Isaiah*, 1.467-73. Cf. Smith, 503, in relation to 29:15 specifically, who highlights God's previous promises in Isaiah's preaching that should have met with trust of God in Judah's leaders and a refusal to rely on plans of human making.

[17] Cf. Delitzsch, *Isaiah*, 2.23, who thinks they sought to avoid hearing "reproof from the word of Jehovah." One might wonder, would they not expect that their plan would eventually come to light when executed if not before and therefore that they would end up facing YHWH's displeasure anyway? It is hard to say. They might have hoped to keep their involvement hidden. But even if not, people tend to deal with what they regard as most urgent first, hoping to be able to deal with later threats when necessary. Moreover, given their low view of YHWH, they seem to have regarded Assyria as a greater threat.

[18] K. Seybold, "הָפַךְ," *TDOT*, 3.423–7 (423); see p. 424 on הֶפֶךְ specifically.

[19] The כִּי in v. 16 is an instance of the conjunction after an interrogative main clause to introduce "a subordinate clause of definition & amplification" (*CHALOT*, s.v. II כִּי, § II. 9). *HALOT*, s.v. II כִּי, § II. 9, cites Isa. 29:16 as an instance of this usage.

As mentioned above, acting on the assumption that they could hide from God implies that they believe God is not all-knowing and all-seeing, as if he were a man, a mere created being rather than the Creator. It implies that he can be outmaneuvered, as if he is not God and they have superior wisdom. Moreover, making their own alternative plan for salvation over against YHWH's plan implies that they believe YHWH lacks understanding of what is best and that they in fact know better about how to achieve salvation. Thus, they pervert the God/man and Creator/creature relationship into the opposite of what it should be, practically denying God as Creator and savior, with man sitting in judgment of God rather than God sitting in judgment of man, man saving himself rather than being saved by God, and man possessing superior wisdom to God.

The rhetorical question of v. 16 implies a negative answer—the potter (representing God the Creator in the implicit analogy) should not be regarded as clay (representing human beings as creations of God). Nor should those who have been made by God deny his being the Creator or his wisdom by trying to escape his judgment. It is this perversion that provides the grounds for the warning that doom will come upon the plotting Judean leaders, leaving that warning and its implicit call to repentance and loyalty to YHWH as the main thrust of the oracle so far.

2.1.b. Isa. 29:17-21

2.1.b.1. Isa. 29:17

These verses begin to describe a reversal that YHWH would bring in contrast to the perverse reversal perpetrated by the Judean leaders, providing another ground for the warning of v. 15. The opening question of v. 17 appears to allude to 10:25 (the only other place מְעַט מִזְעָר [in a very little while] occurs in Isaiah) and the prophecy of which it is a part (10:5-34), which promises imminent judgment against Assyria and an end to its oppression of Judah.[20] This allusion combines with the explication of v. 17's imagery in the following verses for the best guidance to interpretation of the enigmatic v. 17.

The reference to Lebanon is best taken as a symbol of the proud and mighty.[21] As Beuken explains,

> Renowned for its imposing cedars (Judg. 9:15; 1 Kgs 5:3; 2 Kgs 14:9; 19:23; Isa. 60:13; Ezek. 17:3; Ps. 29:5; 37:35; 92:13; 104:16) and its lofty mountain peaks (Jer.

---

[20] So Beuken, *Isaiah*, 105-6, 117-18, who provides detailed corroboration of the allusion; Smith, *Isaiah*, 1.504; Balogh, "Blind," 52.

[21] So Oswalt, *Isaiah*, 1.538; Beuken, *Isaiah*, 119, though he also thinks that Lebanon further signifies Jerusalem (so also Balogh, "Blind," 51-2). This is possible, but speculative, with no clear identification of Jerusalem with Lebanon in the Old Testament, despite Solomon's house being known as "the house of the forest of Lebanon" due to the use of wood from Lebanon in its construction. E. J. Young, *The Book of Isaiah* (3 vols.; Grand Rapids, MI: Eerdmans, 1965-72), 2.325, thinks Lebanon refers to "the mountainous wild country" of Judah, but this misses Isaiah's actual usage of the term.

18:14; 22:6), Lebanon was also a symbol for those who opposed YHWH in their arrogance, those who would ultimately taste humiliation (Isa. 2:13; 10:34; 14:8; 33:9; 37:24; Jer 22:23; Ezekiel 31; Zech. 11:1-3; Nah. 1:4f.).²²

In this light, the cutting down of the forest would naturally symbolize humiliation, which seems to be the significance of the turning of Lebanon into a fertile field (כַּרְמֶל),²³ a substantially more meager agricultural phenomenon. Regarding the fertile field as a forest (יַעַר) would then symbolize the raising of the humble to honor and prosperity.²⁴

This reading of v. 17 is confirmed by the following verses, which describe, inter alia, a negative reversal for wicked oppressors from oppressing to perishing on the one hand, and a positive reversal for the righteous oppressed from being oppressed to joy and well-being on the other hand.²⁵

2.1.b.2. Isa. 29:18-21

2.1.b.2.a. Background of Isa. 29:18 in 29:9-14

Isa. 29:18 alludes to another Isaian prophecy, this time to the oracle that immediately precedes the present one—29:1-14. Verses 9-14 are most pertinent:

> ⁹ Wait²⁶ and be astounded! Blind yourselves and be blind! Become drunk, but not [with] wine! Stagger, but not [from] intoxicating drink!²⁷ ¹⁰ For YHWH has poured out upon you a spirit of deep sleep, and he has shut your eyes, the prophets, and he has covered your heads, the seers. ¹¹ To you the whole vision has become like the words of a sealed book when they give it to the one who knows how to read,²⁸ saying, "Please read this aloud," and he says, "No, I cannot, for it is sealed,"

---

[22] Beuken, ibid. Oswalt, ibid., also mentions Isa. 35:2 and 60:13.
[23] Oswalt, *Isaiah*, who cites Isa. 2:13; 10:34; 37:24. This reading is partly confirmed by the allusion to the prophecy of 10:5-34, which equates the destruction of Assyria with the felling of Lebanon and the cutting down of lofty trees (or perhaps branches) and the thickets of the forest (10:33-34).
[24] Beuken, *Isaiah*, 120, contends that יַעַר does not mean "forest" but a practically useless and common thicket (used here to indicate that fruitfulness will be the common state). However, the evidence does not bear that out as the only or even the dominant meaning of the term, at least in Isaiah. It typically means "forest" in Isaiah, most strikingly in the passage to which Beuken agrees this oracle alludes, the prophecy of 10:5-34 (see 10:19, where יַעַר is paired with כַּרְמֶל and both are characterized by glory; 10:19, which speaks of the trees of the forest; 10:34, which speaks of "the thickets of [סַבְכֵי] the forest"; on 10:34, see further n. 22 above).
[25] No matter how one interprets v. 17, the reversal of the fortunes of the righteous and wicked clearly dominates the following verses.
[26] Many emend the MT from הִתְמַהְמְהוּ (wait) to הִתַּמְּהוּ (be astounded) on the basis of contextual factors. But the MT is supported by the LXX, Syriac, Targums, and Vulgate, and makes fine sense contextually. Therefore, its reading should be retained.
[27] The MT reads indicatives concerning drunkenness and staggering in v. 9, but the MT's vowel pointing is not original to the text and imperatives fit the context better given the preceding imperatives and the use of the second person in the preceding and following sentences. Moreover, the LXX supports imperatives (as do, e.g., Oswalt, *Isaiah*, 1.529; R. E. Clements, *Isaiah 1-39* [NCBC; Grand Rapids, MI: Eerdmans, 1980], 238; NIV; ESV; RSV; NRSV; NAB) with its reading of κραιπαλήσατε.
[28] In the Hebrew text, literacy and illiteracy in these verses is literally referred to as knowing or not knowing a book, respectively.

¹² or they give the book to the one who does not know how to read, saying, "Please read this aloud," and he says, "I do not know how to read." ¹³ Then my Lord said, "Because this people draws near to me with his mouth, and with his lips they honor me, but his heart is far from me, and their fear of me is a commandment taught by men, ¹⁴ therefore behold, I will again deal wonderfully with this people [with] wonder upon wonder. So the wisdom of his wise men will perish and the discernment of his discerning men will keep hidden."

This section begins with a call to wait, an act that will bring about astonishment, presumably when the prophecy of 29:1-8 is fulfilled. This call to waiting and astonishment is followed by similar calls to spiritual blindness as well as spiritual (rather than alcoholic) drunkenness and staggering. Indeed, the three pairs of imperatives are probably roughly synonymous, with the second imperative of each pair indicating the consequence of the first.²⁹

"Waiting" in this context probably connotes doing nothing about what Isaiah has been preaching,³⁰ an unfaithful response fueled by unbelief. Given the unbelief inherent in such a response, astonishment will result when Isaiah's prophecy comes true, especially as its fulfillment would be nothing short of miraculous and a matter of life and death. Self-blinding would be to similarly ignore (turn a blind eye to) Isaiah's call to covenant faithfulness, and being blind would be the resulting state of refusal to believe. Getting drunk similarly refers to taking on a state of improper spiritual reasoning and decision-making, leading to staggering in the form of both stubborn refusal to trust in YHWH's word through Isaiah and any ensuing calamity. Blindness and drunken staggering bring out the disastrous folly of rejecting the Lord and his ways.

The arresting feature about Isa. 29:9, of course, is that it calls upon Isaiah's audience to reject his message. As many commentators recognize, this is an instance of rhetorical irony,³¹ in which the prophet states the opposite of what he means.³² More specifically,

---

²⁹ Cf. Smith, *Isaiah*, 1.499, who holds that the first two pairs of imperatives are synonymous and, citing GKC § 110f., that the syntax employed implies that the second imperative of both pairs indicates a consequence of the first in the pair. This seems correct. But we would add that the third pair is also synonymous, though the consequential significance of the second imperative in that instance is not implied by the syntax employed but by the semantic content (staggering is obviously the result of drunkenness).

³⁰ Beuken, *Isaiah*, 92, notes that the negative sense of מהה "involves to hesitate in making a decision which one is being urged to make on religious grounds (Gen. 19:16; Ps. 119:60 ...)."

³¹ So, e.g., Smith, *Isaiah*, 1.498-9; Clements, *Isaiah*, 238; Young, *Isaiah*, 2.315; Beuken, *Isaiah*, 91, 93; J. A. Alexander, *Commentary on the Prophecies of Isaiah* (2 vols. in 1; Grand Rapids, MI: Zondervan, 1975), 1.465; G. C. I. Wong, "Make Their Ears Dull: Irony in Isaiah 6:9-10," *TTJ* 16 (2008), 24-34 (27); cf. Goldingay, *Isaiah*, 161. Delitzsch, *Isaiah*, 2.20, takes a different view, viz. that these imperatives communicate a "judicial sentence of obduracy." Kaiser, *Isaiah*, 270-2, seems to favor an irony view but thinks it possible that Isaiah's word only prophesied his hearers' fate.

³² This is not the only type of irony used in the Bible but the kind used here. On the use of irony in Scripture, see E. M. Good, *Irony in the Old Testament* (Philadelphia, PA: Westminster, 1965), a seminal work of which there is a second edition from 1981 I have not consulted; E. W. Bullinger, *Figures of Speech Used in the Bible: Explained and Illustrated* (Grand Rapids, MI: Baker, 1968), 807-15; B. Hollenbach, "Lest They Should Turn and Be Forgiven: Irony," *Bible Translator* 34.3 (July 1983), 312-21 (314-16), though his definition of irony seems too restrictive; J. L. Wilson, "Irony," *HBD*, http://www.studylight.org/dic/hbd/view.cgi?number=T3067; C. J. Sharp, *Irony and Meaning in the Hebrew Bible* (ISBL; Bloomington: Indiana University, 2009). For a recent survey of scholarly approaches to irony, see Sharp, 10-28. My own approach is decidedly author-oriented

the prophecy utilizes that form of irony known as sarcasm. The type of irony/sarcasm used here is the type that comes as a last resort at persuasion after repeated attempts to convince someone of a course of action that is best for them but which are met with ongoing stubborn resistance.

It is like a father who loves his wayward son dearly and wants nothing more than for him to flourish and has persistently tried to persuade him to be self-disciplined and studious, but has had his many admonitions ignored and watched his son do very poorly in school, finally saying to his son, "Go ahead, ignore what I have told you! Don't study; flunk out of school and live in poverty all your life!"[33] The father obviously would not want his son to obey those imperatives literally. Rather, in a last-ditch effort, he would hope that his sarcasm would shock his son and motivate him to do the very opposite, as unlikely as it might be to work. At the same time, such sarcastic irony expresses frustration and disdain for the actions of those who are addressed and gives indication of what their present actions are and/or are like and/or may result in. The offensive behavior in view in Isaiah is summed up well in v. 13—hypocrisy and hearts that are far from God.

Thus, in effect, these sarcastic imperatives of Isa. 29:9 call upon Isaiah's audience to heed YHWH's message through Isaiah and to act accordingly with repentance and covenant faithfulness.[34] Verse 10 furnishes a reason for doing so in a striking metaphor that is in keeping with the metaphors of blindness and drunkenness of v. 9 but now has YHWH as its agent. However, before considering how v. 10 supports v. 9, we must ask, what could it mean that YHWH had poured over his people a spirit of deep sleep? In keeping with the spiritual sloth, blindness, drunkenness, and staggering of v. 9, a spirit of deep sleep clearly refers to the same type of phenomenon. It suggests an attitude or tendency[35] (רוּחַ) toward spiritual ignorance and sloth and insensitivity, and so also towards failure to believe and act on YHWH's word. The action of pouring such an attitude would then be one that fosters the attitude.

The following clauses appear to elaborate on the meaning of the divine outpouring of sleep, explicating it with still more metaphors, now as shutting Judah's eyes, identified as the prophets, and covering Judah's heads, identified as the seers.[36] This identification of Judah's prophets and seers portrays them as those who provide Judah with spiritual vision, knowledge, and leadership. To have shut and covered them would

---

rather than reader-oriented; see Abasciano, *Romans 9.1-9*, 21–2, for my position on the issues of author, text, and meaning. On irony in Isaiah specifically, see Good, *Irony*, 115–67.

[33] Cf. Wong's ("Irony," 25) example.
[34] Isaiah 29:9 appears to allude to 6:10, part of Isaiah's inaugural vision and commissioning, a passage that is also best understood as employing rhetorical irony. On irony in 6:9-10, see Good, *Irony*, 136–7; Wong, "Irony"; Hollenbach, "Irony"; R. B. Chisholm Jr., "Divine Hardening in the Old Testament," *Bsac* 153 (Oct.–Dec. 1996), 410–34 (430–3). Of course, 6:9-10 is a difficult text that has occasioned a variety of views, and there are even different forms of the irony view. For a survey of approaches, see D. E. Hartley, *The Wisdom Background and Parabolic Implications of Isaiah 6:9-10 in the Synoptics* (Studies in Biblical Literature, 100; New York: Lang, 2006), chapter 1.
[35] On this meaning of רוּחַ, see *HALOT*, s.v., § 7.
[36] As Oswalt, *Isaiah*, 1.529 n. 3, notes, it is customary for commentators to regard the reference to the prophets and seers as incorrect glosses. But there is no objective evidence against their originality and their awkwardness argues more for than against it. In any case, our concern is the final form of the text; see n. 1 above.

most naturally be to have cut them off from the divine revelation that grounded their prophetic identities and enabled them to provide spiritual knowledge and leadership.[37] The act of pouring out a spirit of deep sleep in v. 10 essentially refers to withholding revelation from the prophets generally,[38] which would naturally foster spiritual ignorance, confusion, and folly due to lack of sound spiritual leadership, an act of ironic and poetic judgment for Judah's covenant unfaithfulness and rejection of the word of the Lord. The cutting off of revelation to the prophets can only be said to have been general because Isaiah (at least) was still receiving revelation and preaching the word of the Lord. Although judging Judah for its resistance to his word by withdrawing it for the most part, YHWH was still holding out the truth to them through Isaiah to lead them to repentance.

But how does withdrawing revelation from the prophets (or removing them altogether) with its ignorance-inducing effects serve as a reason to heed Isaiah's ironic call to repentance (i.e., how does v. 10 support v. 9)? It delivers a limited form of judgment, giving a foretaste of fuller judgment to come, in order to shake the people into repentance. Returning to our earlier example of a father dealing with a son who is failing at school because of laziness, imagine that the father had been helping his son with his homework and going over class material with him. But just as his son ignored his father's admonitions to self-discipline and studiousness, so also he paid little attention to his father's tutoring, though it was of more benefit to him than no tutoring. In such a situation, one can easily imagine the father cutting off his son from tutoring as a natural consequence and last-ditch attempt to motivate his son to finally heed his admonitions.

---

[37] Cf. Smith, *Isaiah*, 1.499; Alexander, *Isaiah*, 1.465. This shares some similarity with passages in Isaiah in which the Lord speaks of cutting off or removing the prophets and other leaders due to the unfaithfulness of the leaders and/or the people they led (3:1-4; 9:14-16). Intriguingly, in ch. 3 the leaders are to be replaced by those who are ignorant and unqualified, which might be thought to parallel the prophets deprived of revelation in ch. 29. Or it may be that shutting/covering the prophets/seers refers to their removal in harmony with chs. 3 and 9. Supporting the idea of revelatory deprivation, see Amos 8:11-12 and Mic. 3:5-7, both of which concern Judah in the same general time period according to a traditional, canonical viewpoint such as Paul undoubtedly would have held. Perhaps both these thoughts should be joined together to posit that we are to assume that the withdrawal of revelation would have brought any sincere prophets to stop functioning, leaving charlatans to take their place. Yet another option would be the preventing of the prophets' ability to understand the word of the Lord.

[38] This construes the three clauses of v. 10 as synonymously parallel. Alternatively, the latter two could be taken as distinct from the first, adding specifically what YHWH would do to the prophets and seers. The latter two are clearly parallel (shutting Judah's eyes/the prophets = covering its heads/the seers) while the first and second clauses are joined by the same coordinating conjunction as the second and third, i.e., ו (and), leaving no syntactical reason to object to the first clause also being parallel. But it is the semantics of the verse that strongly commends the threefold parallelism. Pouring out a spirit of deep sleep is obviously equivalent to shutting eyes, and we have already seen that the latter two clauses are synonymous. Beuken, *Isaiah*, 94–5, observes that the figure of covering the head alludes to the practice of pulling a blanket over the head to help bring on sleep. In any case, covering of the head would be practically equivalent to and entail the covering of the eyes. Some, particularly older commentators along with the KJV, have construed the syntax of the verse differently, grouping deep sleep and shut eyes together of the people, and then both the prophets and seers with covering (so Young, *Isaiah*, 2.314, 316–17; Alexander, ibid.; cf. Motyer, *Isaiah*, 239). But few favor this now, and the resulting two sections of the verse would still likely be synonymous.

Verses 11-12 indicate that the lack of spiritual leadership intensified by God's judgment added to the spiritual ignorance and insensitivity of Judah, exacerbating the people's difficulty in understanding Isaiah's prophecy of woe and weal in 29:1-8.[39] It is as if the prophecy could not be read.[40] Verse 13 appears to explain why—the people's heart was far from God. Their worship[41] of him was merely external and rote, centered on man-made rules. It is again like a resistant student, who does not trust his teacher, thinks very differently than the teacher, has no interest in what the teacher has to say, and so would naturally experience confusion and difficulty in understanding what the teacher says even while going through the motions of the external behaviors required for the teacher's class.

Verse 13 also appears to serve as the basis of the judgment of covering the prophets. The people's unloving, disinterested hearts issued forth in resistance to YHWH's word, bringing divine judgment in the form of withdrawal of that word. Yet more expressly, the hypocritical, unloving hearts of v. 13 provide the basis of further judgment to come,[42] described by v. 14—miraculous action by YHWH that will nullify the wisdom of Judah's wise men. This miraculous action will probably also constitute a blessing for God's people in the astonishing merciful provision of salvation,[43] but the emphasis here is on judgment in the form of showing up the counsel of Judah's wise men as folly.

2.1.b.2.b. The Meaning of Isaiah 29:18-21

In 29:18-21 Isaiah continues describing the reversal that God will work among his people and specifying its result, continuing the grounding of the warning of v. 15. The reference to the deaf hearing words of a book and the eyes of the blind seeing (v. 18) promises the reversal of the hardening judgment of vv. 10-12, which spoke of Judah's eyes being shut and their inability to understand "the words of a sealed book," which was equated in v. 11 with Isaiah's vision in 29:1-8 (see above on v. 11).[44] Thus,

---

[39] I speak of intensification and exacerbation because, in the larger context of Isaiah, the judgment on the prophets was not only due to the people's hardheartedness but also due to the prophets' hardheartedness, who were therefore already substantially spiritually obtuse and providing poor spiritual leadership (see the prophecies in chs. 3 and 9). Thus, both the people and their spiritual leaders would already have trouble coming to grips with Isaiah's messages like a student who pays little attention to his teacher would have trouble understanding the teacher's lectures. But then replacing the teacher with an ignorant buffoon for most lectures would exacerbate the students' difficulty in understanding lectures by the knowledgeable teacher. However, the emphasis here in 29:9-14 is on the people's responsibility. Yet again, the prophets were part of the people and there is no hint of holding the people responsible and not the prophets.

[40] But even this inability to understand was meant to move the people to pay attention to Isaiah's message and therefore understand it, just as a lack of understanding often motivates people to pay closer attention to what is being said so as to come to understand.

[41] Literally, "fear" (ירא).

[42] N.b. "because" (יַעַן כִּי) at the beginning of v. 13 and "therefore" (לָכֵן) at the beginning of v. 14.

[43] The text does not say specifically what wonder God will perform, but it is most likely salvation from Assyria in 701 BCE; see Isaiah 36-37. Cf. Smith, *Isaiah*, 1.500 with 1.497, who also insightfully suggests that the reference could be back to the promise of salvation earlier in the prophecy (29:5-7), which was itself most likely in reference to the Assyrian threat.

[44] On the sealed book referring to the vision recorded in 29:1-8, see Beuken, *Isaiah*, 89, 121, and cf. the natural sense of most of the English translations of חָזוּת הַכֹּל. The reference could be broader, such as to "the entire course of messages which have to do with the fortunes of the nation" (Young, *Isaiah*, 2.317; see Alexander, *Isaiah*, 1.465, for further possibilities). But it is more natural to take it of the

v. 18 most likely refers to the people of Judah finally understanding Isaiah's prophecy due to its fulfillment and seeing that their trust should have been in YHWH all along.[45] Their brush with the gloom and darkness of destruction and death at the hands of Assyria and YHWH's deliverance of them would cut through the gloom and darkness of their spiritual ignorance.[46]

As a result of the fulfillment of Isaiah's prophecy of judgment and salvation, and the ensuing spiritual enlightenment it would bring, "The humble will increase [their] joy in YHWH, and the poor will rejoice in the Holy One of Israel" (29:19). Keeping with the theme of reversal, this verse presents a synonymous parallelism that highlights the blessed reversal that the devout poor would experience when YHWH fulfills his word.[47] Presumably, this would apply to the poor who were already devout as well as those who trusted in YHWH as a result of his salvation from Assyria. The joy would come from the further salvation from oppression that God would provide by cutting off the wicked who perpetrated oppression and would not themselves repent and become obedient to YHWH (29:20-21).

2.1.c. Isa. 29:22-24

As a result and part of the wondrous reversal described in 29:18-21 (n.b. "therefore" [לָכֵן] beginning v. 22), God's people would no longer be ashamed (v. 22).[48] That is, they

---

prophecy of which it is a part, though the vision itself can be thought representative of Isaiah's preaching in general—woe and weal with exhortation to repentance/covenant faithfulness and/or of Isaiah's messages in chs. 28–33, which deal with the same theme in the context of the Assyrian threat.

[45] Pace Beuken, *Isaiah*, 121-2, this would include any of the hardhearted who had formerly refused to accept God's word, including the Judean leaders who are addressed in 29:15, but would now turn to YHWH in repentance. Part of the reason for addressing them in the first place is to urge them to repent. Moreover, blindness and so on was applied to the people of Jerusalem (probably as representative of all of Judah) not just certain individuals like the leaders. And here, blindness is depicted as healed. With an obvious allusion to the earlier blindness motif, 29:18 is best taken of healing the blindness referred to formerly. The language is economical, speaking of God's treatment of the righteous and wicked, respectively, but without implying that there could be no transfer from one category to the other. Much of Isaiah's and the rest of the prophets' ministries were taken up with calling God's people to turn from wickedness to righteousness. So one of the fundamental principles of Old Covenant theology is likely assumed here, that of repentance unto forgiveness, and the text best understood according to the pattern of Isa. 1:21-31, which portrays YHWH as purifying his people by destroying those who will not repent (n.b. 1:27-28). As Beuken (127–9) himself recognizes, the statement in 29:24 that the erring would come to right applies to the leaders addressed in v. 15. On the other hand, some of the people and the leaders would not repent and would thus constitute the wicked who are said to be cut off.

[46] "Gloom" (אֹפֶל) and "darkness" (חֹשֶׁךְ), as often, symbolize a state of suffering and misery. In this context, that has a twofold concrete expression—the devastation and misery brought by Assyria's military campaign against Judah on the one hand, and Judah's miserable spiritual ignorance and poverty on the other.

[47] That עֲנָוִים is best taken as referring to the humble/devout poor rather than merely the poor is suggested by the fact that their joy would be in YHWH (Beuken, *Isaiah*, 122), by related judgment on the wicked (vv. 20–21), and by the typical use of the term in the prophets (see E. Gerstenberger, "ענה," *TDOT*, 10.230-52 [242, and esp. 244]; L. J. Coppes, "עָנָה," *TWOT*, 2.682-4 [682–3]).

[48] While 29:22-24 appears to be a result of vv. 18–21, it appears to be the type of result that is inherent to the cause so that its description amounts to a further explanation of the cause. See the parallel to vv. 18-19 noted below.

would cease bearing both the divine disapproval due to walking contrary to YHWH's Law and the disgrace of various afflictions upon them born of his judgment. Rather, they would enjoy God's blessing, represented by seeing their children in their midst (v. 23), most likely a reference to fruitfulness in fertility[49] given by God ("the work of my hands"), one of the blessings of the covenant when God's people are faithful to it (see, e.g., Num. 20:9). Moreover, they would sanctify the Lord (i.e., treat him as holy, setting him apart as supreme and acting accordingly with trust, obedience, covenant faithfulness, etc.) and stand in awe of him (v. 23). This is roughly equivalent to v. 19's rejoicing in the Lord. For many, this would constitute yet another reversal, described in 29:24: "And ones who err in spirit will know understanding, and ones who grumble will learn instruction."[50] This is roughly equivalent to v. 18's deaf and blind hearing and seeing. Rather than persisting in wickedness and being destroyed by YHWH, many of the wicked would repent and submit to YHWH,[51] probably including some of Judah's leaders who were in view in 29:15-16 and guilty of perverting the proper relationship to the Creator.[52]

2.1.d. Summary/Conclusion

The main point of Isa. 29:15-24 is the implicit call to the leaders of Judah to rely on the Lord's plan of salvation rather than their own, urged by the explicit warning against trying to hide their self-reliant plans from YHWH (v. 15), which aimed at avoiding his judgment for their unfaithfulness. This call/warning is grounded in (1) v. 16's assessment of such behavior as perverse for its reversal of the creator/creature relationship and low view of God, and (2), the future reversal YHWH would bring

---

[49] So Oswalt, *Isaiah*, 1.541.
[50] Cf. H. Wildberger, *A Continental Commentary: Isaiah 28–39* (trans. T. H. Trapp; Minneapolis, MA: Fortress, 2002), 117, who sees v. 24 as an "expansion of the reference to hallowing the name of God." Verse 24 appears to use the *w-qatalti* form for logical rather than temporal consecution (on which, see P. Joüon and T. Muraoka, *A Grammar of Biblical Hebrew* [SB 14/1–14/2; 2 vols.; repr. with corrections, Rome: Editrice Pontificio Istituto Biblico, [1991] 1993], § 119e). I would classify the usage as an explanatory *w-qatalti* or perhaps as a concluding/summarizing one comparable to the uses of *wayyiqtol* discussed in Joüon and Muraoka, § 118i–j. However, it is probably more natural grammatically to take v. 24 as sequentially consequent to v. 23. While I think the context favors the interpretation described above, it could be, as Michael Brown suggested to me in personal correspondence, that the text intends to convey that God will judge the wicked in the midst of Israel but at the same time, he will bring restoration to his people, as a result of which those who have erred—apparently in distinction from the brazenly wicked—will be enlightened. Another possibility (sparked in my mind by personal correspondence with A. Philip Brown II) is that this poetic text has some intentional ambiguity to it that allows for multiple possibilities, such as Israelites sanctifying YHWH's name as equivalent to some of the erring and grumbling gaining understanding and accepting instruction due to seeing the blessing of YHWH, and some of the erring and grumbling seeing that turn to YHWH by others of the erring and grumbling and consequently turning to him themselves.
[51] Verse 24 appears to qualify the statement of vv. 20–21 that the wicked would be cut off.
[52] Beuken, *Isaiah*, 127–9, argues that those in view as turning to proper relationship with YHWH in 29:23-24 are "the self-willed policy makers of vv. 15f.," pointing out that the text employs terms used "in accusations and proclamations of judgment concerning the ruling classes" elsewhere in what he calls "Proto-Isaiah" (128). It seems too restrictive to limit the change of heart to the rulers, but they probably are especially in view.

to pass of humbling/punishing the proud and mighty, exalting/blessing the humble/devout/poor, and bringing his people to see his trustworthiness and to treat him as holy (vv. 17-24). Isaiah presents two interrelated reasons as a compelling motivation to repent of self-reliance and doubt concerning God's plan of salvation, and to trust in the Lord and be faithful to his holiness: YHWH's destruction of those who acted arrogantly like the Judean leaders, on the one hand, and his salvation and blessing of those who trusted in him, on the other.

As for the inner logic of vv. 17-24, v. 17 gives a general statement of the humbling of the proud and exaltation of the humble/devout entailed in the coming salvation from Assyria. Verses 18-21 then give the result of v. 17. Verse 18 indicates that the people would finally come to see the truth of Isaiah's prophecy and YHWH's trustworthiness, which itself would join with salvation from Assyria to bring joy to the humble/devout (v. 19) as would the cutting off of the wicked/oppressors who would not repent (vv. 20-21), leaving delight in YHWH as the chief idea in vv. 17-21, supported by the spiritual understanding of God's people and the judgment of the wicked. Verses 22-24 specify the result of vv. 17-21 and also further explicate them. Due to YHWH's blessing upon his people, they would treat him as holy, including the erring among them who would now yield to YHWH.

2.2. Isa. 45:9 in Its Old Testament Context

Isa. 45:9 begins the discrete passage of Isa. 45:9-13,[53] which is part of a broader section of the book that deals with YHWH's plan to restore his people through the pagan king Cyrus (chs. 40-48). Oswalt helpfully describes the broad flow of the bulk of the final form of the book of Isaiah:

> The recurring theme in chs. 7-39 was that God could be trusted in the face of the threats from the surrounding nations. Yet the people of Israel were continually tempted to trust other nations to help them. God's response was to say that those other nations would fail them and the result would be destruction, sometimes from the very nation trusted for help (8:5-8; 30:1-5; etc.). Nevertheless, Isaiah had declared, God's trustworthiness was so great that even after the well-deserved destruction had come, God would not forsake his own, but would deliver them from what had overtaken them (9:1-6 [Eng. 2-7]; 30:9-33; etc.).
>
> Chapters 40-55, especially chs. 40-48, take up the latter part of the theme, showing how this truth will work itself out in the reality of the coming exile ...

---

[53] As Smith, *Isaiah*, 2.260, notes, the versions disagree on the text at many points, resulting in significant question as to the original text. Our approach is conservative, seeing emendation to something different than is present in any of the versions as a last resort. Oswalt, *Isaiah*, 2.206 n. 30, observes that the text of 45:9 "is notoriously difficult." His conclusion makes the best sense: "LXX and Targ. differ markedly from MT but also from one another. This suggests that neither has a clear textual tradition on which it depends but is simply trying to make sense of a difficult original, which the MT probably represents accurately"; cf. J. Goldingay and D. Payne, *Isaiah 40-55: A Critical and Exegetical Commentary, Volume 2* (ICC; London: T&T Clark, 2006), 34.

Chapters 40–48 particularly address the questions concerning God's ability and desire to deliver that the exile would pose ... The basic content of chs. 41–48 can be stated. God will demonstrate his absolute superiority over the idols by doing something new, something unheard-of to that point: causing a people, his people, to return from exile (41:1–44:22). He will do this by destroying proud Babylon through Cyrus, a previously unknown ruler who will not come from any of the established kingdoms of the Mesopotamian valley (44:23–47:15).[54]

Most scholars (including Oswalt) add that Isaiah 40–48 (or some part thereof) reflects that Israel rejected YHWH's announcement of deliverance because of his choice of Cyrus as Israel's deliverer.[55] Isa. 45:9-13 focuses on this very issue, warning God's people with an oracle of woe against challenging his plan for them and asserting that he would use the man of his choosing to redeem his people.[56] The passage thus falls naturally into two sections:[57]

1. 45:9-10 Woe to the one who challenges God's plan for his people (i.e., restoration by the pagan king Cyrus)!
2. 45:11-13 In the face of challenge to his plan for his people, the Sovereign God will use the man of his choosing to redeem his people.

The very next verse after 45:9-13 introduces the theme of the conversion/salvation of the nations (45:14; see also vv. 20–25),[58] a logical progression from the idea of using

---

[54] Oswalt, *Isaiah*, 2.45–6. A. Laato, *The Servant of YHWH and Cyrus: A Reinterpretation of the Exilic Messianic Programme in Isaiah 40–55* (CBOT, 35; Stockholm: Almqvist & Wiksell, 1992), 188, regards the main theological thesis of Isaiah 40–55 to be "that Israel should put its confidence in YHWH who give [sic] his people a new beginning through Cyrus."

[55] See, e.g., Oswalt, *Isaiah*, 200, 208–11; Goldingay and Payne, *Isaiah*, 31–41; S. M. Paul, *Isaiah 40–66: Translation and Commentary* (ECC; Grand Rapids, MI: Eerdmans, 2012), 259–64; R. E. Watts, "Consolation or Confrontation? Isaiah 40–55 and the Delay of the New Exodus," *TynBul* 41.1 (1990), 31–59 (31); Laato, *Cyrus*, 188–9; K. Baltzer, *Deutero-Isaiah: A Commentary on Isaiah 40–55* (trans. M. Kohl; Hermeneia; Minneapolis, MA: Fortress, 2001), 232, 237; W. Brueggemann, *Isaiah 40–66* (WBCo; Louisville, KY: Westminster John Knox, 1998), 78–80; C. Westermann, *Isaiah 40–66: A Commentary* (trans. D. M. G. Stalker; London: SCM, 1969), 165–8; R. N. Whybray, *Isaiah 40–66* (NCBC; London: Marshall, Morgan & Scott, 1975), 107–9. I think it is fair to say that this is the consensus position. However, a few have challenged it and suggested that Israel objected to something else other than the choice of Cyrus; so Smith, *Isaiah*, 2.242–3, 260–7; J. L. Koole, *Isaiah, Part 3, Volume I: Isaiah 40–48* (trans. A. P. Runia; HCOT; Kampen: Kok Pharos, 1997), 448–62. For detailed support of the consensus, see Watts, "Consolation or Confrontation," 41–4.

[56] Smith, *Isaiah*, 2.260, speaks of two woe oracles due to the term occurring twice, but it is better to recognize one oracle with woe issued twice. Others think the text utilizes the disputation form associated with the word רב (e.g., B. D. Naidoff, "The Two-fold Structure of Isaiah 45:9-13," *VT* 31.2 [1981], 180–5; Westermann, *Isaiah*, 165; C. R. Seitz [cited by Smith, ibid.]). But the oracle warns against humans disputing against God's plans. At the same time, the passage does offer disputation against the people's viewpoint. This is probably an example of a mixed form, incorporating some elements of the woe oracle and the disputation speech. For a concise description of these forms, see M. A. Sweeney, *Isaiah 1–39 with an Introduction to Prophetic Literature* (FOTL, 16; Grand Rapids, MI: Eerdmans, 1996), 28.

[57] Smith, ibid., indicates that there is widespread agreement on this twofold structure.

[58] On these texts having the conversion/salvation of the nations in view, see, e.g., Oswalt, *Isaiah*, 2.215, 220–5. Concerning 45:20-25, he notes that most commentators agree that it is about the salvation of the world (220). On 45:14 taking this view, see also, e.g., Paul, *Isaiah*, 264; Smith, *Isaiah*, 2.269–71;

the Gentile king Cyrus to deliver Israel. Indeed, as Jan Koole has observed, in 45:6 "the worldwide recognition of Yahweh as the only God is his purpose in granting success to Cyrus."[59]

2.2.a. Isa. 45:9-10

As 29:15-24, this oracle begins with the cry of "Woe!" (הוֹי), indicating lament and pointing toward fatal judgment from the Lord that would bring grief upon the objects of his displeasure.[60] In this context, it signals a warning. The verse then identifies those who are liable to such divinely inflicted grief: "Woe to the one who contends with his fashioner, a clay pot among[61] clay pots of the ground!" (45:9a). The oracle, aimed at God's covenant people, identifies those marked for judgment as those (among God's people) who contend against him. The text does not state the content of the disputation at this point, but this emerges with increasing specificity as the passage proceeds. However, 45:9a does already implicitly give the essential basis of YHWH's rebuke of those standing against him in its identification of him and them—that YHWH is their Creator and they are his lowly creation.

Referring to YHWH as יֹצְרוֹ (his fashioner) is a way of referring to YHWH as the creator of the one who contends against him. "Fashioner" perhaps captures the sense here slightly better than "Creator" because the figure that will immediately be employed is that of a potter shaping clay in an ongoing process. Referring to the objector as "a clay pot among clay pots of the ground" stresses his identity as a creature and his corresponding lowly estate. He is just a creature, and merely one among others for that matter. Isaiah expands on the significance of these identifications in 9b, giving a ground for the warning issued in 9a.

The justification of 9a's warning comes in the form of a rhetorical question that expects a strong and obvious negative answer: "Will the clay say to its fashioner, 'What are you doing?' or your work [say], 'He has no hands?'" (9b).[62] The question "What are you doing" is neither neutral information gathering nor positive interest,

---

P. D. Hanson, *Isaiah 40–66* (IBC; Louisville, KY: John Knox, 1995), 108; Motyer, *Isaiah*, 363–4; Young, *Isaiah*, 2.207–8; and cautiously, Goldingay and Payne, *Isaiah*, 42–5.

[59] Koole, *Isaiah*, 468; cf. similarly, e.g., Oswalt, *Isaiah*, 2.203; Whybray, *Isaiah*, 106; Westermann, *Isaiah*, 161; Paul, *Isaiah*, 256; Smith, *Isaiah*, 2.257; Motyer, *Isaiah*, 359; Young, *Isaiah*, 2.199; Brueggemann, *Isaiah*, 76.

[60] On the woe cry used here, see further 2.1.a. above concerning its use in Isa. 29:15-16. Even Goldingay and Payne, *Isaiah*, who think the "woe" here "is the exclamation of a teacher reproving a resistant and stupid pupil" (*Isaiah*, 34), concede that the word's "common association with death makes it strike a worrying note here" (31).

[61] Literally, "with."

[62] The Hebrew here is difficult and tolerant of more than one translation. Fortunately, the overall point of the questions remains the same no matter which option is chosen for their specific meaning—that the creature should not challenge the decisions of the Creator for how he shapes the creature. The uncertainty concerns the text after the first question: וּפָעָלְךָ אֵין־יָדַיִם לוֹ, which could also be taken thus—"and your work has no hands," or thus—"and your work, there are no hands for it," which could have the same meaning as the previous option or, alternatively, could mean that there are no hands for doing the work, which could be a more roundabout way of saying that the potter has no hands. For the translation I have adopted, see Oswalt, *Isaiah*, 2.207, who also notes that 1QIsa[a] reads ופו עולכה אין אדם ידים לו ("as for your worker[s], not a man has hands").

but antagonistic criticism[63] implying that the fashioner of the clay is shaping the clay wrongly. The illustration shows the absurdity of God's people objecting to his shaping of their situation. It is his inherent right as their Creator (in terms of their existence both physically and as his people), and their inherent responsibility as his creation is to submit to his sovereignty. Clay will never object to the potter's fashioning. And God's people should never object to his plans for them.

The second half of the question turns the listeners' own experience against any possible attitude of rebellion against God's designs. It asks them to consider whether their own work would ever charge them with "having no hands," that is, with having no skill or ability.[64] Again, that would be absurd. It is just as absurd for any of God's people to challenge his dealings with them.

Verse 10 is synonymously parallel to v. 9, repeating the warning cry of "woe!" and presenting the same basic basis for it as 9b but using a slightly different metaphor: "Woe to the one who says to a father, 'What are you fathering?' or to a woman, '[With] what are you in labor?!'" (45:10). This version of the thought draws on the deep-seated Israelite conviction that children should honor and obey their parents (Exod. 20:12; 21:15, 17; Isa. 1:2-4; 30:9) as well as the sheer absurdity of the idea of a baby that is being born challenging its father or mother about its make-up.[65] The point is again that none of God's people should by any means object to his plans for them; that would be outrageous in the extreme.

Whereas v. 9a issued the warning cry and implicitly gave its basis through identification of its issuer and its addressees, and then unpacked the logic of that implicit basis in 9b, v. 10 now explicates the basis of the warning cry through the identifications it makes. Thus, v. 10 both restates v. 9 as a whole and also joins 9b in unpacking the implicit basis for the woe cry of 9a contained in 9a's identifications of addresser and addressees. The fashioner/creator/potter/parent in Isaiah's illustration represents YHWH, and the clay/child is the member of God's people who contends that YHWH is shaping his people wrongly. Oswalt captures the logic of vv. 9–10: "To disagree with God's ordering of one's life or one's world is not merely a matter of preference or outlook. At bottom, it is a refusal to let God be God, a reversal of roles, in which the creature tries to make the Creator a servant to carry out the creature's plan."[66] Drawing out the sense of the warning communicated

---

[63] English has the same basic idiom.
[64] Cf. Oswalt, *Isaiah*, 2.209. On יָד (hand) as "ability," see BDB, s.v., § 2; R. H. Alexander, "יָד," *TWOT*, 1.362–4 (363).
[65] Although the text does not explicitly indicate that the questioner is the child of the father or mother, the point seems implicit in this context following on the illustration of clay that talks back to its fashioner, and some translations even make this explicit (so NIV, NET, KJV, NKJV, NLT, HCSB, JPS). Smith, *Isaiah*, 2.262–3, suggests an interesting intermediate reading of a child questioning his own parent about a sibling. But this misses the rhetorical strategy employed by the author of painting the objectors in the most absurd light, just as in v. 9. However, it may be that the text means to encompass both possibilities given its corporate orientation. Nevertheless, a child questioning his own parent's fashioning of himself remains the primary image. In this sort of corporate context, that amounts to an Israelite challenging YHWH's treatment of him entailed in YHWH's treatment of the people.
[66] Oswalt, *Isaiah*, 2.208.

by the cry of "woe," he colorfully adds, "A persistent refusal to allow God to be God, to establish the terms of our relationship with him, as in Gen. 3, will result in a funeral—our own."[67]

2.2.b. Isa. 45:11

Isa. 45:11 continues the rebuke of those who reject YHWH's plans for his people: "¹¹ Thus says YHWH, the Holy One of Israel and his fashioner, 'Ask me about the things to come concerning my sons. Indeed, concerning the work of my hands you shall command me!'" The message now adds the designation "Holy One of Israel" to repetition of the identification of YHWH as Israel's fashioner, doubly stressing YHWH's authority and right to do as he wishes with his people.[68] The two halves of the substance of the verse are synonymously parallel and chiastic. In light of the hostile questions from rebellious Israelites envisioned in 45:9-10 and the obviously inappropriate commanding of YHWH referred to in 11b, the imperative "ask me" (שְׁאָלוּנִי) undoubtedly refers to the same sort of hostile questioning that challenges the wisdom or righteousnesses of YHWH's dealings with his people.[69] Asking YHWH about his sons in such a way is tantamount to telling him what to do with them, who are the work of his hands, which is equivalent to acting like the potter and treating him as if he is clay. "The things to come" refers to YHWH's announced plans for his people.[70] The chiastic structure runs thus:[71]

---

[67] Ibid.
[68] Cf. ibid., 210.
[69] It is possible that the text enjoins straightforward questioning of YHWH (so, e.g., Koole, *Isaiah*, 457; Goldingay and Payne, *Isaiah*, 38) to invite the declaration of YHWH's plans given in vv. 12–13, but this runs counter to the contextual factors mentioned above. Some have suggested emending the vocalization of הָאֹתִיּוֹת to read the interrogative marker הֲ instead of the definite article, yielding a question rather than a command (Smith, *Isaiah*, 2.263). This would alleviate the tension of YHWH commanding Judah to do that for which he is rebuking them, but the harder reading is normally to be followed, and Oswalt, *Isaiah*, 2.207 n. 35, points out that the suggestion is "without ms. support." While rejecting an emendation, Smith, 263–4, points out that a question can be signaled without a written interrogative marker by intonation or context, and thinks a question most likely here. However, this does not sit comfortably with the imperative form שְׁאָלוּנִי. Others emend the imperative to a perfect or an imperfect (Koole, ibid.), though this is also without ms support and eases the reading too conveniently. Most commentators and translations opt for a question here, but this seems to be to resolve the tension the imperative poses and misses Isaiah's use of irony, which we also saw in the context of Isaiah's use of the potter/clay imagery in ch. 29. Thankfully, both an ironic imperative and a question come to the same basic meaning of disapproving what is mentioned. Koole, ibid., rejects an ironic sense, but his suggestion of taking the imperfect תְּצַוֻּנִי (you shall command me) as an oxymoron (458) seems little different except that it loses some explanatory power; it is better to take it as an imperatival imperfect.
[70] The LXX takes הָאֹתִיּוֹת (the things to come) as the object of the participle of יצר, yielding "Creator of the things to come," but the MT is most likely; see Oswalt, ibid., who includes the evidence from Qumran in his analysis; Koole, *Isaiah*, 456.
[71] Some construe the quotation of YHWH along these lines: "Ask me about the things to come. Concerning my sons and concerning the work of my hands command me!" (so Goldingay and Payne, *Isaiah*, 37–8; Motyer, *Isaiah*, 362; Young, *Isaiah*, 3.205). But the parallel and chiastic structure supports the decision of most translations to take "concerning my sons" with the preceding verb. Fortunately, the overall meaning remains the same with either reading.

(A) Ask me
(B) concerning my sons
(B') concerning the work of my hands
(A') command me.

The striking thing about this verse is that it commands those opposed to YHWH's plan to do the very thing for which he is rebuking them. This is another example of Isaiah's use of sarcastic irony, which purposely states the opposite of the meaning that is intended in order to stress that meaning by stating it in a shocking way that also expresses disdain for the attitudes and/or actions it seeks to discourage. We observed this literary technique in our exegesis of 29:15-24, and it is used similarly here.[72] Its expression in this context is similar to a father dealing with a resistant child, and having explained that the child's attitude was foolish and dangerous, telling him to go ahead and put that attitude into action. Isaiah has indicated that the attitude and actions of the rebellious among his people are fatally dangerous ("woe!"; vv. 9–10) and explained their folly in it all (it's like a pot taking issue with its potter, etc.). By telling them to continue on in their dangerous folly, Isaiah is in effect urging them to abandon their absurd distrust of and opposition to YHWH and his plan and to rather trust in and embrace them. This now becomes the main point of the passage, the natural logical conclusion to the warnings against such folly and the explanatory support of those warnings.

2.2.c. Isa. 45:12-13

Verses 12-13 now support Isaiah's denunciation of the opposition to YHWH's plan for his people and that denunciation's implicit call to abandon that opposition by giving reasons for doing so. Verse 12 entails three supporting points: "I myself made the earth, and I created man upon it. I, my hands, stretched out the heavens, and I have commanded all their host." First, reference to YHWH as creator of all things (heaven, earth, man, and the heavenly host) again implies his right and authority to do as he wishes with his creation as well as his creation's responsibility to submit to his plan for them. Second, YHWH's creation of all things implies his great wisdom and thus that his people should realize that his plan is best and trust his wisdom. Third, YHWH's creation of all things implies his supreme power and that his plans will surely be accomplished. Those who oppose his plan should repent of that stance and embrace YHWH's way because it will indeed come to pass.

Verse 13 is an extension of this last implication in that it specifies what that plan is that YHWH will certainly bring to pass. And in specifying that, it also implicitly reveals what the rebellious members of God's people objected to: "'I myself have stirred him up in righteousness and I will make all his ways level. He himself will build my city and he will let my exiles go free without price and without bribe,' says YHWH of hosts" (45:13). The oracle refers to the pagan king Cyrus, as 45:1 indicates. He is the one YHWH would move[73] to rebuild Jerusalem and to set God's people free to return from

---

[72] See Section 2.1.b.2.a. for elaboration on this literary technique as it is used by Isaiah.
[73] There is little reason to take the verb עוּר here to refer to raising up Cyrus onto the scene of human history (so seemingly Young, *Isaiah*, 3.206, and possibly Oswalt, *Isaiah*, 2.210) or to power (so

exile to the land God had given them,[74] granting him success in his undertakings (= making all his ways level) so as to be able to accomplish YHWH's redemptive purpose for his people.[75]

Isaiah specifies that YHWH's actions toward and use of Cyrus would be righteous (צֶדֶק).[76] This undoubtedly comes as a response to the challenge to YHWH and his plan of salvation that Isaiah has been addressing. Some among God's people contended that YHWH's plan (announced by Isaiah) to deliver his people through the Gentile king Cyrus was not right.[77] There is some question of what צֶדֶק (righteousness) means in this context, whether rightness[78] or divine plan[79] or victory[80] or faithfulness.[81] But the dominant contextual issue of contending against YHWH's plan strongly suggests that the primary sense here is rightness or correctness in relation to YHWH's plan and actions concerning Israel, most specifically, of his choice of Cyrus to be their savior. Yet, the sense of faithfulness can be a specific expression of rightness and is probably in view here as a lesser, background accent since the restoration through Cyrus that Isaiah has announced is an expression of the faithfulness of God to his covenant with his people.

Now we might wonder why any of God's people would object to God's choice of Cyrus as the deliverer of his people. But it is not hard to imagine that a Gentile, pagan conqueror would defy the people's expectations for their deliverer. We need only think of the New Testament's portrayal of Jesus as not meeting his people's expectations for the Messiah to see how vehement opposition to one deemed unworthy could be.[82] And Jesus was a Jew while Cyrus would be an unclean pagan Gentile. J. A. Motyer explains more of the rationale well:

> By using a Gentile conqueror to liberate Israel it was not only the pride of the nation that was threatened but the Lord's promises. Under a Gentile liberator the people

---

Motyer, *Isaiah*, 362). The sense is rather that of moving/inspiring/prompting to action. As Smith, *Isaiah*, 2.264, notes, "This verb is typically used of God's unusual moving of unexpected people to do his will." Moreover, it is the use of Cyrus to accomplish the specific actions identified that is at issue.

[74] Paul would surely have taken the prophecy to refer to the future in relation to Isaiah's time. Such a view is possible, and in the modern era would normally involve taking the perfect tense verb in the verse as a prophetic perfect, indicating that the future action of God communicated by the verb was already settled and certain. On the prophetic perfect in Hebrew, see GKC, § 106m-o; B. K. Waltke and M. O'Connor, *An Introduction to Biblical Hebrew Syntax* (Winona Lake, IN: Eisenbrauns, 1990), § 30.5.1.e; Joüon and Muraoka, *Biblical Hebrew*, § 112h.

[75] On יָשַׁר in the piel + דֶּרֶךְ meaning "to make successful"; see BDB, s.v. יָשַׁר, pi. § 1.

[76] Alternatively, righteousness could be describing Cyrus and his actions (Whybray, *Isaiah*, 109, e.g., refers it to his motives). But the prepositional phrase "in righteousness" (בְּצֶדֶק) normally modifies the verb in its sentence, and that is most appropriate here in the context of countering contention against YHWH.

[77] On this, see the introduction to this general section (2.2) above and further below.

[78] Oswalt, *Isaiah*, 2.211, though his appeal to Whitley is puzzling; seemingly Goldingay and Payne, *Isaiah*, 40.

[79] C. F. Whitley, "Deutero-Isaiah's Interpretation of Ṣedeq," *VT* 22.4 (1972), 469–75 (473). Baltzer, *Deutero-Isaiah*, 237, gives the nuance of "order," and G. A. F. Knight, *Deutero-Isaiah: A Theological Commentary on Isaiah 40–55* (Nashville, TN: Abingdon, 1965), 138–9, that of "saving purpose."

[80] Paul, *Isaiah*, 263.

[81] Seemingly Smith, *Isaiah*, 2.265, and Young, *Isaiah*, 3.206.

[82] See Brueggemann, *Isaiah*, 75–6, for some intriguing parallels between God's choice of Cyrus and Jesus.

would in principle return to the same situation from which they had been deported. The times of the Gentiles would continue in Jerusalem. There would be no sovereign state, no Davidic revival! The Cyrus-plan was the death knell to all such hopes.[83]

In response to objections to YHWH's plan, YHWH insists that he will rightly bring Cyrus to allow his people to return to the Promised Land and even rebuild its capital, all without any payment or ostensive incentive ("without price and without bribe"). That he will see to it that Cyrus does this without any motivating benefit further testifies to the power of YHWH at which the rebellious Israelites should stand in awe and bow in submission, underscoring the certain success of his plan of salvation and the folly of opposing it, including his choice of a deliverer.

2.2.d. A Contextual Concern for the Salvation of the Gentiles

Isaiah 45:9-13 is surrounded by concern for the salvation of the nations. Isaiah 45:6 indicates that one of the main purposes of YHWH's choice of Cyrus as the deliverer of his people was for the world to know that YHWH is the only true God.[84] As Motyer observes, "World-wide *(from the rising of the sun to the place of its setting)* knowledge of God was promised through Abraham and his descendants (Gn. 12:1ff.; 22:18) and the Davidic king (Ps. 72:8-11), and Isaiah is linking these very treasured ideas with Cyrus. This must be kept in mind as we come to verses 9-13."[85] Indeed, the rebellious Israelites seem to have been objecting in part to God's plan of salvation because his choice of a savior involved Gentiles in his people's salvation and continuing condition. After addressing this objection, Isaiah 45 naturally moves to a fuller treatment of the salvation of the Gentiles in vv. 14-25.[86] The specifics of that treatment lie beyond the scope of this investigation, but this concern for the salvation of the Gentiles that envelops Isa. 45:9-13 clarifies the resistance to God's choice of a savior for his people as, in effect, resistance to his plan for the salvation of the nations.[87]

2.2.e. Summary/Conclusion

Isaiah 45:9 implies the fundamental point of 45:9-13, which comes to explicit though ironic expression in v. 11: that those who object to God's plan of salvation/choice of a

---

[83] Motyer, *Isaiah*, 361 (whose comments also strengthen support for a secondary nuance of "faithfulness" to צדק in 45.13). Cf. Oswalt, *Isaiah*, 2.208; Paul, *Isaiah*, 259-60; Brueggemann, ibid. Smith, *Isaiah*, 2.242, 260, thinks it implausible that any Hebrew would object against one who would do such great good for them. But he neglects the very plausible rationales routinely offered by commentators. Moreover, the people's objection is against YHWH's plan to restore them in this particular way in the future, not specifically against the prospect of Cyrus doing them good.
[84] On 45:6, see the references in n. 59 above.
[85] Motyer, *Isaiah*, 359.
[86] On 45:14-25 concerning the salvation of the Gentiles, see the references in n. 58 above.
[87] This is not to say necessarily that such resistance was *intentionally* opposed to the salvation of the Gentiles, but was at least practically so. On the other hand, according to the book, Isaiah's preaching included this theme of light to the Gentiles. Hence, it may well be that opposition to blessing for the nations was part of the rationale for resistance to YHWH's plan of salvation; cf. the book of Jonah.

deliverer should abandon their distrust of and opposition to YHWH and his plan and rather trust in and embrace them. Isaiah 45:9 implies this point by warning against contending with the Lord. Verses 9–11 employ the figures of Creator and creation, potter and clay, parent and child, to ground this warning and the call to turn from distrust and opposition to trust and submission. These figures show the absurdity and perversity of God's people objecting to his plan of salvation and his choice of their deliverer; clay does not charge that the potter is shaping it wrongly. Verses 12–13 then provide further grounding for the call to repent of rebellion against the Lord's plan of salvation and to trust in it by drawing attention to YHWH's identity as the omnipotent Creator (v. 12) and reasserting his plan of deliverance with certainty. The surrounding context of the passage reveals that rejection of God's plan of salvation was in effect resistance to his plan to save the Gentiles.

2.3. Jer. 18:6 in Its Old Testament Context

2.3.a. Exegesis

Jer. 18:6 is situated in the larger passage of 18:1-12.[88] Scholars routinely observe that it is difficult to discern the organizing structure of the book of Jeremiah beyond some general, prominent features.[89] The book falls most naturally into two main sections, chs. 2–24 and 26–51, with ch. 25 serving as a literary hinge between the two sections, ch. 1 serving as an introduction, and ch. 52 serving as an epilogue.[90] Both sections contain the themes of judgment and restoration, but the first section is known for its emphasis on judgment and the second for its emphasis on restoration.[91] The passage of our concern falls in the first section, which Christopher Wright describes thus:

> In chapters 1–24 the message of Jeremiah is almost entirely one of relentless tearing down. The prophet systematically dismantles all the main pillars of the edifice of Israel's faith. By their persistent rebellion and unrepentant wickedness, the people have nullified the things they trusted in. The terrible and terrifying reality was that they had turned the great truths of their faith into deception and

---

[88] Jer. 18:1-12 is virtually universally recognized by scholars as a discrete passage in the final text of the book.
[89] See e.g., P. C. Craigie, P. H. Kelley, and J. F. Drinkard, Jr., *Jeremiah 1–25* (WBC, 26; Waco, TX: Word, 1991), xxxi–xxxiii; J. A. Thompson, *The Book of Jeremiah* (NICOT; Grand Rapids, MI: Eerdmans, 1980), 27; F. B. Huey, *Jeremiah, Lamentations* (NAC, 16; Nashville, TN: Broadman, 1993), 24–6; T. E. Fretheim, *Jeremiah* (SHBC; Macon: Smyth & Helwys, 2002), 17–22. C. J. H. Wright, *The Message of Jeremiah* (SBT; Downers Grove, IL: IVP, 2014), 26, observes that "much modern scholarship has assumed … that the book is a rather chaotic assembly of texts with no apparent chronological or thematic order." For an intriguing suggestion of a rationale for the lack of structure in the book, see Fretheim, 19, 22. There is good reason to think that chs. 18–20 have been grouped together for thematic reasons; see L. C. Allen, *Jeremiah: A Commentary* (OTL; Louisville, KY: Westminster John Knox, 2008), 212–13; Craigie et al., *Jeremiah*, 240–1.
[90] See Fretheim, *Jeremiah*, 18. Cf. Wright, *Jeremiah*, 27; L. C. Allen, "Jeremiah: Book of," *DOTP*, 423–41 (425).
[91] See Fretheim, *Jeremiah*, 19.

lies. Over these chapters Jeremiah effectively undermines all the old foundations of their security: their redemption from Egypt and the gift of land; the temple; the Sinai covenant and law; their election from among the nations; the king on David's throne. All of these are "attacked"—not because they were not "true," but because they had become the false security of a people determined to defy the very reason for them and the spiritual, ethical and social implications of them.[92]

Jer. 18:1-12 fits squarely into this section and its concerns with a warning of judgment for a stubborn and rebellious Israel and a call to repentance that is expected to go unheeded. The passage combines multiple prophetic speech forms, including symbolic action report, vision-oracle report, oracle of salvation, oracle of disaster, and call to repentance.[93] The most prominent form in the passage is the symbolic action report. But it is an unusual version in that the form normally reports a symbolic action taken by the prophet whereas in Jeremiah 18 the report is of an action taken by someone else (a potter) that YHWH assigns symbolic meaning. Hence, Leslie Allen observes that the passage is a hybrid of a symbolic action report "and a vision-oracle report ... in which Yahweh draws Jeremiah's attention to everyday phenomena and then explains their significance."[94]

The structure of Jer. 18:1-12 is relatively straightforward following along the lines of the symbolic action report form.[95] There are two basic sections: the report of the symbolic action (vv. 1-4), and the divine interpretation of the action (vv. 5-12).[96] The basic action that Jeremiah sees is that of a potter making clay into a vessel, but that turns out differently than the potter desires ("it was spoiled in the hand of the potter"; v. 4a), leading him to remake it into a different vessel according to his own discretion ("So he remade it [into] another vessel as was right in the eyes of the potter to make"; v. 4b).[97] The interpretation is that YHWH can deal with Israel as the potter dealt with the clay, a point implied strongly by the rhetorical question of 18:6a, which clearly expects an affirmative answer: "'Can I not do to you as this potter, house of Israel?'—a declaration of YHWH." The point is then stated positively by the assertion of 18:6b, which draws out the implication of the preceding question and makes it explicit: "Behold, as the clay

---

[92] Wright, *Jeremiah*, 27-8.
[93] On these various forms, see, succinctly, C. M. Toffelmire, "Form Criticism," *DOTP*, 257-71 (263); Allen, "Jeremiah," 426-32; *Jeremiah*, 213. P. R. Davies, "Potter, Prophet and People: Jeremiah 18 as Parable," *HAR* 11 (1987), 23-33, classifies Jeremiah 18 as a parable, but this seems to miss the mark.
[94] Allen, *Jeremiah*, 213.
[95] On the specifics of the form, see Allen, "Jeremiah," 428-9.
[96] See Craigie et al., *Jeremiah*, 242, for a more detailed outline of four main sections along with subsections.
[97] Fretheim, *Jeremiah*, 270, notes that most scholars take v. 4 iteratively. However, most English translations take it punctiliarly, there is nothing in the context demanding an iterative, and an iterative does not sit well with the converted imperfect (וַיַּעֲשֵׂהוּ) describing the potter's remaking activity. Davies, "Potter," 24-5, notes that the text does not actually indicate whether the action is iterative or not. In any case, the issue does not affect the theological interpretation the text gives to the action observed. On a different point, Fretheim, 270-1, notes that some scholars differ on whether the clay that is used for God's renewed shaping activity is the same clay (Israel), which will eventually be made into the vessel God originally intended, or if it is another clay/people, which will replace the original/Israel. But the text seems clear that it is the same clay that will be given a different destiny, which is the view that Fretheim and most commentators rightly take.

in the hand of the potter, so are you in my hand, house of Israel." The point is that God can change his intention toward the people based on their actions.[98] Specifically, on the one hand, his will is to ordain good for those whom, because of their wickedness, he had slated for destruction but have turned from their evil to good. On the other hand, his will is to ordain calamity for those for whom he had good planned but who turn from good to evil:

> [7] At a moment, if I declare concerning a nation or concerning a kingdom to uproot and to tear down and to destroy, [8] and if that nation of which I spoke turns from its evil, then I will change my mind concerning the calamity which I intended to do to it. [9] But at a moment, if I declare concerning a nation or concerning a kingdom, to build up and to plant, [10] and if it does evil in my eyes, not listening to my voice, then I will change my mind concerning the good [with] which I intended to do good to it. (vv. 7–10)

As stated, the principle applies to any nation. Terence Fretheim observes,

> Israel's particular history is placed within the context of the wider creation. This theme stands in continuity with the use of the "natural" image of God the Creator as a potter. The way in which God acts toward Israel is not unique among the nations of the world (so also 12:14-17; 16:16-21; 17:5-11; 27:1-11). Whether it is Israel or any other people, God will turn away from a judgment word upon human repentance, just as God will turn away from a promised blessing upon rejection of a divine word. The use of this creational motif relates to Israel's questions to God regarding fair treatment (2:35; 5:19; 9:12-16; 16:10-13; 31:27-30). Given the consistent worldwide pattern of God's ways of working, Israel cannot bring God into court claiming unjust treatment.[99]

---

[98] So the vast majority of commentators concerning the final form of the text. Allen, *Jeremiah*, 214, and R. P. Carroll, *The Book of Jeremiah: A Commentary* (OTL; London: SCM, 1986), 372, think that v. 6 originally referred to God's sovereign control but that in the final form of the text, vv. 7–11 take the meaning in a different direction, one of conditionality; cf. Davies, "Potter," 25–7. But this seems an unlikely interpretation even apart from vv. 7–11. The action that Jeremiah sees is a potter remaking clay into a different vessel than first intended due to the clay getting spoiled in the first fashioning attempt. The unmistakable conditional thrust of vv. 7–11 only confirms and explicates the conditional sense of the previous verses. P. G. Ryken, *Jeremiah and Lamentations: From Sorrow to Hope* (Preaching the Word; Wheaton, IL: Crossway, 2001), 294–6, serves as an unusual and shocking example of denying a prominent theme of the text and reading theology into it, seeming to deny that human beings can influence God to change his intention by their actions and taking the theological point to be that God can do whatever he wants with humanity. But to be fair, the quotation from Thompson to which Ryken responds is perhaps overstated or at least in need of some qualification. J. Calvin, *Jeremiah and Lamentations* (CCC; Wheaton, IL: Crossway, 2000), 109–10, was wiser to simply ignore the strong conditionality of the passage that runs counter to his theology rather than expressly deny its presence in the text. T. E. Fretheim, "The Repentance of God: A Study of Jeremiah 18:7-10," *HAR* 11 (1987), 81–92 (81), has observed that scholars have often judged Jer. 18:7-10 to be unsatisfactory, being too abstract or rigid or the like (see Fretheim's article for a compelling rebuttal to such a view). But this only confirms its strong sense of conditionality as such scholars cannot deny its presence in the text but then object to the text itself.

[99] Fretheim, *Jeremiah*, 271–2.

The principle of God's conditional dealing with humanity is then specifically applied to God's people (Judah), whom YHWH had slated for calamity because of their wickedness, in order to urge them to repentance: "And now, do say to the people of Judah and concerning the inhabitants of Jerusalem, saying, 'Thus says YHWH, "Behold, I am fashioning calamity against you and devising a plan against you. Do turn back, each one from his evil way, and make your ways and your deeds good"'" (18:11). The clear implication is that if they repent, then God will change his plan of judgment against them to a plan of blessing. The image is one of a strong divine sovereignty that nevertheless allows for genuine human free will/choice and is responsive to it. Wright captures a balanced view of the text:

> The overall message is that while God remains sovereign over end results, he takes into full account the way people respond to what he says. The relationship is not one of absolute divine sovereignty of a deterministic nature, nor is it one in which there is no plan or control at all. God's sovereignty responds to human choices; human actions affect the way God implements God's plans. Or as Brueggemann puts it, returning to the target of our text, "God is free and can respond and … Judah's obedience is of decisive importance. In light of both these affirmations, Judah is exhorted to choose carefully how it will act, for its future depends on its actons. Yahweh's responsive sovereignty and Judah's determinative obedience are both constitutive of Judah's life." "*Responsive sovereignty*" is an excellent phrase to capture what is portrayed here.[100]

The passage makes it clear that God is sovereign and can do as he wishes with Israel/Judah. And it makes it equally clear that what he will do with them, whether blessing or curse, is conditioned on what they do, whether they repent or not. These points are made in order to urge the audience to repentance, which is the main thrust of the text to this point.

There are two main questions that bear on how v. 12 is to be taken: "But they will say, 'It is hopeless! For we will walk after our own plans and we will each carry out the stubbornness of his evil heart.'" First, there is a question of whether the verse states what the people *will* say or whether it reports what they said or what they say in response to Jeremiah. The MT has a converted perfect construction ("they will say") while the targum, Syriac, and LXX seem to have read a converted imperfect ("they said" or "they kept saying" or perhaps "they keep saying"). Any of these are possible, but the MT seems most natural since there is no particular indication of a change of speaker.[101] Yet happily, the overarching concern of the text remains the same with each option, stressing the people's wickedness. In our view, v. 12 emphasizes the people's wickedness as YHWH reveals that they will not heed his warning and call to repentance through Jeremiah but will stubbornly persist in their own evil plans.

---

[100] Wright, *Jeremiah*, 213.
[101] The converted imperfect reading requires a change of speaker from the Lord to the editor/narrator since it involves informing the reader about what happened in response to Jeremiah giving the prophecy the Lord tasked him with delivering.

A second question about the meaning of v. 12 concerns the way to take the niphal participle נוֹאָשׁ (It is hopeless!). The word has the sense of despair about it and is used here as an interjection.[102] Used in this way, it carries the nuance of hopelessness.[103] The question is whether it communicates a stubborn recalcitrance[104] or an inability to act differently[105] or both.[106] In other words, does the anticipated response of the people assert that the call to (or thought of) repentance is hopeless because they simply and defiantly *will not* heed it, or is it a claim that they cannot help themselves?

Though not conclusive, the fact that the word employed carries a sense of despair to it seems to slightly favor a claim of inability as part of the meaning. However, the text clearly views the people's response as wicked and unjustified. It is unlikely that the quotation of the people is what they would literally say, owning up to stubborn evil.[107] Rather, the quotation appears to attempt to characterize the reality behind what the people's response will be. The result is an emphasis on their wickedness for stubbornly refusing to heed the call to repentance, and this is the most fundamental aspect of their anticipated response. But it is compatible with the people's response including a claim of helplessness as long as such a claim is seen as an expression of the people's sinful recalcitrance, making the weak excuse that they cannot help it. This seems to be the most likely sense of v. 12, a stubbornly defiant response that includes the claim of not being able to act otherwise.

All of this formally leaves the emphasis of the passage on the wickedness and culpability of the people since they could repent and be spared but stubbornly refuse to repent. But rhetorically, this then practically turns attention back on the call to repentance, providing a negative example that spurs motivation to either continue in righteousness or repent of sin.[108]

---

[102] See *HALOT* and BDB, s.v. יָאַשׁ; Huey, *Jeremiah*, 182 n. 32.
[103] BDB, ibid.; *CHALOT*, s.v. יָאַשׁ.
[104] So most commentators.
[105] So Craigie et al., *Jeremiah*, 243.
[106] Huey, *Jeremiah*, 182 n. 32, mentions the possibility of it being both along with a third nuance of indifference, which he finds in both Holladay and Rashi.
[107] Unless it were a sarcastic denial of needing to repent. But since the quotation is most likely anticipating their response, this seems less likely than the view I take below.
[108] It is important to keep in mind two levels of purpose in Jeremiah. There are the original purposes of the oracles in their original settings in Jeremiah's ministry, when they were first spoken and prior to their inclusion in the book. And there are the purposes of the author/compiler of the final form of the book for which he included its various passages. Unfortunately, the original author and historical setting of the book itself are extremely uncertain. While Jeremiah might have had a purpose for a rebellious Israel to repent, e.g., the compiler of the book might have included the same passage to encourage the original readers of the book to remain faithful to the Lord if they were not apostate as the Israel of Jeremiah's day was. Allen, "Jeremiah," 439, compares the situation to the Gospels, which record stories of Jesus that took place a generation earlier and so often involve both the original purpose of Jesus's words and the purpose the Gospel author wanted to accomplish among his contemporary audience by telling them of Jesus's words. When discussing Paul's use of Jeremiah in Chapter 4 of this volume, we might draw on either purpose depending on what is relevant to Paul's discourse. Of course, these two levels of purpose might often coincide. For example, the compiler of the final form of the book might have included a prophecy from Jeremiah calling for repentance in order to call his own contemporary audience to repentance.

2.3.b. Summary/Conclusion

Jeremiah 18:1-12 has two basic sections. First, in vv. 1-4, there is a report of an action God will assign symbolic meaning to—a potter making clay into a vessel that turns out differently than the potter desires, leading the potter to remake it into a different vessel according to his own discretion. Second, there is the divine interpretation of the action (vv. 5-12). The interpretation is that YHWH can deal with Israel as the potter dealt with the clay, a point implied strongly by the rhetorical question of 18.6a and then stated positively by the assertion of 18:6b. The point is that God can change his intention toward the people based on their actions.

Jeremiah 18:1-12 issues a warning of judgment for a stubborn and rebellious Israel and a call to repentance that is expected to go unheeded. The main point of Jer. 18:1-12 is to urge repentance and obedience to the Lord, grounded in the threat of judgment, the ability to escape it through repentance, and the shameful wickedness of failing to heed God's gracious call to repentance. Jeremiah 18.6 sums up the basis for the call to repentance—YHWH's ability and right to deal with Israel as he sees fit, namely, to change his intention toward them from blessing to curse if they walk contrary to his will and from curse to blessing if they repent and walk in accordance with his will.

2.4. Conclusion

A summary of the exegesis of each text that we have analyzed in this chapter has been provided respectively at the end of each exegetical section: Section 2.1.d for Isa. 29:16, Section 2.2.e for Isa. 45:9, and Section 2.3.b for Jer. 18:6. Therefore, there is no need to summarize the exegesis of those texts here; the reader is directed to those locations for summaries of the exegesis of those texts. Instead, we will limit ourselves to a few broad observations. First, both texts from Isaiah have to do with objection to God's chosen means of salvation for his people. Isaiah 29:16 uses the potter/clay metaphor after 29:15 warns those who object to God's chosen means of salvation and try to avoid God's judgment. The chosen means of salvation to which they objected was essentially faith in the form of reliance upon the Lord for well-being, which prohibited reliance on other nations for well-being, such as Egypt.

The means of salvation God chose for his people and that they rebelled against in the context of Isa. 45:9 was the deliverer he selected for them, the Gentile king Cyrus. His Gentile ethnicity and all that went with it hardened Israel to God's plan of salvation and provoked Israel's rejection of it. God chose Cyrus partly to bring the world to know he is the only true God. In effect, Israel's resistance to God's choice of a savior for them was resistance to God's plan of salvation for the Gentiles.

Jer. 18:6 is a heavily conditional passage. It uses the potter/clay metaphor to argue for God's right to judge Israel if they remain unrepentant and to bless them if they repent. It portrays God as wanting Israel to repent and uses the potter/clay imagery to call Israel to repentance. The language of molding and making in all three Old Testament background texts primarily refers to God's shaping of the situation of Israel. In the Isaiah texts, that takes the form of being subject to the conditions of his plan of salvation. In Jeremiah 18, that takes the form of consignment to judgment versus blessing.

3

Interpretive Traditions Relating to the Old Testament Potter and Clay Texts

Having exegeted the relevant potter/clay texts from the Old Testament in their original contexts (Isa. 29:16; 45:9; and Jer. 18:6), it is now time to turn to the most pertinent ancient interpretive traditions that relate to these passages.

3.1. Sirach

The second-century BCE Book of Sirach, written in the tradition of Jewish wisdom literature, uses the analogy of God being like a potter and man being like clay in his hand in 33:13.[1] The verse appears in a section that highlights the use of opposites in the divine order of things and explains God as the source of their differences, including the difference between the godly and the sinner (33:7-15):

> [7] Why does a day surpass another, when all the daylight in a year is from the sun? [8] By the Lord's knowledge they were separated, and he made seasons and feasts different. [9] Some of them he exalted and sanctified, and some of them he placed in a number of days. [10] And all men are from the ground, and from the earth Adam was created. [11] In fullness of knowledge the Lord separated them and made their ways different. [12] Some of them he blessed and exalted, and some of them he sanctified and brought near to himself; some of them he cursed and brought low, and he turned them out of their place. [13] As a potter's clay in his hand—all his ways are according to his good pleasure—so men are in the hand of the one who made them, to recompense them according to his judgment. [14] Good is the opposite of evil, and life the opposite of death; so the sinner is the opposite of the godly. [15] And so look at all the works of the Most High, two by two, one the opposite of the other.[2]

---

[1] Sirach 27:5 mentions potter and vessel, and 38:29-30 mentions the potter, but neither passage construes God as the potter; neither one is relevant to Rom. 9:20-21.

[2] My translation.

Some take this text deterministically.[3] For example, John Piper notes that no ground in people is mentioned for the divine blessing and curse in 33:12 and argues that the point of v. 13 "is that his [God's] choices in determining which vessels or which persons serve which ends are based on his own secret wisdom, not on the free choices of men."[4] But this is an unlikely reading.[5] Ben Sira exhibits a strong doctrine of free will and directly contradicts that type of sentiment:

> [11] Do not say, "Because of the Lord I left the right way"; for he will not do what he hates. [12] Do not say, "It was he who led me astray"; for he had no need of a sinful man. [13] The Lord hates all abominations, and they are not loved by those who fear him. [14] It was he who created man in the beginning, and he left him in the power of his own inclination. [15] If you will, you can keep the commandments, and to act faithfully is a matter of your own choice. [16] He has placed before you fire and water: stretch out your hand for whichever you wish. [17] Before a man are life and death, and whichever he chooses will be given to him. [18] For great is the wisdom of the Lord; he is mighty in power and sees everything; [19] his eyes are on those who fear him, and he knows every deed of man. [20] He has not commanded any one to be ungodly, and he has not given any one permission to sin. (Sir. 15:11-20; NRSV)

As Alexander Di Lella states of 33:11-13,

> This text seems to say that God has decreed for each person either a blessed or a cursed destiny, independent of the person's free choice. But Ben Sira stops far short of attributing human sin to God and of saying that divine predestination destroys human freedom to choose between good and evil. In fact, the most likely meaning of 33:12cd, "Others he curses and brings low, and expels them from their place," is that God curses some people because they have chosen the path of wickedness; it is not that they are wicked because God has cursed them.[6]

---

[3] So J. Piper, *The Justification of God: An Exegetical and Theological Study of Romans 9:1–23*, 2nd ed. (Grand Rapids, MI: Baker, 1993), 197; J. Corley, *Sirach* (NCBCOT, 21; Collegeville, MN: Liturgical, 2013), 90; J. R. Wagner, "'Who Has Believed Our Message?'": Paul and Isaiah 'in Concert' in the Letter to the Romans" (PhD thesis, Duke University, 1999), 85.
[4] Piper, ibid.
[5] In favor of a nondeterministic reading of Sirach 33, see P. W. Skehan and A. A. Di Lella, *The Wisdom of Ben Sira* (AB, 39; New York: Doubleday, 1987), 83; J. G. Snaith, *Ecclesiasticus* (CBCNEB; Cambridge: Cambridge University Press, 1974), 162; A. C. Thornhill, "To the Jew First: A Socio-historical and Biblical-Theological Analysis of the Pauline Teaching of 'Election' in Light of Second Temple Jewish Patterns of Thought" (PhD thesis, Liberty University, 2013), 52–3 (There is a published version of this dissertation [*The Chosen People: Election, Paul, and Second Temple Judaism* (Downers Grove, IL: IVP, 2015)], but due to its thematic approach, it is not as convenient to use for research that seeks information about specific ancient authors/works.); J. Klawans, *Josephus and the Theologies of Ancient Judaism* (Oxford: Oxford University Press, 2012), 61.
[6] Skehan and Di Lella, *Wisdom*, 83.

Moreover, as Sigurd Grindheim has pointed out, Ben Sira understands "the divine election as based on the ethical and religious character of the elect."[7] Furthermore, the background of 33:10-15 is probably covenantal and its focus actually corporate.[8] "In fullness of knowledge" (v. 11) probably includes the Lord's knowledge of the character and actions of people by which he decides "their different ways" (v. 11), that is, their destinies,[9] as exemplified in v. 12. Thus, in v. 12, "Some of them he blessed and exalted" refers to Abraham and his descendants (viz. Israel), "some of them he sanctified and brought near to himself" refers to Israel's priesthood (or possibly Israel generally), and those who get cursed, brought low, and turned out of their place refers to "the Gentiles in general, who were not chosen as Israel had been, and in particular the Canaanites, whom the Lord had expelled 'from their place.'"[10]

Verse 13 with its potter/clay analogy, then, does not have in view God creating some people as good and some as evil or creating them with an unconditionally determined destiny. Rather, it articulates God's sovereign right as the Creator to recompense people for their deeds as he deems right, that is, according to his good pleasure (κατὰ τὴν εὐδοκίαν αὐτοῦ). The very language of the verse demands such a reading with its use of "judgment" (κρίσις) and especially "recompense" (ἀποδοῦναι).[11] Following on v. 13, vv. 14–15 imply that the respective opposite destinies of the sinner and the godly that result from God's judgment complete their being opposites and are in line with God's wise, praiseworthy ordering of creation with opposites.

Piper implicitly raises the possibility that Sir. 33:13 alludes to Jer. 18:6, and this seems probable given Jeremiah's prominence as a prophetic book, the language of being in the potter's hand, and this language having to do with God's sovereign right to judge as it does in Jeremiah.[12] The language of potter and clay coupled with the theme of God's right to judge gives some reason to think that Paul alluded to Sir. 33:13. However, Jer. 18:6 is much more likely in view because it has greater verbal similarity with Rom. 9:20-21,[13] it is the more prominent passage as part of a book that was more widely

---

[7] S. Grindheim, *The Crux of Election* (WUNT, 2.202; Tübingen: Mohr Siebeck, 2005), 37. Grindheim seems to take Sir. 33:10-13 as affirming unconditional divine predestination and sees this as conflicting with the book's clear and strong teaching of human free will in 15:11-20, construal of the latter theme being strengthened by Grindheim's finding that Ben Sira held to a conditional election. But Grindheim does not consider the possibility that 33:10-13 falls short of affirming unconditional predestination and is actually in harmony with the rest of the book's teaching.

[8] Cf. Wagner, "Concert," 85; Skehan and Di Lella, *Wisdom*, 400-1. Contra Piper, *Justification*, 196-7, who views the passage as individually focused. Besides the points made below, Piper misses the generality of the text as well as its employment of groups and types. Certainly it applies to individuals, but secondarily as each one fits into his respective group.

[9] On "different ways" as "different destinies," see Skehan and Di Lella, *Wisdom*, 400; cf. Snaith, *Ecclesiasticus*, 162.

[10] See Skehan and Di Lella, ibid. (including the final quotation); Wagner, "Concert," 85; cf. Corley, *Sirach*, 90.

[11] Cf. Thornhill, "Election," 42 n. 27.

[12] For the scale of probability used in this investigation for appraising allusions, see Abasciano, *Romans 9.1-9*, 24.

[13] As demonstrated by the following comparison of the texts of Rom. 9:20-21, Jer. 18:6, and Sir. 33:13 using these formatting codes:

bold = same word but different form between Romans and Jeremiah
italics = same word but different form between Romans and Sirach
single underline = Romans and Jeremiah correspond exactly (unless qualified by bold)

recognized as Scripture[14] and is alluded to by Sir. 33:13 itself (as just mentioned), and it has greater thematic coherence with Rom. 9:20-21. Both Jer. 18:6 and Sir. 33:13 deal with God's right to judge, but the whole context of Jer. 18:6 is tied up with that theme and has especially to do with God's right to judge *Israel*, whereas the theme is less of a focus in the context of Sir. 33:13.

It is possible that Paul alludes to Sir. 33:13,[15] but it seems superfluous given the probability that he alluded to the more fitting and prominent Jer. 18:6. It would be more accurate to say that Paul joined Sir. 33:13 in alluding to Jer. 18:6. However, if he did allude to Sir. 33:13, it would support the position that in Rom. 9:20-21 Paul speaks about and defends conditional action toward Israel on God's part rather than unconditional action since conditionality is inherent to Sir. 33:13. On the other hand, if we are correct that Paul does not allude to Sirach in Rom. 9:20-21, it is still virtually certain that he knew Sir. 33:13 and likely that it formed part of the general background of his sense of the potter/clay metaphor, especially that it signifies God's right to judge inter alia.

3.2. Jubilees

The second-century BCE Book of *Jubilees* does not contain a potter/clay reference, but the second volume of Charlesworth's *The Old Testament Pseudepigrapha* lists Jer. 18:8 ("and if that nation of which I spoke turns from its evil, then I will change my mind concerning the calamity which I intended to do to it"), which falls in the context of

> double underline = Romans and Jeremiah agree exactly while Sirach has the same word but a different form
> dotted underline = Jeremiah and Sirach share the same different form of the same word as Romans
> Rom. 9:20b-21: μὴ ἐρεῖ τὸ πλάσμα τῷ πλάσαντι, τί με ἐποίησας οὕτως; [21] ἢ **οὐκ** ἔχει ἐξουσίαν ὁ κεραμεὺς **τοῦ** πηλοῦ ἐκ τοῦ αὐτοῦ φυράματος ποιῆσαι ὃ μὲν εἰς τιμὴν σκεῦος ὃ δὲ εἰς ἀτιμίαν;
> Jer. 18:6 LXX: εἰ καθὼς ὁ κεραμεὺς οὗτος **οὐ** δυνήσομαι τοῦ ποιῆσαι ὑμᾶς οἶκος Ισραηλ; ἰδοὺ ὡς ὁ πηλὸς **τοῦ κεραμέως** ὑμεῖς ἐστε ἐν ταῖς χερσίν μου
> Sir. 33:13 LXX: ὡς πηλὸς κεραμέως ἐν χειρὶ αὐτοῦ πᾶσαι αἱ ὁδοὶ αὐτοῦ κατὰ τὴν εὐδοκίαν αὐτοῦ οὕτως ἄνθρωποι ἐν χειρὶ τοῦ ποιήσαντος αὐτοὺς ἀποδοῦναι αὐτοῖς κατὰ τὴν κρίσιν αὐτοῦ

---

[14] Many scholars believe that the Jewish canon of Scripture was in essence closed in the second century BCE (rightly in my opinion), comprised of the books of the Hebrew Bible, the traditional Jewish canon, which has also come to make up the Protestant OT. Even more scholars believe that the Jewish canon was not closed until the second century CE, and that various other books, like Sirach, were considered authoritative in the first century CE. For an overview of the state of the discussion of the canon, see S. Dempster, "Canons on the Right and Canons on the Left: Finding a Resolution in the Canon Debate," *JETS* 52.1 (March 2009), 47–77. Representatives of the two views mentioned above can be found in ibid., 48 nn. 7–8. Even on the expansive view of the Jewish canon in the first century, although many first-century Jews would seem to have regarded Sirach as authoritative, others would seem to have rejected it as such (even if they still respected it), and it was ultimately excluded from the Jewish canon of Scripture. Brief discussions of its canonicity in the first century may be found in Skehan and Di Lella, *Wisdom*, 20; M. Phua, "Sirach, Book Of," *DOTWPW*, 720–8 (721).

[15] Though not a common position, some scholars think Paul specifically draws his potter/clay imagery at least in part from Sir. 33:13: L. E. Keck, *Romans* (ANTC; Nashville, TN: Abingdon, 2005), 236; E. E. Johnson, *The Function of Apocalyptic and Wisdom Traditions in Romans 9–11* (SBLDS, 109; Atlanta, GA: Scholars, 1989), 132–3; C. G. Kruse, *Paul's Letter to the Romans* (PNTC; Grand Rapids, MI: Eerdmans, 2012), 384–5 (seemingly).

Jeremiah's potter/clay reference, as a significant parallel to *Jub.* 5:17 ("And for the children of Israel it has been written and ordained, 'If they return to him in righteousness, he will forgive all of their sins and he will pardon all of their transgressions'").[16] But this does not look like a specific allusion. There is no significant verbal correspondence and no specific thematic parallel apart from the general principle of repentance and forgiveness articulated. It would seem more to be a case of Jer. 18:8 being an example of one of a number of Old Testament texts that give voice to the basic principle affirmed by *Jub.* 5:17 and serves as part of its scriptural background, the doctrine of God's forgiveness being granted upon human repentance. Nevertheless, it is still instructive to pay attention to the context of *Jub.* 5:17, rooted as it is in the Old Testament concept of repentance/forgiveness and texts like Jer. 18:8, which itself sums up the doctrine to a certain extent and is a specific application of the principle expressed in Jer. 18:6.[17]

Jubilees 5:12-13, 15 is particularly enlightening:

> [12] And he made for all his works a new and righteous nature so that they might not sin in all their nature forever, and so that they might all be righteous, each in his kind, always. [13] And the judgment of all of them has been ordained and written in the heavenly tablets without injustice. And (if) any of them transgress from their way with respect to what was ordained for them to walk in, or if they do not walk in it, the judgment for every (sort of) nature and every kind has been written ... [15] He will judge concerning every one: the great one according to his greatness and the small one according to his smallness, and each one according to his way.

Several elements of this broader context stand out as noteworthy. It speaks of (1) God's purpose for people not to sin; (2) God's judgment of people having been already ordained and written down in Heaven; (3) God's judgment being without injustice; (4) people being able to transgress against what has been ordained and to not walk in what was ordained for them; and (5) God's judgment of people as based upon what they do. Most of these elements run counter to the ideas of divine determinism and unconditional election. God's purpose being for people not to sin is contrary to them because, of course, people (including God's people) do sin. One might think that God's judgment of people having been already ordained and written down in Heaven would support determinism and unconditional election, but the passage makes clear that people can act differently than is ordained for them to act. It appears that, for the author of *Jubilees*, God's ordaining of people's actions refers to his determination of what people should do, but are able to do or not to do, and that his prior judgment of people's actions refers to his prior determination of the judgment due for various sins that people might or might not commit (cf. Jn 12:47-49). God's judgment being based

---

[16] See O. S. Wintermute, "Jubilees: A New Translation and Introduction," in *OTP*, 2.35–142 (65); all translations of Jubilees in this investigation are Wintermute's. The parallel is also noted by R.H. Charles, *The Book of Jubilees or the Little Genesis* (London: Adam and Charles Black, 1902), 45 n. 17.

[17] I.e., Jer. 18:8 specifies part of the application of 18:6's principle of God's power and right to make of Israel what he wills based on their actions as being to relent from the calamity he intended against it.

on what people do makes it conditional. The concern for the justice of God's judgment adds a further contact point with Romans 9.

3.3. Testament of Naphtali

The second-century BCE *Testament of Naphtali*[18] uses the potter/clay analogy in ch. 2 to highlight God's knowledge of human beings:

> [2] For just as a potter knows the pot, how much it holds, and brings clay for it accordingly, so also the Lord forms the body in correspondence to the spirit, and instills the spirit corresponding to the power of the body. [3] And from one to the other there is no discrepancy … [4] And just as the potter knows the use of each vessel and to what it is suited, so also the Lord knows the body to what extent it will persist in goodness, and when it begins in evil. [5] For there is no form or conception which the Lord does not know since he created every human being according to his own image … [7] As there is a distinction between light and darkness, between seeing and hearing, thus there is a distinction between man and man and between woman and woman. [8] One cannot say they are one in appearance or in rank, for God made all things good in their order … [9] Thus my children you exist in accord with order for a good purpose in fear of God; do nothing in a disorderly manner, arrogantly, or at an inappropriate time. [10] If you tell the eye to hear, it cannot; so you are unable to perform the works of light while you are in darkness.[19]

It is clear that the text uses the potter image to refer to God as Creator, a role that gives him total knowledge of every human being. It is interesting that the author compares the potter's knowledge of the fitting use of each vessel he creates to God's knowledge of each person's tendency to good and evil. One wonders if this analogy implies that God creates people in such a way as to determine when they do good and when they do evil. But the author develops the thought in a different way that runs contrary to such an implication. He keeps the focus upon God's knowledge of humans beings as he grounds God's knowledge of human tendency to good and evil in God's creation of human beings in his own image (v. 5), which can hardly include a tendency to evil.

---

[18] This dating concerns the presumed original form of the book. Dating the *Testament of Naphtali* is complicated because, as is well recognized, the final form of the *Testaments of the Twelve Patriarchs* came from Christian hands, and there has been debate over whether it is a purely Christian work or originated as a Jewish work later redacted by Christians; see, e.g., H. W. Hollander and M. de Jonge, *The Testaments of the Twelve Patriarchs: A Commentary* (SVTP; Leiden: Brill, 1985), 82–5; H. C. Kee, "Testaments of the Twelve Patriarchs: A New Translation and Introduction," in *OTP*, 1.775–828 (777–8); J. L. Kugel, *Traditions of the Bible: A Guide to the Bible as It Was at the Start of the Common Era* (Cambridge, MA: Harvard University Press, 1998), 946–7; Thornhill, "Election," 72–4. However, as Thornhill observes, "While there is little doubt now that its origins were Jewish, the extent to which the 'Jewishness' of the *Testaments* is recoverable is debated" (73), leaving conclusions about Second Temple Judaism based on it worth drawing but tentative (74).

[19] Kee's (*Testaments*, 811) translation with the exception of the end of v. 4 (καὶ πότε ἄρχεται ἐν κακῷ), which I have translated more literally as "and when it begins in evil" (so also Hollander and de Jonge, *Testaments*, 300) in place of Kee's looser translation, "and when it will be dominated by evil."

A person's heart and so forth, particularly whether it is set upon God's Law or Beliar's, distinguishes him as good or evil (vv. 6–8). This is part of the order God has ordained for his creation and the author's audience exists for good in the fear of God (v. 9). Moreover, all of this serves as the basis for exhortation to righteous living (vv. 9–10). Because God knows the good and evil actions of human beings, and because God has so ordered creation that obedience versus disobedience to his Law distinguishes one as good or evil, and because one exists for good in the fear of God, one should do everything properly, knowing that living in darkness prevents one from performing the works of light.

3.4. Psalms of Solomon

The first-century BCE *Psalms of Solomon* uses the imagery of potter and vessel in 17:23 in an allusion to Ps. 2:9, speaking of the Davidic king smashing "the arrogance of sinners like a potter's jar."[20] The verse is not likening God to a potter, but it does liken wicked Gentiles (or at least their arrogance) to pots. The imagery seems to emphasize the weakness and devastation of sinners and their arrogance before God's judgment (as it is executed by his duly authorized representative, the king of his people). The psalm envisions that just as an earthenware pot is easily broken and smashing it utterly ruins it, so will the Gentiles/sinners and their arrogance be easily broken and utterly ruined by the king God establishes over his people. The reference is not particularly relevant to Paul's use of the potter/clay metaphor, but it does contribute to an understanding of the type of associations that were present in the figure in Paul's sociocultural milieu. *Psalms of Sol.* 17:23 testifies to the metaphor of people as vessels or pots conveying a sense of weakness, lowliness, and fragility.

3.5. Qumran

While there does not seem to be an obvious direct reference to God as a potter in the non-biblical Dead Sea Scrolls, 1QS 11:22 and 4Q511 frgs. 28–29 line 4 join a number of Qumranic *Hodayot* (thanksgiving hymns) in employing the image of mankind as molded clay, which implies God as the fashioner.[21] Generally, these texts use the figure

---

[20] All translations of *Psalms of Solomon* in this investigation are from R. B. Wright, "Psalms of Solomon: A New Translation and Introduction", in *OTP*, 2.639–70, which also treats the date of the book (640–1).

[21] 4Q511 does not actually contain the word "clay" (חמר) clearly but is judged to have been originally present by F. García Martínez and E. J. C. Tigchelaar, *The Dead Sea Scrolls Study Edition*, 2 vols. (Leiden: Brill, 1997–8), 1032, and is implied by the verb "to mold" (קרץ). Among the *Hodayot*, see 1QH^a 9:21-23; 11:23-25; 12:29; 18:3-7; 19:3; 20:24-32; 22:11; 23:12. With the exception of 1QH^a 22:11, this list appears in Wagner, *Heralds*, 57 n. 46. For non-biblical Qumran scrolls, I have followed Martínez and Tigchelaar's referencing system and translation. 4Q386 frg. 1 col. III.1-2 (drawn to my attention by Anthony Chadwick Thornhill in personal correspondence) likens Babylon to a pot but does not seem to imply God as its fashioner. The figure is used to depict Babylon in a lowly/weak way in contrast to God and his power over the nation.

of man as clay (with the implication that God is the potter) to highlight humanity's sinfulness, inadequacy, and extremely low estate before God, who is on the other hand the all-knowing, all-wise, all-powerful, sovereign, and highly exalted Creator. It is interesting that themes associated with Romans 9 appear in the broader contexts of some of these passages, such as divine sovereignty (a pervasive theme), divine faithfulness (1QH[a] 22:13), divine foreknowledge (1QH[a] 9:7-8), predestination/determinism (1QH[a] 9:19-20), eternal destiny (1QH[a] 11:21-22), the elect (1QS 11:17), divine justice and/or questioning/challenging God's judgment (1QH[a] 9:25-26; 12:30-31; 19:7; 20:19-21, 27-28), and the glory of God (1QS 11:20; 1QH[a] 9:10; 11:34-35; 12:28; 18:10-12; 19:6, 8, 10; 20:15, 22; 4Q511 frg. 28). Particularly noteworthy among Qumran texts using the potter/clay metaphor are those that associate the figure with a lack of right to answer back to God since Rom. 9:20-21 contains a similar distinctive sentiment.

1QS 11:21-22 reads, "As what shall one born of woman be considered in your presence? Shaped from dust has he been, maggots' food shall be his dwelling; he is spat saliva, moulded clay, and for dust is his longing. What will the clay reply and the one shaped by hand? And what advice will he be able to understand?" The text does not specify the nature of the human reply envisioned. But in the context of the psalm, which emphasizes God's supreme knowledge and man's inability to even understand God or his thoughts, it seems to be a general notion, communicating that man has nothing to offer or contribute to God.[22] 1QH[a] 9:25-26 gets more specific with its reference to man replying to God:

> [19] ... And in the wisdom of your knowledge you have determined their course before [20] they came to exist. And in accordance with [your] wi[ll] everything happens, and without you nothing occurs. *Blank* [21] These things I know through your knowledge, for you opened my ears to wondrous mysteries although I am a creature of clay, fashioned with water, [22] a foundation of shame and a source of impurity, an oven of iniquity and a building of sin, a spirit of error and depravity without [23] knowledge, terrified by your just judgments What can I say that is not known? Or declare which has not been told? Everything [24] has been engraved before you with the stylus of remembrance for all the incessant periods and the cycles of the number of everlasting years in all their predetermined times, [25] and they will not be hidden, and will not be lacking from before you. How will a man count his sin? How will he defend his iniquities? [26] How will an unjust respond to a just judgment?[23]

---

[22] Wagner, *Heralds*, 69–71, makes an intriguing case for 1QS 11:22 specifically alluding to Isa. 29:16/45:9 from which, he proposes, it crafted its rhetorical question. But the psalm lacks the context of conflict between God and his people in the biblical passages and employs its rhetorical question differently. It is questionable whether שוב ever took the meaning "to dispute" (as Wagner takes it) prior to rabbinic Hebrew. Indeed, it may be (and I think it more likely) that it does not refer to a verbal reply at all but carries a more typical sense of the verb, that of returning (here in the sense of giving back [to God]), which accords with the thrust of the text in any case. Be that as it may, the allusion is possible, but it is more likely that the Isaiah passages form part of the general biblical background to the hymn rather than being specifically in view.

[23] 1QH[a] 9:19-26. Brackets indicate "text restoration, sometimes minimally preserved in the manuscript" and "*Blank*" indicates a blank space left in the ms. (García Martínez and Tigchelaar, *Scrolls*, xxi).

First, we note that the context is deterministic (though this is not specifically linked to humanity-as-clay metaphor). God determines the course of people before they exist.[24] Second, the human reply to God contemplated here appears to be one that attempts to defend against God's just judgment. The implication of these rhetorical questions is that human beings have no defense against the righteous judgment of God and have no right to challenge it because of man's sinfulness and God's perfect knowledge and justice. 1QH^a 20:26-35 speaks similarly:

> The creature of clay must return to the dust, [27] ... What will dust and ash[es] reply? [... How] can it understand [28] his [wo]rks? How will he stand up the one who reproaches him? ... [29] ... They can [not] [30] recount all your glory, or stand up before of your anger. There is no reply [31] to your reproach, for you are just and there is no-one before you. What is he (to do that), he who returns to his dust? [32] I have kept silence, for what can I say about this matter? In accordance with my knowledge /I spoke/, spat saliva, one fashioned from clay. What [33] can I say unless you open my mouth? How can I understand unless you teach me? What can I pro[pose] [34] if you do not open my heart? How can I keep a straight path unless you steady [my] ste[ps]? How [35] can [my] steps stay secure [unless you] strengthen [me] with strength? And how can I rise [unless ...][25]

Clearly the relevant material from Qumran associates the potter/clay metaphor with mankind's lowly, sinful, ignorant position, bereft of any right to challenge God, who is perfectly just, and his righteous judgment.

3.6. *Wisdom of Solomon*

Wisdom of Solomon 15:7 (*c.* first century BCE or CE) employs potter/clay imagery as part of a polemic against idolatry carried out at length in ch. 15 of the book: "A potter kneads the soft earth and laboriously molds each vessel for our service, fashioning out of the same clay both the vessels that serve clean uses and those for contrary uses, making all alike; but which shall be the use of each of them the worker in clay decides."[26] As Piper comments in relation to Rom. 9:21,

> What is remarkable about this is that the potter's making two different sets of vessels for clean and unclean uses from the same clay is so close in thought to Rom 9:21 as to seemingly demand some sort of allusion to this text on Paul's part. But what is frustrating is that the *meaning* of Wis 15:7 has almost nothing in common

---

[24] It is possible that we are to understand that the determination in view is based on divine foreknowledge and fixes the destiny of the person conditionally (nondeterministically). But on balance, it seems more likely that the psalm is deterministic.
[25] Parentheses indicate "explanation required for the meaning of the English text," and slash marks demarcate "legible or illegible text inserted between the lines by the copyist" (García Martínez and Tigchelaar, *Scrolls*, xxi).
[26] All translations of *Wisdom of Solomon* in this investigation are from the NRSV.

with Paul's meaning. The context has to do with idolatry and the potter illustrates the idol-maker who makes a god from the same clay as all his other vessels (15:8). The point is the absurdity of idol worship because the idol-maker is "better than the object he worships" (15:17).[27]

The power and freedom of the human potter to fashion vessels and assign their purpose exacerbates his folly in then worshiping the very idol over which he himself exercised such power.

While Wisd. 15:7 itself does not liken God to a potter[28] or carry a specific meaning that is similar to Rom. 9:21, it does give insight into an ancient conception of the relationship between potter and clay that is likely to inform Paul's application of it to God and man, namely, that it is the potter's prerogative to assign as he sees fit the purpose of vessels he has fashioned. Moreover, Wisd. 15:7's broader context does imply God as the potter and people as clay vessels formed by him. Verse 8 says, "With misspent toil, these workers form a futile god from the same clay—these mortals who were made of earth a short time before and after a little while go to the earth from which all mortals are taken, when the time comes to return the souls that were borrowed." And v. 11 indicates that idol-making potters "failed to know the one who formed them and inspired them with active souls and breathed a living spirit into them." In light of v. 7, these verses imply the ironic criticism that the idol-making human potter exercises sovereignty over the gods he makes out of clay, yet fails to recognize the God who made him out of clay or to submit to his sovereignty. And as

---

[27] Piper, *Justification*, 195–6; emphasis original. Emphasis in quotations in this study are original unless otherwise noted. While Piper assumes an allusion by Paul to *Wisdom* a possibility, A. Sherwood, "Paul's Use of the Old Testament in Romans 9:6-29: God's Judgment Upon Israel's Idolatry" (MCS thesis, Regent College, 2007), 106 (a published version of this work has appeared, though it does not appear to differ in substance from the dissertation, where I interact with it; I have chosen to reference the dissertation because it is much more convenient to use than the ebook version of the published version available to me: *The Word of God Has Not Failed: Paul's Use of the Old Testament in Romans 9* [SSBL; Bellingham: Lexham, 2015], ProQuest Ebook Central), judges that there is a strong case for a late date for the *Wisdom of Solomon* such as would make an allusion by Paul almost impossible. However, the scholarly consensus gives a wide time span for a possible date of the book, sometime between 220 BCE and 50 CE (J. A. Linebaugh, *God, Grace, and Righteousness in Wisdom of Solomon and Paul's Letter to the Romans: Texts in Conversation* [NovTSup, 152; Leiden: Brill, 2013], 28; P. Enns, "Wisdom of Solomon," *DOTWPW*, 885–91 [885], identifies a narrower range of 100 BCE to 50 CE as the consensus), and it is hard to fix a specific date with certainty, though most scholars do seem to favor an early first-century date. Linebaugh, 28–9 n. 11, thinks a more specific date of c. the first decade of the first century is most likely (following McGlynn), and notes that fresh support for that dating has recently emerged. Thus, it seems entirely possible that Paul knew *Wisdom*, and there is no solid dating barrier to the possibility. However, there is question as to whether Paul would have considered *Wisdom* as part of Scripture; see n. 14 above on the state of the canon in the first century, which applies to *Wisdom* as much as to Sirach. If Paul did not consider *Wisdom* to be Scripture, then it is less likely (though far from implausible) that he would allude to it in the context of Romans 9, which is structured on and grounded in allusion to Scripture. Apart from the disputed nature of the book, and in light of the most likely timing of the book (early first century), one might also wonder if there was time for the book to reach scriptural status by the time Paul wrote Romans.

[28] On the figure of the potter in *Wisd*. 15:1-13, see M. McGlynn, *Divine Judgment and Divine Benevolence in the Book of Wisdom* (WUNT, 2.139; Tübingen: Mohr Siebeck, 2001), 159–65.

Ross Wagner has observed, it may be that the use of the potter/clay metaphor in Isaiah and Jeremiah lies in the background of the author's usage:

> if the use of the potter/clay metaphor in Isaiah and Jeremiah was familiar to the author of Wisdom, as it most likely was, it is possible that in Wisdom 15:7 there is an intentional and ironic allusion to these prophetic depictions of Israel's God. The idolaters reject the knowledge of the true creator and their own status as creatures of clay in God's hands (15:8), and instead make themselves out to be the creators of their own gods, masters of their own destinies. Wisdom would thus reflect a *reapplication* to the human sphere of a metaphor borrowed by the prophets from human society in order to speak of God's relationship to creation.[29]

But any conception of man as clay and God as potter in *Wisdom* is likely not a form of unconditional election or divine determinism. Greg Schmidt Goering goes so far as to say that "Pseudo-Solomon's understanding of election rests less on divine determinism and divine caprice and more on human initiative in the divine human relationship. One might even say that humans elect God."[30] That may be overstated. Anthony Chadwick Thornhill seems to express a more balanced perspective:

> while the author upholds the traditional belief in God's choosing of Israel, and does not extend much, if any, hope to Israel's enemies, the overall picture of the book is that God desires all people to repent and seek Wisdom, and that the gift of Wisdom will be afforded to all who ask for her. The few instances of language which seems deterministic must ... be read in light of the whole and major thrust of the book ... God's choice of Israel [in the thought of *Wisdom of Solomon*] is best thought of in corporate terms in that only those faithful to the covenant will receive its blessings.[31]

John Piper thinks Paul probably took some of the surface structures of his language in Rom. 9:21 from *Wisd.* 15:7,[32] but the language is simply not close enough (basic corresponding elements without regard to whether they are exact or loose have been underlined and Rom. 9:20b has been added for fuller comparison):

Rom. 9:20b-21: μὴ ἐρεῖ τὸ πλάσμα τῷ πλάσαντι· τί με ἐποίησας οὕτως; ἢ οὐκ ἔχει ἐξουσίαν ὁ κεραμεὺς τοῦ πηλοῦ ἐκ τοῦ αὐτοῦ φυράματος ποιῆσαι ὃ μὲν εἰς τιμὴν σκεῦος ὃ δὲ εἰς ἀτιμίαν;
Wisd. 15:7: καὶ γὰρ κεραμεὺς ἁπαλὴν γῆν θλίβων ἐπίμοχθον πλάσσει πρὸς ὑπηρεσίαν ἡμῶν ἓν ἕκαστον ἀλλ᾽ ἐκ τοῦ αὐτοῦ πηλοῦ ἀνεπλάσατο τά τε τῶν καθαρῶν

---

[29] Wagner, "Concert," 86 n. 110; cf. Piper, *Justification*, 196.
[30] G. S. Goering, "Election and Knowledge in the Wisdom of Solomon," in G. G. Xeravits and J. Zsengellér (eds.), *Studies in the Book of Wisdom* (JSJSup, 142; Leiden: Brill, 2010), 163–82 (182).
[31] Thornhill, "Election," 166–7.
[32] Piper, *Justification*, 196.

ἔργων δοῦλα <u>σκεύη</u> τά τε ἐναντία πάντα ὁμοίως τούτων δὲ ἑτέρου τίς ἑκάστου ἐστὶν ἡ χρῆσις κριτὴς ὁ πηλουργός.

Given the lack of semantic similarity, one would expect more substantial verbal similarity for *Wisdom* to have been a source for Paul's language in Rom. 9:20 or 21, particularly because other texts with substantial verbal and semantic similarity were at hand.[33] There is substantial verbal linkage between Rom. 9:20-21 and *Wisd.* 15:7 but not enough to signal an allusion without semantic parallel. It is noteworthy that only *Wisd.* 15:7 among the major potential Rom. 9:20-21 background texts shares the term "vessel" with the NT text (the singular nominative σκεῦος in Romans and the plural accusative σκεύη in *Wisdom*). However, it is a natural word to arise in connection with the potter/clay metaphor. Again, if there were not other texts with substantial verbal and semantic similarity at hand, then we might think an allusion probable here.

Even more striking is the similarity of *Wisd.* 15:7's "fashioning out of the same clay both the vessels that serve clean uses and those for contrary uses" to Rom. 9:21's "to make from the same lump one a vessel unto honor and another unto dishonor." Yet if Paul were alluding, without semantic coherence one would expect some distinctive vocabulary from this clause in *Wisdom* to appear in Rom. 9:21 beyond the word "vessel," such as ἀναπλάσσω (to fashion), which does not appear in biblical literature and only a few times in other ancient Jewish literature (Sib. Or. 11:198; Jos. Asen. 8:11; 15:4), rather than Paul's ποιῆσαι (to make), or καθαρός (clean) and ἐναντίος (contrary) rather than Paul's τιμή (honor) and ἀτιμία (dishonor), ἔργον (use), or even the τέ ... τέ construction rather than Paul's ὃ μὲν ... ὃ δέ. All things considered, we may conclude that *Wisd.* 15:7 is a possible allusion in Rom. 9:20-21, but that we do not think it is in fact an allusion.[34] If Paul does allude to *Wisd.* 15:7 in Rom. 9:20-21, then its significance would probably be to serve as an analogy to the human sphere of potters and clay, supporting God's right as the Creator of humanity and Israel to assign the fate of people in the sense of assigning blessing or curse to them, mercy or judgment, covenant relationship or condemnation.

3.7. Pseudo-Philo/Liber Antiquitatum Biblicarum

Writing in the first century CE,[35] Pseudo-Philo alludes to Isa. 29:16 and/or 45:9 in *LAB* 53:13 (most likely both passages are in view). The allusion comes in the book's retelling

---

[33] D. A. Campbell, *The Deliverance of God: An Apocalyptic Rereading of Justification in Paul* (Grand Rapids, MI: Eerdmans, 2009), 777–8, is convinced that *Wisdom* is "implicitly involved in much of the argument" (777) of Rom. 9:6-29. But the parallels are too general to conclude that Paul had *Wisdom* in view rather than that he merely attended to traditions and themes common to first-century Jews. For a consideration of the relationship between Romans 9 and *Wisdom*, see W. Sanday and A. C. Headlam, *A Critical and Exegetical Commentary on the Epistle to the Romans*, 10th ed. (ICC; New York: Charles Scribner's, 1905), 267–9.

[34] Remember our scale of probability for allusions: clear, probable, possible, or improbable; see further Abasciano, *Romans 9.1-9*, 24.

[35] On the dating of *LAB*, see concisely, D. J. Harrington, "Pseudo-Philo: A New Translation and Introduction," in *OTP*, 2.297–377 (299). For additional introductory literature on *LAB*, see Abasciano, *Romans 9.1-9*, 74 n. 101.

of the call of Samuel the prophet (ch. 53). The high priest Eli discerned that God was speaking to Samuel for the first time and instructed Samuel on how to respond properly to God speaking to him. After Samuel heard the word of the Lord to him, which was one of judgment upon Eli and the corrupt priests under him,[36] and reluctantly shared it with Eli, Eli replied, "Will the object formed answer back him who formed it? So I cannot answer back when he wishes to take away what he has delivered as a faithful giver. Holy is he who has prophesied, for I am under his power" (*LAB* 53:13). Here Pseudo-Philo has Eli use Isa. 29:16 and 45:9 to make the point that he, as one created by God, did not have the right to question God's judgment upon him. The figure of God as the one who forms and man as that which is formed indicates that man is under God's power, subject to his judgment.[37]

3.8. Philo

Philo (*c.* 20 BCE–50 CE) appears to explicitly use the language of God as a potter only once (*Quaest. in Gen.* 1:4) but speaks of human beings as clay (or made from clay) a number of times (which, of course, implies God as potter).[38] Platonist that he was, Philo tended to use the image of man as clay to depict humanity in what he considered its lesser attributes: molded rather than directly made (*Quaest. in Gen.* 1:4; *Op. Mund.* 1:135), physical/corporeal (pervasive in the references in n. 38 of this chapter), perceptible to the physical senses (*Op. Mund.* 1:134-35), mortal (*Op. Mund.* 1:135), earthly rather than heavenly (*Leg. All.* 1:31), lacking God's image (*Quaest. in Gen.* 1:4; *Leg. All.* 1:31; *Plant.* 1:44), corruptible (*Quaest. in Gen.* 1:4), fragile (*Spec. Leg.* 3:58), and in great need of divine assistance (*Rer. Div. Her.* 1:58).[39] Interestingly, Philo considered the fragility of a clay vessel (κεραμεοῦν ἀγγεῖον; *Spec. Leg.* 3:58) to make it fit for symbolizing the sinful act of adultery because the punishment for adultery is death, the reasoning apparently being that something so easily destroyed makes a good symbol for an act that invites destruction. Philo's one explicit reference to God as potter clearly has God as Creator in view but does not yield any relevant further insight into the divine role or its relationship to humanity.

---

[36] While this is discernible in *LAB* 53, it is much clearer in the biblical text.

[37] It is possible to take Eli to say that he is under the prophet Samuel's power, though hardly anyone does; see H. Jacobson, *A Commentary on Pseudo-Philo's Liber Antiquitatum Biblicarum with Latin Text and English Translation* (2 vols.; Leiden: Brill, 1996), 1129–30. However, even on that interpretation, Eli would still be indicating himself to be under God's power since the prophet represents God and wholly derives his power from him.

[38] *Quaest. in Gen.* 2:56; *Op. Mund.* 1:134-37; *Leg. All.* 1:31; *Plant.* 1:44; *Migr. Abr.* 1:3; *Rer. Div. Her.* 1:58; *Spec. Leg.* 3:58.

[39] On Philo's dual conception of human nature, see D. M. Hay, "Philo's Anthropology, the Spiritual Regimen of the Therapeutae, and a Possible Connection with Corinth," in R. Deines and K.-W. Niebuhr (eds.), *Philo und das Neue Testament: Wechselseitige Wahrnehmungen I. Internationales Symposium Zum Corpus Judaeo-hellenisticum. 1.-4. Eisenach/Jena, Mai 2003* (WUNT, 172; Tübingen: Mohr Siebeck, 2004), 127–42 (130-4); G. E. Sterling, "Different Traditions or Emphases? The Image of God in Philo's *De Opificio Mundi*," in G. A. Anderson, R. A. Clements, and D. Satran (eds.), *New Approaches to the Study of Biblical Interpretation in Judaism of the Second Temple Period and in Early Christianity* (STDJ, 106; Leiden: Brill, 2013), 41–56 (50-5).

3.9. Life of Adam and Eve

The first-century book *Life of Adam and Eve* employs the idea of man having been made of clay in 27:2, where Adam speaks to God after having received God's word of judgment for his sin in the garden: "Cast me not from your presence, whom you formed from the clay of the earth; and do not withhold your grace from him whom you nurtured."[40] The theme is used to emphasize Adam as created by God in an effort to persuade God to be merciful in light of the Creator/creature relationship and the benevolence God had previously bestowed in that relationship. This is reminiscent of the use of the potter/clay metaphor in Isa. 64:8 and is probably drawn from it.

3.10. Rabbinic Literature

Wagner has demonstrated that the Isaiah Targum interpretively linked Isa. 29:16 and 45:9.[41] The exact same phrase occurs in both passages ("Is it possible that the clay should say to its maker, 'You did not make me?'" / חשיבין קדמי האפשר דיימר טינא לעבדיה לא עבדתני) and "includes a number of features found in one or the other of the Hebrew passages but not in both."[42] He rightly concludes that this suggests Paul could have made the same connection between the two texts.[43] What Wagner does not mention in his book is that Targ. Isa. 29:16 and Jer. 18:6 are also interpretively linked,[44] showing it plausible that Paul could have alluded to Isa. 29:16, 45:9, and Jer. 18:6 all at once as well.[45] As Wagner describes it, the Targum employs "in Isaiah 29:16a and Jeremiah 18:6b an identical phrase which is itself composed of elements drawn from the Hebrew texts of both verses."[46] The phrase is: "Behold, as clay in the potter's hand, so are you regarded before me" (הא כמא דטינא ביד פחרא כין אתון חשיבין קדמי). However, a look at Wagner's own helpful comparison chart of the Hebrew and targumic texts reveals that only one word of that phrase (regarded/חשיבין) is drawn from the Hebrew

---

[40] Translation of *L.A.E.* in this investigation is from M. D. Johnson, "Life of Adam and Eve: A New Translation and Introduction," in *OTP*, 2.249–95. The dating of *L.A.E.* is very uncertain, with a span between 100 BCE and CE 200 most likely according to Johnson (252), who thinks the late first century most likely.

[41] Wagner, *Heralds*, 59–62. On the inclusion of the targums with rabbinic literature, see M. McNamara, *Targum and New Testament: Collected Essays* (WUNT, 279; Tübingen: Mohr Siebeck, 2011), 68. Cf. *DNTB*, which includes its entry on targumim under rabbinic literature; see further section 1 of that entry (B. D. Chilton, "Rabbinic Literature: The Targumim," *DNTB*, 902–9 [902–1]) for a concise discussion of the relationship between rabbinic Judaism and the targumim. For our approach to rabbinic literature and appropriate caveats, see Abasciano, *Romans 9.1-9*, 12–13; and *Romans 9.10-18*, 32 n. 44.

[42] Wagner, *Heralds*, 60. Translations from Targum Isaiah in this investigation are those of B. D. Chilton, *The Isaiah Targum: Introduction, Translation, Apparatus, and Notes* (TAB, 11; Wilmington: M. Glazier, 1987).

[43] Wagner, *Heralds*, 61–2.

[44] Wagner, "Concert," 81–2, does mention it in his doctoral dissertation, however. I observed it independently before noticing it in his dissertation.

[45] Targum Jeremiah 18:12 does not contain the note of inability that some find in the biblical verse.

[46] Ibid., 81.

text of Isa. 29:16 and that the bulk of it is drawn from the Hebrew text of Jer. 18:6.[47] This is important because (1) allusion to Isa. 29:16 by Paul in Rom. 9:20-21 is clearer than allusion to Jer. 18:6, and (2) reference to Jer. 18:6 in Targ. Isa. 29:16 is especially apparent, increasing the likelihood of reference to Jer. 18:6 when reference to Isa. 29:16 is present. Combined with the targumic linking of Isa. 29:16 and 45:9, the further linking to Jer. 18:6 justifies Wagner's conclusion: "Through the use of these composite phrases, the targumists establish a three-way relationship among these potter-clay texts, with Isa. 29:16 as the middle term, suggesting that Isaiah 29:16, Isaiah 45:9, and Jeremiah 18:6 have been read in light of one another. A similar interpretative move appears to lie behind Paul's allusion to the potter-clay metaphor in Romans 9."[48]

Interestingly, Targ. Isa. 45:9 at first uses the potter/clay imagery differently than the biblical text.[49] In the first part of the verse, the potter makes idols and a warning is issued to those who trust in them for good. So the potter represents idol-making human beings, and the clay represents idols in Targ. Isa. 45:9a. But the second half of the verse switches to using the imagery as the biblical text does, portraying God as a potter (though not using the word) and clay as human beings (presumably who are part of his people) who trust in idols. Rather than taking the rebellion against God at issue to be an objection to God's plan of salvation or choice of redeemer, the targum appears to regard it as idolatry, so that it is idolatry that is equivalent to telling God, "You did not make me" and so on. Using the metaphor of such different referents within the same verse shows its flexibility.

We saw that Isa. 29:9-14 provides important background for understanding the passage in which Isa. 29:16 lies (see Section 2.1.b.2.a. in Chapter 2 of this volume). Targum Isaiah 29:10 strengthens the biblical verse's expression of divine involvement in Israel's wicked ways, speaking of God casting a spirit of deception or error (טעו) among them instead of Isaiah's pouring out a spirit of deep sleep upon them. The targum interprets Isaiah's language of the shutting/covering of Judah's eyes/prophets/heads/seers as God hiding himself from the prophets and hiding (i.e., removing) the scribes and teachers of the Law. Rather than it being Isaiah's vision specifically that has become inscrutable, it is *all* prophecy that has become inscrutable.

There is little of significance for background to Paul's use of the potter/clay in the rest of rabbinic literature. *Genesis R.* 24:1 cites Isa. 29:16 but takes a relatively straightforward approach, elaborating on the verse with examples, namely the created object objecting to its creator and the plant objecting to its planter. *Genesis R.* 24:1 also cites Isa. 29:15, giving a straightforward illustration of trying to hide counsel from God. Isaiah 29:17-18 also receive interpretations here in *Gen. R.* 24:1: Isa. 29:17's fruitful field as a royal palace and its forest as a multitude of men, and v. 18's book as the book of the generations of Adam referred to in Gen. 5:1.

---

[47] See ibid., 82.
[48] Ibid.
[49] On the other hand, Targ. Isa. 45:14 follows along with the biblical text's affirmation of Gentile conversion (Isa. 45:14) and even strengthens it by classifying its Gentile confession of faith as thanksgiving to God.

Many of the rabbinic references that are related to the context of Isa. 29:16 are appeals to Isa. 29:15 for its mention of darkness. Typically, the appeals to Isa. 29:15 link the wicked to darkness (*Exod. R.* 14:2; *Lev. R.* 27:1; *Num. R.* 1:1; 9:1, 45; in 2:10 idolatry is darkness) and/or speak of the hiddenness of their deeds (*Num R.* 9:1, 45; *t. B. Qam.* 7:2; *Pesiq. Rab. Kah.* 9:1). *Genesis R.* 1:6 appeals to Isa. 29:15 to support the interpretation that "the deep things" in Dan. 2:22 refers to the deeds of the wicked. *Song of Songs R.* 1:1 cites Isa. 29:15 to prove that the lowly men of Prov. 22:29 are the wicked. And in *Gen. R.* 2:3, the darkness of Gen. 1:2 symbolizes the generation of Enosh while in *Exod. R.* 14:2 it is the deep, which is Gehinnom (Hell).[50]

Rabbinic reference to Jer. 18:6 is more substantive in relation to our concerns. *Yerushalmi Ber.* 9:3 and *Gen. R.* 72:6 cite Jer. 18:6 to prove that God can do anything he wants with a human being, specifically mentioning changing the sex of a child in the womb, which serves as a reason to pray for a male child while it is still in the womb. While the details are not very relevant, these rabbinic texts interpret Jer. 18:6 to indicate a vast extent to God's sovereignty. Even though the interpretation is distant from the original meaning of the Old Testament text, it brings us into the general realm of one of the main themes of both Jer. 18:6 and Romans 9–11, the sovereignty of God.

Another rabbinic tradition that appeals to Jer. 18:6 and comes into the sphere of concerns found in Romans 9 appears in *b. Ber.* 5:1 and *b. Sukkah* 5:4. It cites Jer. 18:6 as one of three verses that show God is responsible for the evil impulse in human beings. This point is used to clear Israel from blame so that its enemies would not have any charge against them. It appears to reflect an interpretation of Jer. 18:6 as indicating a divine sovereignty that at least controls the moral orientation of human beings. It is surprising to see responsibility assigned to God for Israel's evil impulse and innocence to Israel when this is the opposite of the biblical emphasis.

3.11. Conclusion

Relevant interpretive traditions related to the Old Testament potter/clay texts tend to use the metaphor of God as the sovereign, wise, and exalted Creator with every right to judge his creatures, and of human beings as lowly creatures who are under God's power and rightly subject to his judgment. Sometimes it is specified that human beings do not have a right to challenge God's judgment (1QS 11:22 [possibly]; 1QH^a 9:25-26; 20:26-35; *LAB* 53:13). A number of the themes found in Romans 9 appear in interpretive traditions we have surveyed, such as God as Creator, divine sovereignty, divine power, divine justice, divine glory, divine knowledge/foreknowledge, divine judgment, divine hardening of human beings, divine responsibility for sin, divine faithfulness, foreordination/predestination/determinism, eternal destiny, the elect, human liability to divine judgment, human responsibility for sin/evil, human arrogance, human lowliness, questioning/challenging God's judgment, and idolatry.

---

[50] Interestingly, *Exod. R.* 14:2 uses an earthenware lid in an analogy employed to show that the wicked are of darkness, but there is no indication that earthenware particularly is mentioned for associations in any way related to the verse's references to clay/pottery.

Particularly noteworthy is: (1) Sirach using the potter/clay metaphor to articulate God's sovereign right as the Creator to recompense people for their deeds as he deems right; (2) *Jubilees'* use of strong language of God's sovereignty and foreordination and judgment in a clearly conditional and nondeterministic sense; and (3) Targ. Isa. 29:16 combining elements of Isa. 45:9 and Jer. 18:6 in its rendering of Isa. 29:16, showing ancient interpretation that associated the three texts. We did not find any particular interpretive tradition that directly influenced Paul's use of the potter/clay metaphor, but we have been able to gain a picture of its usage in contemporary literature, some of which is surely similar to Paul's. This is not to say Paul was not influenced by general understandings of the potter/clay metaphor in his cultural milieu (such as is seen in *Wisd.* 15:7's assumption that it is a potter's prerogative to assign as he sees fit the purpose of vessels he has fashioned)—he undoubtedly was. But it is to say that any such influence cannot be traced to any specific extrabiblical text.

4

Intertextual Exegesis of Romans 9:19-24

Having analyzed the Old Testament texts to which Paul alludes in Rom. 9:19-24 in their original contexts and having surveyed ancient interpretive traditions related to these passages, we will now compare the forms of Paul's allusions with their Old Testament wording and then seek to draw on what is relevant from our research to explicate what Paul has written in Rom. 9:19-24.

4.1. Textual Comparison of Rom. 9:20-21; Isa. 29:16; 45:9; and Jer. 18:6

In Rom. 9:20-21, we appear to be dealing with both quotation and more general allusion. So the relevant texts do not always contain extensive verbal correspondence. But the textual comparison will help us to discern what verbal correspondence may be present and to assess the significance of the way in which Paul has worded his allusions. Later in this chapter, we will argue that there is substantial semantic correspondence between Rom. 9:20-21 and its context on the one hand, and Isa. 29:16, 45:9, and Jer. 18:6 and their contexts on the other. Therefore, conclusions in the present section on textual comparison about Paul alluding to these texts or his wording having been influenced by them take this factor into account.

The following formatting codes have been used to identify similarities and differences between the texts of the New Testament, LXX, and MT, listed without indication of correspondence to the other texts. The word "correspond(ence)" by itself does not necessarily indicate exact correspondence but at minimum indicates substantial correspondence, such as the same word though not necessarily the same form of the word.[1]

Italics: Verbal correspondence with differing forms of the same word(s); this code
    combines with other codes
<u>Double Underline</u>: NT, Isa. 29:16 LXX, and Isa. 45:9 LXX correspond exactly

---

[1] Cf. the less detailed tables in Wagner, *Heralds*, 58, and Shum, *Romans*, 204, and the helpful listing in H. Hübner, *Gottes Ich und Israel: Zum Schriftgebrauch des Paulus in Römer 9–11* (Göttingen: Vandenhoeck & Ruprecht, 1984), 152.

<u>Single Underline</u>: NT and Isa. 29:16 LXX correspond exactly
<u>Dotted Underline</u>: NT and Isa. 45:9 correspond exactly
<u>Dot Dash Underline</u>: NT, Isa. 29:16 LXX, and Jer. 18:6 LXX correspond
<u>Wave Underline</u>: All Greek texts correspond
<u>Dash Underline</u>: NT and Jer. 18:6 LXX correspond with differing forms of the same word; code only shown in the text of Jeremiah and not used when the wave underline is used
Bold: NT and Jer. 18:6 LXX correspond exactly; when present with italics, the italics do not apply to the relationship between NT and Jer. 18:6 LXX

Rom. 9:20b-21 μὴ ἐρεῖ τὸ πλάσμα τῷ πλάσαντι, *τί με ἐποίησας* οὕτως; ²¹ ἢ οὐχ ἔχει ἐξουσίαν **ὁ κεραμεὺς** *τοῦ πηλοῦ* ἐκ τοῦ αὐτοῦ φυράματος **ποιῆσαι** ὃ μὲν εἰς τιμὴν σκεῦος ὃ δὲ εἰς ἀτιμίαν;

Isa. 29:16 LXX οὐχ ὡς ὁ πηλὸς τοῦ κεραμέως λογισθήσεσθε; μὴ ἐρεῖ τὸ πλάσμα τῷ πλάσαντι οὐ σύ με ἔπλασας ἢ τὸ ποίημα τῷ ποιήσαντι οὐ συνετῶς με ἐποίησας;

Isa. 29:16 MT הָפְכְּכֶם אִם־כְּחֹמֶר הַיֹּצֵר יֵחָשֵׁב כִּי־יֹאמַר מַעֲשֶׂה לְעֹשֵׂהוּ לֹא עָשָׂנִי וְיֵצֶר אָמַר לְיוֹצְרוֹ לֹא הֵבִין

Isa. 45:9 LXX ποῖον βέλτιον κατεσκεύασα ὡς *πηλὸν* *κεραμέως* μὴ ὁ ἀροτριῶν ἀροτριάσει τὴν γῆν ὅλην τὴν ἡμέραν *μὴ ἐρεῖ ὁ πηλὸς τῷ κεραμεῖ τί ποιεῖς* ὅτι οὐκ ἐργάζῃ οὐδὲ ἔχεις χεῖρας

Isa. 45:9 MT הוֹי רָב אֶת־יֹצְרוֹ חֶרֶשׂ אֶת־חַרְשֵׂי אֲדָמָה הֲיֹאמַר חֹמֶר לְיֹצְרוֹ מַה־תַּעֲשֶׂה וּפָעָלְךָ אֵין־יָדַיִם לוֹ

Jer. 18:6 LXX εἰ καθὼς **ὁ κεραμεὺς** οὗτος οὐ δυνήσομαι τοῦ **ποιῆσαι** ὑμᾶς οἶκος Ισραηλ; ἰδοὺ ὡς *ὁ πηλὸς* τοῦ κεραμέως ὑμεῖς ἐστε ἐν ταῖς χερσίν μου

Jer. 18:6 MT הֲכַיּוֹצֵר הַזֶּה לֹא־אוּכַל לַעֲשׂוֹת לָכֶם בֵּית יִשְׂרָאֵל נְאֻם־יְהוָה הִנֵּה כַחֹמֶר בְּיַד הַיּוֹצֵר כֵּן־אַתֶּם בְּיָדִי בֵּית יִשְׂרָאֵל

4.1.a. Comparing the Greek Texts

In the following discussion, the Old Testament references refer to the LXX unless otherwise stated. We will begin by working through the correspondences between Rom. 9:20-21 and Isa. 29:16, and give attention to correspondences to the other Old Testament texts as seems fitting along the way. After finishing discussion of correspondences with Isa. 29:16, we will attend to any correspondences with the other texts that remain to be discussed.

All three Old Testament texts have some level of verbal correspondence with Rom. 9:20b-21. But Isa. 29:16 contains the most extensive correspondence in the string of words, μὴ ἐρεῖ τὸ πλάσμα τῷ πλάσαντι. With the use of a verbatim sequence of that many words in Rom. 9:20b,[2] it is hard not to regard their presence as a quotation regardless of whether there is contextual/thematic correspondence. However, Paul does not explicitly indicate that he is quoting. Hence, we have an informal, exact quotation from Isa. 29:16 in Rom. 9:20.[3]

---

[2] The first two words (μὴ ἐρεῖ) also occur in Isa. 45:9, but not the final four.
[3] For the terminology and classification system of quotations used in this investigation, see Abasciano, *Romans 9.1-9*, 16.

That is not the only correspondence with Isa. 29:16. We will review the rest of the correspondences in the order of their appearance (for the most part) in Rom. 9:20-21. The next is με ἐποίησας, which is an exact correspondence but functions a little differently. In Rom. 9:20, the words are modified by an adverb and part of a challenging question that Paul indicates (by use of an incredulous question) would be outrageous for a molded thing to put to its molder. In Isa. 29:16, the words are used absolutely and part of a statement that the prophet indicates (by use of an incredulous question) would be outrageous for a molded thing to say to its molder.

The conjunction ἤ comes next and might be thought too minimal to be of any significance. But it is only shared by Rom. 9:21 and Isa. 29:16, and it is critical to the dual-question structure of each passage. On the other hand, Paul takes his second question in a different direction. Isaiah merely adds another, similar question whereas Paul moves to a question that addresses the problem raised by the first. Still, given the correspondences of theme and vocabulary, it seems most likely that Paul drew his dual-question structure and its use of the conjunction ἤ from Isaiah.

Romans 9:21, Isa. 29:16, and Jer. 18:6 all use οὐ(χ) in a question in order to indicate that an affirmative answer is expected. Each question gets at a similar idea about God's sovereignty and human relationship to it. Isaiah 29:16 is the most distant in meaning from Rom. 9:21, asking a question that clarifies the status/position of God's people before him. Jeremiah 18:6 is much closer in specific meaning to Rom. 9:21, implicitly setting forth God's right to judge/treat Israel as he sees fit.[4] Romans 9:21 communicates the same specific meaning in different words, and then works out the principle in greater detail, specifying that this divine right includes the prerogative "to make from the same lump one a vessel unto honor and another unto dishonor."

Paul's question about whether the potter has authority or right over the clay is very similar to Jeremiah's question of whether God is able to deal with Israel as a potter does his clay. Indeed, both questions could be translated along the lines of whether God has the power to act as contemplated. Nonetheless, the unmarked meaning of Rom. 9:21's ἐξουσία would emphasize the idea of God's right or authority while the unmarked meaning of Jer. 18:6's δύναμαι would denote God's ability. However, in context both words bring out both God's ability and right to act as specified, though Paul's lexical choice emphasizes God's right/authority and LXX Jeremiah's word choice more basically calls attention to God's ability with the contextual connotation of his right. All of this leaves the expressions close enough to conclude that Paul probably framed the question of Rom. 9:21 partly from Jer. 18:6.

All the Greek texts contain some form of the word κεραμεύς with the article.[5] But only Jer. 18:6 has the exact same form as Rom. 9:21, the nominative ὁ κεραμεύς.[6]

---

[4] The Israel addressed in both Isaiah and Jeremiah was the southern kingdom of Judah. But we will not particularly differentiate between the northern and southern kingdoms of Israel in this chapter. "Israel" is the name of the covenant people of God and is most appropriate in discussing Paul's discourse in Romans 9–11. A qualification that will be used at times and can be helpful in light of Paul's discourse in Romans 9 is the specification "ethnic Israel."

[5] Indeed, Isa. 45:9 and Jer. 18:6 contain the word twice, though one of its occurrences in Isa. 45:9 is anarthrous.

[6] *Wisdom* 15:7 has the nominative κεραμεύς but lacks the article and appears in a statement rather than a challenging question. Reference to "the Greek texts" in this discussion concerns only the Old

While use of a word in a different case would be perfectly natural in an allusion for the purposes of fitting the word into its new context, Jer. 18:6 alone using the same form as Rom. 9:21 strengthens the case that Paul alludes to it. The case is strengthened even further by the fact that the word's occurrence in Jer. 18:6 comes in a portion of the verse that we have already concluded above served as a source for Paul's framing of the question of Rom. 9:21.

Paul's second use of the verb ποιέω is similar. All the Greek texts contain some form of the word,[7] but only Jer. 18:6 has the exact same form as Rom. 9:21, the infinitive ποιῆσαι. And it again occurs in a portion of Jer. 18:6 that we have already seen likely served as a source for Paul's framing of the question of Rom. 9:21. In addition to sharing the exact form as Rom. 9:21, Jer. 18:6 is also closer in usage to the former than is either of the Isaiah texts. Both Paul and Jeremiah use the word in a question that directly implies God's right or power to do as he chooses with his people. But Isa. 29:16 uses the word in a substantival participle (τῷ ποιήσαντι) of God as the maker of Israel (in the sense of fashioning their situation) in a statement that challenges God's fashioning action, placed within a question implying the absurdity of such challenges. And Isa. 45:9 uses the word about God making Israel (again in the sense of fashioning their situation) in a question that voices an objection to God's fashioning action, also set within a question implying the absurdity of such objections. The meaning of ποιέω is basically the same in each instance, but the usage is most similar between Rom. 9:21 and Jer. 18:6. Perhaps setting translations of the relevant portions of the texts in parallel will help show the point. The translation of the relevant occurrences of ποιέω has been underlined.

Rom. 9:21: "Or does not the potter have the right over the clay <u>to make</u> from the same lump one a vessel unto honor and another unto dishonor?"
Isa. 29:16b: "Will the molded thing really say to the molder, 'You did not fashion me,' or the thing made <u>to the maker</u>, 'You did not make me wisely?'"
Isa. 45:9c: "Will the clay really say to the potter, 'What <u>are you making</u>?'"
Jer. 18:6a: "Just as this potter, am I not able <u>to make</u> you, house of Israel?"

In light of all of this, it seems probable that Paul's use of ποιῆσαι draws on Jer. 18:6, strengthening the conclusion that Paul alludes to the verse in Rom. 9:21.

The words ὁ πηλός occur in every Greek text, but no other text uses the same form as Rom. 9:21, the genitive τοῦ πηλοῦ.[8] Paul combines this genitive construction with ὁ κεραμεύς, yielding ὁ κεραμεὺς τοῦ πηλοῦ. Interestingly, Isa. 29:16 and Jer. 18:6 have the same phrase with the cases inverted: ὁ πηλὸς τοῦ κεραμέως. Isaiah 45:9 also has the nominative ὁ πηλός (the word's second occurrence in the verse), but paired with the dative of ὁ κεραμεύς, yielding ὁ πηλὸς τῷ κεραμεῖ. In the word's first occurrence

---

Testament texts laid out at the beginning of Section 4.1 (Isa. 29:16; 45:9; Jer. 18:6), not extracanonical texts such as *Wisd.* 15:7, though some comparative observations concerning *Wisd.* 15:7 will be made in the notes. For comparison of *Wisd.* 15:7 to Rom. 9:20b-21, see Section 3.6 in Chapter 3 of this volume.

[7] *Wisdom* 15:7 lacks the word altogether.
[8] *Wisdom* 15:7 also uses the genitive, specifically τοῦ αὐτοῦ πηλοῦ.

in Isa. 45:9, the verse has the anarthrous accusative πηλόν paired with the anarthrous genitive κεραμέως. These differences from Rom. 9:21 are simply due to the syntactical needs of the different contexts and the different ways the authors have formulated their discourse.

The last correspondence to note is the word τί, shared only by Rom. 9:20 and Isa. 45:9.[9] This raises the question of whether Paul's use of τί reflects the influence of Isa. 45:9. One point that counts against the suggestion is that the word has different meanings in the respective contexts. In Isa. 45:9, it means "what," but in Rom. 9:21 it means "why?"[10] However, the difference is only superficial. τί occurs in a question in each context, and both questions challenge God's fashioning of his people, implying the same basic point. Paul words it, "Why did you make me like this?" whereas the Isaiah passage words it, "What are you making?" The presence of the word in only Rom. 9:21 and Isa. 45:9 among the biblical potter/clay texts in similar questions is more compelling than its minor difference in meaning. At least it earns a hearing for there being a connection that is either verified or invalidated by the presence or absence of contextual thematic correspondence. Our judgment is that there is such correspondence (see later in this chapter) and that Paul probably drew his use of τί from Isa. 45:9.

4.1.b. Comparing the Greek Texts to the Hebrew Texts

As for the relationship of the Septuagintal texts to the Hebrew, they appear to be loose translations in Isaiah, which fits with the tendency of the LXX in general in that book.[11] The relationship of LXX Jeremiah to the Hebrew textual tradition is much more complicated.[12] But happily, the LXX of Jer. 18:6 reflects a Hebrew text that was reasonably close to the MT for that verse. The variations in the LXX texts of Isaiah and Jeremiah from the Hebrew as represented by the MT carry relatively minimal impact with respect to the overall meaning of the verses.

Taking Isa. 29:16 (from which Paul quotes in Rom. 9:20) as an example, the LXX omits a number of elements, such as the MT's "Your perversity!" and its question, "Should the potter be regarded as clay?" When it comes to the clay's objections to the potter's work, the LXX uses the second person (the clay speaking *to* the potter) whereas the MT uses the third person (the clay speaking *about* the potter), and the last part in

---

[9] *Wisdom* 15:7 has the nominative form τίς (τί is accusative) with a different meaning and uses the word in a very different way.

[10] D.-A. Koch, *Die Schrift als Zeuge des Evangeliums: Untersuchungen zur Verwendung und zum Verständnis der Schrift bei Paulus* (BHT, 69; Tübingen: Mohr Siebeck, 1986), 144, thinks the difference (demanded by οὕτως) shows that Paul's wording did not come from Isa. 45:9 (cf. similarly, Sherwood, "Romans 9:6-29," 104). But Wagner, *Heralds*, 59 n. 50, does not think it enough to prevent the conclusion that Isa. 45:9 shaped Paul's wording along with Isa. 29:16 in Rom. 9:20. D. J. Moo, *The Epistle to the Romans*, 2nd ed. (NICNT; Grand Rapids, MI: Eerdmans, 2018), 622, ProQuest Ebook Central, thinks it probable that Isa. 45:9 contributed to Paul's language.

[11] On the relationship of the LXX to the MT as well as the LXX's free translation style in Isaiah, see briefly Smith, *Isaiah*, 1.49-53; H. G. M. Williamson, "Isaiah: Book of," *DOTP*, 364-78 (371-2).

[12] On the relationship between the Hebrew and Greek texts of Jeremiah, see Craigie et al., *Jeremiah*, xli-xlv; Thompson, *Jeremiah*, 117-20; and more recently, but less cautiously, Allen, "Jeremiah," 434-7.

the MT envisions the clay charging God with not understanding while in the LXX the clay charges God with not making the clay wisely. Paul clearly quoted from the LXX of Isa. 29:16, though the part he quotes largely accords with the Hebrew of the MT. There does not appear to be any significant differences between the Greek Old Testament texts of Isaiah and Jeremiah as represented by the LXX and the relevant Hebrew texts of the Old Testament as represented by the MT to call for special attention to one or the other for considering potential alternatives in meaning that might have formed Paul's or his readers' understanding of the Old Testament background of Rom. 9:20-21.[13]

4.2. Intertextual Exegesis of Rom. 9:19-24

Having examined material relevant to the Old Testament background of Paul's discourse in Rom. 9:19-24 and conducted a comparison of the New Testament text with its intertexts, we are now ready to begin our direct exegesis of the passage.

4.2.a. The Argument of Rom. 9:1-18

It is important to keep in mind that the exegesis of Rom. 9:19ff. that we are picking up here is a continuation of the exegesis of Rom. 9:1-18 laid out in my previous two volumes. In summary,[14] those studies found that in Romans 9–11 Paul was concerned about uniting a predominantly Gentile Roman church containing a substantial minority of Jews behind his gospel for his future mission to Spain along with its Jew-prioritizing methodology. Toward this end Paul defends the gospel he has presented in Romans 1–8 against its most compelling objection—that it would render God unfaithful to his covenant promises to Israel since the vast majority of Jews had not received the fulfillment of those promises even though the promises had been realized in the elect messianic community, the Church of Jews and Gentiles. So after exulting in the church's possession of all the blessings of God for his chosen people (Rom. 8), Paul declares his profound grief over the cursed state of his fellow Jews (9:1-3), who are separated from Christ and therefore cut off from the covenant and its promises, their election nullified, and are devoted to destruction under the eschatological wrath of God (9:3). As the clarifying, climactic expression of Paul's immense grief, 9:3 stands as the main point of 9:1-5 with its allusion to Moses's intercession on behalf of idolatrous Israel in Exod. 32:32. Romans 9:4-5 then ground Paul's grief by recognizing that the (Jewish) people who have been excluded from the covenant and its blessings are, all things being equal, the very people to whom

---

[13] Use of the term "reader" does not imply that the majority of Paul's original audience actually read the letter, though some surely did. We recognize that most of the original audience probably heard the letter read rather than reading it themselves. But we use the term "reader" as a general designation for those who read or heard the letter.

[14] Here I can provide only a substantive sketch of the basic meaning and logical flow of Rom. 9:1-18 with a view toward setting the context for an exegesis of 9:19-24, leaving out much detail about Paul's intention. For a full account of the meaning of this passage, see Abasciano, *Romans 9.1-9* and *Romans 9.10-18*. Much of what I say in this summary is simply restated from the latter volume.

the promises most properly belong as the historic bearers of the divine election. This is all the more tragic following on the heels of Romans 8, since mostly Gentiles are participating in the eschatological fulfillment of the name and blessings of election celebrated there.

Having raised the problem of God's faithfulness in Rom. 9:1-5, Paul then states his main thesis for all of chs. 9–11 in 9:6a: the promises of God to Israel have not failed. Romans 9:6b-9 ground this programmatic statement. More specifically, 9:6b ("not all who are from Israel are Israel") provides what also turns out to be a programmatic statement, which Paul fleshes out over much of the rest of chs. 9–11, to the effect that not all ethnic Israelites are part of the true Israel, to whom the covenant promises were actually made. The point is stated more clearly though again negatively in 9:7a ("nor [is it] that all [who are his] children are the seed of Abraham") and stated positively through the quotation of Gen. 21:12 in 9:7b ("but in Isaac your seed will be called"). As the positive statement of Paul's point and his chief scriptural proof text, Gen. 21:12/Rom. 9:7b becomes the thrust of his argument to that point. It speaks of the calling of God's covenant people as his naming/identification of them as his own, the true heir to the covenant promises. Romans 9:8 ("it is not the children of the flesh who are children of God, but the children of the promise are regarded as seed") then gives an interpretation of 9:7b, summing up and explaining all of 9:6b-7, becoming Paul's practical main point in support of 9:6a. That point is that God does not (nor did he ever) regard mere physical descendants of Abraham ("children of the flesh") as heir to the covenant promises, but he regards those who believe the promises ("children of the promise") as the true heir to them (i.e., the true Israel). That is, as it pertains to the present time of eschatological fulfillment, all and only those who believe in Christ are regarded as God's covenant people to whom the promises were made. Finally, 9:9 supports Paul's interpretation of Gen. 21:12 in 9:8 by quotation of Gen. 18:10, 14, showing that Isaac and the covenantal descendants of Abraham represented by him would be identified through promise rather than ancestry. Thus, Paul's response to the charge against God's faithfulness through 9:9 is that God never guaranteed enjoyment of the promises to ethnic Israel, but only to spiritual Israel, which means, in the context of Romans, all who believe in Christ.

Romans 9:10-13 add to the support Paul adduced from Gen. 18:10, 14 for the contention of Rom. 9:8 that only those who believe in Christ are the covenant seed of Abraham/*rightful* heirs of the covenant promises by furnishing an even stronger example than the Sarah/Isaac/Ishmael example given in 9:7 of the principle that covenant heirship has always depended on God's call and promise rather than ancestry—the example of Rebekah, Jacob, and Esau from Genesis 25. Despite Esau's natural right as the firstborn to inherit the covenant and its promises, God sovereignly chose Jacob over Esau for the privilege, as was his divine right, a right that was underscored by the prenatal timing of the announcement of God's choice. Paul argues that the purpose of God in announcing his choice before the twins were born was to ensure that the fulfillment of his purpose to bless the world would proceed on the basis of his sovereign right to name whomever he wants as his covenant people rather than on the basis of human works or ancestry. This purpose statement (found in 9:11c-12b) is the main point of vv. 10–13 and serves as the essence of 10–13's support of the principle enunciated in 9:8 that only those who believe in Christ are rightful covenant heirs.

Defending God's right to name his people based on faith rather than works/ancestry, Paul explains in 9:10-13 how God could justly do so as well as why he acts in this way. God retains the right to choose who his people are according to his own good pleasure (for any or no reason whatsoever) because the election of his people depended wholly on his sovereign will from the beginning through his election of Jacob, the covenant head, and therefore remained subject to the dictates of his own will. Consequently, he is able to righteously call only those who believe in Jesus Christ the seed of Abraham if he so chooses. Basing the fulfillment of God's purpose to bless the world on his sovereign call rather than on works/ethnicity makes that fulfillment possible, for it enables God to call his people based on faith rather than works/ethnicity and thereby include Gentiles in the blessings of Abraham. However, this entails the grievous corollary of the rejection of unbelieving ethnic Israel from the covenant, an element of Paul's argument that is expressed ironically, starkly, and concisely by his citation of Mal. 1:2-3 ("Jacob I loved, but Esau I hated") in support of the principle of God's sovereignty over election manifested in Gen. 25:23/Rom. 9:12 and articulated in the purpose statement of Rom. 9:11c-12b ("in order that the purpose of God in election would continue not by works, but by the one who calls").

Romans 9:14-18 then supports vv. 10-13 by addressing the objection to this sharpened statement of sovereign divine election that God choosing his people without regard to works or ancestry would make him unrighteous through violation of his covenant promises to Israel. Paul vehemently denies that God is unrighteous (v. 14) and supports his assertion with two quotations of Scripture that point to their original Old Testament contexts. The first quotation comes from Exod. 33:19b ("I will have mercy on whomever I have mercy, and I will have compassion on whomever I have compassion"), answering the charge of divine unrighteousness from the perspective of God's nature as well as the nature of Israel's election from its beginning. In its original context Exod. 33:19b means that God has mercy on whomever he chooses based upon whatever conditions he establishes, most specifically referring to the mercy of corporate covenantal election of the people of God. The quotation defends the righteousness of God in sovereign election by pointing to the fact that the fundamental nature of Israel's election involved its subjection to the sovereign will of God and his definition of Israel/his people according to his own good pleasure. Moreover, the covenant itself contained the principle that God would have mercy on those who repent of their sin, maintain covenant relationship with him, and are connected to his righteous and faithful covenant mediator, and that he would reject those who are otherwise. Finally, Exod. 33:19b reveals the very nature of God when relating to sinful humanity to be both merciful and also sovereign in determining the beneficiaries of the divine mercy, including any conditions for choosing them.

Romans 9:16 ("[it is] not of the one who wills nor of the one who runs, but of the mercy-bestowing God") presents Paul's inference from and interpretation of Exod. 33:19b/Rom. 9:15, drawing the logical stress of his argument in 9:15-16 in support of the denial of divine unrighteousness in 9:14. The verse most specifically means that the bestowal of mercy that is the election of God's covenant people is (rightly) at the discretion of the mercy-bestowing God, as are any stipulations he chooses to lay down for the bestowing of his mercy. Whereas 9:15-16 took up the positive side of God's sovereignty in election, Rom. 9:17 ("for this very purpose I raised you up, that I might show my power in you and that my name might be proclaimed in all the earth") gives further scriptural support for God's righteousness in sovereign election with special reference to its negative side—covenantal rejection and hardening. The second quotation that Paul employs in 9:14-18 for the righteousness of God's sovereign election comes from Exod. 9:16 where it is part of a statement of God's incomparable power and sovereignty in forestalling fatal judgment on Pharaoh despite his arrogant rebellion against the Lord, a statement formally aimed at bringing Pharaoh to acknowledge YHWH's supremacy and to submit to the divine will.

In Exodus, the judgment and hardening of Pharaoh facilitates the election of the people of God and the fulfillment of God's covenant promises. Just as Paul has used other figures from salvation history as types of unbelieving and rejected ethnic Israel in his argument in Romans 9, so in 9:17-18 he puts forth Pharaoh as a type of hardened, unbelieving, and rejected ethnic Israel. His quotation suggests that just as God hardened Pharaoh to bring about the renewed election of his people and to advance his plan for fulfilling the climactic covenant promise of blessing all the nations in Abraham, so he has hardened unbelieving ethnic Israel in the time of covenant fulfillment to accomplish the same purposes. Paul's typology therefore vindicates God's righteousness consisting in faithfulness to his covenant promises to Israel vis-à-vis God's election of the church by faith apart from works or ancestry and rejection of unbelieving ethnic Israel despite its works and ancestry. For it conveys that, far from violating God's covenant promises to Israel, the hardening and rejection of ethnic Israel actually contribute to fulfilling them.

Informed by his quotations from Exodus, Paul speaks of the proclamation of God's name and power in the sense of the proclamation of his incomparable sovereignty, supreme divinity, presence, nature, goodness, and glory. Notably, this especially includes the proclamation of God's grace and mercy, which for Paul would undoubtedly involve the proclamation of his sovereign plan for the bestowal of God's grace and mercy in Jesus Christ to all who believe, whether Jew or Gentile.

We found the hardening of Pharaoh in Exodus to be nondeterministic, and in harmony with that, Paul's invocation of hardening in Rom. 9:17-18 has specific reference to God making ethnic Israel of his day unyielding to the claims of the gospel message by means of God's sovereign act of making elect status conditional on faith in Christ apart from works or ancestry. Just as the hardening of Pharaoh was a judgment on Pharaoh's sin and rebellion against God, so Paul's use of Pharaoh as a type of unbelieving ethnic Israel intimates that God's choice of faith as the exclusive basis of covenant membership was meant partly to bring judgment upon Israel for the very ethnocentrism, pride, and self-reliance that would lead them to seek to establish their own righteousness, take offense at Christ, and become resistant to accepting the gospel of salvation by faith. Moreover, just as God made Pharaoh's own freely rebellious will to serve as its own punishment in the execution of ironic and poetic justice, so Paul's typology would suggest that God was now making ethnic Israel's own freely formed zeal for establishing their own righteousness by the Law to serve as its own judgment.

But even more so, the hardening of ethnic Israel was ironically for the purpose of fulfilling God's covenant promises to his people, most markedly culminating in the blessing of all the nations of the earth by including them in the covenant and its blessings along with believing Jews. For this cause of hardening—election by faith—is the very means for opening salvation up to the Gentiles while keeping salvation open for the Jews as well.

In its original context, Exod. 9:16 contributes to encouragement to the original audience of Exodus to reject idolatry and be loyal to YHWH and his covenant with Israel. Paul cites it partly to encourage his own audience in the time of eschatological fulfillment to reject the idolatry of trusting in a means of mediating God's covenant, presence, and blessing other than God had ordained for the present eschatological age, Jesus Christ, and to be loyal to God and his covenant with Israel in its eschatological expression of the gospel and the New Covenant in Christ. Indeed, Paul labored, as did Moses in Exodus 32–34, to bring rejected Israel to the restoration of covenantal election and blessing in a new covenant established primarily with the Covenant Mediator and mediated to the people only through connection with him. He did so by going to the Jew first with the gospel of Christ (Rom. 1:16) and also, in the hope of provoking his kinsmen to jealousy and consequent faith, by magnifying his gospel ministry to the Gentiles (11:13-14). In pursuit of this gospel ministry he now defends his gospel against its most pressing objection—that its truth would make God unrighteous in the sense of unfaithful to his promises to Israel—as he seeks to win support from the Christians in Rome for his upcoming Jew-prioritizing mission to Spain and the gospel that will stand at its heart.

Romans 9:18 ("So therefore, he [rightly] has mercy on whom he desires, and he [rightly] hardens whom he desires")[15] sums up vv. 15–17 and their support for v. 14's denial of the unrighteousness of God in election by faith apart from works or ancestry. Verse 14 itself defends the affirmation of election by faith apart from works or ancestry in vv. 11c–12b, which in turn supports the affirmation of v. 8 that only those who believe in Christ are the covenant seed of Abraham/*rightful* heirs of the covenant promises, which in turn supports v. 6a's affirmation of God's faithfulness to his covenant promises to Israel. In the next stage of Paul's argument (9:19-29), he will move to consider an objection to the principle annunciated in 9:18.

4.2.b. Romans 9:19: The Objection to the Argument of Rom. 9:14-18

4.2.b.1. Diatribe and Rhetoric

Now in Rom. 9:19, employing the diatribe,[16] Paul brings up an objection to his argumentation (given in vv. 15–18) in support of v. 14's denial of unrighteousness in God: "You will say to me then, 'Why does he still find fault? For who has resisted

---

[15] The addition of "rightly" in brackets conveys the sense of Rom. 9:18 in context.
[16] On the diatribe, which is a method of instruction that Paul uses here, see my previous comments in Abasciano, *Romans 9.10-18*, 168, along with the literature cited there.

his purpose?'"[17] This is the most vivid use of the diatribe—employing an imaginary interlocutor to pose an objection to a teacher's viewpoint so that the teacher could answer the objection. The use of the conjunction οὖν (then) signals that the objection Paul now considers arises inferentially from what he has just been saying in vv. 14–18, and particularly from its stark summary expression in v. 18, especially its final clause asserting that God "hardens whom he desires."[18] Thus, the blame in view concerns hard-heartedness, which, in context, is equivalent to stubborn rejection of Christ.

Most interpreters construe the sense of v. 19 to be something like "Why does God blame us for being hardhearted if he irresistibly hardened our hearts?" that is, "Why does God blame us for doing what he irresistibly caused us to do?"[19] C. H. Dodd, who construed the text in this way, thought the objection to be correct and famously commented concerning Paul's appeal to the potter/clay metaphor in response, "It is a well-worn illustration. But the trouble is that a man is not a pot; he *will* ask, 'Why did you make me like this?' and he will not be bludgeoned into silence. It is the weakest point in the whole epistle."[20] The questions are rhetorical, and on the above approach, they implicitly assert that God would be unrighteous to find fault with people for doing what he irresistibly causes them to do—in this case, reject Christ—and that Paul's position is therefore wrong. However, while the questions are clearly rhetorical, this line of interpretation assumes that the hardening spoken of in 9:17-18 is irresistible/deterministic. Yet, our exegesis of those verses found that their concept of hardening is not deterministic.[21] If our exegesis there is correct, then that invalidates the typical

---

[17] It is very difficult to decide whether οὖν in 19b (τί [οὖν] ἔτι μέμφεται;) in P⁴⁶ B D F G it vg^mss is original. These are weighty mss but counterbalanced by the array of ms evidence for omission of the word (so R. Jewett, *Romans: A Commentary* [Hermeneia; Minneapolis, MN: Fortress, 2007], 587). C. E. B. Cranfield, *A Critical and Exegetical Commentary on the Epistle to the Romans* (ICC; 2 vols.; Edinburgh: T&T Clark, 1975-9), 489 n. 4, thinks οὖν an addition "possibly due to a copyist's being accustomed to the frequent occurrence of τί οὖν in Romans." Jewett counters that the deletion of οὖν is stylistically likely due to its presence in the preceding sentence. However, that just as easily argues for Paul having left the word out originally. The question is further complicated by the fact that it is easy to imagine that οὖν could have been accidentally added (dittography) or omitted (haplography) due again to the word's occurrence in the preceding sentence. Given such uncertainty, it is probably best to follow the simplest/shortest reading, which omits οὖν and happens to yield the most satisfactory style. Happily, a decision does not affect the basic sense of the verse.

[18] As Jewett, *Romans*, 590 notes, "The sharply formulated conclusions of the preceding verse, in fact, was [sic] intended to provoke these questions and thus to move Paul's argument forward."

[19] So, e.g., Moo, *Romans*, 620; Cranfield, *Romans*, 489-90; Piper, *Justification*, 185-6, 189-92; Jewett, *Romans*, 591; Schreiner, *Romans*, 493-4; C. H. Dodd, *The Epistle of Paul to the Romans* (London: Collins, 1959), 171; C. G. Kruse, *Paul's Letter to the Romans* (PNTC; Grand Rapids, MI: Eerdmans, 2012), 383-4; H. Räisänen, "Römer 9–11: Analyse eines geistigen Ringens," ANRW 2.25.4 (1987), 2891-939 (2903). By using the term "irresistibly," I do not mean to imply that the idea in view is that God would force people to do something they do not want to do even while doing it. The term as I use it is neutral and could be used of such a forced action but does not in itself indicate such. I use the term to bring out the idea of God making it so that someone will certainly do what he intends them to do *and* will not be able to act otherwise/will not be able to avoid doing what God intends them to do, which he could accomplish, e.g., by effectually causing them to desire most to do what he intends them to do.

[20] Dodd, ibid.

[21] See esp. Abasciano, *Romans 9.10-18*, 200-19.

understanding of v. 19 articulated above.[22] It is more likely that Paul's thought here moves along slightly different lines already voiced in the epistle.

4.2.b.2. Romans 9:19 in Light of Rom. 3:1-8

Most interpreters regard Rom. 3:1-8 as a brief discussion that is resumed at length in chs. 9-11.[23] Indeed, in our exegesis of 9:14 we demonstrated the parallel nature of 3:1-8 and 9:1-29[24] and observed the same basic movement in Romans 2-3 and 9:1-29 from the ideas of (1) God choosing his people apart from works or ancestry, (2) Jews being rejected by God for their unbelief even though possessing great salvific advantage, and (3) God using Jewish unrighteousness to display his righteousness, to the question of whether God is unrighteous to condemn those whose unrighteousness is made to accomplish his will of glorifying his righteousness. This is the basic question taken up in 3:5, 7, and now in 9:19.[25]

---

[22] However, even if one disagrees with our conclusion about the nondeterministic nature of hardening in 9:17-18, the larger thrust of our exegesis, contending that Romans 9 defends God's right to choose his people by faith, can still be maintained, especially in light of the OT background to 9:20-21 we will discuss later in this investigation. Some scholars argue that 9:19ff. show that unconditional election is in view because the question and answer of 9:19ff. would not make sense if election is conditional (so Schreiner, *Romans*, 494; Moo, *Romans*, 618). But it makes good sense with conditional election that there might be objection to irresistible judicial hardening and consequent judgment even if hardening is temporary and reversible and ultimate judgment is avoidable. I am pleased that since I argued that God's hardening of Pharaoh's heart in Exodus is not irresistible/deterministic, a major commentary on Exodus has appeared that fully agrees with the point; see now Alexander, *Exodus*, 163-71.

[23] See Abasciano, "Romans 9:1-9," 84 n. 125, for an extensive list of scholars who support this view. Works published since that list was drawn up which join this consensus include D. R. Wallace, *Election of the Lesser Son: Paul's Lament-Midrash in Romans 9-11* (Minneapolis, MN: Fortress, 2014), 48, 61, 73, 86 n. 47; C. S. Keener, *Romans* (NCCS, 6; Eugene, OR: Cascade, 2009), 115; C. Stenschke, "Römer 9-11 als Teil des Römerbriefs," in F. Wilk and J. R. Wagner (eds), *Between Gospel and Election: Explorations in the Interpretation of Romans 9-11* (WUNT, 257; Tübingen: Mohr Siebeck, 2010), 197-225 (206-7); A. Sherwood, *Romans: A Structural, Thematic, and Exegetical Commentary* (Bellingham: Lexham, 2020), 479 n. 1; cf. T. Holland, *Romans: The Divine Marriage: A Biblical-Theological Commentary* (Eugene, OR: Pickwick, 2011), 296. For a rare objection to this view, see J. N. Aletti, *God's Justice in Romans: Keys for Interpreting the Epistle to the Romans* (trans. P. M. Meyer; *SB*, 37; Rome: Gregorian and Biblical Press, 2010), 178, though even he acknowledges unquestionable commonalities between 3:1-4 and chs. 9-11.

[24] See Abasciano, *Romans 9.10-18*, 169-71. That discussion is assumed in the present one.

[25] Cf. J. A. Fitzmyer, *Romans: A New Translation with Introduction and Commentary* (AB, 33; New York: Doubleday, 1993), 568; Keener, *Romans*, 120; P. Stuhlmacher, *Paul's Letter to the Romans: A Commentary* (trans. S. J. Hafemann; Louisville, KY: Westminster John Knox, 1994), 150; J. Munck, *Christ and Israel: An Interpretation of Romans 9-11* (Philadelphia, PA: Fortress, 1967), 56-8; J. R. Edwards, *Romans* (NIBCNT; Peabody, MA: Hendrickson, 1992), 239; N. T. Wright, "Romans," in L. E. Keck (ed.), *The New Interpreter's Bible*, X (NIB, 10; Nashville, TN: Abingdon, 2002), 393-770 (641), who thinks 9:19 echoes 3:6, and Räisänen, "Analyse," 2903, notes similarity to 3:6. K. Haacker, *Der Briefe des Paulus an die Römer* (THKNT, 6; Leipzig: Evangelische Verlagsanstalt, 1999), 195, notes 3:5 and 7 for comparison. U. Luz, *Das Geschichtsverständnis des Paulus* (BevT, 49; Munich: Kaiser, 1968), 237, notes similarity to 3:5ff. B. Byrne, *Romans* (Sacra Pagina, 6; Collegeville, MN: Liturgical, 1996), 299, recognizes the similarity of form to 3:7, but thinks the grounds in 9:19 to be "somewhat different." W. M. Greathouse and G. Lyons, *Romans 9-16: A Commentary in the Wesleyan Tradition* (NBBC; Kansas City, MI: Beacon Hill, 2008), 61-2, think Paul answers the objection of 9:19 in 2:1-3:20 and assumes that background here.

In Romans 2-3, Paul moves from the notion of God's approval apart from works or ancestry (2:17-29; cf. 9:1-13)[26] to that of Jewish privilege (3:1-2; cf. 9:3-5) to the question of whether Jewish unfaithfulness will nullify the faithfulness of God (3:3; cf. 9:6). Answering that question with his characteristic μὴ γένοιτο, Paul reveals that Jewish unrighteousness shows forth the righteousness of God (3:4-5; cf. 9:17-18). This in turn raises the question of whether God is unrighteous to inflict his wrath on those whose unrighteousness glorifies his righteousness (3:5). The questions of 3:5 taken together are generally parallel to 9:19: "But if our unrighteousness demonstrates the righteousness of God, what shall we say? That the God who inflicts wrath is unrighteous?" But 3:7 expands on 3:5 with a specific example and brings out the parallel with 9:19 more clearly: "But if through my lie the truth of God abounds to his glory, why then am I still judged as a sinner?" The questions of Paul's hypothetical objector in 9:19 taken together—"Why does he still find fault? For who has resisted his purpose?"—carry the same basic sense, though intensified due to God's role in provoking the hard-heartedness that he uses to manifest his righteousness and glorify his name.[27] However, the concern is not with God blaming people for rebellion that he irresistibly caused them to commit—Paul has not indicated that God irresistibly causes anyone to resist him.[28] Rather, the objection is that it would be unrighteous for God to find fault with those whose unrighteousness he provokes (by making elect status conditional on faith in Christ apart from works or ancestry) and uses to manifest his righteousness and glory.

---

[26] On possible objection to this characterization, see Abasciano, *Romans 9.10-18*, 170 n. 77.

[27] It is critical to understand that in speaking of God *provoking* Israel's hard-heartedness, I do not mean an irresistible provoking, but that God took action that Israel responded to by becoming hard-hearted. It can therefore be said that God's action provoked Israel and that he hardened them without the implication that he irresistibly provoked or hardened them. One might wonder how God uses Jewish sin to show his power and proclaim his name. See ibid., 214–16, for a full explanation. In addition to what I say there, the following note from my chapter, "Romans 9, Election, and Calvinism," in D. L. Allen and S. W. Lemke (eds.), *Calvinism: A Biblical-Theological Critique* (Nashville, TN: B&H, 2022) is relevant (slightly adapted here): First, just as in Rom. 3:4-7, it is through God's judgment on Jewish sin, showing his power in judgment and the justice of his character/name. Second, hardening and election by faith apart from works or ancestry are so intertwined in this context that to speak of one of them is to speak of the other, since election by faith is what hardens (keep in mind that such hardening is resistible). Speaking of them is also to speak of Israel's sin, for hardening from the human side is stubborn rebellion against the Lord and his gospel and is itself sin. Thus, hardening from the divine side in the form of the proclamation of election by faith apart from works or ancestry, which brings along with it hardening from the human side in the form of resistance to the gospel on the part of many Jews, brings about the display of God's power in judgment on the hardened and in salvation for those who believe. Similarly, it also brings about the declaration of God's name/character in the judgment and mercy of the gospel.

[28] This is another instance in Romans 9 in which one's prior exegesis in the chapter is crucial for one's exegesis of the text at hand. We saw this phenomenon in connection with 9:16 and 18 (see Abasciano, *Romans 9.10-18*, 187 and 216, respectively). If one finds unconditional election in 9:6-15, then one will likely find 9:16 to be an articulation of unconditional election. If one finds unconditional election in 9:15-16, then one will tend to conclude that 9:18 refers to unconditional hardening. And if one believes that 9:18 speaks of unconditional hardening, then one will tend to assume that 9:19 raises an objection to unconditional hardening and that what follows is a defense of God's justice in irresistibly hardening people and punishing them for their resulting hard-hearted rebellion that he irresistibly caused.

Paul has already shown a concern to take up later in the epistle matters raised in the first part of ch. 3. In ch. 6, he addresses at length the question he raises in 3:8 ("Shall we actually say … 'Let us do evil that good may come?'"), a question he raised in answer to the question of 3:7 ("But if through my lie the truth of God abounds to his glory, why then am I still judged as a sinner?"). That strengthens the suggestion that 9:19 is taking up the basic question of 3:5 and 7. It is further strengthened by the fact that Paul's answer to the question in 9:19 appears to complement and expand on his answer given in 3:6.

In 3:6, Paul answers the objection that God would be unrighteous to inflict his wrath on those whose unrighteousness glorifies his righteousness via God's judgment by pointing to the biblically axiomatic truth that God will judge the world: "May it never be! For then how will God judge the world?" The logic of this reply is to deny that God is unrighteous to inflict wrath on those whose unrighteousness glorifies his righteousness on the basis that (1) since sin does indeed have the effect of glorifying God via his judgment as Paul showed with Scripture in v. 4,[29] and (2) it is (biblically) unquestionable that God will in fact judge the world,[30] the objection is false because it therefore implies that God should not judge the world. Since the objection is based on God getting glory from his judgment on sin, which he does, its contention that such judgment is unrighteous undermines the very concept of judgment.[31] Significantly, Paul's answer to the objection of 9:19 complements the answer he gives in 3:6 to the same basic question. Whereas in 3:6 Paul answers the objection with the basic point that God must judge, now in 9:20-21, he deepens that response with the points that God

---

[29] See F. Godet, *Commentary on St. Paul's Epistle to the Romans* (trans. A. Cusin and T. W. Chambers; New York: Funk & Wagnalls, 1883), 136–7.

[30] See Cranfield, *Romans*, 184–5, which represents the most common view of Paul's meaning (though see Moo, *Romans*, 201). Although separate, I find numbers 1 and 2 complementary. For the various views on offer, see Moo, 201 and n. 541. Views that take the reference to the world to be related to the fact that the objection arises out of consideration of judgment on Jewish sin do not take sufficient account of how general and wide-ranging the principle set forth in 3:4 is. It is not as if Paul meant to assert that only judgment on *Jewish* unrighteousness magnifies God's righteousness or, to use Paul's example from 3:7, that only Jewish lies highlight God's truth.

[31] Piper, *Justification*, 128, argues that God's righteousness in judgment is not in view based on the claim that the objection Paul would be considering is too implausible to have ever been suggested. But 3:5 responds to 3:4 and its talk of God being proved right in his judgment (cf. Moo, *Romans*, 198–9; Schreiner, *Romans*, 173). Schreiner, 173–4, thinks righteousness in judgment is in view but feels the sting of Piper's argument. However, his solution reads too much into what Paul says in 3:5-6, taking the objection to be something different than Paul articulates. It is better to take the objection to be just as Paul states it. While the objection Paul addresses is totally implausible, it is not unlikely to have been made. Totally implausible arguments are not infrequently made in any number of contexts. Often, the rhetorical framing of implausible arguments gives them a superficial plausibility that takes some reflection, even if minimal, to see through, and they can be quite influential. Take, for example, the superficial but influential argument in our own time that there is no absolute truth, which is easily and simply countered by pointing out that the claim is itself an absolute truth claim. Phrasing like "God should not judge people for unrighteousness that glorifies him" sounds reasonable on the surface. But Paul can dispense with the objection by asking a simple question: "then how will God judge the world?" (3:6). That he offers such a simple, brief response supports the view that he is dealing with an implausible objection that is easily dispatched. Verse 8 also supports this, since Paul adds consideration of an allegation against his teaching that is so absurd that he does not even dignify it with a response except to express his contempt for it, merely countering that those who make the allegation deserve condemnation.

is the Creator and human beings are his creation, and thus, judging is his prerogative, and challenging his judgment on sin is challenging the Creator/creature distinction.

4.2.b.3. Jewish Concerns

In our exegesis of Romans 9, we have seen that Paul's argument is oriented toward especially Jewish concerns about his gospel and its implications. Indeed, in 9:14-18 we saw that Paul used the diatribe to address objections to his argument that might arise especially from a Jewish point of view.[32] While the objection Paul considers now is of a more general nature, focusing in on the logic of his argument, it is still put into the service of opposition that arises from distinctively Jewish concern,[33] particularly the concern that Paul's gospel entails that God has been unfaithful to his promises to Israel. Paul uses the second-person singular to address an individual imaginary interlocutor who objects to his argument, enabling him to involve his audience in a heightened exchange over his argument without their being necessarily identified with the arrogant perversity of the objection.[34]

As mentioned earlier, the questions of v. 19 are rhetorical. The first ("Why does he still find fault?") implicitly asserts that God would be unrighteous to blame those

---

[32] See Abasciano, *Romans 9.10-18*, 167–224. Cf. now R. N. Longenecker, *The Epistle to the Romans: A Commentary on the Greek Text* (NIGTC; Grand Rapids, MI: Eerdmans, 2016), 775–6, who, based on the extremely heavy concentration of biblical quotations in Romans 9–11 compared to the rest of Paul's writing, proposes that "when Paul speaks directly to those who had been influenced by Jewish or Jewish Christian theology, ways of thinking, and religious language (as had been the ethnically mixed congregations of believers in Jesus at Rome), he uses OT quotations, OT allusions, and biblically based aphorisms to support his arguments and his presentations (as in 1:16–4:25 and 9:1–11:36)." For a caveat on speaking about the "Jewish point of view" and the like, see Abasciano, *Romans 9.10-18*, 172–3 n. 89.

[33] Cf. J. Morison, *Exposition of the Ninth Chapter of the Epistle to the Romans: A New Edition, Re-written, to Which Is Added an Exposition of the Tenth Chapter* (London: Hodder and Stoughton, 1888), 147–8; J. D. G. Dunn, *Romans* (WBC, 38; 2 vols.; Dallas, TX: Word, 1988), 555; Moo, *Romans*, 620 n. 248; J. Cottrell, *Romans*, II (CPNIVC; Joplin: College Press, 1998), 110, who discusses the reasons for this view more extensively than most. Jewett, *Romans*, 590, sees no tie to Jewish concerns here, but that untethers the passage from its context. R. M. Thorsteinsson, *Paul's Interlocutor in Romans 2: Function and Identity in the Context of Ancient Epistolography* (ConBNT, 40; Stockholm: Almqvist & Wiksell, 2003); and R. Rodríguez, *If You Call Yourself a Jew: Reappraising Paul's Letter to the Romans* (Eugene, OR: Cascade, 2014), both suggest the unusual view that Paul's fictive interlocutor in Romans is not Jewish, but in Thorsteinsson's case, a Gentile considering becoming a proselyte to Judaism, and in Rodríguez's case, a Gentile who has become a proselyte to Judaism. These approaches run counter to what our exegesis has found. But even if one finds one of these proposals persuasive, we would still expect the interlocutor to have Jewish concerns, whether considering adopting Jewish thought or especially having adopted it. For brief, incisive critiques, see A. P. du Toit, "Review of R. M. Thorsteinsson, *Paul's Interlocutor in Romans 2: Function and Identity in the Context of Ancient Epistolography*," *Neot* 38.1 (2004), 152–4, on Thorsteinsson, and on Rodríguez, see P. Esler, "Review of *If You Call Yourself a Jew: Reappraising Paul's Letter to the Romans*," *RBL* (May 2017), https://www.sblcentral.org/home/bookDetails/10048. B. J. Oropeza, "Is the Jew in Romans 2:17 Really a Gentile? Second Thoughts on a Recent Interpretation," *Academia Letters*, Article 444 (2021), https://doi.org/10.20935/AL444, critiques this sort of view in not only Thorsteinsson and Rodríguez, but also M. Thiessen, M. Zetterholm, and P. Fredriksen.

[34] See Jewett, *Romans*, 590–1.

whose unrighteousness he provokes (by making elect status conditional on faith in Christ apart from works or ancestry) and then makes accomplish his will of manifesting his righteousness and glory. The adverb "still" (ἔτι) in the question has an adversative thrust, indicating that, granting the truth of Paul's teaching in 9.14-18 for the sake of argument, God nevertheless finding fault is contrary to expectation[35] because it would make him unrighteous.

4.2.b.4. Echoes of Job

Some interpreters think that Paul alludes to one passage or another in the Book of Job.[36] But suggestions vary,[37] which in this case probably reflects a general allusion to Job's language rather than to any specific text in the book. Wagner has captured the significance of Job for Rom. 9:19-21 skillfully:

> The imaginary interlocutor who objects to Paul's theodicy does so in language laden with overtones of Job's heart-rending protests against the apparent injustice of God. By framing his interlocutor's objection in terms reminiscent of Job's complaints, Paul stacks the deck in his favor, subtly portraying such questions as outrageous, both on the grounds that, for Paul at least, no one can claim to be blameless before God and because the questions themselves are improper for a mere creature to ask of the creator.[38]

The Book of Job reveals Job's questioning of God's justice as totally preposterous and invalid. Job repents and puts his hand over his mouth when faced with God's awesome power and wisdom (Job 40:3-5; 42:1-6). By coloring the present objection to his gospel with accents of Job's ill-advised accusations against God, Paul intimates that the objector should likewise repent and put his hand over his mouth.

4.2.b.5. Romans 9:19b

The second question of the verse ("For who has resisted his purpose?") provides support[39] for the implicit assertion of the first question that God should not blame those whose unrighteousness he makes accomplish his purpose of glorifying his righteousness, by underscoring that God's purpose is accomplished by their rebellion,

---

[35] On this use of ἔτι, see LN, § 89.135; *ALGNT*, s.v. ἔτι.
[36] Byrne, *Romans*, 298, says that the potter/clay image used by Paul "is brought forward simply to illustrate and evoke a basic biblical dogma—one emerging above all from the Book of Job." On *Wisd.* 12:12 as a possible allusion in Rom. 9:19, see note 124 below.
[37] L. T. Johnson, *Reading Romans: A Literary and Theological Commentary* (New York: Crossword, 1997), 161, thinks Paul alluded to Job 9:12. Jewett, *Romans*, 592, thinks Paul echoes both Job 9:12 and 35:2 in Rom. 9:20. Dunn, *Romans*, 556, points to Job 9:19 as possibly in Paul's mind in Rom. 9:19; cf. similarly, Byrne, *Romans*, 299. Byrne additionally finds the first question of Rom. 9:20 "strongly reminiscent" of Job 38:2-3; 40:1-2. Without suggesting that Paul specifically alluded to these texts, Wagner, *Heralds*, 56–7 nn. 42, 45, 47, mentions Job 9:19; 10:9; 30:19; 33:6, 9-10; 38:3; 40:2, 4b-5; 42:6.
[38] Wagner, *Heralds*, 56.
[39] N.B. the use of γάρ (for).

and accomplished certainly. The rhetorical question implies that no one has ever resisted God's purpose (in the sense intended by the question).[40] The verb ἀνθίστημι means "to resist, oppose"[41] and can have the sense of "*successfully* resist/oppose"[42] as it most likely does here.[43] It is unlikely that the objection refers to *mere* resistance or opposition to God's will or purpose since (1) it arises out of 9:17-18's contemplation of actual resistance to God as exemplified in Pharaoh and taking place in unbelieving Israel's rejection of the gospel, (2) the objection itself is a form of resistance to God,[44] and (3) it is self-evident that human beings have resisted God. Indeed, Paul refers to possible human resistance to God in Rom. 13:2 using the same word that he uses here.[45] As Piper observes, it is so obvious to everyone that human beings do resist God by acting against his will "that it is utterly implausible that the objector would be affirming that no one has ever resisted God in this sense. Everyone has."[46] Thus,

---

[40] Cf. Jewett, *Romans*, 591. On the sense intended by the question, see below. The wording of the question does not in itself rule out anyone ever having resisted God's purpose in the past since the perfect tense verb includes the present results of the verbal action. But it is the wording in this context that conveys that sense.

[41] BDAG, s.v. ἀνθίστημι.

[42] See Lev. 26:37; Deut. 7:24; 9:2; 11:25; Josh. 1:5; 7:13; 23:9; Judg. 2:14; 2 Chron. 20:6; 20:12; Jdt. 11:18; Ps. 76:7; Job 41:2-3; Wisd. 11:3; Sir. 46:7; Hos. 14:1; Mic. 2:7-8; Obad. 1:7; Mal. 3:15; Isa. 3:9; Jer. 27:24, 29; Dan. 10:13; Jas 4:7.

[43] Cf. F. L. Forlines, *Romans* (RHBC; Nashville, TN: Randall House, 1987), 276; Cottrell, *Romans*, 111.

[44] On (2), see R. T. Forster and V. P. Marston, *God's Strategy in Human History*, 2nd ed. (Eugene, OR: Wipf and Stock, 2000), 72, 78-9 n. 11, though they take the view that the objector has misunderstood Paul's teaching in Romans 9, which disagrees with the notion that God's will cannot be resisted in the sense intended by the objection. This is possible—Piper, *Justification*, 189-92, is too dismissive of the view (see below)—but Paul does not indicate that the objection misunderstands him on that point (rightly pointed out by Piper), which would immediately rip the ground out from under it. Cottrell, *Romans*, 111-13, does not agree that the objector's second question misunderstands Paul but does think that the objector misunderstands Paul on another point, "assuming that this purposive will of God applied to Israel's salvation status (9:3) as well as to the nation's historical role in accomplishing God's redemptive plan" (112) when Paul only has the latter in mind. Against the view that Paul does not have salvation in view, but historical role only, see my exegesis of Rom. 9:1-18 in my two previous volumes on Romans 9; see esp. *Romans 9.1-9*, 185-6. Our analysis of vv. 21-24 in this volume will also support the point. Rodríguez, *Jew*, 184-6, thinks the interlocutor misunderstands Paul on another matter, viz. that Paul sees mercy and hardening as balanced when he in fact saw mercy as dominant. While it is true that the note of mercy is dominant in Romans 9, the text gives no indication that the interlocutor misunderstands this or that Paul seeks to correct such a misunderstanding.

[45] Forster and Marston, *Strategy*, 72, 78-9 nn. 8, 11, point to Lk. 7.30 ("But the Pharisees and the lawyers rejected for themselves the purpose of God, not having been baptized by him [John]") as a plain scriptural statement that God's will is not irresistible. But Piper, *Justification*, 190 n. 5, disputes this, arguing that the verse means "that the plan of salvation preached by John the Baptist was accepted by some and rejected by others" without suggesting that an individual can frustrate God's purpose for that individual. However, in context, the purpose of God in Lk. 7:30 has to do with John the Baptist's ministry of preparing the way for Christ through his message calling all Israel to repentance. So the purpose of God in context includes God's purpose for all Israel to repent. For the Pharisees to reject for themselves that purpose was still to reject God's purpose for them, specifically God's purpose for them to repent and live in faithful adherence to the kingdom of God. Piper's characterization of the purpose in view is therefore misleadingly reductionistic for consideration of the question being addressed and his conclusion is accordingly inadequate.

[46] Piper, *Justification*, 191. Ironically, this point actually gives some support to Forster and Marston's position described in note 44 above, for the fact that it is so obvious that people can resist God's will in some significant sense could explain why Paul would not explicitly address the contention that God's will is irresistible even though disagreeing with it. Piper's own solution is not as obvious as

Leroy Forlines comments, "The verse does not suggest that a person cannot resist God's purpose in the sense of *opposing* God's purpose. Rather, no one can *defeat* God's purposes. A person can disobey God and will be held responsible for his disobedience. However, God has purposes that are carried out in spite of disobedience."[47] More than that, God has purposes that are accomplished *as a result* of human disobedience inter alia. Moreover, God has purposes that required action that was bound to harden Israel, namely making election to be by faith in Jesus Christ rather than works or ancestry. It is partly this provocative exercise of divine sovereignty that sparks the current objection. Why should God judge people for disobedience that was bound to result from the fulfillment of his purpose? And why should God judge people when their disobedience facilitates the accomplishment of his purpose?

The question, "For who has resisted his purpose?" then, serves to emphasize that God's purpose of glorifying his righteousness has been and remains accomplished. So v. 19 is essentially asking what God is complaining about since he unfailingly gets what he wants out of Jewish unrighteousness. It is arguing that it is wrong for him to find fault for unrighteousness that he uses to accomplish his purpose and in a sense benefits from.

The word for purpose used here, βούλημα, is uncommon.[48] While most translations render the word as "will" in 9:19 ("For who has resisted his *will*?"), the word carries a more specific nuance of "intention/purpose/plan."[49] In light of the inexorable nature of the purpose in view, the word seems to refer here to an instance of what some scholars have called "the decretive will of God" or the like.[50] However, this is not to be taken in the deterministic sense of an exhaustive decree that unconditionally determines all that ever happens.[51] Nothing in the context suggests such a notion. Rather, the idea is that God might allow humans beings a choice in any number of situations, but when he decides to make something happen, there is nothing anyone can do to stop him. That is the purpose of God that cannot be successfully resisted.[52]

The purpose of God in view is best taken as the specific purpose of God most immediately identified just prior to 9:19—the manifestation of God's power and the proclamation of his name in all the earth (9:17). For the objection voiced in 9:19

---

he supposes, but seems somewhat contrived (cf. Godet's [*Romans*, 356] opinion of the same view as articulated by Hofmann). He argues that Paul's position was that it can be said that no one resists God's will because God effectually wills their resistance to his will (so also Schreiner, *Romans*, 494). Interestingly, Cranfield, *Romans*, 489–90, sees that very position as the objection that the objector is articulating. Piper's position here is not impossible, but it is hardly natural or obvious.

[47] Forlines, *Romans*, 276.
[48] Piper, *Justification*, 192; L. Morris, *The Epistle to the Romans* (Grand Rapids, MI: Eerdmans, 1988), 363 n. 80; G. Schrenk, "βούλημα," *TDNT*, 1.636–37 (636); Dunn, *Romans*, 556.
[49] Morris, ibid.; Schrenk, ibid.; Jewett, *Romans*, 591; Cottrell, *Romans*, 111; Forlines, *Romans*, 276; Dunn, ibid.; W. Sanday and A. C. Headlam, *A Critical and Exegetical Commentary on the Epistle to the Romans*, 10th ed. (ICC; New York: Charles Scribner's, 1905), 259; D. Müller, "βούλομαι," *NIDNTT*, 3.1015–18 (1017); A. T. Robertson, *Word Pictures in the New Testament* (Nashville, TN: Broadman, 1932–3, 1960), s.v. Rom. 9:19, https://www.studylight.org/commentaries/eng/rwp.html.
[50] Cottrell, ibid.; Piper, *Justification*, 192, who cites examples of both exegetes and systematic theologians.
[51] Rightly, Cottrell, *Romans*, 112–13.
[52] But see below about whether the notion of ability is in view.

responds to the principle articulated in 9:18, which is drawn in part from this purpose identified in 9:17. Some think the perfect tense used in the question of 9:19b ("For who has resisted his will?") should be taken as gnomic, expressing a general principle.[53] Romans 9:19 does respond to a general principle (9:18), and Paul appeals to a general principle in 9:15. But Paul employs a mix of specific statements and general principles in Romans 9. The verb in 19b seems more likely to be an extensive perfect, emphasizing a completed past act that has continuing results in the present,[54] since it relates to the specific purpose of God described in 9:17 that is concretely connected to the situation of unbelieving ethnic Israel in Paul's day. Moreover, the gnomic perfect is rare.[55] Furthermore, 9:19ff. have the hardening and judgment of Israel spoken about in the previous verses especially in view. And we have already seen that the objection in 19a is asking specifically why God finds fault with hardened Jews who have rejected Christ. Consequently, although a general principle could be in view, the specific situation of unbelieving ethnic Israel is more likely in view.[56]

The use of the perfect tense keeps unbelieving ethnic Israel's opposition to Paul's gospel in Paul's time in view, though in this context it seems to emphasize the completed act of opposition.[57] Its use in 9:19b contributes to the nuance of the resistance that

---

[53] So Jewett, *Romans*, 591; Moo, *Romans*, 620 n. 250. Jewett notes that some translate with the present tense or with reference to the ability to resist ("who can resist?") to capture this nuance. Moo's (*Romans*, 610 n. 250) assumption that the gnomic perfect carries "no past-referring significance" is incorrect. As Wallace, *Greek*, 580, states, "The aspectual force of the [gnomic] perfect is usually intact, but now it has a distributive value."

[54] On the extensive perfect, see Wallace, *Greek*, 577. An intensive perfect (on which, see ibid., 574–6), which emphasizes the results or state in the present coming from a past act, could rather be the sense here. A decision depends on whether one thinks the past act of resisting God or the continuing state of resistance in the present is more emphasized.

[55] Ibid., 580.

[56] Happily, a decision does not affect the overall exegesis. Our interpretation of 9:19-24 otherwise is consistent with either a general principle or a specific situation being in view in 19b, though a specific reference coheres best with the rest of our exegesis. But if a general principle is in view in 19b, it is being applied to the specific situation of unbelieving Jews in Paul's time. Our general exegesis can also cohere with the purpose in 9:19 having reference to God's purpose in general, encompassing any purpose of God, though again, the specific purpose from 9:17 coheres best with the rest of our exegesis. If the reference itself is to a specific situation rather than a general principle applied to a specific situation, it probably still implies a general principle on some level. In other words, if asked if 19b refers to a general principle, Paul would say something like, "No, it refers to the fact that no Jews, by rejecting Christ, have prevented God from accomplishing his purpose of manifesting his name and power. But now that you mention it, of course it is an abiding principle that no one prevents this purpose of God from being accomplished."

[57] As mentioned above, this would be an extensive perfect; cf. note 54 above. It could be that the perfect tense here is one of wholly present force as Sanday and Headlam, *Romans*, 259; and Cranfield, *Romans*, 490 take it; ἀνθίστημι is the type of verb that can be used in that category of perfect, on which see, e.g., Wallace, *Greek*, 579–80. But it seems that more is being said. It is not merely that no one successfully resists God in the present, but that no one has successfully resisted God in the past with a resultant continuing opposition in the present, as the traditional/majority conception of the force of the perfect tense (for which, see, e.g., Wallace, 572–4) as it would apply here would suggest (though the nature of the perfect tense in Koine Greek is hotly debated among grammarians; see D. A. Carson [ed.], *The Perfect Storm: Critical Discussion of the Semantics of the Greek Perfect Tense under Aspect Theory* [SBG, 21; New York: Peter Lang, 2021]). This enhances the portrayal of the resistance that is being asked about as successful; see further below. It should be noted that I take a nuanced traditional view of the Greek tenses as represented by grammarians such as Wallace, Rijksbaron, Fanning, Blass, Debrunner and Funk, Zerwick, Robertson, and so on, what is probably still the majority position. As I stated in B. J. Abasciano, "Does Regeneration Precede

is contemplated as successful since the perfect includes the continuing results of the completed action in the speaker's present. Of course, as mentioned earlier, the rhetorical question of 19b strongly implies negation of its verbal idea; it implies that God's purpose of manifesting his name and power has not been successfully resisted.

Some translations translate ἀνθέστηκεν as "can resist," but this is inaccurate; the wording of the text is about what has in fact happened and the continuing results ("who has resisted?").[58] Robert Jewett thinks this is "an overly sharp distinction."[59] But is there not a substantial distinction between the concepts of what people can do and what they in fact do? Piper argues, "But surely this difference is of no great consequence. If no one has ever resisted, it is precisely because no one can."[60] It is probably true in this case that no one has ever successfully resisted God's purpose of manifesting his name and power because no one can. But the question for exegesis is what Paul intended to convey and what he directs attention to. The fact that the objection he describes asks about what has been done rather than what can be done fixes the text's focus on the former. If Paul wanted to talk about ability, then he could have simply used the language of ability. On the other hand, he could very well have been trying to capture both ideas by indicating that no one has ever successfully resisted God's purpose. But even if one thinks so, or that Paul's point is mainly about ability, that should be treated as a matter of interpretation, not translation. Paul would be making the point by implication in the manner of Piper's reasoning mentioned above rather than by direct statement. But in light of our reading of Romans 9 through 19a, including the background of Romans 3, combined with Paul's explicit language speaking of what has happened rather than of ability, we conclude that Paul's focus is on what has happened, specifically whether or not God's purpose has been prevented from being accomplished by unbelieving ethnic Israel's rejection of Christ.[61]

Faith? The Use of 1 John 5:1 as a Proof Text," *EQ* 84.4 (2012), 307–22 (309 n. 9): "One critical but sometimes overlooked point in the debate about time in the Greek tenses is that 'both ancient and modern Greeks have unanimously affirmed that temporal significance is normally communicated by Greek verbs'" (Roy E. Ciampa and Brian S. Rosner, *The First Letter to the Corinthians* [Pillar New Testament Commentary; Grand Rapids, MI: Eerdmans, 2010], 44, note their references to ancient Greek authors who commented on time in Greek verbs). If ancient authors writing in Greek considered themselves to normally be communicating time through their use of tense, then the fact that authorial intention determines meaning (a point that is itself disputed, but rightly is still probably the standard assumption of exegetes) demands that we regard Greek verbs as normally communicating time.

[58] See Cranfield, *Romans*, 490; Moo, *Romans*, 600 n. 63 (1st ed.; in his second edition, Moo, 620 n. 251, has softened his view; he still notes that "the Greek does not explicitly justify" the notion of ability but now thinks it "still gets the basic point"); Fitzmyer, *Romans*, 568; Dunn, *Romans*, 556; Sanday and Headlam, *Romans*, 259. If the perfect tense here is one of wholly present force, then the wording of the text would be about what in fact happens (that would also be the case for a gnomic perfect) or is happening ("who resists?" or "who is resisting?").

[59] Jewett, *Romans*, 591 n. 33.

[60] Piper, *Justification*, 189 n. 3. See also Schreiner, *Romans*, 500 n. 3.

[61] I would suggest applying here the principle of lexical semantics known as "maximal redundancy" (the meaning of a polysemous word in a specific context is most likely the meaning that contributes least to the passage in which it is used) even though it is normally applied to the lexical meaning of a specific word. In light of our exegesis to this point, the notion of inability is not necessary to account for the objection. Of course, this is not a lexical rule and is not in itself conclusive. But it adds to support for a reference that does not intend to invoke the notion of inability. On the principle of maximal redundancy, see M. Silva, *Biblical Words and Their Meaning: An Introduction*

In context and in light of our exegesis of Rom. 9:14-18, the fullest and most specific sense of v. 19 is best taken along the following lines: if God (resistibly) hardens Israel by making elect status conditional on faith in Christ apart from works or ancestry in order to bring about the fulfillment of his plan to fulfill his covenant promises and glorify his name, and no one has prevented the accomplishment of his intention of glorifying himself with the result that through Israel's stubborn rebellion his faithfulness and glory are indeed magnified, then it would be unrighteous of God to find fault with hardened Israel since their stubborn rebellion serves his purposes. Or again, in the words of Rom. 3:5 and 7, "But if our unrighteousness demonstrates the righteousness of God, what shall we say? Is the God who inflicts wrath actually unrighteous? ... But if through my lie the truth of God abounds to his glory, why then am I still judged as a sinner?" and in their summary form in 9:19, "Why does he still find fault? For who has resisted his purpose?"

4.2.c. Romans 9:20-21: The Potter and the Clay

4.2.c.1. Romans 9:20a: Who Do You Think You Are?

Paul begins his reply to the objection of 9:19 with this: "²⁰ O man, on the contrary, who are you, the one who answers back to God? Will the thing molded really say to the molder, 'Why did you make me like this?' ²¹ Or does the potter not have the right over the clay to make from the same lump one a vessel unto honor and another unto dishonor?" This response reflects that the objection is insolent; the objector arrogates to himself the right to pass judgment on God and would deny him the right to judge his own creation and do with them as he sees fit. The language of the verse conveys a strong tone of rebuke, evident from the very first words.

The interjection ὦ ('O') normally expresses emotion,[62] and here colors with passion the whole question that it begins.[63] While the opening address, ὦ ἄνθρωπε (O man), can carry the polite sense of "sir" or "my dear sir" in dialogue,[64] in this context it clearly stresses the objector's lowly place as a human being in contrast to God. As many have

---

to *Lexical Semantics*, rev. and exp. (Zondervan Academic, 2010), chapter 6, in the sec. on "Unintended Ambiguity," http://search.ebscohost.com.gordonconwell.idm.oclc.org/login.aspx?direct=true&db=nlebk&AN=1524650&site=ehost-live&scope=site. Happily again, a decision on whether Paul has inability in mind does not affect the overall exegesis, which is consistent with Paul invoking inability even if a focus on what has in fact happened coheres best with our exegesis. The notion of inability would intensify the objection, emphasizing that God irresistibly accomplishes his purpose, which would in turn emphasize that his purpose is certainly accomplished. But it would not really alter the basic objection.

[62] BDAG, s.v. 1a. On ὦ more fully, see BDF, § 146.

[63] See BDF, § 146.2; Jewett, *Romans*, 592.

[64] See Cranfield, *Romans*, 490, who recognizes that is not the case here. Some mss omit μενουνγε (P⁴⁶ B D* F G 629 latt) and the majority of mss place it before ω ανθρωπε (including ℵ² D² K L P 33 104 365 1175 1241 1505 2664 sy^h). But as ibid., n. 8, argues, these "look like attempts to make an easier text" since it is unusual for μενουνγε to follow the vocative (so also Jewett, *Romans*, 587; Moo, *Romans*, 609 n. 190; Longenecker, *Romans*, 798–9). It is possible that the omission of μενουνγε in some mss is to be explained as haplography due to μοι ουν in the previous verse. The presence of μενουν in B is an obvious accidental alteration of μενουνγε, perhaps from haplography due to πε at the end of the preceding word, ἄνθρωπε, or simply mistaking μενουνγε for its milder form.

observed, "there is surely a conscious contrast between ὦ ἄνθρωπε and τῷ θεῷ (the first and last words of the sentence), so that the translation 'man' or 'O man' is required."[65] Indeed, the placement of ὦ ἄνθρωπε at the beginning of the sentence before μενοῦνγε lays emphasis on this humbling address.

The reprimanding tone is intensified by the use of the emphatic adversative particle μενοῦνγε (on the contrary).[66] The word was used in answers to emphasize, or as here, to correct.[67] The tone is intensified even more by the question, "Who are you?" The modern English equivalent in sense would be, "Who do you think you are?"[68] The position of "you" in the question in the Greek text is emphatic, drawing further attention to the interlocutor's arrogance. The next phrase, "the one who answers back to God," shows just how severe the hypothetical objector's arrogance is, taking it upon himself to sit in judgment of God and to challenge his very right to judge. No wonder that Jewett observes, "Paul's question resonates with Jewish warnings about the fear of God and with Greco-Roman warnings about the dangers of pride before the deity."[69]

"Answering back" (ἀνταποκρίνομαι) to God in this context carries the sense of disputing or contradicting him.[70] One might wonder if it is fair for Paul to characterize his interlocutor as contradicting God when the contention is really that Paul's claims about God's actions are what logically entail unrighteousness in God's judgment. The Christian believer (not to mention Paul himself) could respond that, as an Apostle of Christ, Paul knew his view to be God's view. Therefore, to challenge his theological position is to challenge God. But Paul has not used that approach with the previous objections he has addressed in Romans 9, and it does not seem be an approach he ever uses when addressing substantive objections.[71] The issue here is probably that Paul views the interlocutor as objecting to an axiomatic biblical principle—God's right and glory in judging human sin—and therefore, unquestionably, to God's own viewpoint and divine prerogative.[72]

Romans 9.20a is another rhetorical question like those of v. 19. "Who are you, the one who answers back to God?" means "you should not answer back to God." In context, more fully and specifically it means that the objector should not dispute God's judgment upon unbelieving ethnic Israel when he glorifies himself and accomplishes his purpose through their rebellion. This is the main point of 9:19-24. Verse 19 evokes the point with its objection to Paul's argument. Verse 20a provides the basic

---

[65] Cranfield, *Romans*, 490.
[66] On μενοῦνγε as emphatic, see LN, § 89.128; Wallace, *Greek*, 673, 761; cf. H. W. Smyth, *Greek Grammar for Colleges* (New York: American Book Company, 1920), § 2901b; Jewett, *Romans*, 592.
[67] BDAG, s.v. μενοῦν.
[68] Indeed, the NJB uses that expression in its translation. Cf. BDAG's (s.v. τίς, τί, 1.?) "(just) who are you?" Jewett, *Romans*, 592, draws attention to the same phrase in Job 35:2, where it is used to challenge presumption.
[69] Jewett, ibid.
[70] See *ALGNT*, s.v. ἀνταποκρίνομαι; LN, § 33.413; LSJ, s.v. ἀνταποκρίνομαι, I; F. Büchsel, "ἀποκρίνω, ἀνταποκρίνομαι," *TDNT*, 3.944-5 (945).
[71] Paul does invoke his own authority in giving authoritative direction to churches (e.g., 1 Cor. 14:36-38; 2 Cor. 13; Galatians, 1-2), but that is another matter.
[72] Cf. Rom. 3:1-8 and discussion of it in Section 4.2.b.2.

response to the objection, in effect asserting that the objection is invalid. And the rest of the passage supports the point of 20a that v. 19's objection to God's judgment on unbelieving ethnic Israel is false.

4.2.c.2. Romans 9:20b-21 in Intertextual Perspective

4.2.c.2.a. Initial Observations

As we saw earlier in this chapter, the first six words of Paul's next sentence ("Will the thing molded really say to the molder") come verbatim from Isa. 29:16 LXX, making an informal, exact quotation.[73] Piper contends that "Paul is not so much citing a text for authority as he is adapting a common metaphor for his own purpose."[74] He bases this on the fact that Paul does not go on to use Isaiah's exact wording in the next clause for what the molded thing (τὸ πλάσμα) says to its molder. But that cannot discount the actual quotation before us. At the very least, it invites examination of the original context of the quotation to see if it actually informs Paul's meaning. Moreover, we have seen very clearly in our study of Romans 9 so far (in the two previous volumes) that Paul's Old Testament quotations and other allusions have been functioning as pointers to their original contexts. It would be surprising at this point if an actual quotation in this chapter did otherwise.

But there is some value in the observation that the phrasing of the clay's words in Paul ("Why did you make me like this?") does not match the phrasing of the clay's words in Isaiah exactly ("You did not fashion me"/"You did not make me wisely"). I would suggest that the explanation for this is that Paul was inspired by multiple potter/clay texts and wanted to allude to all of them, namely, Isa. 29:16, 45:9 in Rom. 9:20, and Jer. 18:6 in Rom. 9:21. Our comparison of these texts and Rom. 9:20-21 led to the conclusion that all of these Old Testament texts contributed to Paul's presentation (see Section 4.1). The verbal similarities are enough to suggest this as a possibility. But contextual thematic correspondence is necessary to confirm it in the cases of Isa. 45:9 and Jer. 18:6. That Isa. 29:16 contributed to Paul's presentation is beyond doubt given

---

[73] See Section 4.1. T. H. Tobin's (*Paul's Rhetoric in Its Contexts: The Argument of Romans* [Peabody, MA: Hendrickson, 2004], 332) denial of a quotation and Schreiner's (*Romans*, 495) assertion that Paul does not specifically depend on any particular text (cf. Piper, *Justification*, 195) are curious given the verbatim match of six words in identical sequence, as is Morris's (*Romans*, 365) uncertainty over which text Paul quotes from, Isa. 29:16 or 45:9. Commentators routinely recognize a quotation here, e.g., Moo, *Romans*, 601; Cranfield, *Romans*, 491; Dunn, *Romans*, 556; Fitzmyer, *Romans*, 568; Jewett, *Romans*, 592. Shum, *Romans*, 205, oddly considers only whether all of Rom. 9:20-21 is a quotation of Isa. 29:16, and so concludes that it is not, but is merely an allusion. He cites Cranfield as holding that there is not a quotation, but this is inaccurate. Cranfield holds that Paul quotes part of Isa. 29:16 followed by material that is merely generally reminiscent of it. On the other hand, Shum, 204, notes that Paul's use of Isa. 29:10 in Rom. 11:8 strengthens the likelihood that Rom. 9:20-21 depends on Isa. 29:16 to some substantial degree. Johnson, *Romans*, 161, appears to be alone (or virtually so) in his assertion that Paul mixed Job 9:12 with Isa. 29:16, and for good reason. As mentioned above, we have a clear quotation of Isa. 29:16 here, but Job 9:12 does not *distinctively* match Rom. 9:20-21 in any way, and there are other texts that are much closer to Rom. 9:20-21 than Job 9:12. But perhaps Johnson took his lead from the likelihood that there are overtones from Job in Paul's language; see below.

[74] Piper, ibid.

his quotation of the verse. That it contributed to his meaning also calls for contextual thematic correspondence. We shall see that such correspondence is profoundly present in each of these Old Testament passages, making it highly likely that all of them contributed to Paul's meaning and that Paul meant to point to all of them in their original contexts.[75]

Wagner rightly points out that the clay's question which Paul articulates—"Why did you make me like this?" (Rom. 9:20c)—paraphrases the second statement of Isa. 29:16 LXX—"You did not make me wisely."[76] But it also paraphrases Isa. 45:9c's question—"What are you making?" Indeed, the question in Rom. 9:20c is closer to Isa. 45:9c than Isa. 29:16 in that the former are questions whereas Isa. 29:16 is a statement. All of these expressions—Paul's and both of Isaiah's—challenge the wisdom or appropriateness of God's treatment of his people. Isaiah 29:16 LXX states the matter straightforwardly albeit negatively. The clay's questions in Rom. 9:20 and Isa. 45:9c are rhetorical questions that are neither friendly nor even neutral requests for information. They implicitly assert that God has acted wrongly in his treatment of his people. In its context, Isa. 45:9c's "What are you making?" implies that the fashioner of the clay is shaping the clay wrongly. Romans 9:20's "Why did you make me like this?" implies that God was unrighteous to fashion the clay as he did.

4.2.c.2.b. Remarkable Broad Thematic Parallels between Rom. 9:20 and Isa. 29:16 and 45:9

Before delving more deeply into the meaning of Rom. 9:20b-c, it would be beneficial to pause and take note of the fact that there is remarkable thematic correspondence between the passage in its context and Isa. 29:16 and 45:9 in their original contexts.[77] For now, we will just sketch the broader parallels besides the potter/clay imagery and then bring out further detail as we explore the meaning-effects of these allusions in relation to Rom. 9:20b-c. Isaiah 29:16 is part of a passage (Isa. 29:15-24) that is situated in a section of Isaiah (chs. 28-33) with the purpose of urging trust in the Lord and in his chosen means of salvation rather than in some means of human making. Isaiah 29:15-24 fits into this purpose by issuing a warning to those who rebel against faith/trust in the Lord alone as his means of salvation for them (precluding reliance on other nations, such as Egypt) and would try to avoid the Lord's judgment on their disloyalty and rebellion against him by attempting to hide their self-reliant plans from him. This warning is issued on the ground that God's blessing would fall upon the righteous (including the fulfillment of his promise of salvation announced by Isaiah),

---

[75] See Chapter 3 of this volume for an assessment of other possible background to Paul's use of potter/clay imagery.

[76] Wagner, *Heralds*, 58. The Hebrew reads, "He [God] does not understand," which is different in its wording but makes the same basic point. Support for επλασας in D and sy^p in Rom. 9:20 is too weak to be read in place of the strongly supported εποιησας; see Longenecker, *Romans*, 799. But Jewett, *Romans*, 587 n. c, notes that it "follows the wording of the LXX of Isaiah."

[77] The reader is urged to refer to the detailed exegesis of these Old Testament texts provided in Chapter 2 of this investigation. We will take up the similarly remarkable connections with Jer. 18:6 when treating Rom. 9:21.

and his judgment upon the wicked, which would lead to vindication of God's holiness, reverence for him among his erring people, and the removal of their hard-heartedness.

Isaiah 45:9 is part of a passage (Isa. 45:9-13) that focuses on one of the major themes of the broader section comprised of Isaiah 40–48, that Israel rejected God's plan of deliverance because of his choice of Cyrus, a Gentile king, as Israel's deliverer. It was the Gentile ethnicity of God's choice (Cyrus) and all that it meant that hardened Israel to God's plan and provoked their rejection of it. Moreover, Isa. 45:9-13 is surrounded by concern for the salvation of the Gentiles. Indeed, Isa. 45:6 indicates that one of the main purposes of YHWH's choice of Cyrus as the deliverer of his people was for the world to know that YHWH is the only true God. Thus, Israel's resistance to God's choice of a savior for his people was, in effect, resistance to his plan for the salvation of the Gentiles. The purpose of Isa. 45:9 and the passage in which it is found (45:9-13) is to urge those who object to God's plan of salvation/choice of a deliverer to abandon their distrust of and opposition to God and his plan and rather to trust in and embrace them.

These parallels to Rom. 9:20-21 and its context are striking and just happen to support the understanding of Romans 9 that I have set forth in my exegesis of the chapter to this point in my two previous volumes on the passage and the present one. I have argued that in Romans 9–11 Paul is defending his gospel of justification by faith apart from works or ancestry against its most pressing objection, that it makes God unrighteous in the sense of unfaithful to his promises to Israel because it denies covenant membership and fulfillment of the promises to unbelieving ethnic Jews and grants these blessings to believing Gentiles (and Jews). In reply to the objection, Paul argues that the fulfillment of God's promises was not given to ethnic Israel qua ethnic Israel, but to spiritual Israel, Israel as the covenant people of God and as defined by promise, faith, and God's call rather than works or ancestry. The point brings Paul to argue for God's sovereign right to name whomever he wants as his covenant people rather than on the basis of human works or ancestry. In context, Paul is arguing for God's right to choose his people by faith rather than works or ancestry and that this (ironically) brings about the fulfillment of God's covenant promises, which had the blessing/salvation of the world as their aim. It is faith in Christ as the condition of covenant membership that allows God to bestow his covenant blessings on Gentiles in addition to Jews, opening up covenant membership/elect status and the salvation that goes with it to all. However, this requires the rejection of unbelieving Jews. Moreover, it is this very separation of ethnicity from covenant membership that was bound to harden, and in fact did harden, the Jews to the gospel message. What we have been describing is Paul's understanding of God's plan of salvation for ethnic Israel and the Gentiles. In Romans 9, Paul is defending God's righteousness in his plan of salvation for Israel in light of the gospel.

Paul has now come to the objection (from the unbelieving Jewish point of view)[78] that God would be unrighteous to condemn Jews for rejecting Christ when his plan of salvation was bound to harden them (due to its offensiveness to their ethnocentrism

---

[78] On the Jewishness of this viewpoint, see Section 4.2.b.3.

and zeal for the Law)⁷⁹ and he would be glorified as a result of their hardening.⁸⁰ The objection is in essence an objection to God's plan of salvation and his right to judge. In response, Paul invokes Isa. 29:16 and 45:9, which concern God's people's objections to his plan of salvation.

Just as, against the backdrop of God's people objecting to his plan of salvation, the broad section in which Isa. 29:16 appears (Isa. 28–33) has the purpose of urging trust in the Lord and in his chosen means of salvation rather than in some means of human making, so Rom. 9:20-21, against the backdrop of God's people objecting to his plan of salvation, has the purpose of urging trust in the Lord and in his chosen means of salvation, Jesus Christ, and faith in him, rather than in some means established by human beings such as ancestry (9:6-13), works (9:12, 32), or their own righteousness (10:3). Moreover, just as Isa. 29:16 issues a warning to those who would try to avoid the Lord's judgment on their disloyalty and rebellion against him, so Rom. 9:20-21 issues a rebuke of the one—represented by the interlocutor—who tries to avoid God's judgment on their unbelief, disloyalty, and rebellion against him in their rejection of Christ.⁸¹ And just as the warning of Isa. 29:16 is issued on the ground that God's blessing would fall upon the righteous and his judgment upon the wicked, so the rebuke of Rom. 9:20-21 is ultimately grounded on God's blessing for the righteous by faith in Christ (9:7-9, 12-13, 15, 18, 23-26, 30, 33; 10:9-13; 11:4-7, 19-20, 22-23) and his judgment upon the unrighteous (i.e., unbelievers; 9:3, 13, 17-18, 22, 28, 31-33; 11:7-10, 20-22).⁸² Furthermore, just as the context of Isa. 29:16 prophesies the reversal of God's hardening judgment upon his people by the fulfillment of his word in the working of his salvation, so the context of Rom. 9:20-21 looks to the reversal of God's hardening judgment upon his people by the fulfillment of his word in the working of his salvation/the gospel.⁸³

Intriguingly, Paul quotes Isa. 29:10 in Rom. 11:8, the Isaian prophecy of God's hardening judgment against Israel that the context of Isa. 29:16 specifically reverses. This corroborates the unity and consistency of Romans 9–11 as well as the natural assumption that the hardening of Romans 9 and 11 are one and the same.⁸⁴ It also

---

⁷⁹ It should be kept in mind that this hardening was neither irresistible nor specifically individual, but corporate in nature and resistible on the individual level. See again, Abasciano, *Romans 9.10-18*, 200–19.

⁸⁰ On how their hardening would glorify God, see ibid., 215.

⁸¹ In the Isaian context, the unfaithful sought to avoid God's judgment by hiding their faithless plans from him. In the Pauline context, the unfaithful (represented by the interlocutor) seek to avoid God's judgment by arguing against its validity.

⁸² One might wonder how divine blessing/judgment constitutes the ultimate basis of the rebuke Paul delivers. The objection to God's judgment is given to support objection to Paul's gospel. Paul's reply implies that the objection is unfounded and so implicitly urges repentance from rejection of the gospel to faith in it. The context of Romans 9 ultimately reveals that the call to embrace Paul's gospel is undergirded by divine covenantal blessing for believers and condemnation for unbelievers.

⁸³ This evidences an anticipatory pattern in Paul's use of the OT that we have seen repeatedly in Romans 9 thus far. We will see it again in our treatment of Paul's use of Jer. 18:6 in Rom. 9:21, where we will take up the phenomenon in more detail in light of its occurrence in Paul's use of both Isa. 29:16 and Jer. 18:6.

⁸⁴ Piper, *Justification*, 176–7, is eager to equate the hardening of these chapters in support of the point that the hardening of Rom. 9:18 damns. But he misses the crucial fact that ch. 11 reveals that Paul hoped to win as many hardened Jews as possible in the present, which contradicts Piper's broader approach of construing hardening as irreversibly leading to final damnation. While Moo, *Romans*,

corroborates something we have seen time and again throughout Romans 9, that Paul's Old Testament allusions in the chapter function as pointers to their original Old Testament contexts. Indeed, what we see here is very much like what Dodd described with regard to the New Testament authors generally in his classic book, *According to the Scriptures: The Substructure of New Testament Theology*.[85] As G. K. Beale describes Dodd's contribution,

> Dodd observed that throughout the New Testament there are numerous and scattered quotes that derive from the same few Old Testament contexts. He asks the question why, given that the same segment of the Old Testament is in view, there are so few identical quotations of the same verse, and secondly, why it is that different verses are cited from the same segments of the Old Testament. He concludes that this phenomenon indicates that New Testament authors were aware of broad Old Testament contexts and did not focus merely on single verses independent of the segment from which they were drawn. Single verses and phrases are merely signposts to the overall Old Testament context from which they were cited.[86]

In light of Dodd's observations, it is striking that in a unified but sprawling section in which Paul talks at different points about Israel's hardening and the reversal of that hardening, he alludes to an Old Testament prophecy of the hardening of Israel at one point and to its distinct counterpart at a different point, which directly follows it in the same original broad context and includes the reversal of that hardening.

The context of Isa. 45:9 also concerns Israel's rejection of God's plan of salvation. But it specifies the reason for Israel's objection to God's plan—opposition to his chosen means of salvation, specifically the man he chose as the deliverer, a Gentile king (Cyrus). Just as the Gentile ethnicity of God's choice of a Gentile savior (Cyrus) and all that it meant hardened Israel of Isaiah's day to God's plan of salvation and provoked their rejection of it, so God's choice of Jesus as savior, and faith in him apart from works or ancestry as the means of participation in God's salvation of his people, hardened Israel in Paul's day to God's plan of salvation (the gospel) and provoked their rejection of it. Moreover, just as one of the main purposes of YHWH's choice of Cyrus as the deliverer of his people was for the world to know that YHWH is the only true God, so one of the main purposes of God's choice of Jesus as the deliverer of his people was for the world to know the saving power and glory of God. Furthermore, just as Israel's resistance to God's choice of a savior for his people in Isaiah's day was, in effect,

---

understands the hardening of Rom. 9:18 and 11:7 to be the same (680), he posits a difference between the hardening of 9:18 and that of 11:25 (599). For brief critique of the latter, see Abasciano, *Romans 9.10-18*, 211 n. 218. On the consistency of Romans 9–11, see Abasciano, "Romans 9:1-9," 112–17.

[85] C. H. Dodd, *According to the Scriptures: The Substructure of New Testament Theology* (London: Nisbet, 1952), see esp. 108–9, 126–7; and cf. Abasciano, *Romans 9.1-9*, 7.

[86] G. K. Beale, "Did Jesus and His Followers Preach the Right Doctrine from the Wrong Texts?" in G. K. Beale (ed.), *The Right Doctrine from the Wrong Texts?: Essays on the Use of the Old Testament in the New* (Grand Rapids, MI: Baker, 1994), 387–404 (390).

resistance to God's plan for the salvation of the Gentiles, so Israel's resistance to Jesus as the savior of all in Paul's day was, in effect, resistance to God's plan for the salvation of the Gentiles. Finally, just as the purpose of Isa. 45:9 and the passage in which it is found (45:9-13) is to urge those who object to God's plan of salvation/choice of a deliverer to abandon their distrust of and opposition to God and his plan, and rather to trust in and embrace them, so the purpose of Rom. 9:20-21 is to urge those who reject God's choice of a savior—Jesus—and God's plan of salvation by faith in him, to abandon their distrust of and opposition to God and his plan and rather to trust in and embrace them. At least this is the rhetorical framing of Paul's rhetoric in the diatribe. But it should be remembered that Paul's implicit exhortation to abandon distrust of and opposition to God and his plan for trust in them is aimed at a hypothetical objector to his teaching for the purpose of encouraging acceptance of his teaching by his audience of Christians in Rome without implying that *they* were rejecting or resistant to his teaching or to Jesus.

4.2.c.2.c. Closer Intertextual Reading of Rom. 9:20

Now that we have sketched the broader parallels between Rom. 9:20b-c and Isa. 29:16 and 45:9 in their contexts apart from the fundamental potter/clay metaphor, we may now attend more closely to the meaning of Rom. 9:20b-c, including its potter/clay imagery, in light of this Old Testament background. We have already seen that Rom. 9:20b ("Will the thing molded really say to the molder") quotes part of Isa. 29:16 and that Rom. 9:20c paraphrases parts of Isa. 29:16 and 45:9. The syntax of Rom. 9:20b (μὴ introducing a question) indicates that a negative answer is expected—the thing molded will not actually say to the molder, "Why did you make me like this?" Even apart from syntactical considerations, the question is unmistakably rhetorical and the answer to it is obvious. Pots do not say anything to their makers let alone argue with them! On its face the analogy portrays objecting to God's judgment on unbelieving ethnic Israel in the matter at hand as absurd,[87] like a pot challenging its potter's fashioning of it. It turns the Creator/creature relationship on its head.

While this thrust is obvious enough in the Romans context alone, the use of the potter/clay imagery in the passages to which Paul alludes enriches understanding of his use of the metaphor. The metalepsis of Isa. 29:16 highlights the perversity of the objection Paul is countering.[88] It is not only that it suggests that the objection to Paul's gospel and God's judgment of unbelieving Israel if that gospel is true turns the divine/human relationship into the opposite of what it is supposed to be. It does suggest that, strengthening the natural surface meaning of the metaphor in the Romans context. But it is also that, with Isa. 29:16 indicating that God is being treated as a creature, the

---

[87] The matter at hand involving inter alia (1) provocation of Israel to hard-heartedness by God's choice of a method of salvation exceedingly offensive to the Jews (faith in Christ apart from works or ancestry, which opens up covenant membership and salvation to Gentiles) and (2) God being glorified by the unrighteousness of unbelieving ethnic Israel, on which see Abasciano, *Romans 9.10-18*, 215, and also n. 27 above.

[88] This emphasis is especially strong in the Hebrew text with its exclamation of "Your perversity!" but still present in the LXX.

metalepsis intimates that the objection practically (1) denies God as Creator because it denies his basic right as Creator to judge his creatures (this is especially clear since the molded thing explicitly denies having been created by God in Isa. 29:16);[89] (2) has man sitting in judgment of God rather than God sitting in judgment of man because it seeks to avoid God's judgment and renders judgment on God's actions; (3) denies God as savior because it serves the rejection of his plan of salvation; (4) has man saving himself rather than being saved by God; and (5) has man possessing superior wisdom to God, because[90] it serves the establishment of a human plan of salvation in place of God's plan.

Given the meaning-effects created by Paul's allusion to Isa. 29:16 with respect to the potter/clay metaphor itself, the transumption of Isa. 45:9 mostly reinforces them. But it adds two nuances. First, since Isa. 45:9 uses the metaphor in reference to the rejection of God's choice of a savior (not just his chosen means of salvation more generally) and his plan for the salvation of the Gentiles, Paul's allusion to the verse contributes to the perception that his use of the metaphor has these same concerns in view vis-à-vis Jesus Christ and his gospel. Second, allusion to Isa. 45:9 adds to the sense of the absurdity of contending against God's judgment by 45:10 setting forth an additional metaphorical illustration, namely a child in the process of being born challenging its father or mother about its constitution.

In Isa. 29:16, "the molded thing" (τὸ πλάσμα/מַעֲשֶׂה) refers to the Israelite who did not trust or accept God's plan of salvation, relied on some other plan, and sought to avoid God's judgment for his disloyalty and rebellion in the matter.[91] The singular is generic, representing any and all who were opposing God in this way.[92] Moreover, the rebuke concerns inter alia the objector's opposition to God's plan of salvation *for Israel*. It has to do in part with God's treatment of Israel as a corporate whole.

A superficial engagement with Isa. 29:16 has led Piper to conclude that "Isaiah is *not* speaking of the nation as a corporate whole, but of the 'perverted' wise men (cf 29:14) in Israel, who in their presuming to hide counsel from God, act as if they were God."[93] This is an eloquent statement of the biblical text's view of the attitude of those in Israel who opposed God's plan. And it is true that the divine rebuke through Isaiah was to the rebellious leaders and that the molded thing in Isa. 29:16 represents them through a representative hypothetical interlocutor. However, their rebellion was to God's plan for his people, and their objection to God's treatment of them ("You did not make me wisely") was to their lot as part of his people. That is, God's treatment of them to which they objected was the situation of all Israel in which they shared precisely because they were part of Israel. Thus, their objection to God's treatment of them was grounded in God's treatment of Israel and was equivalent to objecting to God's treatment of

---

[89] Note also the strong emphasis on God as Creator in Isa. 45:12.
[90] This final reason applies to both numbers (4) and (5).
[91] More specifically, the reference is to Judean political leaders who secretly planned to ally with Egypt and to rely on it to save Judah from Assyria.
[92] The point is obvious enough but confirmed by the plural address in the Greek and Hebrew texts of Isa. 29:16 just prior to the potter/clay reference: "your [plural] perversity" in the Hebrew text and "Will you [plural] not be regarded as clay of the potter" in the LXX.
[93] Piper, *Justification*, 195.

Israel as a corporate whole.[94] Paul's allusion to Isa. 29:16 confirms his corporate focus in Romans 9 and in this stage of his argument. At issue is God's treatment of Israel, whether he has been faithful to his promises to them if Paul's gospel is true.

4.2.c.2.c.1. Molding and Making
The Old Testament background can also shed light on the meaning of Paul's language of molding[95] and making.[96] One might assume that this language is used in the sense of God bringing the individual rebel or the group of rebels into existence as human beings. And indeed, that seems to be part of the picture in Isa. 29:16 and 45:9 on some level. But recalling that in each case the rebels' protest[97] has to do with God's dealings with his people as a corporate whole, the concept of God as Israel's creator is much more in view. That does not refer to God bringing individual Israelites into existence as human beings, but to his choosing Israel and constituting her as a nation. In the words of Edward Young, "In speaking of Him as the Creator of Israel, Isaiah refers not to creation as such but to the act whereby God brought a band of slaves from Egyptian bondage into the wilderness and made of them His own peculiar people."[98]

At the risk of oversimplification, it can be said that God's creation of Israel refers to his election of Israel. This is noteworthy because we have contended that the main objection to God's faithfulness to which Paul is responding in Romans 9 is to Paul's gospel's conception of the divine election, that it is based on faith rather than works or ancestry. Invoking the imagery of God as the Creator of Israel and the Israelite objector to God's ways as created by God (as part of Israel) reinforces Paul's argumentation in the previous verses to the effect that it is God's right to choose whom he will as his covenant people and to set forth any conditions he chooses for covenantal election.

There is one more sense to the language of molding and making in its Old Testament context to consider: the shaping of Israel's situation, whether that be one of blessing or woe. This is probably the most prominent sense in both Isaiah passages. In Isa. 29:16, the rebels are admonished for behavior that implies disapproval of the situation God had Israel in, namely military vulnerability with a prohibition of seeking foreign alliance for the purpose of national security, and a demand for reliance on God for protection. When Isaiah critiques their actions as implying that they were acting as if God, the potter, were rather clay and not their fashioner or maker, or that God had erred in his making of them, it reveals an understanding of God fashioning and making them as (especially) his shaping or causing to some degree or another their

---

[94] Morris, *Romans*, 365, more simply and directly contends that the passage has to do with Israel as a nation; he seems to be followed by Cottrell, *Romans*, 115.

[95] πλάσμα/πλάσσω are used in Rom. 9:20 and LXX Isa. 29:16; cf. יצר in the MT.

[96] ποιέω is used in Rom. 9:20-21 and the LXX of Isa. 29:16 and 45:9; cf. עשה in the MT of those LXX verses.

[97] One might note that there is no formal protest on the part of the rebels in Isa. 29:16. However, the rebellious actions of the leaders confronted there implicitly protest/contend against God's will and plan.

[98] Young, *Isaiah*, 3.166, commenting on Isaiah's use of the terminology in 44:2. Cf. his comments on 43:1. Oswalt, *Isaiah*, 2.165 n. 8, notes "that the paralleling of 'make' [עשה] and 'form' [יצר] occurs only in the Book of Isaiah (22:11; 27:11; 44:2; 45:18)."

situation to be what it was, a situation of which they disapproved and sought to take into their own hands.

The meaning of molding and making as shaping Israel's situation comes out all the stronger in Isa. 45:9. There Israel is admonished for objecting to God's plan for Israel's salvation. Thus, when Isaiah critiques Israel's objection as challenging God as to what he was making, using verb tenses of ongoing action,[99] it is clear that what the text considers to be God's molding and making of Israel is his activity in the process of shaping their situation. In Isaiah 45, that would especially include his plan for their salvation (involving his choice of a savior) and the situation that would leave them in, still under foreign domination.

Saying that the language of molding and making in the sense of shaping Israel's situation is the most prominent sense of the language in Isa. 29:16 and 45:9 is not to deny that the senses of bringing people into existence as human beings or creating Israel as a nation by choosing them and constituting them as a nation are not in view at all. All of these senses are intertwined and likely in view to one degree or another. Indeed, these senses build on one another. Creation as bringing people into existence is most basic and foundational to the other two conceptually. Creation/election of Israel as a nation builds on God's authority and power as the Creator of humanity. And the shaping of Israel's fortunes relies on his authority and power as the Creator of humanity and Israel, and also builds on his role as the Creator/elector of Israel. While all three of these senses seem to be in play in the language of molding and making in the Old Testament passages, contributing to the point that it is perverse and illegitimate to challenge God's dealings with his people, the meaning of shaping the destiny of Israel is foremost because their rebellion was most immediately against God's shaping of their situation. However, because of the organic interconnection of the various senses of God as the maker or former of his people, rebellion against God shaping their situation is a strike at his identity as the Creator of human life and the Creator of Israel as a nation. Still, reference to God as the molder or maker or Creator of his people is not a direct reference to his identity as the Creator of humanity or to his activity of bringing people into existence.

Most specifically, when God is referred to as the potter, all of these senses are probably invoked to one degree or another in accordance with our discussion above. But God as the Creator of Israel, who is therefore the shaper of Israel's situation (or God as the shaper of Israel's situation rooted especially in his identity as Israel's Creator), is probably paramount due to the corporate national context and intensified authority of his special relationship to Israel. However, when God's molding/making activity is referred to, it seems to be in reference to his shaping of Israel's situation in line with the observations made above.

This Old Testament background suggests that Paul's use of molding and making language in Rom. 9:20, which refers to God's molding/making activity, primarily has to do with God's shaping of the situation of unbelieving ethnic Israel/Jews, specifically

---

[99] In Hebrew, the imperfect tense (מַה־תַּעֲשֶׂה [What are you making?]) and a verbless clause (לוֹ אֵין־יָדָיִם [he has no hands]) that takes its temporal reference from the context, the previous imperfect verb. In the LXX, present tenses.

with regard to God's plan of salvation, his sovereign and offensive/hardening decision to make election by faith in Christ apart from works or ancestry, his choice of a savior, and given its being the most immediate contextual concern, especially his judgment on unbelieving Israel. The senses of bringing people into existence as human beings and creating Israel as a nation by choosing them and constituting them as a nation linger in the background insofar as God as the potter is implicit in the verse. Of course, as an analogical reference, potter and clay are generic references to literal potters and clay in both Isaiah and Paul. And just as Isaiah applied the analogy to God as Creator and rebellious Israelites as clay, so Paul's use of the analogy clearly applies it to God (the potter), unbelieving Jews, and Paul's diatribal interlocutor (clay), who represents those in opposition to Paul's gospel, a stance that is fueled by Jewish concerns. All of this will be confirmed even more strongly when we examine the meaning-effects of Jer. 18:6 in the next verse, Rom. 9:21.

4.2.c.2.d. Romans 9:21: The Potter's Right

As we have noted, the rhetorical question of Rom. 9:20b-c ("Will the thing molded really say to the molder, 'Why did you make me like this?'") makes the point that the creature should not challenge the Creator's plans for or treatment of the creature.[100] Paul now asks another rhetorical question making the same basic point from a different angle: "Or does the potter not have the right over the clay to make from the same lump one a vessel unto honor and another unto dishonor?" (9:21). The question begins with the conjunction ἤ (or), which can be used, as here, "to introduce a question which is parallel to a preceding one or supplements it."[101] In this case, 9:21 supplements 20b-c in making the same basic point from a different perspective. The two questions are two sides of the same coin. The question of 9:20b-c makes the point with respect to the right of the clay/creature—it is not right for the creature to dispute God's plans for or treatment of or judgment of the creature. The question of 9:21 makes the point with respect to the right of the potter/Creator. It draws the logical stress over 9:20b because it is more prominent and pointed due to being more specific and more in line with the focus on God in Romans 9, leading naturally into the following verses, which seem to pick up especially 9:21 for interpretation and explanation.

The syntax of 9:21 (οὐκ introducing a question) indicates that an affirmative answer is expected—the potter (God) does have the right over the clay (his creatures) to make from the same mass one a vessel unto honor and another unto dishonor. But just as with 9:20b, even apart from syntactical considerations, the question here in 9:21 is

---

[100] This does not mean that anything the Creator does to the creature is automatically right no matter what it is. In biblical thought, it would be unrighteous of God, e.g., to be unfaithful to his promises to Israel. Indeed, Paul takes such a charge of moral wrongdoing on God's part to be so serious that he focuses three chapters of Romans (chs. 9–11) on answering it (not to mention other, smaller sections) in defense of divine righteousness. This is not the type of action to which Paul's interlocutor objects, but rather decisions that affect the creature which would normally be thought to be within the divine prerogative, such as conditions for divine acceptance and judgment of human behavior.

[101] BDAG, s.v. ἤ, 1.d.⊃; cf. *ALGNT*, s.v. ἤ, 1.c.

unmistakably rhetorical and the answer to it is obvious. It is absurd to think that a potter would not have a right to make what he sees fit out of the clay with which he works. Likewise, it is absurd to think that God does not have the right to decide the fate of his creatures or to judge them for sin even if he somehow obtains glory from it.

Paul speaks of God's right (ἐξουσία) over the clay. The word ἐξουσία can refer to right, authority, or power. But in light of the context, in which Paul is defending God's righteousness, the meaning "right" is most appropriate here, as most translations render ἐξουσία in Rom. 9:21. More specifically, the "right to control something" is the intended sense.[102] And more specifically still, in this context, the word is used of God's right to control the destiny of the people he has created, whether that be to covenantal blessing or to curse/judgment.

4.2.c.2.d.1. Broad Intertextual Insights from Jer. 18:6

Earlier (see Section 4.1), we concluded from textual comparison of Isa. 29:16, 45:9, Jer. 18:6, and Rom. 9:20-21 that Jer. 18:6 contributed to Paul's formulation of Rom. 9:21. That conclusion assumed the discussion of semantic correspondence between Rom. 9:21 and Jer. 18:6 that we are about to begin. We have already seen that there is remarkable thematic coherence between Rom. 9:20-21 and Isa. 29:16, 45:9. The thematic correspondence between Rom. 9:21 and Jer. 18:6 is also remarkable, perhaps even more so in that its theme answers the objection Paul is addressing even more directly than the passages from Isaiah. While those passages in one way or another address the illegitimacy of objecting to God's plan of salvation, and the objection to God's judgment that Paul is addressing in Rom. 9:20-21 is an outgrowth and expression of that very phenomenon, Jer. 18:6 specifically addresses God's right to judge and naturally carries implications of the illegitimacy of human objection to that divine right.

Jeremiah 18:6 is part of a passage (Jer. 18:1-12) that issues a warning of judgment and a call to repentance for a stubborn and rebellious Israel. The main point of the passage is to urge repentance and obedience to the Lord, grounded in the threat of judgment, the ability to escape it through repentance, and the shameful wickedness of failing to heed God's gracious call to repentance. It lays great stress on the wickedness and culpability of Israel since they could repent and be spared, but stubbornly refused to repent.

Jeremiah 18:6 sums up the basis for the main point of the passage (the call to repentance/covenant faithfulness): "'Can I not do to you as this potter, house of Israel?'—a declaration of YHWH. 'Behold, as the clay in the hand of the potter, so are you in my hand, house of Israel'" (Jer. 18:6). In light of Jer. 18:7-11, that basis articulated in general summary form by 18:6 is God's ability and right to deal with Israel as he sees

---

[102] See BDAG, s.v. ἐξουσία, 3; Dunn, *Romans*, 557. BDAG lists the word's occurrence in Rom. 9:21 under meaning 1 ("a state of control over something") rather than meaning 3 ("the right to control or command"), however, Paul is not so much addressing whether the potter/God has control over the clay/creatures—that is not in question—but his right to do with them as he sees fit. Contrast Jewett's (*Romans*, 594) use of "power" as the basic gloss for ἐξουσία and W. Foerster's ("ἐξουσία," *TDNT*, 2.562-74 [567]) position to which Jewett refers, that its connotation in 9:21 is "the absolute power of God."

fit, namely, to change his intention toward them from blessing to curse/judgment if they walk contrary to his will and from curse to blessing if they repent and walk in accordance with his will, a policy that slated Israel for ruin at the time of Jeremiah's prophecy.[103] In response to a challenge to God's right to judge unbelieving Israel for its rejection of the gospel, Paul now alludes to an OT passage that argues for God's right to judge Israel.

Just as Jer. 18:6 serves as part of the grounding for 18:1-12's call to Israel to turn from covenant unfaithfulness to submission to the Lord and his ways, so Paul's allusion to it serves as part of the grounding for his implicit call to turn from covenant unfaithfulness in the form of rejection of Christ and his gospel to submission to God's ways in Christ and the righteousness of his judgment upon unbelieving ethnic Israel. And just as Jeremiah called Israel to repent based on God's intention to destroy them for their evil rebellion and to spare them if they would repent, so the implicit appeal of Rom. 9:20-21 to repent of opposition to the gospel (in the form of objection to God's judgment on unbelieving Jews for their rejection of the gospel) is ultimately based in part on God's intention to bless those who believe in Christ (9:7-9, 12-13, 15, 18, 23-26, 30, 33; 10:9-13; 11:4-7, 19-20, 22-23) and to judge those who reject Christ (9:3, 13, 17-18, 22, 28, 31-33; 11:7-10, 20-22).[104]

Further thematic contact between the contexts of Rom. 9:21 and Jer. 18:6 can be seen in the possibility of escaping God's judgment. As we saw in our exegesis of Rom. 9:18, the hardening of Romans 9–11 is reversible, and Paul holds out hope in Romans 11 that through his ministry hardened Jews would turn from their hard-heartedness and come to faith in Christ.[105] Indeed, Paul has already alluded to multiple Old Testament passages in Romans 9 with the intertextual significance of God's purpose to embrace those whom he had rejected, including apostate Israel;[106] that includes the potter/clay passage from Isaiah 29 Paul just quoted in v. 20! The Jeremian context heavily stresses the possibility of escaping God's judgment by repentance. This thematic connection confirms our detection of both the motif earlier in Romans 9 and Paul's allusion to Jer. 18:6 in Rom. 9:21.

To the attentive reader, Paul's allusion to Jer. 18:6 conveys that unbelieving ethnic Israel need not finally end up under the judgment to which the interlocutor objects. As Richard Hays argues,

> the effect of the allusion ... resonates deeply with Paul's wider argument about God's dealings with Israel. The parable suggests that the potter's power

---

[103] Here is how the grounding works in the passage. Jeremiah 18:6 asserts that God can do as he wishes with Israel, which is then clarified in the following verses as him being able to change his intention toward the people based on their actions. The text then specifies further concerning God's power and right over Israel that (1) God's policy is to change the destiny of a nation from curse to blessing or vice versa based on the nation's submission to or rebellion against him, and (2) God is planning to bring ruin on Israel. All of this grounds the passage's call to Israel for repentance.

[104] On the reasoning behind taking the implicit appeal of Rom. 9:20-21 to be based in part on divine blessing/judgment, see note 82 above.

[105] See Abasciano, *Romans 9.10-18*, 211–14.

[106] See ibid., 213, and the references there to detailed discussion in my two previous volumes on Romans 9.

is not destructive but creative: the vessel may fall, but the potter reshapes it. The parable, spoken in prophetic judgment upon Israel, is simultaneously a summons to repentance and a reassurance of the benevolent sovereignty of God, persistently enacted in his love for his people Israel even in and through the pronouncement of judgment. Thus, the allusion to Jeremiah 18 in Rom. 9:20-21, like other allusions and echoes earlier in the text, anticipates the resolution of Paul's argument in Romans 11. The reader who recognizes the allusion will not slip into the error of reading Rom. 9:14-29 as an excursus on the doctrine of the predestination of individuals to salvation or damnation, because the prophetic subtexts keep the concern with which the chapter began—the fate of Israel— sharply in focus.[107]

In light of the heavily conditional nature of the context of Jer. 18:6, Paul's allusion to the passage tinges his reply to the interlocutor's objection with a sense of conditionality. This adds an additional support for Paul's defense of God's righteousness in election, showing of mercy, and hardening. While the objection Paul is addressing is not focused on Jewish inability to avoid God's judgment, the point that they can avoid it weakens the interlocutor's charge in a supplementary way.[108]

The sense of conditionality receives some support from 2 Tim. 2:20-21, which uses similar language and a vessel/clay metaphor with respect to people:

> Now in a great house, there are not only gold and silver vessels, but also wooden and clay, and some unto honor and some unto dishonor. Therefore, if anyone cleanses himself from these [ungodly ways of false teachers described in vv. 14–18], he will be a vessel unto honor, sanctified, useful to the Master, prepared for every good work.

The similarity in language is striking: the term "vessel" (σκεῦος) applied to people, the phrases "unto honor" (εἰς τιμήν) and "unto dishonor" (εἰς ἀτιμίαν) in reference to vessels/people and in the same basic, larger syntactical construction ("one a vessel unto honor and another unto dishonor" using ὅ μὲν ... ὅ δέ in Romans, and "some unto honor and some unto dishonor" using ἃ μὲν ... ἃ δέ in 2 Timothy), the specific phrase "vessel unto honor" (σκεῦος εἰς τιμήν in 2 Tim. 2:21 and εἰς τιμὴν σκεῦος in

---

[107] R. B. Hays, *Echoes of Scripture in the Letters of Paul* (New Haven, CT: Yale University Press, 1989), 66, though labeling the Creator's power as creative rather than destructive is a false dichotomy. In the picture Paul paints, it is both, though God's greater concern is positive (cf. Ezek. 18:23, 33). I would also not say that it is so much the prophetic subtexts' focus on Israel's fate as much as their corporate orientation that steers the intertextually attentive reader away from an individualistic predestinarian reading.

[108] Perhaps an analogy would be helpful: Consider a judge on a bench trial who benefits from the publicity of condemning a hated, high-profile criminal. A detractor argues that the judge is unjust because he benefited from his judgment against the criminal. This is then answered by saying, "It is the judge's right and duty to judge crime even if it benefits him to do so [equivalent to the main thrust of Paul's use of the potter/clay metaphor]; and besides, the criminal did not have to commit the crime and so could have avoided condemnation [equivalent to the supplementary point Paul's Jeremian potter/clay allusion conveys]."

Rom. 9:21), and the term ἑτοιμάζω (to prepare), cognate to 9:23's προετοιμάζω (to prepare beforehand).

Of course, the majority of scholars believe that Paul did not write 2 Timothy. But there is a "significant minority" that hold it to be from Paul,[109] rightly in my opinion.[110] If Paul did not write 2 Timothy, then that reduces the potential significance of 2 Tim. 2:20-21 for understanding Rom. 9:21, but not completely since it would still be early Christian literature, associated with Paul no less, that could evidence similar thought patterns and tradition. Moreover, a number of scholars who regard 2 Timothy as pseudonymous nonetheless think that it was written by one or more disciples or admirers of Paul who sought to continue and apply Paul's own thought.[111] Thus, to one degree or another, 2 Tim. 2:20-21 is potentially helpful for understanding Rom. 9:21.

Piper agrees that Paul wrote 2 Timothy, but he thinks "it is of little help in interpreting Rom 9:21" because of the difference in context and in the metaphor.[112] But that conclusion is premature. It is true that the context and the use of the metaphor are different. But that does not necessarily mean that there are not aspects of Paul's use of the metaphor and language that might be relevant to Paul's use of the metaphor in a different context. Piper correctly points out concerning the 2 Timothy passage that (1) it does not mention the vessels being from the same lump, (2) the vessels it mentions are not all of clay, and (3) the different vessels refer to the faithful versus the unfaithful in the church.[113] But his construal of Paul's point as being merely that, "There are 'genuine' (1 Cor 11:19) and false brethren in the visible church," is lacking.[114] Howard Marshall captures the metaphorical application of 2 Tim. 2:20 more accurately, suggesting that it concerns "people [in the church] who hold to the truth and to godliness and are therefore useful and destined for honour in contrast to those who hold to error and ungodly conduct and therefore are useless and destined for judgment."[115] Second Tim. 2:21 then brings out the point of the metaphor's use, which is not particularly to assert that there are genuine and false believers in the church, but to encourage sound faith and godly action based on the point that God's purpose and destiny for the individual are contingent on the individual's faith/actions.[116] This

---

[109] I. H. Marshall, with Philip H. Towner, *A Critical and Exegetical Commentary on the Pastoral Epistles*, rev. ed. (ICC; Edinburgh: T&T Clark, 1999), 57-8.

[110] In favor of Pauline authorship, see P. H. Towner, *The Letters to Timothy and Titus* (NICNT; Grand Rapids, MI: Eerdmans, 2006), 55-112 (very cautiously); W. D. Mounce, *Pastoral Epistles* (WBC, 46; Nashville, TN: Nelson, 2000), lxxxiii-cxxix. For a review of recent literature in English on the pastoral epistles, see C. J. Bumgardner, "Paul's Letters to Timothy and Titus: A Literature Review (2009-2015)," *STR* 7.2 (Winter 2016), 77-116. He also gives references for review of prior literature. It is interesting to note that more of the most recent and forthcoming scholarship on 2 Timothy favors Pauline authorship than rejects it; see ibid., 77-86.

[111] For a description of this sort of approach, see Marshall, *Pastoral*, 80-1.

[112] Piper, *Justification*, 204. He also notes that most commentators leave "2 Tim 2:20 out of account when trying to explain Rom 9:21." On the other hand, Godet, *Romans*, 360, thinks 2 Tim. 2:20 "completely parallel"; cf. S. Lyonnet, "De doctrina praedestinationis et reprobationis in Rom 9," in S. Lyonnet, *Etudes sur l'Epître aux Romains* (AnBib, 120; Rome: Editrice Pontificio Istituto Biblico, 1989), 274-97 (288-9).

[113] Piper, ibid.

[114] Ibid.

[115] Marshall, *Pastoral*, 761.

[116] Schreiner, *Romans*, 501 n. 20, seems to try to avoid the conditionality of the text in his description of the passage and its immediate context. But that runs against the plain reading of the text. Verse

text is not directly relevant to Rom. 9:21 as if it addresses the same issue or makes the same point. But it does show Paul using the metaphor of people as vessels with the understanding that God's treatment of the vessels/people is conditional on their actions. That increases the likelihood that he could have used the metaphor in that way in Rom. 9:21.

The intertextual undercurrent of conditionality emanating from Paul's allusion to Jer. 18:6 is related to another theme that will come into greater focus later on in Paul's argument in addition to the notion of the reversibility of Israel's hard-heartedness— Israel's responsibility, guilt, and wickedness in their unbelief. The typical assessment of Romans 9-11 takes the basic thrust of 9:30-10:21 as laying the blame for Israel's fall fully on Israel.[117] Whether it is the main thrust or not (I think it is), Israel's responsibility and guilt are prominent themes in 9:30-10:21. As noted earlier, the context of Jer. 18:6 lays heavy stress on the wickedness and culpability of Israel since they could repent and be spared but stubbornly refused to repent. Paul's allusion subtly casts unbelieving ethnic Israel as both extremely wicked and fully responsible for their condemnation before God. That contributes to the vindication of God's judgment on them against the interlocutor's objection.

Like Paul's Isaian potter/clay allusions, his allusion to Jer. 18:6 is corporately focused. Even Piper, who argues for an individual focus in the relevant OT and Jewish texts when he at all can, concedes that Jer. 18:1-6 "has reference to God's dealings with Israel as a nation."[118] This is yet another of Paul's allusions that confirms his corporate focus in Romans 9 and in this stage of his argument. His concern is not the predestination of individuals to salvation or damnation (as Hays observed),[119] but the defense of God's treatment of Israel in light of the gospel. More specifically, Paul's defense has to do with the faithfulness of God to his covenant promises to Israel if his gospel of justification and election by faith is true. More specifically still at this precise point in Paul's argument, Paul is addressing the righteousness of God's judgment against unbelieving ethnic Israel on the supposition that his Jew-hardening gospel is true. Paul's allusion to Jer. 18:6—which evokes for the ideal reader God's right to judge, Israel's ability to escape his judgment through repentance, the great guilt and wickedness of Israel, and God's desire for Israel's repentance, all in a corporate context—vindicates God's righteousness in his judgment on Israel's unbelief and in the gospel.

---

20 indicates that there are people in the church unto honor and people in the church unto dishonor. Based on that truth (οὖν), Paul indicates what will bring one to be unto honor—cleansing oneself from the false doctrine and practice of the false teachers mentioned in vv. 14-18. Repentance and faith (expressed in this context by naming the name of the Lord, departing from iniquity [v. 19], and cleansing oneself [v. 21]; cf. the mention of faith in v. 18) is the condition for being a vessel unto honor.

[117] See C. K. Barrett, "Romans 9.30-10.21: Fall and Responsibility of Israel," in L. de Lorenzi (ed.), *Die Israelfrage nach Röm 9-11* (Monographische Reihe von "Benedictina" Biblisch-ökumenische Abteilung, 3; Rome: Abtei von St Paul vor den Mauern, 1977), 99-121 (99). A look at more recent literature confirms that Barrett's observation still holds: see, e.g., Longenecker, *Romans*, 827; Wallace, *Election*, 105; Kruse, *Romans*, 392.

[118] Piper, *Justification*, 194.

[119] See the extended quotation of Hays, *Echoes*, 66, above.

4.2.c.2.d.1.a. Blind Luck?

Recognizing the meaning-effects of Paul's allusion to Jer. 18:6 might cause some scholars who believe Paul is arguing for unconditional individual election to bristle because those meaning-effects run directly counter to their interpretation of Rom. 9:19-21. Indeed, such scholars typically deny that Jeremiah 18 or any of the biblical potter/clay passages are part of the specific semantic background behind Rom. 9:19-21, or at least that their contexts hold any significance for the verses beyond the metaphor itself and its obvious meaning of God's sovereignty over his creation.[120] But as Shiu-Lun Shum has observed, most scholars have posited that such texts have shaped Paul's thought in Rom. 9:20-21.[121]

Isaiah 29:16 is the text most frequently recognized as background for Paul's thought here, undoubtedly because he actually quotes it. Isaiah 45:9 and Jer. 18:6 are the texts most frequently recognized after Isa. 29:16. These two texts are recognized at about the same frequency by scholars, Jer. 18:6 perhaps a little more often.[122] Each is sometimes taken as the foremost of all the potter/clay background texts for Rom. 9:20-21, and Jer.

---

[120] See Piper, *Justification*, 194–9; Moo, *Romans*, 623; Schreiner, *Romans*, 495–6. Though holding a different perspective on election in Romans 9, Cranfield, *Romans*, 491–2, thinks Paul makes his own independent use of the biblical image. Talking about OT texts as the semantic background of Paul's discourse is a way of talking about the specific meaning of the OT texts contributing to the meaning of what Paul says.

[121] Shum, *Romans*, 204–5. The OT texts he lists as being the type of text most scholars think have shaped Paul's thought here in addition to Isa. 29:16 are Jer. 18:6, Isa. 64:8, and Isa. 45:9. He mentions one extra-OT text, *Wisd.* 15:7.

[122] Scholars who think Paul's thought was shaped at least in part by Jeremiah 18 include Hays, *Echoes*, 65–6; Wagner, "Concert," 81–4; Kruse, *Romans*, 384–5; M. A. Seifrid, "Romans," in Beale and Carson (eds), *Commentary*, 607–94 (645); Origen (see G. Bray [ed.], *Ancient Christian Commentary on Scripture: New Testament, VI: Romans* [ACCSNT, 6; Downers Grove, IL: IVP, 1998], 251–2); E. H. Plumptre, "The Potter and the Clay: Jer. xviii. 1-10; Rom. ix. 19-24," *Expos* 1.4 (1876), 469–80; J. C. O'Neill, *Paul's Letter to the Romans* (Harmondsworth: Penguin, 1975), 158 (seemingly); J. Murray, *The Epistle to the Romans* (NICNT; 2 vols. in 1; Grand Rapids, MI: Eerdmans, 1959–65), 2.32; D. Moody, "Commentary on Romans," in C. Allen (ed.), *The Broadman Bible Commentary, Vol. 10* (BBC, 10; Nashville, TN: Broadman, 1970), 231; J. Ziesler, *Paul's Letter to the Romans* (TPINTC; Philadelphia, PA: TPI, 1989), 246 (seemingly); Godet, *Romans*, 359; Lyonnet, "Praedestinationis," 282; C. M. Pate, *Romans* (TTCS; Grand Rapids, MI: Baker, 2013), 193; A. F. Johnson, *Romans* (EvBC; Chicago: Moody Bible Institute, 2000), 178 (seemingly); V. Reasoner, *A Fundamental Wesleyan Commentary on Romans* (Evansville, IN: FWB, 2002), 426–30; Keener, *Romans*, 120 n. 16 (seemingly); C. L. Bence, *Romans: A Bible Commentary in the Wesleyan Tradition* (Indianapolis, IN: WPH, 1996), 169; J. D. Strauss, "God's Promise and Universal History: The Theology of Romans 9," in C. H. Pinnock (ed.), *Grace Unlimited* (Minneapolis, MN: Bethany, 1975), 199; Munck, *Israel*, 58 (seemingly); Wallace, *Election*, 87–9; Forlines, *Romans*, 276; Stuhlmacher, *Romans*, 149 (seemingly, though he stresses *Wisd.* 11:23 and 12:3-22 much more as background); B. Klappert, "Traktat für Israel (Römer 9–11)," in M. Stöhr (ed.), *Jüdische Existenz und die Erneuerung der christlichen Theologie* (Munich: Kaiser, 1981), 58–137 (74, 128 n. 67); B. Witherington III with D. Hyatt, *Paul's Letter to the Romans: A Socio-rhetorical Commentary* (Grand Rapids, MI: Eerdmans, 2004), 257 n. 43; F. J. Leenhardt, *The Epistle to the Romans: A Commentary* (London: Lutterworth, 1961), 257 (seemingly); Forster and Marston, *Strategy*, 73–4; F. Belli, *Argumentation and Use of Scripture in Romans 9–11* (AnBib, 183; Roma: Gregorian and Biblical Press, 2010), 99 n. 124; F. F. Bruce, *The Epistle to the Romans* (TNTC, 6; Grand Rapids, MI: Eerdmans, 1963), 189. Scholars who think Paul's thought was shaped at least in part by Isaiah 45 include Moody, "Romans," 231; Forster and Marston, *Strategy*, 72–3; Dunn, *Romans*, 556; Kruse, *Romans*, 384–5 (seemingly); Keener, *Romans*, 120; Barrett, *Romans*, 175; Cottrell, *Romans*, 114–15; Holland, *Romans*, 329; Pate, *Romans*, 193; Bruce, *Romans*, 189; Seifrid, "Romans," 644–5; Munck, *Israel*, 58–9; Stuhlmacher, *Romans*, 149; Tobin, *Rhetoric*, 333 (seemingly); Godet, ibid.; Leenhardt, *Romans*, 255–7; Lyonnet, "Praedestinationis," 283; Murray, *Romans*, 2.32; R. H. Mounce, *Romans* (NAC, 27; Nashville, TN: Broadman & Holman, 1995), 201; Longenecker, *Romans*, 819 (seemingly);

18:6 is more often taken as such than Isa. 45:9.[123] Finally, after these three texts *Wisd.* 15:7 is the next most recognized text for background to Paul's thought in these verses.[124] But as we concluded in Section 3.6 of Chapter 3 in this volume, while there is a possible

---

Wagner, *Heralds*, 58–71; Strauss, "Romans 9," 199; Ziesler, *Romans*, 246 (seemingly); Byrne, *Romans*, 300; G. R. Osborne, *Romans* (IVPNTC; Downers Grove, IL: InterVarsity Press, 2004), 252.

[123] For interpreters who appear to take Jer. 18:6 as primary, see from the previous note, the works by Hays, Forlines, Origen, Plumptre, Klappert, Reasoner, Wallace, Bence, Witherington, and Forster and Marston. For those who take Isa. 45.9 as primary, see C. Hodge, *Commentary on the Epistle to the Romans*, rev. ed. (Grand Rapids, MI: Eerdmans, 1886), 494 (on Rom. 9:20); Sanday and Headlam, *Romans*, 259 (on Rom. 9:20); Holland, *Romans*, 329 (on 9:19-20); Keener, *Romans*, 120. Forster and Marston, *Strategy*, 72–3, discuss both Isa. 45:9 and Jer. 18:6 while leaving out any mention of Isa. 29:16. Morris, *Romans*, 365, is unsure of whether it is Isa. 29:16 or 45:9 that Paul quotes. Byrne, *Romans*, 300, recognizes that the introductory part of the second question in Rom. 9:20 is quoted from Isa. 29:16 but thinks that the rest is based on Isa. 45:9. However, Jewett, *Romans*, 593, follows Koch, *Schrift*, 144, in finding it unnecessary to appeal to Isa. 45:9 on verbal or thematic grounds, though he fails to discuss the verbal element shared by Rom. 9:20 and Isa. 45:9 but missing from Isa. 29:16 (τί). On the other hand, Jewett's comment in reference to Isa. 29:16 that "Since Paul wishes to concentrate on human resistance to divine selectivity, Isaiah's concerns about whether the clay was molded at all (v. 16c), or was molded wisely (v. 16e), are extraneous" shows a grave insensitivity to the function of those concerns in the Isaian context; see our exegesis of the passage in Section 2.1 in Chapter 2 of this volume.

[124] Scholars who think Paul alludes to *Wisd.* 15:7 include Johnson, *Function*, 132–3; Dunn, *Romans*, 557; Campbell, *Deliverance*, 777–8; Kruse, *Romans*, 384–5 (seemingly); Keck, *Romans*, 235–6; Belli, *Argumentation*, 99 n. 124 (Paul alludes but is not dependent); Lyonnet, "Praedestinationis," 283; Greathouse and Lyons, *Romans*, 62; Osborne, *Romans*, 252 (seemingly); Stuhlmacher, *Romans*, 149; Sanday and Headlam, *Romans*, 259; Cranfield, *Romans*, 492 (though he thinks Paul's use of the similitude is distinctly his own); Ziesler, *Romans*, 246 (seemingly); Jewett, *Romans*, 594; Shum, *Romans*, 206; M. Black, *Romans* (NCB; London: Marshall Morgan and Scott, 1973), 131; D. A. deSilva, "Wisdom of Solomon," *DNTB*, 1268–76 (1274). Occasionally, a scholar will think Paul alludes rather to *Wisd.* 12:12 (so Barrett, *Romans*, 175) or to both 12:12 and 15:7 (so Jewett [12:12 in Rom. 9:20 (592) and 15:7 in Rom. 9:21 (594)]; Kruse, ibid. [seemingly]; Campbell, ibid.). I regard *Wisd.* 12:12 as a possible allusion in Rom. 9:19, but not an actual one. The verbal similarity is relatively minimal, mainly τίς ἀντιστήσεται (who will resist?) in the question "who will resist your judgment?" compared to Rom. 9:19's τίς ἀνθέστηκεν (who has resisted?) in the question "who has resisted his purpose?" (τί ἐποίησας and a second occurrence of ἐποίησας also appears in *Wisd.* 12:12 while τί με ἐποίησας occurs in Rom. 9:20 and ποιῆσαι in 9:21, but the terminology is used differently in the two contexts). Though the verbal similarity is minimal, the thematic similarity of the context in *Wisdom* 12 is substantial, arguing for God's righteousness in judgment. But combined with factors considered in assessment of *Wisd.* 15:7 (see Section 3.6 in Chapter 3 of this volume), the verbal similarity is probably too minimal to regard *Wisd.* 12:12 as a specific allusion (although we do join most scholars in seeing an allusion to Exod. 32:32 in Rom. 9:3 without any verbal similarity, but the Exodus text is so much more prominent as to be a probable allusion; see Abasciano, *Romans 9.1-9*, chapter 3). If it is an allusion, then its context would be quite illuminating for exegesis of Rom. 9:20-21, including its stress on the justice of God's judgment, grounded in part in his care for all people, his desire for the wicked to repent, and his granting opportunity to them to repent. It would only add support to our exegesis of Romans 9. There are other texts that are often referred to in lists of general background for Paul's potter/clay metaphor, but we are talking here about texts that are affirmed (at least implicitly) as specifically alluded to by Paul in Rom. 9:19-21. Inclusion in a commentator's listing of various texts as part of the Jewish or cultural background of the potter/clay image, or inclusion in a list of texts for comparison to Paul's comments in Rom. 9:19-21 was not enough to merit inclusion in this paragraph and its notes. The next most frequently considered text for specific background to Paul's thought here is Sir. 33:13, but it is rarely affirmed as an actual allusion, though Johnson, ibid. (seemingly), and with reference to 33:7-13, Schreiner, *Romans*, 496 (seemingly), and with reference to 33:10-13, Lyonnet, "Praedestinationis," 283 (seemingly), do affirm it; B. Mayer, *Unter Gottes Heilsratschluss: Prädestinationsaussagen bei Paulus* (Würzburg: Echter, 1974), 200, thinks 33:10-13 close to Paul's thought here. For analysis of potential extrabiblical background texts for Rom. 9:19-21, including *Wisd.* 15:7 and Sir. 33:13, see Chapter 3 of this volume (Section 3.1 on Sirach and Section 3.6 on *Wisdom*).

allusion to *Wisd.* 15:7 in Rom. 9:21, it does not rise to the level of a probable allusion. That leaves us with Isa. 29:16 as a certain allusion (more specifically, a quotation), and Isa. 45:9 and Jer. 18:6 as probable allusions.

Objections to these as allusions at all or as allusions that hold significance for Paul's argument have failed to pay close enough attention to the original contexts of the Old Testament texts. John Piper has given more attention to arguing against these texts as shaping Paul's thought than most,[125] and Aaron Sherwood has similarly devoted more attention than most to arguing against Isa. 45:9 and Jer. 18:6 as formative background.[126] But Piper simply does not attend to the Old Testament texts in much detail. As for Sherwood, he makes the puzzling, erroneous claim that τί ποιεῖς is the only verbal overlap between Rom. 9:20b and Isa. 45:9.[127] They also share μὴ ἐρεῖ. Perhaps Sherwood means verbal overlap not also found in Isa. 29.16, but he does not specify that.

Moreover, Sherwood excludes Rom. 9:21 from consideration, but including it for comparison yields additional verbal similarity with Isa. 45:9 (see Section 4.1). Sherwood also claims that the context of Isa. 45:9 lacks the theme of God's judgment on Israel present in Isa. 29:16 or any common theme that is applied similarly. But there is more than one problem with that claim. First, it is false (see our exegesis of Isa. 45:9 and its context in Section 2.2 of Chapter 2 in this volume). Isaiah 45:9 begins as a threat of judgment! Moreover, judgment forms the background of the prophecy. It concerns Israel's objection to God's plan to deliver them from his judgment upon them in the exile.

Second, it is based on an invalid premise employed by Sherwood, namely that Isa. 45:9 must contribute the same theme as Isa. 29:16 and apply that theme in the same way if it is an allusion. But why would that be necessary? Isaiah 45:9 could be an additional allusion that contributes something distinctive to Paul's meaning. In this case, it contributes both agreement with Isa. 29:16 in certain respects and distinctive associations.

Third, Isa. 29:16 and 45:9 are similar thematically beyond the theme of judgment. Indeed, John Oswalt observes that the two texts make the same argument from slightly different perspectives.[128] Most notably, they both utilize the potter/clay metaphor to rebuke opposition to God's plan and means of salvation for Israel. Concerning Jer. 18:6 and its context, Sherwood makes the same sort of puzzling, false claim about verbal coherence that he did in relation to Isa. 45:9. In this case he claims that there is no verbal overlap between Jer. 18:5-11 and Rom. 9:20-21.[129] In the published version of his work, he does concede that "there is limited shared vocabulary."[130] But what is verbal overlap if not shared vocabulary? He cannot correctly mean that there is no verbal coherence that is distinctively shared by Rom. 9:20-21 and Jer. 18:6 in

---

[125] See Piper, *Justification*, 194–5.
[126] See Sherwood, "Romans 9:6-29," 104–5.
[127] On the difference Sherwood cites in the meaning of τί between the two texts as counting against Isa. 45:9 as background, see Section 4.1.a.
[128] Oswalt, *Isaiah*, 2.209.
[129] Sherwood, "Romans 9:6-29," 105.
[130] Sherwood, *Romans 9*, lxiv.

comparison to other possible background texts, for there is, minor as it may be (see again Section 4.1.a).

Sherwood also makes the astonishing claim that Jer. 18:5-11 does not refer to God's judgment on Israel. He concedes that the passage "employs the potter/clay metaphor to spell out in principle God's *right* to judge Israel"[131] but bafflingly does not consider that as having to do with God's judgment. He appears to hold another invalid premise (cf. the one mentioned above in relation to Isa. 45:9) to the effect that only a specific act of accomplished judgment counts as part of the theme of judgment. His conclusion that Jer. 18:5-11 is contextually dissimilar to Rom. 9:20-21 is very perplexing because a challenge to God's right to judge Israel is precisely what Paul is responding to with the potter/clay metaphor in Rom. 9:20-21.

We have found striking parallels between the Old and New Testament contexts, which we have laid out earlier in this chapter. To borrow a turn of phrase from Richard Hays, these parallels can hardly be cases of blind luck.[132] We will not rehearse all of those parallels here, but when Paul is defending God's righteousness in his plan of salvation for Israel by means of the gospel, are we to think that it is a mere coincidence that the OT potter/clay text Paul quotes from (Isa. 29:16) has to do with Israelite objection to God's plan of salvation and his chosen means of salvation? When Paul is defending his gospel with Jesus Christ as Lord and Savior at its center, offensive for its granting of righteousness by faith in Christ (the Stumbling Stone; Rom. 9:32) apart from works or ancestry, are we to regard it as a fortuitous accident that Isa. 45:9, which uses the potter/clay metaphor and has some substantial verbal similarity to Rom. 9:20, also has to do with Israelite objection to God's plan of salvation and his chosen means of salvation, specifically his choice of a savior with Gentile associations? Or when Paul is responding specifically to an objection to God's right to judge Jews who have rejected the gospel, are we to think that he just happens to use the potter/clay metaphor in language with some substantial verbal similarity to Jer. 18:6, which uses the potter/clay metaphor and argues for God's right to judge Israel? We could multiply these sorts of questions targeting various parallels we have observed, but that would be repetitive. The point is that the thematic coherence with Rom. 9:20-21 that we have observed in these passages is too substantial to be accidental in light of Paul's attention to the Old Testament in Romans 9 and the presence of some verbal coherence. Just as Targ. Isa. 29:16 draws on Isa. 29:16, 45:9, and Jer. 18:6, so does Paul.[133]

4.2.c.2.d.1.b. *Intertextual Anticipation*
We have noted that Paul's use of Isa. 29:16, and now Jer. 18:6, has adumbrated themes he will come to express explicitly later in Romans 9–11. In the case of his use of Isa. 29:16, Paul subliminally anticipates the theme of the reversal of hardening. In the case of his use of Jer. 18:6, Paul anticipates the theme of the guilt and responsibility of Israel as well as the theme of the reversal of hardening. All of this is in line with a pattern of Pauline interpretive activity that has been observed by Richard Hays in other texts

---

[131] Sherwood, "Romans 9:6-29," 105.
[132] See Hays, *Echoes*, 72.
[133] See Section 3.10 in Chapter 3 of this volume.

and that we have seen at work repeatedly in Romans 9—Paul's OT allusions frequently anticipate the next or otherwise later stage of his argument.[134] As Hays describes it, "an unvoiced element of the explicitly cited text subliminally generates the next movement of discourse."[135] That this is a Pauline interpretive practice strengthens the probability of an allusion to Jer. 18:6 here since the proposed allusion falls in line with that practice. And in properly circular fashion, seeing that practice in play here in Rom. 9:21 further confirms that this is indeed a Pauline practice and that his use of Scripture was contextual and evocative of additional associations of unstated elements of the original contexts of his allusions.

4.2.c.2.d.2. Further Details of an Intertextual Reading of Rom. 9:21
Now that we have described the fundamental parallels between Rom. 9:21 and Jer. 18:6 in their contexts, we may now move on to considering the remaining details of the text of Rom. 9:21 along with any insight we might discover from the Jer. 18:6 background.

4.2.c.2.d.2.a. Molding and Making in Light of Jer. 18:6
As we saw earlier, the Isaian background of Paul's potter/clay metaphor suggests three complementary senses for the meaning of his language of molding and making: bringing people into existence as human beings, creating Israel as a nation by choosing them and constituting them as a nation, and shaping Israel's situation, with the last being the most prominent sense of the terminology in both Isaiah and Paul (see Section 4.2.c.2.c.1). Paul's allusion to Jer. 18:6 greatly strengthens the conclusion that shaping Israel's situation is the primary meaning of the terminology as Paul uses it in 9:20, and now in 9:21 especially in the sense of shaping Israel's situation for good or ill (employing only ποιῆσαι), for that is the meaning of it in the verse from Jeremiah to which he alludes here. In fact, the two other senses mentioned above appear to have largely if not altogether receded from view in Jer. 18:6.[136] In the Jeremiah context, God making Israel refers to him either uprooting it/tearing it down/destroying it (i.e., inflicting calamity on it) in judgment or building it up and planting it (i.e., doing good to it) (Jer. 18:7-10). Paul's use of the language in Rom. 9:20 likely accords with the use of the language in the Isaiah texts he alludes to in that verse (Isa. 29:16, 45:9)—having to do with God as the Creator of human life, even more, the elector and founder of Israel, and primarily, as the determiner of Israel's situation. But in 9:21, which alludes to Jer. 18:6, Paul's use of the language likely accords with Jer. 18:6's use of it to refer almost exclusively to God's conditional shaping of Israel's (or any nation's) situation/fate,[137] whether to blessing or to judgment. This point has implications for what Paul means by honor and dishonor in 9:21.

---

[134] See Abasciano, *Romans 9.1-9*, 230.
[135] Hays, *Echoes*, 70.
[136] They are probably entailed on some level by the sense of shaping Israel's situation, as discussed in Section 4.2.c.2.c.1.
[137] The degree to which Gentiles come into view would impact the degree to which God's identity as the Creator of humanity also comes into view as grounding God's authority to determine the situation of Gentiles.

4.2.c.2.d.2.b. *Εἰς: For or Unto?*

In light of this meaning of Paul's making language, the most appropriate translation of εἰς in the phrases εἰς τιμὴν and εἰς ἀτιμίαν in 9:21 is "unto," conveying the use of εἰς to indicate the result of an action.[138] Thus, Paul asks, "Or does the potter not have the right over the clay to make from the same lump one a vessel unto honor and another unto dishonor?" (Rom. 9:21). BDAG suggests "into," "to," and "so that" as glosses for this usage, but does not specify "unto" as an option. However, that is probably because it is now archaic. Yet "into" and "so that" do not fit the context and "to" could be misconstrued to indicate purpose in English. Indeed, most translations and interpreters take εἰς here to indicate the use/purpose for which the vessels are made, translating with "for."[139] Either sense fits with our understanding of Romans 9 in general and 9:19-21 specifically.

If purpose is in view, the idea would be that God's shaping activity has the purpose of bestowing honor/blessing or dishonor/judgment upon this or that vessel. If result is in view, the idea would be that God's shaping activity has the result of bestowing honor/blessing or dishonor/judgment upon this or that vessel. Each sense probably entails the other to some degree in this context. But the question remains as to whether these senses are equally present, and Paul's εἰς is meant to do double duty, or if not, which idea is primarily in view. The metaphor itself apart from contextual considerations probably fits most naturally with an indication of the use for which the vessel is made. But the Old Testament background uses the metaphor in a way that fits better with an indication of result of blessing or judgment, and it is more likely that Paul uses it similarly as he draws on its use in Isaiah and especially Jeremiah.

4.2.c.2.d.2.c. *From the Same Lump, unto Honor or Dishonor*

Paul's phrase "from the same lump" (ἐκ τοῦ αὐτοῦ φυράματος) clearly refers to a lump *of clay* and is best taken as applying to humanity as a whole, the mass of humanity, as the vast majority of commentators appear to take it.[140] This is strongly supported by the fact that Paul applies the principle of 9:21 to Jews and Gentiles in the verses that follow. It is also supported by my contention, argued for in my two previous volumes, that Paul's argument in Romans 9 has had Gentiles in view from the beginning.

There is debate over what Paul means by a vessel unto honor (εἰς τιμὴν) versus unto dishonor (εἰς ἀτιμίαν). The basic metaphorical image itself is clear. A potter has

---

[138] On which, see BDAG, s.v. εἰς, 4e.
[139] In accordance with ibid., 4d rather than 4f.
[140] Many commentators fail to consider the question directly of what "the same lump" refers to but reveal their opinion implicitly in their discussion of the meaning of Rom. 9:21. Dunn, *Romans*, 557, and Godet, *Romans*, 358, do give explicit attention to the question, adopting the view I take above. Alternatively, the phrase could be taken to apply to Israel (so Cottrell, *Romans*, 117, 119; Forster and Marston, *Strategy*, 73–5; Osborne, *Romans*, 252). One would think that more commentators who hold that Paul's discussion of election has been about election within Israel would adopt that approach. This would receive support from Paul's use of φύραμα to refer to a lump of dough in 11:16, where "Almost all scholars agree" that it "stands for the Jews" (Moo, *Romans*, 717). But even there, the following verses go on to consider, in essence (using the metaphor of an olive tree and branches), how Gentiles can be added to that lump of dough. Yet most definitively, the context here in ch. 9 is against it; see below. Godet refers to the view and rejects it.

the right to make from the same lump of clay one vessel that will receive honor and another that will receive dishonor.[141] But there is disagreement over the meaning of the metaphor as to the form of honor/dishonor Paul envisions for the metaphor's application. Some regard it as applying to God's appointment of people or nations to positive/noble or negative/ignoble historical roles or circumstances.[142] Others think it applies to eschatological, eternal destiny, that is, salvation versus damnation.[143] I find that the evidence best supports the latter view.

4.2.c.2.d.2.c.1. Assessing Support for the Historical Roles View

In favor of the historical roles view, it has been argued, first, that the potter/clay metaphor itself demands that Paul is talking about the use to which God puts the vessels he shapes, since potters make vessels to be used and not to be destroyed.[144] But this is pressing the metaphor too far. Few metaphors carry all of the aspects of the physical reality from which they come. It is critical to determine which aspects of the literal reality translate into the meaning of the metaphor. Besides, vessels are sometimes made for destruction, such as pieces made for target practice or vessels that will be thrown away with the waste they store.[145] But even apart from such considerations, the eternal destiny position can also view the matter as including God's use of the vessels, in this case to bring glory to God, to express his love and justice, and so on.

---

[141] Most would say that the honor/dishonor results from the use to which the vessel is put (so, e.g., BDAG, s.v. τιμή, 2b). But there is reason to question whether usage of the vessel is particularly in view here; see below. Forster and Marston, *Strategy*, 74-5, offer the unusual view that the honor or dishonor are to God rather than to the respective vessels. But that does not fit with the context in Romans 9 of God as the agent who makes vessels unto honor or dishonor. Are we to think of God as making vessels unto his own dishonor? Forster and Marston rely on the usage of the language in 2 Tim. 2:20-21 where it is more feasible that the idea is that the vessel brings honor or dishonor to God since it speaks of a person making himself into a vessel unto honor. But even there, commentators tend still to see the honor or dishonor as accruing to the vessel/human being (see, e.g., Marshall, *Pastoral*, 760) or as descriptive of its purpose or usage (see, e.g., Mounce, *Pastoral*, 531).

[142] So Cranfield, *Romans*, 492; Sanday and Headlam, *Romans*, 260; Munck, *Israel*, 58-9; Dunn, *Romans*, 557; Morris, *Romans*, 366; Leenhardt, *Romans*, 256-7; Holland, *Romans*, 330; Byrne, *Romans*, 299-300 (see esp. on v. 18). Some scholars state that Paul does not have eternal destiny in view, but do not state specifically what he has in mind; see, e.g., Fitzmyer, *Romans*, 569; Jewett, *Romans*, 594; Moody, "Romans," 231 (seemingly); P. J. Achtemeier, *Romans* (IBC; Atlanta, GA: John Knox, 1985), 161-5 (seemingly, though he does not specifically address the meaning of honor and dishonor). But if it is not eternal, then it must be some sort of temporal role or circumstance.

[143] So Piper, *Justification*, 200-2; Moo, *Romans*, 622-3; Schreiner, *Romans*, 495-6; Cottrell, *Romans*, 119; Osborne, *Romans*, 252-3; G. Shellrude, "The Freedom of God in Mercy and Judgment: A Libertarian Reading of Romans 9:6-29," *EQ* 81.4 (2009), 306-18 (314 n. 14).

[144] Cranfield, *Romans*, 492; Morris, *Romans*, 366; Leenhardt, *Romans*, 256; cf. Dunn, *Romans*, 557. Piper, *Justification*, 193-4, is especially helpful in identifying the arguments in favor of the historical roles view.

[145] Cf. on 2 Tim. 2:20, Marshall, *Pastoral*, 761; Mounce, *Pastoral*, 531. This is not to suggest that Paul is speaking about God bringing people into existence for the purpose of destroying them. It is simply to address the claim that Paul does not apply the potter/clay metaphor to eternal matters because potters do not make vessels to be destroyed.

Piper adds the point that

> Destruction is not the opposite of existence; it is the opposite of *glorious* existence (9:22f). And that is all that the metaphor of 9:21 requires. If ἀπώλεια means an eternal, inglorious existence in hell, then the objection that God could not make persons for such ἀπώλεια, since potters do not do that sort of thing, is not true. For potters do make vessels which are fit for inglorious uses outside the house.[146]

Piper's specific view of Paul's meaning is problematic,[147] but his point here, that the potter/clay metaphor does not itself inherently preclude application of it to eternal destiny, is valid. On the other hand, a crucial point that undermines the argument that Rom. 9:21 must have only historical roles in view and supports the idea that eschatological blessing versus judgment is in view is the fact that the Old Testament background in Jer. 18:1-12 does speak of God, represented as a potter, making Israel unto blessing or destruction in judgment. That leads us to consideration of the next argument for the historical roles view, which involves the Old Testament background.

A second argument in favor of the historical roles view is that the Old Testament background deals with Israel as a nation rather than with individuals.[148] This is true depending on how it is meant,[149] but it does not require the historical roles view. Advocates of the redemptive historical approach are vague on the reasoning here,[150] but the thought seems to be that since the texts Paul alludes to in 9:20-21 have to do

---

[146] Piper, *Justification*, 201-2.
[147] He takes Paul to refer to God bringing individuals into existence in order to destroy them.
[148] See Munck, *Israel*, 58; Dunn, *Romans*, 557; E. H. Gifford, *Epistle of St. Paul to the Romans* (London: John Murray, 1886), 173; Witherington, *Romans*, 256-7 (n.b. note 43); cf. Hays, *Echoes*, 66.
[149] As long as it is understood properly, not excluding individuals altogether, but including individuals secondarily as members of the nation and recognizing that the individual members of the nation are impacted by the group's circumstances. A distortion of this sort of point that excludes individuals altogether from a corporate view does not seem to come out much in scholarly treatment of Rom. 9:20-21 specifically, but it does often come out in discussion of corporate vs. individual election in Romans 9. Opponents of the corporate election view often level criticism at such a distorted version, thinking that pointing out references to individuals refutes it. But a proper corporate view takes account of individuals and is completely compatible with references to individuals. See Abasciano, *Romans* 9.1-9, esp. 41-4, 183-9; *Romans* 9.10-18, esp. 58-62, 67-8; "Election"; criticism of my view in T. R. Schreiner, "Corporate and Individual Election in *Romans* 9: A Response to Brian Abasciano," *JETS* 49/2 (June 2006), 373-86 (henceforth, "Response"); and my follow-up to Schreiner's reply in Abasciano, "Misconceptions." In the first major commentary to give substantial attention to the debate over corporate vs. individual election in light of the exchange between me and Schreiner, Kruse, *Romans*, 391-2, unfortunately misrepresents my view as holding that there is no election of individuals to salvation. However, one of the primary points of my article is that a proper, biblical conception of corporate election unto salvation does not exclude the election of individuals, but rather entails it as a consequence of membership in the elect corporate people. Indeed, Kruse even lists this point in his recounting of my arguments for corporate election despite also indicating that my view excludes individuals. In his conclusion concerning the issue, Kruse rejects the corporate view based partly on the incorrect notion that it holds "that there is no such thing as the election of individuals, only communities" (392). See further my response to Kruse: B. J. Abasciano, "Corporate Election Misrepresented in the Pillar Commentary on Romans by Colin G. Kruse," August 31, 2012, http://evangelicalarminians.org/brian-abasciano-corporate-election-misrepresented-in-the-pillar-commentary-on-romans-by-colin-g-kruse/.
[150] Cf. the observation of Shellrude, "Freedom," 314 n. 14, that advocates of the redemptive historical approach tend to be vague about how the point of the potter/clay metaphor works out in detail.

with temporal realities for Israel, such as the role they play in God's plan, or temporal blessing or ruin of the nation, then temporal, historical realities must be what Paul has in view in Rom. 9:21 as well. But even though the Old Testament background Paul relies on would influence his meaning and helpfully guide us in understanding it, it must be remembered that the New Testament context should take precedence in guiding our understanding of how Paul is using the Old Testament background. There is ambiguity in how to apply this principle in specific instances. But I would submit that when a New Testament passage has eternal judgment in view, and allusion is made to an Old Testament text that deals with temporal judgment, if application is to be made, what the Old Testament text has to say about judgment should be applied to the eternal judgment being discussed in the New Testament text. Of course, this begs the question of whether eternal judgment is part of what Paul is talking about in Romans 9, a point we will address below when discussing support for the eternal destiny view.

A third, related argument in favor of the historical roles view is that the context of Romans 9 deals with Israel as a nation.[151] Advocates of the redemptive historical approach again tend to be vague on the reasoning here, but the thought seems to be that Israel's national identity is a historical, temporal matter, hence the honor and dishonor in view are as well.[152] But that is simplistic. As the saying goes, the devil is in the details. Paul does discuss the nation of Israel in Romans 9, but he addresses other themes as well. The question is, what specifically is Paul saying about the nation of Israel? And how does that relate to the other topics he is discussing? The point is too general[153] and calls for exegesis of the context to assess it. My exegesis of the context in my two previous volumes and the present one leads me to reject the argument as support for the historical roles view of honor and dishonor in Rom. 9:21.[154] The following discussion of support for the eternal destiny view will explain why.

4.2.c.2.d.2.c.2. Support for the Eternal Destiny View

It is more likely that honor and dishonor in 9:21 involve salvation and damnation, respectively. In our exegesis of Romans 9 to this point,[155] we have seen that Paul has had a corporate concept of election to salvation in mind. In fact, Paul began the discussion of which 9:21 is a part with his intense grief that unbelieving ethnic Israel is separated from

---

[151] See Dunn, *Romans*, 557 ("it is Israel's sense of *national* distinctiveness which Paul seeks to counter"); Gifford, *Romans*, 173; N. T. Wright, *The Climax of the Covenant: Christ and the Law in Pauline Theology* (Edinburgh: T&T Clark, 1991), 238–9; "Romans and the Theology of Paul," in D. M. Hay and E. E. Johnson (eds.), *Pauline Theology III: Romans* (Minneapolis, MN: Fortress, 1995), 30–67, see the section on Romans 9–11; Achtemeier, *Romans*, 163–5. Though the Wright and Achtemeier references do not discuss 9:21's honor and dishonor specifically, their approach implies this sort of understanding.

[152] Wright, ibid. Wright is clearer and more detailed than most advocates of the redemptive historical approach concerning what he thinks is going on in this section with God's historical usage of Israel. But Wright's view is somewhat unique.

[153] Cf. Piper, *Justification*, 199.

[154] Though he holds to a different specific view of the details, cf. again Piper's response to this argument for the historical roles view (ibid.).

[155] The following discussion of prior parts of Romans 9 as well as Romans 9 as a whole and Romans 9–11 relies on the exegesis of Rom. 9:1-18 and related research in my two previous volumes. I refer the reader to these for support of my view of Romans 9 appealed to here.

Christ and therefore cut off from the covenant and its promises, devoted to destruction under the eschatological wrath of God (9:1-3). It is concern for ethnic Israel's exclusion from the New Covenant and its salvation that raises the problem Paul addresses in Romans 9-11, the question of God's faithfulness to his promises to Israel in light of Paul's gospel. The concern undergirds Paul's entire discussion in Romans 9-11.[156]

Moreover, the identity of the true people of God/the true Israel is central to Paul's defense of the faithfulness of God vis-à-vis his gospel. Paul is concerned to clarify who are the true Israel = the covenant people of God = the seed of Abraham = the called = the children of the promise (9:6-9). Hence, the language of "election unto salvation" is imprecise in relation to Romans 9. More precisely, in Romans 9 election is about corporate election of a people unto covenant partnership/relationship with God. But the New Covenant entails salvation as one of its primary benefits. So election unto covenant partnership entails election unto salvation, and it is accurate enough to use the language of "election unto salvation" as long as the fuller, covenantal context is kept in mind.

The concern over salvation for Israel and the Gentiles pervades Romans 9-11. But a couple more instances of the theme beyond what I have already mentioned stand out for special attention. Verses 22-23 concern eternal destinies and interpret and apply 9:20-21. We will take up the question of whether 9:22-23 concern eternal destinies later when we take up the focused exegesis of those verses. For now, we will assume that they do and assess the suggestion that 9:22-23 interpret and apply 9:20-21. That this is in fact the case is strongly suggested by 9:22-23 following immediately upon 9:21 and taking up the same language of vessels (σκεῦος), contrasting two types, one positive and the other negative. It is hard not to conclude that 9:21's vessel unto honor (εἰς τιμὴν σκεῦος) is the equivalent of 9:23's vessels of mercy (σκεύη ἐλέους) prepared beforehand for glory, and 9:21's vessel unto dishonor (εἰς ἀτιμίαν [σκεῦος]) is the equivalent of 9:22's vessels of wrath (σκεύη ὀργῆς) prepared for destruction.[157] Beyond the vessel language and the contrast between negative and positive alternatives in relation to the vessels, there is a natural connection between the idea of honor (9.21) and glory (9.23), and between dishonor (9.21) and wrath and destruction (9.22). Indeed, as Schreiner points out, the word for honor that Paul uses (τιμή) "designates eternal life in 2:7, 10, where it parallels the term δόξα," the word Paul uses for glory in 9.23.[158] Moreover, in 2:7-10 honor, glory, and eternal life are set in contrast to eschatological wrath (ὀργή, the word for wrath Paul uses in 9:23) and rage.

Two more passages in chs 9-11 to note are 9:33 and 10:11, which quote from Isa. 28:16, through which Paul indicates that the one who believes in Jesus "will not be dishonored" (οὐ καταισχυνθήσεται). Being dishonored in 9:33 is parallel to not attaining the salvific state of righteousness and to a state of stumbling and falling. Conversely, being dishonored/shamed in both 9:33 and 10:11 is set in contrast to salvation in some way. Immediately after Paul's first reference in 9:33 to faith saving

---

[156] Cf. esp. Schreiner, *Romans*, 496.
[157] Dunn, *Romans*, 558, appeals to δέ at the beginning of 9:22 to suggest that the vessels of v. 21 are not identical to the vessels of vv. 22-23. But this is rather strained; see the discussion of 9:22 later in this chapter.
[158] Schreiner, *Romans*, 497.

from dishonor, he affirms that his prayer and desire for Israel is for their salvation (10:1). In 9:33 and 10:11, being dishonored refers to eschatological condemnation (cf. Mk 8:38; Lk. 9:26).[159]

Thus, we conclude that honor and dishonor in Rom. 9:21 have to do with salvation and damnation. As mentioned earlier, Paul's use of Jer. 18:6 supports this conclusion because its context speaks of God, represented as a potter, making Israel unto blessing or destruction in judgment. Alluding to that Old Testament text in this context brings application to the blessing of eschatological salvation and to eschatological judgment. But recalling the more precise concept of election unto covenant partnership active in Romans 9 mentioned earlier helps us to grasp more precisely the meaning of honor and dishonor in 9:21. Keeping in mind Paul's corporate orientation in Romans 9, God making unto honor in v. 21 most precisely means God embracing a people as his covenant partner and the bestowal of the covenant blessings wrapped up in that; it is the equivalent of covenant election and its blessings, including salvation. God making unto dishonor here means the judgment of eternal condemnation, which will fall upon those who do not have the New Covenant to save them from God's wrath against sin.

4.2.c.2.d.2.d. *The Corporate Orientation of Rom. 9:21*

We have already noted the corporate orientation of Rom. 9:20-21 at various points in our exegesis of these verses. But it remains for us to consider more fully the implications this has for the basic meaning of 9:21. When Paul talks about the potter having the right to make from the same lump one a vessel unto honor and another unto dishonor, the vessels he speaks of refer to groups made from the mass of humanity.[160] The question is in effect asking, does God not have the right to honor a people by embracing them as his own and blessing them accordingly on the one hand, and to condemn a people for their sin on the other? In other words, does God not have the right to save one people (on whatever conditions he chooses) and to judge another people? Does God not have the right to choose who his covenant people are and to condemn those who are not in covenant relationship with him for their sin even if judging them glorifies him and even if the condition for covenant membership he laid down was so offensive to the Jews that many of them hardened to the gospel? The obvious answer from application of the Old Testament texts Paul has alluded to and from the metaphor itself is yes, of course God has such a right, refuting the interlocutor's objection voiced in 9:19.

Some might be inclined to argue that the separation of humanity into two groups implies individualistic election, which forms the two groups.[161] But this founders on the false assumption that a corporate view excludes individuals from its scope and on a failure to grasp the nuanced nature of biblical election. I have addressed these

---

[159] Cf. ibid., 541.
[160] T. R. Schreiner, "Does Romans 9 Teach Individual Election unto Salvation? Some Exegetical and Theological Reflections," *JETS* 36 (1993), 25–40 (34) (henceforth, "Election"), takes Paul's use of the singular σκεῦος along with other uses of the singular in Romans 9 as evidence that specific individuals are in view. But this is misguided and naive. See Abasciano, "Election," 358–60, for a rebuttal.
[161] Cf. with respect to the remnant, the approach of Schreiner, ibid.; Piper, *Justification*, 199. See Abasciano, "Election," 360–1, for a rebuttal of this line of argument.

issues extensively in my two previous volumes on Romans 9 and elsewhere,[162] and so I will only comment briefly here. First, it should be noted that while corporate election views the group as primary, it includes individuals by virtue of their membership in the group. Accordingly, second, mention of individuals is not inconsistent with corporate election, which could always speak of the inclusion or exclusion of individuals vis-à-vis the covenant without shifting the locus of election itself to the individual. Third, in this instance, we do not even have a mention of individuals specifically. It is simply assumed that making two or more groups from one entails individually choosing each person for each group. But that begs the question of whether the choice of these groups was made corporately or individualistically, which leads to the next point.

Fourth, biblical corporate covenant election refers to the election of a group as a consequence of the choice of an individual who represents the group, the corporate head and representative. The group is elected as a consequence of its identification with this corporate representative. Individuals are chosen as a consequence of their identification with the people, and more fundamentally, with the individual corporate head. They and the group share in the election of the corporate head. Fifth, as some commentators have pointed out, the mass of humanity in view is a sinful humanity already worthy of God's judgment and under his condemnation.[163] His embracing of a people as his covenant partner from that mass of sinful humanity, bestowing salvation upon them as part of that covenant relationship, in effect "make[s] from the same lump one a vessel unto honor and another unto dishonor." All of this is perfectly consonant with corporate thought in general and corporate election in particular.

4.2.d. Romans 9:22-24: Paul's Interpretation and Application of Rom. 9:20-21 and the Potter/Clay Metaphor

Paul continues in 9:22-24:

> [22] But if God, desiring to show his wrath and to make known his power, endured with much patience vessels of wrath prepared for destruction, [23] and in order that he might make known the riches of his glory upon vessels of mercy, which he prepared beforehand for glory, [24] whom he also called—us—not only from Jews but also from Gentiles ...

4.2.d.1. A Difficult Sentence

This is an incomplete sentence, but not accidentally so. Paul begins the sentence as a conditional, with a protasis using the conditional particle εἰ, but never supplies the apodosis. As Cranfield observes,

---

[162] See my *Romans 9.1-9*, esp. 183–9 (cf. 41–4); *Romans 9.10-18*, esp. 58–62; and most fully, "Election"; and "Misconceptions." Cf. the corporate approach to Romans 9–11 of Thornhill, *Election*, 232–53 (232–43 on Romans 9); and C. Müller, *Gottes Gerechtigkeit und Gottes Volk: Eine Untersuchung zu Römer 9-11* (FRLANT, 86; Göttingen: Vandenhoeck & Ruprecht, 1964), 75–8; and to Rom. 9:6-24 of Mayer, *Heilsratschluss*, 213–14.
[163] Murray, *Romans*, 2.32; Hodge, *Romans*, 495; Morris, *Romans*, 366; Barrett, *Romans*, 175.

Attempts have indeed been made to construe v. 23 or v. 24 or even Τί οὖν ἐροῦμεν; in v. 30 as an apodosis; but these must be rejected, the resulting sentences being much too forced to be acceptable. Such expedients are unnecessary anyway, since ellipsis of the apodosis of a conditional sentence is fairly common in classical Greek and occurs several times in the NT.[164]

Taking v. 23 as the apodosis involves taking καί at the beginning of the verse as "then, so"[165] or "also"[166] and understanding an expression such as "he did so" as implicit, yielding translations such as "then [he did so] in order to" or "[he did so] also in order to." But as Piper points out, "The then-clause of this construction does not seem to follow from the if-clause."[167] Moreover, it relies on the words regarded as implicit being so strongly assumed or obvious that the construal of καί depends on it, such as taking καί in its less common usage as an adverb ("also") modifying an unstated verb. On the other hand, taking v. 24 as the apodosis is simply implausible, a fact that becomes evident if one tries to read it as a then-clause. As for the beginning of v. 30, it is simply too far away with too much material between it and what can reasonably be regarded as the protasis to be taken seriously as the apodosis.

Some take v. 22 and v. 23 (or 23–24 or 25) as distinct incomplete sentences to which the reader or translation is to supply the missing material,[168] but this unnecessarily complicates already complicated Greek grammar. There is nothing that particularly indicates two sentences; it is grammatically more natural to read only one. The main alternative to the approach we have taken above (vv. 22–24 as one incomplete sentence)[169] is to take vv. 22–23 as one incomplete sentence, with v. 24 starting a new sentence.[170] But the syntax of v. 24 indicates that the verse continues the sentence it is in rather than beginning one (see below on v. 24). The simplest, most straightforward, and most likely approach to 9:22-24 is to read the verses together as one incomplete sentence, requiring the reader to supply from the context what Paul leaves unstated, the apodosis of his conditional construction.[171]

I mentioned above that Paul's use of an incomplete construction is not accidental. By doing so, he draws the reader in to think his thought with him, to grasp it more fully for herself, and to be more likely to own it. It functions similarly to a rhetorical

---

[164] Cranfield, *Romans*, 492. Moo, *Romans*, 624 n. 273, mistakenly identifies Cranfield and Murray as supporting vv. 22–23 as the protasis when they actually think it is vv. 22–24. The omission of καί at the beginning of v. 23 in B 326 lat Or$^{(1739mg)}$ is probably an attempt to smooth out the original text.

[165] So, e.g., A. Nygren, *Commentary on Romans* (Philadelphia, PA: Muhlenberg, 1949), 372.

[166] So, e.g., G. Stählin, "The Wrath of Man and the Wrath of God in the NT," *TDNT*, 5.419-47 (426).

[167] Piper, *Justification*, 206.

[168] So, e.g., NIV ("^{22} [What] if God ...?^{23} [What if] he did this to ...?"; brackets added to show additions to the Greek); NET; NRSV. Although complicating the Greek grammar, this option does make for a smoother text in English translation.

[169] Also held by, e.g., Cranfield, *Romans*, 492; Murray, *Romans*, 2.33; Barrett, *Romans*, 176; Godet, *Romans*, 359, 362; Hodge, *Romans*, 495–7; NASB; ESV; RSV. Even Schreiner, *Romans*, 503, who thinks that v. 24 begins a new paragraph acknowledges that v. 24 is syntactically connected to v. 23.

[170] Held by, e.g., Moo, *Romans*, 624; Dunn, *Romans*, 550–1, 558, 570; Fitzmyer, *Romans*, 572.

[171] On the omission of the apodosis in a conditional construction, which is a form of aposiopesis, see BDF, § 482. If the καί at the beginning of 9:23 is retained, as the consensus would have it, BDF, § 467, would also find a case of anacoluthon in 9:22-23.

question, making its point implicitly, which can sometimes make a point more powerfully; understatement can move the listener to seize upon a point more forcefully to compensate for the lack of directness or emphasis employed by an author.

Most scholars translate 9:22-23 or 24 as a question (or multiple questions), beginning 9:22 with something like, "What if God?" But there is no explicit indication of a question.[172] A question is probably implicit. But translating it as a question makes explicit what Paul leaves implicit. It is more appropriate to leave it implicit in translation and to explain it as part of the meaning of the text in exegesis. In line with interpreting and applying 9:21, and with the questions Paul asked in 9:20-21, the implicit apodosis of 9:22-24 is something like, "then does he not have the right to do so?" Adding that to the verses gives us,

> [22] But if God, desiring to show his wrath and make known his power, endured with much patience vessels of wrath prepared for destruction, [23] and in order that he might make known the riches of his glory upon vessels of mercy, which he prepared beforehand for glory, [24] whom he also called—us—not only from Jews but also from Gentiles[, then does he not have the right to do so?].

The obvious implicit answer is, yes, he has the right to do so. The point made by 9:22-24 is that God has the right to do all that is mentioned in the verses, which in context includes pouring out his wrath on the unbelieving (which applies especially to unbelieving Jews) and giving the riches of his glory to believers, a group consisting of both Jews and Gentiles.

4.2.d.2. The δέ of Rom. 9:22

The conjunctive particle δέ follows the conditional particle εἰ at the beginning of v. 22. Some commentators take the conjunction here as adversative and argue that it indicates a substantial element of contrast with v. 21 such that the thought of vv. 22-23 differs somewhat from the thought of v. 21.[173] But as Douglas Moo comments, "this seems overly subtle."[174] δέ does not necessarily indicate a contrast when it is used, but can just as readily indicate continuation and/or transition (represented in translation by "and" or "now," or as in most translations of 9:22, left untranslated). Therefore, an adversative sense for δέ cannot be validly appealed to here for clear support of there being a difference of thought in 9:22-23 in some degree of opposition to the thought in 9:21.[175] The δέ allows for there to be a contrast but does not demand it; it

---

[172] The particle εἰ at the beginning of v. 22 can indicate a question, but in that case, it would not indicate a condition, leaving Paul asking about what God did do. This is possible, but virtually no one supports this option. It does not fit as well into Paul's rhetorical strategy and stress on defending God's righteousness in election and the gospel. P. Ellingworth, "Translation and Exegesis: A Case Study (Rom 9,22ff.)," *Bib* 59 (1978) 396–402 (399), does not specifically support taking εἰ as interrogative here, but does suggest that it should at least be considered.

[173] So Cranfield, *Romans*, 493; Sanday and Headlam, *Romans*, 261; Dunn, *Romans*, 558.

[174] Moo, *Romans*, 624.

[175] That includes Dunn's (*Romans*, 558) suggestion that the vessels of v. 21 are not identical to the vessels of vv. 22–23.

suggests contrast or mere continuation as possibilities, but the precise nuance of the conjunction must be determined from context.

Moreover, even if there is a contrast intended, what that contrast is must be determined from the context. The contrast could be one that relates to some aspect of what precedes other than Paul's potter/clay metaphor or the main point of 9:21. For example, the contrast could be to the objection from 9:19 Paul is still answering. Verse 19 voices the objection of the interlocutor to Paul's statement in v. 18 that God has mercy on or hardens whom he desires. He then uses a strong adversative particle as he begins his response in v. 20a and employs the potter/clay metaphor in a series of rhetorical questions through v. 21. As he turns to explain and apply the potter/clay metaphor, it would be quite natural to pick up the note of contrast to the objection itself again by use of a conjunction. Whether this is more likely than a note of continuation and/or transition is hard to say. But on balance, continuation and/or transition seems more likely.

However, there is another adversative option that I think is more likely for δέ here than the contrast option just discussed or mere continuation or transition. Before identifying that, it should be noted that the features of contrast on the one hand and continuation or transition on the other are not mutually exclusive as elements of the text. Indeed, as the *ALGNT* states, δέ is used "most commonly to denote continuation and further thought development, taking its specific sense from the context *and*; contrast *but*; transition *then, now* (with no temporal sense)."[176] The particle can denote continuation and further thought development with a nuance of mere continuation, or contrast, or transition. In 9:22, Paul is continuing his response to the objection of v. 19 and transitioning to an explanation and application of his potter/clay metaphor. But the question before us now is, what specific nuance does δέ have here?

I would suggest that the δέ of 9:22 denotes continuation and further thought development with a nuance of contrast between the unobjectionable point of 9:21 and the offensive idea that God has a right to call a people consisting of Gentiles as well Jews as his own covenant partner, an idea found in 9:24, at the end of the sentence begun in 9:22. As we have seen throughout our exegesis of Romans 9 so far, this is at the heart of the issue Paul is dealing with in the chapter, God's right to call his people by faith rather than works or ancestry, resulting in the exclusion of unbelieving ethnic Jews from the covenant and its salvation, and the inclusion of believing Gentiles. This is what has called God's faithfulness to his promises to Israel into question and, due to its extreme offensiveness to Jewish sensibilities, hardened ethnic Israel to Christ. Using the potter/clay metaphor, Paul has just shown in 9:20-21 that God has the right to choose who he wants as his people and to condemn those he wants to condemn for their sin. Paul now applies this unobjectionable point to the details of his gospel, which include the exceedingly offensive notion that the covenant people have been called from Gentiles as well as Jews apart from works or ancestry. Paul's use of δέ expresses the contrast between the ideal that his potter/clay metaphor has established (God's right to save one group and condemn another

---

[176] *ALGNT*, s.v. δέ, 1.

according to his discretion) and the challenge its application in such an offensive way brings.

To offer an analogy: It would be like asking an employee who hates to clean the company office, "Does your boss not have the right to tell you what to do at work?" and then following that up with, "*But* what if he tells you to clean the office?" The word "but" in that last question expresses the contrast between the principle as presumably rather obvious and acceptable, and its application as obviously sound but difficult to accept.

4.2.d.3. Desiring to Show His Wrath and to Make Known His Power

The participial phrase "desiring to show his wrath and to make known his power" (θέλων ὁ θεὸς ἐνδείξασθαι τὴν ὀργὴν καὶ γνωρίσαι τὸ δυνατὸν αὐτοῦ) modifies the main verb of the sentence, "endured" (ἤνεγκεν). The participle θέλων has occasioned much discussion.

4.2.d.3.a. The Participle θέλων

"Desiring" translates the adverbial participle θέλων, which has been rendered by translations variously as desiring (ESV, NRSV, HCSB), willing (NASB, NET, KJV), wanting (NKJV, CSB, LEB), wishing (NAB), and choosing (NIV).[177] With the participial phrase, we encounter two major, intertwined questions of interpretation: (1) Is the participle θέλων (desiring) causal or concessive?[178] (2) How does the participial clause of 9:22 relate to the purpose clause of 9:23?[179]

---

[177] Jewett, *Romans*, 595 n. 82, thinks that "wanting" is most appropriate idiomatically, but curiously that "willing" is most appropriate theologically due to Paul's use of the word in 9:18 (I regard desire and want as normally synonymous). However, the word can be taken of desiring/wanting in 9:18 too, just as in our exegesis. But even if "to will" is the specific meaning in 9:18, some small difference of nuance in 9:22, which is indeed related to 9:18, would not be unusual. "Willing" is not an ideal translation here because the word often has a sense of reluctant or neutral consent to it in English (e.g., John's boss was willing to grant his request for a raise; Mary was willing to let her daughter go to the party instead of study). That can also encourage a concessive reading of the participle, which is one of the main ways it can be taken (see below). But the sense of "willing" in 9:22 is not reluctant, neutral, or passive but a positive desire, something God wants to do. Dunn, *Romans*, 558, thinks the participle would be read as a relative, but that is not its grammatical function here. It has all the marks of an adverbial participle and would be abnormal for a participle that could function as a relative in this context; one would expect the article in that case. Moreover, Paul could have used a relative if he wanted to convey a relative sense.

[178] This question is addressed in the current section. Jewett, *Romans*, 595; and Luz, *Geschichtsverständnis*, 242–4, take the participle as purposive (final). But this is very unlikely because the idea of purpose would especially include the action of the participle (desiring) as a purpose of the main verb, not just the infinitives it introduces. A translation of this option should show its implausibility: "If God, for the purpose of willing to show his wrath and to make known his power, endured." While it is true that the infinitives are ultimately purposes of God's endurance here (see below), that is not expressed by the grammar or the participle but is logically implied by the meaning of what is said. Luz, 243, also mentions a modal option for the participle, but quickly rejects it because it would still carry a purposive sense. Godet, *Romans*, 359–60, mentions a temporal sense as a possibility but notes that is little different than the concessive view, which he favors.

[179] This question is addressed partially in the present section and more fully in Sections 4.2.d.8.a and 4.2.d.9.

If the participle is concessive, then the sense is: "But if God, *although* desiring to show his wrath and to make known his power, endured with much patience vessels of wrath prepared for destruction." The idea would be that God endured the vessels of wrath *despite* his desire to show his wrath and to make his power known. Given that desire, one would expect God to pour out his wrath on the vessels of wrath, not endure them patiently. A concessive use of the participle would express the contrast between God's desire and his surprising, tolerant, patient action toward the vessels of wrath. With respect to question 2 above, it would also mean that the infinitive phrases of 9:22's participial clause (to show his wrath and to make known his power) are not indicated as purposes of God in his enduring the vessels of wrath; the purpose clause of 9:23 would alone indicate the purpose of his patience with the vessels of wrath.[180]

If the participle is causal, then the sense is: "But if God, *because of* desiring to show his wrath and to make known his power, endured with much patience vessels of wrath prepared for destruction." The idea would be that God endured the vessels of wrath *because of* his desire to show his wrath and to make his power known. With regard to the relationship between the participial clause of 9:22 and the purpose clause of 9:23 (see question 2 above), this would conceptually join the infinitive phrases of 9:22 ("to show his wrath and to make known his power") with the purpose clause of 9:23 as purposes God sought to accomplish by enduring the vessels of wrath rather than bringing destruction on them immediately.[181] That is because a causal participle of a verb meaning "to desire" here introduces actions God *desired* to accomplish by the action of enduring the vessels of wrath, which makes them equivalent to purposes he aimed to accomplish by that endurance.[182]

---

[180] Cranfield, *Romans*, 493, speaks of this as "coupling πολλῇ μακροθυμίᾳ and the ἵνα γνωρίσῃ clause together."

[181] Ibid., specifies the options for this as either coupling together the participial clause of 9:22 and the purpose clause of 9:23 or "taking ἵνα γνωρίσῃ [of 9:23] as equivalent to an infinitive after θέλων, and so as parallel to ἐνδείξασθαι and γνωρίσαι [of 9:22]." In the latter case (supported by Murray, *Romans*, 2.35; Piper, *Justification*, 206–7), it would not only be a conceptual coupling, but also grammatical, with ἵνα of 9:23 as grammatically dependent on 9:22's θέλων (desiring). But Cranfield rightly finds that the word order makes the latter option "rather unnatural" (n. 3). Grammatically, it is far more likely that ἵνα depends on the nearby indicative verb ἤνεγκεν (he endured) of 9:22 rather than the distant participle θέλων. Morris, *Romans*, 108, mentions another possibility—that ἵνα depends on κατηρτισμένα (prepared), "prepared for destruction and in order that he might make known." Morris omits the "and" (καί) from his translation for this option, which reflects its difficulty; it makes for a more awkward construction than the other options. It is a possibility that virtually no one supports. It is more likely that a subordinating conjunction will relate to the main verb of the sentence than to an attributive participle, especially preceded by καί. Context, of course, must decide the question. But here, the Old Testament background and the context press a focus on God's patient endurance (spoken of in the language of raising up in 9:17) with the vessels of wrath and God's purposes in that. Moreover, patience with vessels of wrath goes along more obviously with the purpose of making known the riches of glory on vessels of mercy than does preparing the vessels of wrath for destruction, even if closer reflection reveals compatibility between the latter two as well.

[182] Puzzlingly, Dunn, *Romans*, 560, claims that the ἵνα/purpose clause of v. 23 being read as following on from the main clause of v. 22 prohibits the infinitives of v. 22 as purposes; rather, they describe what God wants. But he gives no explanation, and it is unclear why we should think the assertion to be true. On the contrary, it misses the specifics of the context observed above involving a participle that even Dunn admits is difficult to take other than as denoting desired purpose (558).

The concessive view has much to commend it. First, there is an obvious apparent contrast between God's desire to show his wrath and power and the restraining of that wrath and power in patient endurance of those who would suffer his wrath. On the other hand, it is not readily apparent how desiring to show his wrath would move God to restrain it. This gives the concessive view a more natural feel on a surface reading of the text. Second, Paul has already indicated earlier in Romans that God's patience (μακροθυμίᾳ) is meant to lead to repentance (2:4). That would seem to explain why God restrained his wrath even though desiring to show it. While he did want to show it, he wanted even more for the vessels of wrath to come to repentance and be spared, for them to become vessels of mercy (cf. Ezek. 18:23, 30-32; 33:11). Paul's use of Jeremiah 18 greatly strengthens the likelihood of this approach, for it clearly presents God's desire for his people to repent and be saved rather than continue in their rebellion and perish, though he would bring calamitous judgment upon them if they would not repent.

Third, the different construction (a participial clause vs. a ἵνα clause) and placement of the alleged expression of purpose in 9:22 versus the clear expression of purpose in 9:23 weighs in favor of viewing these two differently placed and distinct grammatical constructions as also distinct in meaning. Why use different constructions if they both express purposes for the same action? And why separate the expressions of purpose when doing so results in awkward syntax by needing to pick up the idea of purpose again with a connective?[183]

Despite the strength of the concessive view, the causal view is ultimately more likely due to contextual considerations.[184] The primary reason is tied up with Paul's use of the Old Testament in 9:17. It must be remembered that the present verses are responding to an objection to Paul's quotation of Exod. 9:16 in Rom. 9:17 and his application of it in Rom. 9:18. Hence, any parallel to 9:17 in 9:22-23 is especially significant. And there is a substantial parallel.

To fully appreciate the parallel, it should be recalled that our exegesis found that Paul's use of ἐξεγείρω (to raise up) in 9:17 carries the sense of "to spare/allow to live" in line with the original context of the quotation.[185] With that in mind, we can lay out the Greek texts of 9:17 and 9:22-23:

Rom. 9:17 Εἰς αὐτὸ τοῦτο ἐξήγειρά σε ὅπως ἐνδείξωμαι ἐν σοὶ τὴν δύναμίν μου καὶ ὅπως διαγγελῇ τὸ ὄνομά μου ἐν πάσῃ τῇ γῇ

Rom. 9:22-23 εἰ δὲ θέλων ὁ θεὸς ἐνδείξασθαι τὴν ὀργὴν καὶ γνωρίσαι τὸ δυνατὸν αὐτοῦ ἤνεγκεν ἐν πολλῇ μακροθυμίᾳ σκεύη ὀργῆς κατηρτισμένα εἰς ἀπώλειαν, 23 καὶ ἵνα γνωρίσῃ τὸν πλοῦτον τῆς δόξης αὐτοῦ ἐπὶ σκεύη ἐλέους ἃ προητοίμασεν εἰς δόξαν

---

[183] A similar question could be put to the concessive option regarding the awkward syntax. But it could be answered that the awkward syntax brings special focus to the purpose clause of 9:23. However, a similar response could be given from the causal option; see below.

[184] Wright, "Romans," 641, suggests that both concessive and causal meanings might be in view, with the concessive as primary. But this seems too difficult because the meanings are contradictory.

[185] See Abasciano, *Romans 9.10-18*, 162-4.

The most obvious parallel is the affirmation in 9:17 of God's purpose to show (using ἐνδείκνυμι) his power (using δύναμις) compared to the affirmation in 9:22 of his desire to show (also using ἐνδείκνυμι) his wrath and make known his power (using δυνατός). But Paul's use of ἐξεγείρω in the sense of "to allow to live" in reference to God allowing Pharaoh (whom Paul uses as a type of unbelieving ethnic Israel) to live even though he was continuing in rebellion against God despite suffering his wrath in the plagues[186] is roughly equivalent to God enduring vessels of wrath with much patience. Thus, 9:17 refers to God enduring the vessel of wrath Pharaoh for the purpose of showing his power. Moreover, in the Exodus context, God allowing Pharaoh to continue living and resisting God served to multiply the pouring out of God's wrath in further plagues culminating in the destruction of the Egyptian forces in the Red Sea.

But the parallels are not exhausted. Romans 9:17 also speaks of God's purpose to proclaim his name in all the earth by his endurance of Pharaoh. And that finds parallel in 9:23's reference to God enduring vessels of wrath for the purpose of making known the riches of his *glory* upon vessels of *mercy*, for the context of Paul's Old Testament quotation in Rom. 9:15 (quoting Exod. 33:19), the application of which he defends by quoting Exod. 9:16, uses the terminology of God's name synonymously with his glory and profoundly associates it with his being merciful.[187] All of this makes it highly likely that as Paul defends his application to unbelieving ethnic Israel of God's actions toward Pharaoh, he now speaks of God enduring vessels of wrath for the purpose of showing his wrath and making his power known.

As mentioned above, Paul has been and still is responding to an objection of his use of Exod. 9:16. It appears that, after refuting the objection with the Old Testament potter/clay metaphor, Paul now constructs his interpretation and application of the potter/clay metaphor on the pattern of Exod. 9:16/Rom. 9:17. Having proved the principle of Rom. 9:17, in 9:22-24 Paul has rephrased the principle in concrete terms related to the specific expression of it that has met with the hypothetical interlocutor's objection, election based on faith rather than works or ancestry so that believing Gentiles and Jews are called children of God but unbelieving Jews are accursed. It is an effective rhetorical strategy because it takes advantage of the principle having been proven and the power of framing an issue in line with the view one is advocating. It is like a preacher using a principle articulated by a Bible verse his audience accepts and rephrasing it in a way that applies it to his audience.[188]

However, there are questions about the causal view of the participle that need to be answered. First, one would normally think that the desire to show wrath is contrary to

---

[186] Though there is not much specific mention in Exodus of the plagues as expressions of God's wrath, the concept is clearly present. And Exod. 15:7 does use the term of the destruction of the Egyptians in the Red Sea, which is seen in the narrative as the climax of the process of God bringing judgment on Pharaoh and the Egyptians in the plagues. Indeed, the plagues are explicitly identified as divine judgments in Exodus (6:6; 7:4; 12:12).

[187] See Abasciano, *Romans 9.1-9*, 64–70; Piper, *Justification*, 84–8.

[188] Consider the example of a preacher saying, "Citing the Old Testament, the Apostle Paul wrote, 'Everyone who calls on the name of the Lord will be saved.' You see, we who have called on the name of the Lord Jesus Christ here at this Church will be saved."

restraining it, not a purpose to be accomplished by restraining it. How can God's desire to show wrath be accomplished by his restraining his wrath? Second, does not the linkage of God's patience with his desire to save the objects of his patience earlier in the epistle (2:4) stand against his patience having the goal of pouring out his wrath in 9:22? And third, how is the different construction and placement of the alleged expression of purpose in 9:22 versus the clear expression of purpose in 9:23 to be explained? Rather than focusing on these questions now, we will address them later on in the course of continuing to address the meaning of 9:22-23.

4.2.d.3.b. Showing His Wrath and Making His Power Known

Paul indicates that God's desire "to show his wrath and to make known his power" led him to endure "with much patience vessels of wrath prepared for destruction." *Showing* (ἐνδείκνυμι) wrath here likely involves more than simply making God's wrath known informationally,[189] but pouring out his wrath openly upon the objects of his judgment, which also shows his wrath/makes it known.[190] The divine wrath referred to is eschatological (i.e., eternal damnation) just as the glory referred to in v. 23 is eschatological (i.e., eternal blessedness).[191] This is supported by our earlier discussion of the vessels unto honor and dishonor in 9:21, which we concluded have to do with eschatological honor and dishonor and are parallel to the vessels of wrath and of mercy in 9:22-23 (see Section 4.2.c.2.d.2.c.2). Adding to that discussion (which the reader is advised to consult in conjunction with what is said here), we note that Schreiner argues compellingly for the sense of eschatological wrath and glory in 9:22-23:

> The "vessels of wrath" (σκεύη ὀργῆς) are destined "for destruction" (εἰς ἀπώλειαν, *eis apōleian*). In Paul's writings, both "wrath" (ὀργή, Rom. 2:5, 8; 5:9; Eph. 5:6; Col. 3:6; 1 Thess. 1:10; 5:9) and "destruction" (ἀπώλεια, Phil. 1:28; 3:19; 2 Thess. 2:3; 1 Tim. 6:9; cf. the verbal form ἀπόλλυναι, *apollynai*, to destroy: 1 Cor. 1:18, 19; 8:11; 10:9, 10; 15:18; 2 Cor. 2:15; 4:3; 2 Thess. 2:10) frequently refer to eschatological judgment. Any notion of historical destiny alone certainly seems forced. Moreover, the corollary "vessels or mercy" (σκεύη ἐλέους) that are destined "for glory" (εἰς δόξαν, *eis doxan*) describes eternal life, for we have seen in Rom. 9:14-18 that the ἔλεος word group often refers to eschatological life, and δόξα does the same (Rom. 2:7, 10; 5:2; 8:18, 21; 1 Cor. 2:7; 15:41; 2 Cor. 4:17; Eph. 1:18; Phil. 3:21; Col. 1:27; 3:4; 1 Thess. 2:12; 2 Thess. 2:14; 2 Tim. 2:10).[192]

---

[189] Meaning 1 in BDAG, s.v. ἐνδείκνυμι.
[190] This falls under meaning 2 in BDAG, s.v. ἐνδείκνυμι. See esp. *ALGNT*, s.v. ἐνδείκνυμι, which describes this meaning thus: "as perpetrating something openly against someone." Cf. the English terminology of "showing mercy," which does not mean simply to make mercy known, but to give mercy, which also shows the mercy/makes it known.
[191] However, these must be understood in light of both inaugurated as well as consummated eschatology; see below.
[192] Schreiner, *Romans*, 496. Moo, *Romans*, 627 n. 284, speaks even more strongly with respect to ἀπώλεια (destruction), which he says "is always used by Paul with reference to final condemnation."

God "making known" (γνωρίζω) his power obviously has a focus on communicating knowledge of God's power. But this "making known" articulated by γνωρίζω can take place not only by verbal communication but also by the carrying out of the action to be made known (see the use of γνωρίζω in 1 Sam. 14:12; 2 Sam. 7:21; 1 Kgs 8:53; 3 Macc. 2:6; Ps. 77:14; 90:12; 98:2; 106:8; Jer. 16:21), in this case, the exercise of God's power. In such cases, the "making known" and the carrying out of the action are one and the same. This can be seen in some passages in the Septuagint that speak of God's power being made known. Third Macc. 2:6 says, "You made known your power when with many and diverse punishments you tried bold Pharao, when he had enslaved your people, holy Israel, at which time you made known your great might" (NETS). The exercise of God's power in judgment made his power known. Psalm 77:14 reads, "You are the God who works wonders; you made known among the peoples your power." The exercise of God's power in working wonders made his power known. In line with the showing of God's wrath involving the pouring out of his wrath, God desiring to make his power known here involves the desire to unleash his power.

But what does God's power refer to here? Given the relationship to Rom. 9:17 we have discussed, it almost certainly carries the same meaning—God the Creator's supreme divine power and sovereignty as expressed in its exercise in judgment and mercy/salvation.[193] Our conclusion concerning 9:17 fits just as well here: God's power in 9:22 that he wants to make known has specific application in Paul's argument

> to the exercise of "the power of God for salvation for all who believe, both to the Jew first and to the Geek" (1.16), which names those who believe in the promise (i.e., children of the promise) as children of God and seed of Abraham (9.6-8) and recipients of the divine elective love (9.13) on the one hand, and on the other hand, the power of God in pouring out the curse of the covenant on unbelieving ethnic Israel (children of the flesh; 9.8), cutting them off from Christ and his people/the seed of Abraham and the covenant promises (9.3-9) and making them objects of the divine hatred that is covenantal rejection (9.13).[194]

One might argue that the pairing of wrath and power in 9:22 suggests that the power in view is limited to God's power expressed in his wrath. But that would be to overlook the inextricable link between God's judgment and salvation that we have found in both the Old Testament background of 9:17 and throughout Romans 9.[195] In Exodus, God's salvation of his people required the divine wrath to be poured out on Pharaoh/Egypt so that they would let Israel go and Israel could be taken by the Lord to the place where they would be chosen by God in a renewed covenant. His saving power was expressed in part by his judging power. In Romans 9, God's salvation of the world required the judgment/rejection of unbelieving Jews so that God could choose his people in a New Covenant in that God's sovereignly established means of New Covenant membership/salvation is faith in Christ apart from works or ancestry.

---

[193] See Abasciano, *Romans 9.10-18*, 197–8.
[194] Ibid., 198.
[195] See ibid., 197.

It could be argued that this explains how God's desire to show his wrath and make his power known motivated him to restrain his wrath. It is easy to see how God's desire to make known his power that includes working salvation would lead him to patiently endure those who need salvation (i.e., the vessels of wrath) in order to accomplish their salvation, making those who submit to his salvation vessels of mercy. (That, I submit, is the main way in which God's desire to make his power known contributed to his decision to endure the vessels of wrath.) But while God desired to exercise his power in salvation, New Covenant salvation required judgment/rejection of those who reject Christ. Because accomplishing salvation required it, God also desired to express his wrath. With God's salvation and judgment as two sides of the same coin in this case, and God's plan of salvation requiring patient endurance of the vessels of wrath, one might say that God's desire to express his wrath and saving power brought him to patiently endure the vessels of wrath.[196]

That seems to be part of Paul's thought, but not the whole of it. One might wonder if the notion of God's desire to save requiring his judgment adequately explains Paul's reference to God's desire to show his wrath; in that case his desire to judge is merely derivative. It is certainly possible, but God's love of righteousness and hatred of sin in the biblical tradition generally and in Paul specifically stand against this (see, e.g., Paul's other references to God's wrath in Rom. 1:18; 2:5, 8; 3:5; 4:15; 5:9; 12:19; 13:4-5). Moreover, it seems clear in the Exodus background that God's judgment on Pharaoh and Egypt was not merely required to save Israel but also something God desired to do. On the other hand, if God's desire to show his wrath is more than derivative of his desire to save, that would seem to leave some of the difficulty of how his desire to show his wrath contributed to his restraining his wrath for a time. But the context of Romans and the Old Testament background offer further insights into Paul's thought here. However, before exploring that (see Section 4.2.d.7 for that exploration), it will be beneficial to attend to the next and final phrase in v. 22, which indicates that God "endured with much patience vessels of wrath prepared for destruction."

On the pattern of God forestalling his final judgment on Pharaoh, allowing him to live (Rom. 9:17 quoting Exod. 9:16), Paul's reference to God enduring "with much patience vessels of wrath prepared for destruction" refers to God patiently tolerating the vessels of wrath by forestalling the pouring out of his wrath upon them in fatal judgment. Grammatically, this is the main clause of the sentence, containing its main verb, the indicative ἤνεγκεν (he endured).[197] "Vessels of wrath" (σκεύη ὀργῆς) is another way of referring to 9:21's "vessel unto honor" (σκεῦος ... εἰς ἀτιμίαν), both corporate references. "Vessel unto honor" is a collective singular, which focuses on the group without any substantial reference to individuals whereas "vessels of wrath" refers

---

[196] This would be like the case of a father who wants to discipline his son for the good of his son learning a valuable lesson he could not learn without the discipline. His son learning the lesson is the primary goal, but it so fundamentally requires the discipline that it can be said that the father wants to discipline his son and teach him a valuable lesson.

[197] The omission of ἤνεγκεν in F G it and Ambst is clearly accidental, though the reason is not apparent. The addition of εἰς in the same witnesses is also clearly accidental, possibly from dittography due to the word's presence elsewhere in the same verse.

to the same group with a regular plural, which retains a corporate focus but portrays the corporate group as made up of individuals.

4.2.d.4. σκεύη ὀργῆς

Various understandings of the phrase σκεύη ὀργῆς (vessels of wrath) have been suggested by interpreters: (1) vessels that deserve wrath;[198] (2) instruments/agents that effect or manifest [God's] wrath;[199] and (3) objects of God's wrath (i.e., vessels that receive wrath),[200] which can stand alone but under which more specific nuances can be classed in that they ultimately see the phrase as indicating that God's wrath falls on the people represented by the vessels, such as vessels destined for wrath,[201] vessels all saturated with wrath,[202] or vessels for wrath (i.e., vessels for which God's purpose is to receive wrath).[203] Senses 1 and 2 above are unlikely. Neither of them matches the parallelism with v. 23's vessels of mercy, which are clearly vessels that receive mercy rather than vessels that deserve or effect mercy.[204] The phrase σκεύη ὀργῆς in 9:22 almost certainly carries the sense that most interpreters assign to it, that of "vessels that are objects of wrath/receive wrath," whether in the present (e.g., "vessels on whom

---

[198] Sanday and Headlam, *Romans*, 261; cf. Wright, "Romans," 642. This would be one way of understanding ὀργῆς (of wrath) as a genitive of quality; see note 206 below.

[199] Munck, *Israel*, 68; A. T. Hanson, "Vessels of Wrath or Instruments of Wrath? Romans IX.22-3," *JTS* 32 [1981], 433–43. This would be another way of understanding ὀργῆς as a genitive of quality; see again note 206 below.

[200] Cranfield, *Romans*, 495; Dunn, *Romans*, 559; Morris, *Romans*, 368. This would be yet another way of understanding ὀργῆς as a genitive of quality; see again note 206 below. Both supporters of this option, Moo, *Romans*, 607 (1st ed.), phrases this as "vessels on whom God's wrath rests," and BDF, § 165, phrases it as "bearers of wrath."

[201] Hodge, *Romans*, 497; Wallace, *Greek*, 101. This would be a genitive of destination, on which, see Wallace, 100–1. Cf. Murray, *Romans*, 2.33 n. 41, who seems to see his own suggestion of a genitive of purpose as equivalent to the sense of destination. Indeed, Wallace treats destination and purpose as the same, including them under the same genitival use, what he calls the genitive of destination or purpose.

[202] Godet, *Romans*, 360–1, which for him is a reference to the content of the vessels in keeping with the metaphor, ultimately meaning that the people represented by the figure of vessels will experience God's wrath. This would be a genitive of content, on which see Wallace, *Greek*, 92–4. But it is necessary neither to extend the metaphor nor the only conception that coheres with the metaphor, and few if any have followed Godet's suggestion.

[203] Murray, *Romans*, 2.33. This would be a genitive of purpose.

[204] Murray, ibid., makes this point based on parallelism with respect to sense 1, and Moo, *Romans*, 607 n. 98 (1st ed.), makes it with respect to sense 2. Perhaps the main reason in favor of sense 2 is that the exact same phrase, σκεύη ὀργῆς, is used with that sense in Jer. 27:25 LXX, and as Dunn, *Romans*, 559, points out, Isa. 13:5 Symmachus. But those texts are unrelated to Rom. 9:22 (though see Hanson, "Vessels," 443, for a rare affirmation that Paul had them in mind). Hanson's view (441) that σκεύη ὀργῆς refers to instruments that manifest God's wrath by either killing Jesus (his death being the supreme manifestation of God's mercy and wrath) or rejecting Christ, which brings God's wrath, seems strained. The suggestion that unbelievers are instruments of wrath by choosing to be objects of wrath due to unbelief is rather indirect and relies on suffering wrath as an essential element of most of the σκεύη ὀργῆς. Certainly the phrase in itself can bear sense 2. But it does not fit the context of Rom. 9:22, on which see the list of reasons supporting sense 3 detailed below; and cf. Jewett, *Romans*, 596, who points to the contextual factor of divine patience. On the meaning of "vessels of mercy" in 9:23, see our treatment of the verse later in this chapter.

God's wrath rests"[205]), in the future ("vessels destined for wrath"), or both.[206] Both present and future wrath are likely in view. Supporting the vessels as objects of wrath (the view of most interpreters) with both present and future wrath involved are the following: (i) that Paul is defending God's judgment upon unbelieving ethnic Israel; (ii) what we have seen about the eschatological nature of the language of wrath, glory, honor, dishonor, destruction, and so on that Paul is using in the context; (iii) that Paul has indicated earlier in the epistle that God's wrath is (presently) being revealed against sinful humanity (Rom. 1:18); (iv) that Paul elsewhere indicates that God's wrath has already come upon unbelieving Jews in some sense (1 Thess. 2:16); (v) that Paul has indicated earlier in the epistle that there will be an ultimate final judgment and pouring out of divine wrath (Rom. 2:5-16; 3:6; 5:9); (vi) the parallel expression, "a vessel ... unto dishonor" in 9:21, which clearly refers to a vessel that is an object of dishonor; and (vii) Paul describes these vessels of wrath as "prepared for destruction" (κατηρτισμένα εἰς ἀπώλειαν).

4.2.d.5. *The Voice and Agency of κατηρτισμένα*

The perfect middle/passive participle κατηρτισμένα (prepared) has been a matter of some debate, mostly focused on the questions of whether it is middle or passive and who performs its action. The main views are: (1) κατηρτισμένα is passive with it being implicit that God performs the action;[207] (2) κατηρτισμένα is passive with it being implicit

---

[205] Moo's (*Romans*, 607; 1st ed.) translation, though he still sees Paul as indicating that such vessels are "prepared by God for eternal condemnation." Moo probably did not intend this to carry a solely present focus, though he does set it against the translation "vessels destined for wrath." Dunn, ibid., thinks the sense is "vessels which are objects of God's wrath *now*" (emphasis mine); cf. E. Käsemann, *Commentary on Romans* (trans. G. W. Bromiley; Grand Rapids, MI: Eerdmans, 1980), 270.

[206] ὀργῆς (of wrath) is probably best construed as a qualitative genitive (so Moo, *Romans*, 625; BDF, § 165; Jewett, *Romans*, 596), which is a rather general and loose category (on the qualitative genitive, see BDF, § 165, and Wallace, *Greek*, 79-81, though he calls it the descriptive genitive). That would give the sense of "vessels characterized by wrath" for the phrase σκεύη ὀργῆς, without specifying the way in which wrath characterizes the vessels in view. In that case, the specific meaning needs articulation in exegesis. Wallace, 79 n. 24, notes that this type of genitive is especially possible when the head noun is figurative, which is what we have here in Rom. 9:22's σκεύη ὀργῆς (the head noun σκεύη [vessels] is clearly figurative). As noted earlier, Wallace, 101, argues for a genitive of destination/purpose in 9:22, but that leaves out the present wrath resting on the unbelieving. Wallace points to the parallel with "prepared for destruction" as support. And indeed, that does support an emphasis on future wrath. However, the vessels' resulting state of ripeness for destruction or God's act of preparing them is not itself future, but present and best considered part of, or intertwined with, God's wrath upon them. Oddly, Moo, 626 n. 281, classifies "destined for wrath" as representing the objective genitive; and Robertson, *Pictures*, s.v. Rom. 9:22, understands the meaning as "objects of God's wrath" and also classifies it as representing the objective genitive. But semantically, the objective genitive receives the action implicit in the head noun, not its own implicit action. Moo and Robertson's classification might be based on taking σκεύη as a verbal noun based on its cognate verb σκευάζω, but that seems strained since σκεύη's meaning is not determined by etymology. I agree that the meaning of the phrase is basically "vessels that are objects of wrath, vessels that receive wrath," but none of the typical genitive categories clearly yields this specific sense (see, e.g., the plethora of genitive categories in Wallace, 72-136).

[207] Held by most interpreters, e.g.: Hodge, *Romans*, 498; Käsemann, *Romans*, 271; Piper, *Romans*, 211-14; Dunn, *Romans*, 560; Moo, *Romans*, 607 (1st ed.), though he has changed his position in the

that the people represented by the vessels perform the action (prepare themselves);[208] (3) κατηρτισμένα is a direct middle and explicitly indicates that the people represented by the vessels perform the action (prepare themselves);[209] (4) κατηρτισμένα is passive with no explicit or implicit indication of the agent of the action;[210] (5) κατηρτισμένα, a perfect passive participle, does not refer to an act of preparing for destruction but to a state of preparation/readiness/ripeness for destruction, giving no indication of an agent of action.[211]

The least likely of these views is view 3 because it relies on the suggestion that Paul uses a direct middle when in Koiné (or Hellenistic) Greek usage of the direct middle was waning as it was replaced by usage of the reflexive active,[212] and in the New Testament, "the direct middle is quite rare and is used almost exclusively in certain idiomatic expressions, especially where the verb is used consistently with such a notion (as in the verbs for putting on clothes). This is decidedly not the case with καταρτίζω: nowhere else in the NT does it occur as a direct middle."[213] Indeed, even in classical Greek the direct middle was "limited to a small group of agentive verbs, which have in common that they denote a *habitual physical treatment*, i.e. a treatment which

---

2nd ed. (p. 627) to Paul deliberately leaving the agent of preparation an open question; Schreiner, *Romans*, 498; Seifrid, "Romans," 646; Kruse, *Romans*, 387.

[208] So John Chrysostom, "The Homilies of St. John Chrysostom, Archbishop of Constantinople, on the Epistle of St. Paul the Apostle to the Romans," in P. Schaff (ed.), *Nicene and Post-Nicene Fathers, Vol. 11: Chrysostom on the Acts of the Apostles and the Epistle to the Romans* (First Series; Peabody, MA: Hendrickson, 1995), 329–564 (468) (This is most likely Chrysostom's view, though he does not address the voice of the participle directly. It is possible that he held view 3. Moo, *Romans*, 627 n. 285, agrees that he held view 2.); Godet, *Romans*, 361; Morris, *Romans*, 368; Mounce, *Romans*, 202 n. 28 (seemingly). Lenski sees Satan as the agent of preparation, and Hendriksen holds it to be a combination of the people themselves and Satan (Morris, 368).

[209] So Strauss, "Romans 9," 200; Cottrell, *Romans*, 126; Prat (cited by Moo, ibid.). Piper, *Romans*, 211, attributes this position to Bengel, but he actually seems to have held view 4 below. Wallace, *Greek*, 417, attributes the view to Chrysostom, but it seems more likely that he held view 2. On the direct middle, see Wallace, 416–18; A. T. Robertson, *A Grammar of the Greek New Testament in the Light of Historical Research*, 3rd ed. (London: Hodder & Stoughton, 1919), 806–8; cf. A. Rijksbaron, *The Syntax and the Semantics of the Verb in Classical Greek: An Introduction*, 3rd ed. (Chicago: University of Chicago Press, 2002), § 43.

[210] Sanday and Headlam, *Romans*, 261–2; Wright, "Romans," 642. K. Müller fits here, whose view Piper, ibid., states as being that "the passive is intended to express a mystery no human can break through."

[211] Cranfield, *Romans*, 495–6; Leenhardt, *Romans*, 258 n. †; Fitzmyer, *Romans*, 570; Byrne, *Romans*, 302, 305–6 (seemingly). This does not mean that the other passive views would not recognize the vessels to be in a state of preparation based on the perfect tense. Nor does it mean that this view excludes action that results in the state of preparation. But it takes Paul to be directing attention to the state rather than the act. Grammatically, this would be classified as either an intensive (or resultative) perfect or a present perfect (on these uses of the perfect, see Wallace, *Greek*, 574–6 and 579–80, respectively). Puzzlingly, Schreiner, *Romans*, 498 (cf. similarly, Wallace, 418), following G. Delling, "καταρτίζω," *TDNT*, 1.476 n. 2, claims that "there is no philological basis for translating the word [καταρτίζω] as 'ripe' or 'ready.'" This is a surprising claim. One of καταρτίζω's basic meanings is "to prepare, make ready" (see *ALGNT*, s.v. καταρτίζω, 2; *BDAG*, s.v. καταρτίζω, 2). The perfect tense is commonly used to denote a state (especially in the participle; see B. F. Fanning, *Verbal Aspect in New Testament Greek* [Oxford: Clarendon, 1990], 416). And the passive leaves the agent of the action unspecified. Therefore, "ready" or "ripe" is a perfectly valid and natural translation.

[212] Wallace, *Greek*, 415–16.

[213] Ibid., 418.

forms part of the more or less normal practice of everyday life (also called verbs of *grooming*)."[214] And καταρτίζω does not fit into that limited group of verbs.[215]

Typically, the chief textual support cited for thinking either that no agent of preparation is implied (views 4 and 5) or that the people who are the vessels of wrath are themselves the implied agents (view 2) is the difference in the language Paul uses to describe the preparation (or preparedness) of the vessels of wrath for destruction versus the preparation of the vessels of mercy for glory. Concerning the preparation (or preparedness) of the vessels of wrath for destruction in v. 22 he uses the perfect passive of καταρτίζω without explicit indication of an agent of action, whereas concerning the preparation of the vessels of mercy for glory in v. 23 he uses the aorist active indicative προ-compound προητοίμασεν with explicit indication of God as the agent who performs the action of preparing. The difference is striking. The suggestion by the views that hold that no agent of preparation is implied is that Paul does not identify an agent of action because he did not intend one to be identified; when he wants to indicate an agent of action in 9:23, he does so explicitly. Some argue that Paul's use of the προ-compound verb προητοίμασεν in the aorist active indicative in 9:23 conveys divine predetermination in contrast to Paul's avoidance of the προ-compound version (προκαταρτίζω) of the verb he uses of preparation here in 9:22 (καταρτίζω) in a passive participle, a προ-compound verb he knew and used in 2 Cor. 9:5, suggesting that 9:22 does not refer to divine predetermination/action.[216]

But the flow of Paul's argument and the Old Testament background lead to the conclusion that God is the primary if not the sole agent of preparing the vessels of wrath for destruction. Paul is still responding to an objection to his quotation of Exod. 9:16 in Rom. 9:17 and his application of it in Rom. 9:18. That objection is in essence an objection to God's right to judge those whose unbelief he uses to glorify himself, particularly in this context, unbelieving Jews. Since Paul is defending God's right to judge Israel, that judgment is destruction here in 9:22, and preparation of that judgment is also mentioned here, it seems likely that God is to be thought of as preparing that judgment. Moreover, God's judgment on Pharaoh stands partly behind the notion of the vessels of wrath here. And God is surely the primary one who prepared destruction

---

[214] Rijksbaron, *Verb*, § 43.1.
[215] Wallace, *Greek*, 418, adds that, "in the perfect tense, the middle-passive form is always to be taken as passive in the NT (Luke 6:40; 1 Cor 1:10; Heb 11:3)—a fact that, in the least, argues against an idiomatic use of this verb as a direct middle." But he must be speaking of the middle-passive form of καταρτίζω specifically, and then that is hardly different from pointing out that the other three uses of the word in the perfect middle-passive form are passive. It does not itself really preclude or even argue strongly against an idiomatic usage of κατηρτισμένα in this instance, nor is such a small number of unified uses strong evidence against a different use in this case.
[216] So Cranfield, *Romans*, 495; Leenhardt, *Romans*, 258 n. †; cf. Jewett, *Romans*, 596; Morris, *Romans*, 368, who does not explain, but does cite absence "of anything equivalent to the prefix for 'before'" as one of the differences that suggest that the people rather than God did the preparing. But this distinction does not seem to hold up; see below, where we will argue that both refer to a form of predestination, but not an absolute/unconditional kind. Jewett's remark that καταρτίζω in the perfect passive "implies action subsequent to the original creation of the vessels" is curious. The context and background imply this, but neither the grammar nor the word itself does. Dunn's (*Romans*, 559) appeal to a basic sense of the word that implies action performed on something already in existence misses that the word's range of meaning is broader and includes the meaning "to create"; see BDAG, s.v. καταρτίζω, 2; Heb. 10:5; 11:3.

for Pharaoh. Furthermore, as Paul responds to the objection, he invokes the potter/clay metaphor, alluding to Jeremiah's use of it, which Jeremiah employed to argue for God's right to judge sinful Israel. And again, in Jeremiah, God is clearly the one who prepares destruction for Israel (or whichever nation walks contrary to his will).

On the other hand, while the judgment/destruction is clearly God's doing, it could be argued that the passive participle is used in v. 22 of the preparation for destruction without explicit indication of divine agency in contrast to use of the active indicative of preparation for glory in v. 23 with its explicit indication of divine agency because, although it is God who will destroy the vessels of wrath, it is not God who prepares them for destruction, but something the vessels of wrath do to themselves. This finds solid support from earlier in Romans when Paul indicated that God's patience (μακροθυμία) is meant to lead to repentance (2:4), "but because of your hardness [cf. the language of hardening in 9:18] and unrepentant heart, you are storing up wrath against yourself on the day of wrath and revelation of the righteous judgment of God" (2:5). Storing up wrath against oneself for the day of God's wrath is a form of preparing oneself for destruction. The concept of patience in both contexts (2:4-5 and 9:22) is noteworthy. In harmony with 2:4-5, it may well be here in 9:22 that, while God's patience was meant to give the opportunity for repentance, continuing in hard-heartedness and unbelief prepares the vessels of wrath for destruction by storing up wrath against themselves, which God will unleash on the day of judgment.

Both of these views that understand an implicit agent for the passive participle κατηρτισμένα, whether God or the vessels/people, have good support, and it is hard to decide between them. But in light of all that we have said, if pushed to choose one, God as the agent seems more likely. The context of defending God's judgment on unbelieving ethnic Israel and the Old Testament background of God preparing judgment weigh more heavily in my judgment than the evidence in favor of the vessels preparing themselves for destruction. However, taking God as the implicit agent of preparation requires an explanation of the difference in Paul's language in describing the preparation of the vessels of wrath in 9:22 versus his description of God's preparation of the vessels of mercy in 9:23.

Perhaps the best explanation that has been given from the God-as-the-agent view is that the difference in language reflects that wrath is subordinate to mercy in God's desires and purpose.[217] This accords with the typical view that the purpose clause of 9:23 articulates God's primary purpose in the actions spoken of in 9:22-23.[218] That is quite possible and reasonable and, in my view, the most likely explanation if God is regarded as the only agent of preparation. But I would suggest a view that is not normally considered and that we have not yet discussed—that both God and the vessels are the implicit agents of preparation.

The view that both God and the vessels are the implicit agents of preparation is supported by there being such good support for each (i.e., God or the vessels) as being the agent (see the discussion above). It is further supported by the Old Testament background. Although we pointed to the Old Testament background as supporting

---

[217] One possibility mentioned by Piper, *Justification*, 213–14; cf. Schreiner, *Romans*, 499.
[218] On the purpose clause of 9:23 as primary, see, e.g., Cranfield, *Romans*, 496.

the God-as-the agent view due to its depiction of God as preparing judgment, it is also true that the Old Testament background in a way also depicts Pharaoh in Exodus and Israel in Jeremiah as preparing themselves for destruction. In Pharaoh's case, it was by his hardening his own heart and his persistent, stubborn rebellion against the Lord in the face of repeated warnings and experiences of judgment. In Israel's case in Jeremiah, it was much the same even if the language of hardening their own hearts is not explicitly used (though cf. Jer. 5:3, "they have made their faces harder than rock"; 6:28). In Isaiah's (3:9) and Jeremiah's (2:17, 19; 4:18) language, Pharaoh and Israel did evil to themselves because their sin provoked God to wrath against them. In Paul's language in Romans (2:5), they were storing up wrath against themselves.

Now there is a greater stress on God preparing Pharaoh and Israel for destruction in the Old Testament background than on Pharaoh and Israel preparing themselves for destruction. But both themes are present. And that suggests that the same may be true here in Rom. 9:22, including a greater stress on God's agency while multiple agencies are in view. Multiple agents (God and the vessels) would also explain the use of the passive. Specifically identifying multiple agents would be obtrusive and unnecessarily complicate an already extremely complex sentence when the most primary agent is already obvious enough from the context and background.[219] Additionally, I would suggest that in contrast to the use of the προ-compound verb προετοιμάζω of 9:23, Paul uses καταρτίζω in 9:22 (in the perfect tense) instead of the προ-compound version of the word (προκαταρτίζω) because Paul has in mind that God's wrath rests on the vessels of wrath in the present along with its culmination in a future, final outpouring of wrath on what Paul calls "the day of wrath and revelation of the righteous judgment of God" (2:5).

4.2.d.6. Destruction and the Nature of Preparation for It

Most interpreters of every stripe rightly agree that destruction here refers to final eschatological judgment, whether in the form of some sort of traditional notion of Hell,[220] which is most likely in my opinion, or in the form of annihilation.[221] But most commentators who regard God as the agent of preparation do not consider exactly what Paul means by preparation for destruction. On the other hand, a view of the nature of the preparation is built into the vessels-as-agents view: the people prepare themselves for destruction by their sin and impenitence, which makes them increasingly fit for the destruction God will inflict on them in his wrath. Since I am arguing that both God and the vessels are in view as agents of preparation for the vessels' destruction, I would affirm that this is part of the nature of the preparation. That also implies at least one

---

[219] Wallace, *Greek*, 435–8, discusses various reasons for the lack of an expressed agent with the passive. Two reasons particularly relevant for this context that he mentions are that the agent is obvious in the context (435–6) and that "An explicit agent would sometimes be obtrusive or would render the sentence too complex, perhaps reducing the literary effect" (436; emphasis removed).

[220] So, e.g., Piper, *Justification*, 201–2; Schreiner, *Romans*, 498; A. Oepke, "ἀπώλεια," *TDNT*, 1.396–97 (397).

[221] So, e.g., Jewett, *Romans*, 596; Dunn, *Romans*, 560 (seemingly and cautiously).

aspect of what God does to prepare the vessels of wrath for destruction—marking their wickedness and impenitence and storing up his wrath against them accordingly.

One might question if this process of preparation fits with the text since Paul uses a perfect participle (κατηρτισμένα) to describe the prepared state of the vessels of wrath, indicating a previous act of preparation with the continuing result of a prepared state. Daniel Wallace seems to be getting at something along these lines when he states that "the lexical nuance of καταρτίζω, coupled with the perfect tense, suggests something of a 'done deal.'"[222] He regards the lexical nuance of καταρτίζω to be *complete* preparation, but that is dubious.[223] But more to the point here, the perfect tense does not address the internal nature of the action, whether it was instantaneous or a process. Nor does it address whether further preparation could be made. It merely describes the prepared state of the vessels as the result of previous action.

On the other hand, any further preparation that might be made is not comprehended in the perfect participle. That would have to be inferred from the context and the nature of the preparation it suggests as it gets applied to the present. Paul speaks of God's patience in the past using the aorist indicative (endured/ἤνεγκεν). But it seems evident that Paul would have regarded this as a continuing phenomenon, not only that God endured the vessels of wrath in the past (the focus of what he says in the text) but that he continues to endure them (application of the past phenomenon he describes to the present), and so any prepared state in the present would then include any further preparation. There is in fact a gnomic quality to what Paul describes in 9:22-23. But if this approach is judged implausible, I would point out that even though I think it is part of the preparation in view, I neither regard it as essential to understanding the text nor as the primary sense of the text.

The Old Testament background can give us additional insight into the nature of the preparation for destruction of which Paul speaks. As mentioned, few who hold God to be the agent of preparation discuss how it is that God prepares the vessels for that fate. However, Piper does give the question attention, helpfully arguing that "since Paul's inference from the Pharaoh story is that 'God hardens whom he wills' (9:18), the most natural suggestion from the context is that 'fitted for destruction' (9:22) refers precisely to this divine hardening."[224] However, my understanding of Paul's conception of divine hardening differs markedly from Piper's. Whereas he understands it to be a matter of God irresistibly causing people to stubbornly resist God and the gospel, I have argued it is best understood in relation to ethnic Israel and as resistible provocation unto stubborn resistance to God and the gospel by means of God making faith in Christ apart from works or ancestry the exclusive basis of covenant membership.[225] That better accords with the manner of hardening in the narrative of Exodus, which portrays God as normally hardening Pharaoh by indirect, natural, strategic actions

---

[222] Wallace, *Greek*, 418.
[223] See the lexicons, e.g., BDAG, s.v. καταρτίζω.
[224] Piper, *Justification*, 212.
[225] See Abasciano, *Romans 9.10-18*, 203–10. Of course, this element of preparation would not apply to Gentiles even though unbelieving Gentiles are surely among the vessels of wrath. As Paul defends God's rejection of unbelieving Jews and his election of believing Gentiles, his focus is naturally on Jews with respect to the vessels of wrath.

such as withdrawing a given plague.[226] Thus, another part of God's preparation of the vessels of wrath for destruction is his making faith in Christ apart from works or ancestry the exclusive basis of covenant membership.

But the primary and most basic aspect of God preparing the vessels of wrath for destruction is suggested by the Jeremian context of Paul's potter/clay metaphor in Rom. 9:21. In Jeremiah, God prepares the objects of his wrath for destruction by slating them for destruction. Jeremiah 18:7 speaks of it as God declaring "concerning a nation or concerning a kingdom to uproot and to tear down and to destroy," 18:8 speaks of it as God intending calamity against a nation, and 18:11 speaks of it as fashioning calamity against Israel and devising a plan against Israel.[227] This is not some form of absolute predesitination. It is a form of divine predestination or, perhaps more technically, a form of divine reprobation—God setting a destiny of destruction for the objects of his wrath. But it is a conditional reprobation that can change upon repentance to a predestination unto blessing and glory, which suggests the same of the preparation of which Paul speaks here in Rom. 9:22. It is slating the vessels of wrath for destruction, though they can repent and become vessels of mercy (which are mentioned in 9:23) until the day of wrath finally comes.

This primary sense of preparation is supported by the immediate context. As we have seen, Rom. 9:22-23 interprets and applies 9:20-21. And 9.20-21 speaks of God as molding and making pottery (a figure for Israel and others), which finds an obvious parallel in God preparing vessels of wrath and vessels of mercy. The language of molding and making carries the sense of consigning to eschatological honor/blessing or dishonor/condemnation. The preparation spoken of in 9:22-23 is to be understood in the same sense, indeed, as a different expression of the same reality, now in terms of preparation and wrath and mercy.

4.2.d.7. How Do God's Desire to Show His Wrath and His Patient Endurance of the Vessels of Wrath Fit Together?

Having examined all of 9:22, we are now in a position to resume consideration of the question of how it is that God's desire to show his wrath contributed to his patiently enduring the vessels of wrath. We have already said that part of Paul's thought seems to be that God's desire to show his wrath was partly motivated by his greater desire to make his power known in salvation since his plan to save the world required faith in Christ apart from works or ancestry as the condition of covenant membership and its salvation, which naturally resulted in judgment/rejection of those who reject Christ (see Section 4.2.d.3.b). But the context of Romans and the Old Testament background offer further insights into Paul's thought here.

We have already seen that, in light of Rom. 2:5, the preparation of the vessels of wrath includes (1) their own continuing sin and impenitence, which stores up wrath

---

[226] See ibid., chapter 2; see ibid., 138–40, for a summary.
[227] Interestingly, some translations of Jer. 18:11 use the language of preparation for God's fashioning of calamity against Israel; so NIV; NET; NJB; L. C. L. Brenton's (*The Septuagint with Apocrypha* [London: Samuel Bagster, 1851], BibleWorks, v. 8) translation of the LXX.

that God will inflict on them at the final judgment; and (2) God consequently marking their wickedness and impenitence and storing up his wrath against them accordingly. Hence, it may be that God's desire to show his wrath motivates him to restrain his wrath temporarily because doing so allows for a greater expression of his wrath given that his patience with the vessels of wrath allows them to store up more and more divine wrath against themselves for the final judgment.[228] Indeed, that seems to be the case, for that is similar to God's actions toward Pharaoh referred to by Rom. 9:17/Exod. 9:16, which is a major part of the background to Rom. 9:22, as we have repeatedly observed. In the Exodus context, God patiently endured Pharaoh and his rebellion by allowing him to continue living, that is, by restraining his fatal wrath, and he did so in order to pour out his wrath more fully upon Pharaoh in additional plagues until the greatest display of his wrath in the conflict would come in the final plague and the destruction of Pharaoh's army. Thus, it seems that Paul is indicating that at least part of God's purpose in patiently enduring the vessels of wrath is to pour out his wrath upon them more fully on the day of judgment in order to best express his sovereign power and righteous character.

But earlier we concluded that part of God's purpose in patiently enduring the vessels of wrath was to lead them to repentance and see them saved, making them vessels of mercy. For, as we have argued, making his power known includes both judgment *and salvation*. Moreover, the next verse (9:23) adds another, climactic purpose to God's patient endurance of the vessels of wrath, and that is to make known the riches of God's glory upon vessels of mercy. Furthermore, as Paul's argument develops, he reveals that (1) his ministry seeks to win those who are currently vessels of wrath to repentance, and so to become vessels of mercy;[229] and (2) God's overarching purpose is "that he might have mercy on all" (11:32). Just as in 2:4, God's patience gives sinners under God's wrath the opportunity to repent, an expression of kindness and forbearance that leads to repentance, which, if exercised, takes the sinners from being under God's wrath to receiving his mercy. But how do these two seemingly opposite purposes of

---

[228] This, along with the previous observation mentioned in the previous paragraph, explains the feasibility of what Witherington, *Romans*, 257, finds hard to imagine—"Paul saying that God endured the vessels of wrath *because* he wanted to show forth his wrath." Piper, *Justification*, 209-10, appeals to 4 Ezra 7:72-74, 2 Macc. 6:12-14, and 1 Macc. 8:1-4, as examples of divine patience meaning "patiently holding back judgment with a view to a greater display of wrath and power" (209). But none of them are valid examples. What the former two are actually examples of is, to use Piper's words, "God being patient with man for some reason other than man's good" (ibid.), while the latter is an example of human patience as a means to conquest. It is not even clear if the notion of patience in 1 Macc. 8:4 involves the idea of restraint of military attack "to secure a greater victory later," or more likely, if it is rather a way of referring to perseverance and/or accepting limitations along the way in a long-term effort of conquest. Thus, while I agree with Piper in that I think that part of the meaning (though Piper thinks it is the whole meaning) of God's patience in Rom. 9:22 is "patiently holding back judgment with a view to a greater display of wrath and power," his appeal to these ancient texts as examples of the idea in Paul's ancient Jewish milieu falls short and does not add much to his case. They are worth noting for comparison but are not examples of the same idea.

[229] One might object to characterizing Paul's later remarks in this way. But it is quite fitting. As we have already mentioned in discussion of 9:22, in Paul's theology unbelievers are under the wrath of God in the present and slated for the ultimate outpouring of his wrath in the future on the day of judgment. Cf. Eph. 2:3 and discussion of it below.

judgment/wrath and mercy/salvation fit together toward the same vessels, the vessels of wrath? Can they fit together?

Some interpreters insist that they cannot fit together, and that the two categories, vessels of wrath and vessels of mercy, are absolute and unchangeable.[230] Schreiner maintains that "the μέν ... δέ ... construction in verse 21 confirms that the two kinds of vessels must be kept distinct."[231] Similarly, Moo invokes "the sharp contrast Paul draws in these verses between the vessels of wrath and the vessels of mercy," and argues that "This contrast would be unfairly diminished ... if we were to assume that the vessels of wrath could have the same ultimate destiny as the vessels of mercy."[232] But this line of argument misses the mark.

The suggestion that a vessel of wrath can change from a vessel of wrath into a vessel of mercy does not in any way compromise the distinctness or contrast between the two kinds of vessels. It does not imply that the vessels of wrath and the vessels of mercy have the same ultimate destiny. The vessels of wrath will suffer wrath/destruction, and the vessels of mercy will receive mercy/glory/salvation. But that does not gainsay that before the day of judgment a vessel of wrath could cease being a vessel of wrath with the accompanying destiny and become a vessel of mercy with the accompanying destiny. In that case, since the former vessel of wrath would no longer be a vessel of wrath, it would not share the fate of the vessels of wrath, but as a vessel of mercy would share the fate of the vessels of mercy. Those who remain vessels of wrath would indeed suffer wrath and destruction on the day of judgment. And those who remain vessels of mercy would receive the glory and blessing promised to the vessels of mercy.

The point can be demonstrated by considering an analogous case. In Pauline thought, there is a radical distinction and contrast between believers/the saved and unbelievers/the lost. But that distinction/contrast is not compromised or lessened in any way by the Pauline belief that an unbeliever can go from unbelief and condemnation to faith and justification and salvation. Indeed, in Eph. 2:1-5, which we cite because of its similar terminology, Paul indicates that believers were "children of wrath" prior to conversion and in a state of salvation and spiritual life after conversion.[233] Yet, surely the two categories of unbeliever/lost and believer/saved remain distinct along with the respective destinies accompanying each one. Numerous Pauline texts could be cited for similar examples, but this should suffice to make the point.

Schreiner adds another argument, boldly asserting in regard to the possibility of the vessels of wrath later becoming vessels of mercy that "The text rules this out explicitly

---

[230] See Moo, *Romans*, 626; Schreiner, *Romans*, 499.
[231] Schreiner, ibid.
[232] Moo, *Romans*, 626.
[233] Notice the similar terminology to that of Rom. 9:22-23 clustering in the context of Eph. 2:3: "children of wrath" (τέκνα ... ὀργῆς, 2:3) (most notably), "mercy" (ἔλεος, 2:4), to "show" (ἐνδείκνυμι, 2:7) divine "riches" (πλοῦτος, 2:7; cf. πλούσιος in 2:4), and "to prepare beforehand" (προετοιμάζω, 2:10); cf. also the use of ἐπί in Eph. 2:7 and Rom. 9:23 (see n. 263 below). Of course, there is debate over the Pauline authorship of Ephesians, which I hold to. But even if one is inclined to reject Pauline authorship, Ephesians may still be regarded as faithful to Paul's teaching. H. Hoehner, *Ephesians* (Grand Rapids, MI: Baker, 2002), 2-61, is notable for providing an extensive defense of the Pauline authorship of Ephesians; see also P. T. O'Brien, *The Letter to the Ephesians* (PNTC; Grand Rapids, MI: Eerdmans, 1999), 4-47.

by describing the vessels of wrath as 'prepared for destruction.'"[234] This is a baffling assertion. It is not at all evident that God having prepared the vessels of wrath for destruction means that they could not be changed from vessels of wrath, who would be destroyed, to vessels of mercy, who would not be destroyed but saved. Schreiner would need to explain why it is that God could not change his preparation of a vessel of wrath.

On the other hand, the actual meaning of God preparing the vessels of wrath that we have seen favors the possibility of vessels of wrath later becoming vessels of mercy. All three aspects we identified of God's preparation of the vessels of wrath are consistent with the vessels being changed to vessels of mercy at a later time prior to the day of final judgment. First, according to Paul's gospel, God marking the wickedness and impenitence of unbelievers and storing up his wrath against them accordingly would change to him not counting their sin against them, forgiveness, and justification if they become believers in Christ (see Romans 3–4). Second, the resistible nature of divine hardening allows for its reversal. Some hardened Jews might have initially been hardened to the gospel due to its offensiveness in making faith in Christ apart from works or ancestry the exclusive basis of covenant membership, but eventually turn from their hard-heartedness to faith in Christ, going from vessels of wrath to vessels of mercy.

Third, the most fundamental aspect of God's preparation of the vessels of wrath—his slating them for destruction—argues strongly for the possibility of vessels of wrath becoming vessels of mercy. For that meaning of preparation emerges from Jeremiah's use of the potter/clay metaphor to which Paul alludes in Rom. 9:21, and one of the main points of that passage is precisely that God will change his slating of his or any people for destruction upon repentance. Indeed, the point is used by Jeremiah to urge Israel's repentance and with the strong implication that Israel can indeed repent and thereby escape God's wrath, which only adds to Israel's wickedness and culpability if they refuse to repent.

Nonetheless, we are still left with the question of how the two purposes of judgment/wrath and mercy/salvation fit together toward the vessels of wrath. Here, too, the Jeremiah background is instructive. In the Jeremiah passage, God desires most that his people would repent and be saved from his wrath rather than continue in their rebellion and perish, though he does desire to bring calamitous judgment upon them if they will not repent. This sort of sentiment can be seen throughout the Bible. Ezekiel provides some especially striking examples:[235]

> "Do I have any pleasure in the death of the wicked," declares the Lord GOD, "rather than that he should turn from his ways and live?" (Ezek. 18:23)

> "Cast away from you all your transgressions which you have committed and make yourselves a new heart and a new spirit! For why will you die, O house of Israel? For I have no pleasure in the death of anyone who dies," declares the Lord GOD. 'Therefore, repent and live." (Ezek. 18:31-32)

---

[234] Schreiner, *Romans*, 499.
[235] These quotations from Ezekiel are from the NASB.

Say to them, "As I live!" declares the Lord GOD, "I take no pleasure in the death of the wicked, but rather that the wicked turn from his way and live. Turn back, turn back from your evil ways! Why then will you die, O house of Israel?" (Ezek. 33:11)

The same sort of impulse can be seen in Rom. 2:4-5, which we, along with most scholars, have already found important for shedding light on 9:22: "Or do you despise the riches of his kindness and forbearance and patience, disregarding that the kindness of God leads you to repentance? But because of your hardness and unrepentant heart, you are storing up wrath against yourself on the day of wrath and revelation of the righteous judgment of God." Here we see that God's patience toward sinners has the purpose of bringing them to repentance.[236] The implication is that their repentance and the divine mercy that would follow upon it is God's preference over judgment. However, if repentance does not occur, then God's desire is to pour out on the unrepentant all the wrath that they deserve, so much so that, as they continue in their sin, he stores it up against them for the final judgment. That is the flip side of the unrepentant storing up wrath against themselves. In other words, what their storing up wrath against themselves means is that their behavior leads God to store up his wrath against them.[237]

Piper argues that "leading" (ἄγω) in Rom. 2:4 should be understood as pointing to repentance in the sense that "everything in nature (Rom 1:18-23; Acts 14:17) and history (Acts 17:26f) and the human conscience (Rom 2:15) is pointing (i.e. 'leading') men to repentance and faith," and there being opportunity to repent (apparently without a purpose for all who are so led to repent).[238] But first, it is hard to see how there is a genuine opportunity for the hardened to repent on Piper's view, since it holds that God prevents them from repenting. Second, Paul never uses the word in the way Piper suggests. As Murray comments, "The assertion that the goodness of God leads to repentance must not be weakened to mean merely that it points us to repentance. The word 'lead' must be given its true force of conducting (cf. 8:14; 1 Cor. 12:2; 1 Thes. 4:14; 2 Tim. 3:6)."[239] To these references, we should add Gal. 5:18 and 2 Tim. 4:11 (cf. Heb. 2:10). Moreover, it is questionable whether the word was ever used by anyone in the weak way Piper suggests. Most scholars now seem rightly to read a conative present here, which indicates an action being attempted but not (yet) completed/successful (and might or might not end up completed/successful).[240]

This presents a problem for those, like Piper, who think Paul teaches unconditional election and irresistible permanent hardening in Romans 9. For Rom. 2:4's indication

---

[236] As most interpreters recognize; so, e.g., Moo, *Romans*, 144; Black, *Romans*, 45; Murray, *Romans*, 1.59-60; Cranfield, *Romans*, 144-5; Witherington, *Romans*, 81; Hodge, *Romans*, 75; Osborne, *Romans*, 61; cf. Piper, *Justification*, 208, who seems to recognize this to be the natural surface reading of the text, but see below.
[237] Cf. Kruse, *Romans*, 122-3.
[238] Piper, *Justification*, 208.
[239] Murray, *Romans*, 1.59-60.
[240] So, e.g., Morris, *Romans*, 113 n. 30, who also cites Moule in agreement; Black, *Romans*, 45; Moo, *Romans*, 144 n. 227. On the conative present, see Wallace, *Greek*, 534-5, who lists Rom. 2:4 as an example; BDF, § 319.

of God's purpose that vessels of wrath repent combined with the notion of God irresistibly preventing their repentance through divine hardening has God purposing two mutually exclusive outcomes, impenitence and wrath versus repentance and mercy. Some theologians resort to a theory of God having two wills (one that is revealed, and a secret one that supersedes the revealed one when they conflict, always comes to pass, and brings about all that happens) to defend the doctrine of exhaustive divine determinism in the face of biblical affirmation of God's desire for all to be saved. That is a dubious position in my judgment.[241]

But even if one were to grant the legitimacy of the two wills theory, purpose is a different matter. While it makes sense that God has conflicting desires (though I would argue that the two wills theory presses the idea beyond coherence), God holding mutually exclusive purposes toward the same situation is not reasonable. Moreover, a two purposes theory contradicts a fundamental premise of Piper's conception of God's sovereignty (exhaustive divine determinism) that God always accomplishes his purpose. There is good reason for the fact that there is no such thing as a "two purposes of God" theory; it is simply not tenable.[242]

The best argument against the possibility of vessels of wrath being changed into vessels of mercy is from the Old Testament background of the divine hardening of Pharaoh's heart. We have already seen that Paul's reference to God's patience with the vessels of wrath develops his earlier reference in 9:17 to God forestalling his final judgment on Pharaoh (quoting Exod. 9:16). Yet the Old Testament context does not show any particular concern for Pharaoh to repent and be changed from a vessel of wrath into a vessel of mercy. In fact, as we observed earlier, God's patience toward Pharaoh was so that he could continue to pour out wrath on him in additional plagues culminating in the destruction of the Egyptian forces in the Red Sea.[243] But we have considered this in our treatment of Rom. 9:18 and concluded that the details of the Old Testament context do not stand against the possibility of, in the language of Rom. 9:22-23, vessels of wrath being changed into vessels of mercy, but actually supports it.[244] In addition to what is said there, we can now add that there is additional Old Testament background that strongly supports the possibility, the Jeremiah 18 background, discussed above.

---

[241] Piper, *Justification*, 192, appeals to the two wills theory in his discussion of 9:19. He argues for the theory at length in John Piper, "Are There Two Wills in God?" in T. R. Schreiner and B. A. Ware (eds.), *Still Sovereign: Contemporary Perspectives on Election, Foreknowledge, and Grace* (Grand Rapids, MI: Baker, 2000), 107–31. For a concise, incisive, and compelling critique of Piper's view, see T. H. McCall, "We Believe in God's Sovereign Goodness: A Rejoinder to John Piper," *TJ* 29/2 (Fall 2008), 235–46 (240–3.)

[242] Piper, *Justification*, 208, appeals to God's dealings with Pharaoh to support his understanding of 2:4, but see below. He also appeals to Rom. 9:14-23, but that presupposes his interpretation of those verses, which our exegesis has found faulty in its relevant argumentation and conclusions; on one's exegesis of Romans 9 in prior verses determining exegesis of later verses, cf. note 28 above.

[243] Some would add that God irresistibly hardened Pharaoh, causing him to rebel against the Lord and suffer his wrath. However, we have argued that the hardening of the Old Testament background was not irresistible; see Abasciano, *Romans 9.10-18*, 75–140, on the Old Testament context, and then 200–19 for discussion in application to the context of Romans 9.

[244] See ibid., 212.

4.2.d.8. Romans 9:23

4.2.d.8.a. Indications of Emphasis

The conjunction καί (and) at the beginning of v. 23 is awkward.[245] This comes through in English with a formal equivalence translation of 9:22-23: "²² But if God, desiring to show his wrath and to make known his power, endured with much patience vessels of wrath prepared for destruction, ²³ and in order that he might make known the riches of his glory upon vessels of mercy, which he prepared beforehand for glory." But I would suggest that this awkwardness is not accidental. It brings emphasis to what Paul now says as it draws attention to it.

We noted earlier that the participial clause of 9:22 is most likely causal, which makes the infinitive phrases of 9:22 ("to show his wrath and to make known his power") join conceptually with the purpose clause of 9:23 as purposes God sought to accomplish by enduring the vessels of wrath rather than bringing destruction on them immediately (see Section 4.2.d.3.a). But the indication of purpose in v. 22, communicated by a participle open to more than one interpretation, is subtler than in v. 23. The purpose clause in 9:23 is clearer in its expression of purpose, employing a ἵνα clause. It is also separated from the purpose clause of 9:22 by substantial intervening material. The connective καί beginning 9:23 picks up the idea of purpose again, resulting in the awkward syntax before us.[246] Moreover, as Cranfield observes, the purpose clause of 9:23 "is extended by means of the two relative clauses which follow," receives further attention from vv. 25–29, and is marked off from the purposes mentioned in 9:22 by its content, "for the manifestation of the wealth of the divine glory is nothing less than the ultimate purpose of God."[247] Indeed, its content is also tied into what has been called the keyword and keynote of Romans 9–11—mercy.[248] All of this brings emphasis to the purpose clause of 9:23, suggesting it to be God's chief purpose in his patient endurance of the vessels of wrath.[249] Furthermore, if, as we have argued, 9:22's reference to making God's power known includes God's saving activity as part of its meaning, then the purpose clause of 9:23 receives even more emphasis by isolating and repeating a salvific purpose to God's patient endurance of the vessels of wrath (making

---

[245] This is routinely recognized; see, e.g., Moo, *Romans*, 609 n. 191; Cranfield, *Romans*, 496 n. 4; Jewett, *Romans*, 587 n. f.; Morris, *Romans*, 368.

[246] Cranfield, ibid., thinks that the stress on the purpose clause of v. 23 would be greater without the καί introducing it because it would stand by itself as a statement of purpose. However, that would still leave the expression of purpose in 9:22 intact and in need of explanation as to how it relates to the expression of purpose in 9:23. To my mind, the awkward syntax created by the addition of καί brings greater emphasis to the purpose clause than omitting καί would.

[247] Ibid.

[248] See ibid., 448; Dunn, *Romans*, 552; Barrett, *Romans*, 175; cf. L. Gaston, "Israel's Enemies in Pauline Theology," in L. Gaston, *Paul and the Torah* (Vancouver: University of British Columbia Press, 1987), 80–99 (97).

[249] I take all of this as intentional on Paul's part. But if not intentional, at the very least, it would still seem to reflect Paul's conception of the dominance of the purpose expressed in 9:23 among the purposes he mentions for God's patient endurance. In favor of the ultimacy of the purpose identified in 9:23, see Cranfield, *Romans*, 496-7, who regards this as clear; Piper, *Justification*, 188-9, who also notes that this is "generally recognized" (214).

known God's saving power in 9:22 and the riches of his glory in 9:23).[250] We need to consider the relationship between the purposes identified in 9:22-23 more specifically. But first we will discuss the meaning of the rest of v. 23 itself.

4.2.d.8.b. The Riches of His Glory

Verse 23 indicates that God's purpose in enduring the vessels of wrath was "to make known the riches of his glory upon vessels of mercy." Paul uses the same word for "to make known" that he did in v. 22—γνωρίζω. And just as there (see Section 4.2.d.3.b), it is likely that here it has in view not simply making information known, but carrying out an action that embodies what is to be made known. In v. 22, it was the exercise of God's power in judgment and salvation that made his power known. Here it is the bestowing of the riches of God's glory upon vessels of mercy that makes those riches known.

But what are "the riches of his [God's] glory" (τὸν πλοῦτον τῆς δόξης αὐτοῦ)? The term πλοῦτος (riches, wealth) is best taken here to refer to abundant blessing/benefit, a figurative extension of its meaning of an "abundance of many earthly goods."[251] This is benefit that comes from God's glory.[252]

---

[250] Paul's choice to use γνωρίζω (to make known) of God's power in 9:22 and glory in 9:23 accords with this observation.

[251] BDAG, s.v. πλοῦτος, 1, lists the more literal meaning but surprisingly does not list the figurative meaning mentioned above, which is quite obvious here, in line with Paul's usage elsewhere in Romans (2:4; 11:12, 33; cf. Eph. 1:7, 18; 2:7; 3:8, 16; Phil. 4:19; Col. 1:27; 2:2), each instance of which has some connection to the usage here (note the frequent reference made to 2:4 in our discussion of 9:22-23 and that the other uses occur within the same extended section of the epistle as 9:23 [Romans 9-11]). Instead, BDAG place Rom. 9:23 under another figurative extension of the former, viz. "plentiful supply of someth.," their meaning 2. But that does not work well here. It is not so much that God wants to make known an abundance of his glory, but that he wants to make known the abundant blessing that his glory is and bestows; cf. *NIDNTTE*, 3.798, which takes the reference to be to "spiritual riches." *ALGNT*, s.v. πλοῦτος, recognizes a meaning similar to the one we are suggesting in 9:23: "spiritual abundance or prosperity," though I would not restrict it to *spiritual* blessing (e.g., the resurrection of the body and inheritance of the New Earth would surely be part of the blessings that God's glory bestows). Interestingly, *ALGNT* cites Rom. 9:23 as an example of the term's usage followed by the genitive to mean something like "abundance of, great amount of, extreme value of something" (emphasis removed). But there is a significant difference between "abundance of, great amount of" (cf. BDAG's meaning 2) and "extreme value of." "Extreme value" is quite possible here but is hard to distinguish from abundant blessing/benefit because the latter is of extreme value and implies the former. Indeed, there is little difference between "value" and "benefit." The former is more abstract, and the latter is more concrete. When there is a noticeable difference between the two in Paul's usage, "benefit" seems to be the more fitting meaning (Rom. 11:12; Eph. 3:8; Phil. 4:19; Col. 2:2) and so is most likely here. H. Merklein, "πλοῦτος," *EDNT*, 3.114-17 (116), correctly speaks of Paul's characteristic usage of the word as theological.

[252] τῆς δόξης is most likely a genitive of source (or perhaps a genitive of production or possession); Moo, *Romans*, 627 n. 286, suggests it is epexegetical or partitive. B. M. Newman and E. A. Nida, *A Handbook on Paul's Letter to the Romans* (UBSHS; New York: UBS, 1973), 189, argue for what may be called an attributive genitive, rendering τὸν πλοῦτον τῆς δόξης αὐτοῦ as "his rich glory" (on the attributive genitive, see Wallace, *Greek*, 86-8). They assert that when an abstract noun is followed by a genitive, "the abstract noun should be interpreted as a qualifier of the noun which appears in the genitive." But this is not evident. In this case it would diminish the metaphor and vividness of Paul's thought. The difference between a subjective genitive or the like and an attributive genitive is brought out well in English translation in speaking of the revelation of "the riches of God's glory" vs. the revelation of "God's rich glory." The former conveys a greater sense of the multiple, magnificent, concrete benefits given to believers by God's glory and thereby gives a greater sense of the richness of God's glory. Cf. Moo, ibid., who rightly argues that "the importance of the concept

What, more specifically, are the riches bestowed by God's glory that are in view? Multiple lines of evidence suggest a complex reality that can be summed up by the Christian tradition's conception of Heaven, human experience of the fullness of all the goodness of the divine nature, the manifold perfections of God,[253] and all the good the almighty God has promised to those who belong to him. This is suggested in part by the nature of the divine glory. As we saw in the Old Testament background to Rom. 9:4-5, 15 (Exod. 32–34),[254] the glory of God refers to the very essence or presence of God in all its fullness, a reality of supreme worth, beauty, and magnificence roughly synonymous with the goodness of God.[255] This suggests that part of what is in view is a general sense of all the good that the awesome divine nature has to offer human beings.

Building on the meaning of the glory of God noted above, we found further that the chief significance of the glory of God in the Old Testament background was to denote God's covenant presence, which bestowed his covenant and election with all of the accompanying blessings.[256] Accordingly, we found Paul speaking earlier in Romans 9 of the glory of God as his manifest presence, which simultaneously establishes his covenant, confers his election, effects his adoption, and bequeaths his blessings.[257] In other words, in addition to the enjoyment of the essence or presence of God itself, the riches of God's glory include the covenant privileges of Israel listed in Rom. 9:4-5.[258]

In addition, we have seen that the glory of God is also used synonymously in the Old Testament background with the goodness and name of God.[259] This suggests further specific significance to the riches of God's glory because, while the name of God in the Old Testament background also refers generally to God and his presence, it includes a more specific sense of God's character as gracious and merciful and sovereign in his bestowal of mercy in the Old Testament background to Romans 9 (Exod. 32–34).[260]

---

of 'glory' in Paul (see esp. Rom. 2:7, 10; 3:23; 5:2; 8:17, 18, 30) and in this context (v. 23b) requires that we preserve its independent significance."

[253] I am indebted to John Piper for the phrase "manifold perfections" in describing the glory of God. See John Piper, *Desiring God*, rev. and exp. (Sisters: Multnomah, 2003), 42, 308; cf. 96.

[254] See Abasciano, *Romans 9.1-9*, 64–5, 124–7; cf. Abasciano, *Romans 9.10-18*, 199. Dunn, *Romans*, 560, thinks Paul here intended an allusion to Exod. 33:18-19 and its use of δόξα. That is plausible but might be going too far. It is probably more accurate to say that Paul is drawing on that same Old Testament background and would expect his audience to understand his use of the word against that background rather than that he is specifically alluding to Exod. 33:18-19. In either case, Exodus (I would say chs. 32–34) provides part of the background for understanding Paul's use of glory here. In light of the observation made above that the glory and name of God are used synonymously in the Exodus context, it is worth noting that the thought carries right on into Paul's quotation of Exod. 9:16 in Rom. 9:17, with its concern for the proclamation of God's name, and that the present verse is still part of Paul's response to the objection to his interpretation and application of Exod. 9:16 in Rom. 9:17-18.

[255] The external evidence for reading χρηστοτητος (i.e., P and (sy^p)) instead of δόξης is too weak to take the variant seriously. It is probably the result of the phrase τοῦ πλούτου τῆς χρηστότητος in Rom. 2:4, a verse we have seen to be highly relevant to 9:22-23.

[256] Abasciano, *Romans 9.1-9*, 64–5, 124–7.

[257] Ibid.

[258] On these, see ibid., 115–42.

[259] Ibid., 64–5, 124–7; Abasciano, *Romans 9.10-18*, 199.

[260] Ibid.

Thus, the riches of God's glory include the bestowal of his grace and mercy. And as we observed in our exegesis earlier in Romans 9, Paul has been speaking of God's mercy in the form of divine covenantal election,[261] confirming that nuance already observed above.

Paul's use of πλοῦτος (riches) elsewhere gives further insight. We have already seen the importance of Rom. 2:4-5 for understanding 9:22-23. It proves helpful again here as it speaks of "the riches of his [God's] kindness and forbearance and patience" in contrast to God's wrath and judgment and is followed by speaking of glory received from God in association with eschatological honor, immortality, eternal life, and peace (2:7, 10), which also brings to mind Paul's affirmation in 8:30 that the church will be glorified.[262] In 11:12, Paul uses the term "riches" to refer to salvation (cf. 11:11). In Ephesians, the glory of God's grace is associated with election (1:4), predestination to adoption, and the good intention of God's will (1:5), and the riches of God's grace are associated with redemption and the forgiveness of transgressions (1:7).[263] In Eph. 2:4-7, Paul speaks of God's great love and mercy flowing forth with the purpose of making known (using the same word as Rom. 9:22 in its reference to making known God's wrath—ἐνδείκνυμι) "in the coming ages the surpassing riches of his grace in kindness to us in Christ Jesus" (2:7). And in Eph. 3:16, with a focus on the present age, the riches of God's glory strengthen believers through God's Spirit in the inner man resulting in Christ dwelling through faith in their hearts, knowledge of God's infinite love, and being filled to all the fullness of God. Also with a focus on the present age, Phil. 4:19 promised the Philippian church that the riches of God's glory would meet their every need. All of this fills out some of the details of the general sense of the riches of God's glory as the experience of ultimate blessing provided by the full presence/essence of God. It includes covenantal election, adoption/sonship, honor, immortality, eternal life, glorification, and experience of God's grace, mercy, love, goodness, kindness, forgiveness, redemption, and more.

---

[261] Abasciano, *Romans 9.10-18*, 185; cf. Abasciano, *Romans 9.1-9*, 61–9, 106–15.

[262] There is some question of whether Rom. 8:30 really affirms the future glorification of the church because it refers to the past in its use of the aorist indicative. Moo, *Romans*, 536 (1st ed.), notes that "Most interpreters conclude … that Paul is looking at the believer's glorification from the standpoint of God, who has already decreed that it should take place." But positing a sudden shift from the human perspective to God's perspective seems ad hoc and unlikely. More likely, it is a proleptic aorist, stressing the certainty of the future action by speaking of it as if it has already happened; on the proleptic aorist, see, e.g., Wallace, *Greek*, 563–4. But it is more natural to read an actual past action if possible, especially given that all the other actions listed in the context are actual past actions (cf. Godet, *Romans*, 327). Taking account of the corporate character of the passage, it is perhaps best to take this in an already-and-not-yet sense, accounting for the past sense of the aorist indicative. It can be said that the church was glorified because her covenant head, Jesus Christ, has been fully glorified just as Paul can say that the church was seated with Christ in the heavenlies in Christ (Eph. 2:6; on the question of Paul's authorship of Ephesians, see note 233 above). At the same time, it can be said that the church has a significant degree of glory during the current age. As Paul mentions in 2 Cor. 3:18, as believers behold the glory of the Lord (in the present), they are increasingly transformed into his image "from glory to glory," transformation that is said to be from the Spirit, whom Peter calls "the Spirit of glory"; cf. Jn 17:22, where Jesus affirms that he gave his disciples the glory that the Father had given him.

[263] On the question of Paul's authorship of Ephesians, see again note 233 above.

4.2.d.8.c. σκεύη ἐλέους

The reason Paul stresses here for God enduring of the vessels of wrath is God's purpose of making known the abundant blessing and surpassing value bestowed by his glory upon those who are the vessels of his mercy. As most scholars recognize, the phrase "vessels of mercy" (σκεύη ἐλέους) almost certainly refers to objects of mercy, that is, those on whom mercy is bestowed.[264] This is supported by the following considerations: (1) Paul is defending God's judgment upon unbelieving ethnic Israel and his right to grant the mercy of covenant membership to those who believe in Jesus (especially Gentiles); (2) the eschatological nature of the language of wrath, glory, honor, dishonor, destruction, and so on that Paul is using in the context and looks toward God dispensing his mercy and so on upon human recipients; (3) the contrast with the eschatological wrath of 9:22; (4) the contrasting parallel phrase "vessels of wrath" in 9:22 meaning objects of wrath (see Section 4.2.d.4); (5) the parallel expression "vessel unto honor" in 9:21, which is best taken as a vessel that is an object of honor; (6) Paul indicates that God's purpose is to make known the riches of his glory upon vessels of mercy, which rather obviously and straightforwardly identifies the vessels of mercy as recipients of divine blessing (presumably the mercy in view); and (7) Paul also describes these vessels of mercy as prepared beforehand for glory (προητοίμασεν εἰς δόξαν), which itself portrays them as objects of mercy in that eschatological glory will be granted to them.

As mentioned earlier, the making known of the riches of God's glory is an action that embodies what is to be made known. The "making known" and the carrying out of the action that makes known are one and the same. God's desire to make known the riches of his glory is also his desire to bestow the riches of his glory on the vessels of mercy, namely the objects or recipients of his mercy. The use of the preposition ἐπί (upon) here is an instance of the word as a "marker indicating the one to whom, for whom, or about whom someth. is done."[265] In this case, the act of making known

---

[264] Like the genitive ὀργῆς (of wrath) in the phrase σκεύη ὀργῆς (vessels of wrath) in 9:22, the genitive ἐλέους (of mercy) in the phrase σκεύη ἐλέους (vessels of mercy) in 9:23 is best classified as a qualitative genitive; context reveals its more specific meaning to be vessels upon which mercy is bestowed. See the discussion of the genitive ὀργῆς in note 206 above, which can be applied to ἐλέους here in v. 23 mutatus mutandis. Munck, *Israel*, 68, considers a meaning of "agents who effect God's mercy" to be just as possible, tying it to the reciprocal dynamic revealed in Romans 11 of the hardening of one group leading to the salvation of a second group, and the salvation of the second group leading to the salvation of the first. This goes along with taking "vessels of wrath" as agents who effect God's wrath, which is itself unlikely (see Section 4.2.d.4). But Munck does not flesh out the details, and it is hard to see how these meanings would reasonably play out in detail in the immediate context based on his comments. Hanson, "Vessels," 441–2, does give details for his view. But his suggestion that believers are instruments of mercy in that they show forth mercy by receiving mercy seems strained. Even Hanson has to admit that an essential aspect of the σκεύη ἐλέους is that they receive mercy. More importantly, the basic approach represented by Munck and Hanson does not match the immediate context, on which see below as well as the list of reasons supporting "vessels that receive wrath" in Section 4.2.d.4.

[265] BDAG, s.v. ἐπί, 14bα. It is similar in this instance to the use of the preposition "on" in the English idiom "to have mercy on (someone)." Cf. the use of the language of pouring out glory on the vessels of mercy in Newman and Nida, *Handbook*, 189. Cf. also the use of ἐπί with ἐνδείκνυμι in Eph. 2:7 in a similar type of statement, speaking of God showing "in the coming ages the surpassing riches of his grace in kindness to us"; this is notable not only because of the similarity in thought but also

the riches of God's glory is done to and for the vessels of mercy. It is done *to* them in that they receive/experience the riches of God's glory. It is done *for* them in that it is meant for their benefit, for them to know cognitively and experientially the supremely valuable benefits of God's glory.[266]

The vessels of mercy are those to whom God grants New Covenant membership and all it entails, including the blessings we mentioned earlier, such as adoption/sonship, eschatological honor, immortality, eternal life, and experience of God's eschatological grace, mercy, love, goodness, kindness, forgiveness, redemption, and so on. This is nothing other than the church, those who believe in Jesus Christ. Paul does not here indicate the basis for God's decision about who he gives this mercy to. But he has already indicated that clearly in the epistle in earlier chapters, earlier in this chapter, later in this chapter, and later in the unified section of Romans 9–11. God gives his saving mercy to those who believe in Jesus Christ, whether that be thought of in terms of justification (e.g., Rom. 3–4), reconciliation (5:10-11), being at peace with God (5:1-2), union with Christ (3:24; 6:5, 11, 23; 8:1) being alive to God (6:11, 13), eternal life (5:21; 6.22-23), having the Holy Spirit (5:5; ch. 8 passim), adoption and sonship (8:15-23; 9:4, 26), heirship (8:17), being children of the promise (9:4, 8-9; cf. 4:13-25), New Covenant membership (9:4, 6-13, 15-16, 25-26; 11:5, 17-24), being/being called God's people (1:6-7; 4:16-18; 8:14-23, 28, 30; 9:4, 6-16, 25-26, 30-33; 11:15, 17-24), attaining righteousness (3:21-22; 4; 9:30-33; 10 passim), salvation (1:16; 5:9-10; 8:24; 9:28; 10:1, 8-13; 11:11; 13:11), or God's kindness (11:22). It is mercy because no one deserves these blessings. Rather, all sin fall short of the glory of God, and deserve his wrath as a result.

4.2.d.8.d. Prepared Beforehand for Glory

Paul indicates that God prepared the vessels of mercy beforehand for glory. The word for preparation used now (προετοιμάζω) is a different word than the one used for preparation in v. 22 (καταρτίζω). We have already considered the suggestion that Paul uses different language concerning preparation in these two verses to indicate that God does not prepare the vessels of wrath for the destruction they will face while he does prepare the vessels of mercy for glory, but concluded that the suggestion is incorrect (see Section 4.2.d.5).[267] However, it still remains for us to offer an explanation for why

---

because ἐνδείκνυμι is used in 9:22 and in parallel with γνωρίζω in 9:22 and 23, while the specific usage we have in 9:23 is γνωρίζω + ἐπί.

[266] If forced to choose between these two facets of the meaning of ἐπί in 9:23 or pressed to say which is more fundamental, I would pick indication of to whom something is done. But it is impossible to separate the two senses in this context. Giving the lavish benefits of God's glory to people is done for their benefit. The former (doing to) entails the latter (doing for), and the latter relies on the former. It is worth noting that from an inaugurated eschatological perspective, God's mercy to the vessels of mercy is not only for them but for all in that the making known of God's mercy to them might move vessels of wrath to repentance, bringing them to become vessels of mercy. Cf. Romans 11's scheme in which the making known of God's mercy to the Gentiles is meant to spur unbelieving ethnic Israel to faith. However, Paul is not concerning himself with such details or nuances here but focusing on the basic categories with which he is dealing, yielding a practical focus on the final, consummated bestowal of mercy and glory.

[267] The suggestion also includes other differences in Paul's language between the two verses: καταρτίζω being in the perfect passive without explicit indication of an agent of action in 9:22, and

Paul uses a different word for preparation in each verse. We cannot be certain of the reason, but it seems most likely that Paul simply chose different words to match the difference of group and destiny between the two verses, vessels of wrath prepared for destruction in v. 22 versus vessels of mercy prepared beforehand for glory in v. 23.[268]

Apart from the προ- prefix on προητοίμασεν in 9:23, this is not to say that either word is more fitting for the nature of the preparation of which it speaks. In other words, Paul could just as well have used ἑτοιμάζω in 9:22 and προκαταρτίζω in 9:23. But using different words helps to highlight the drastic difference between the two groups and their respective destinies.

As for the προ- prefix on προητοίμασεν, a number of scholars note that it contributes to a sense of divine predestination or predetermination in the word in this context.[269] That is true, but only as a matter of emphasis rather than as an essential element. That is, the very notion of God preparing people for eschatological glory is a form of divine predestination in the sense of God setting a particular destiny for those people (see below on the meaning of preparation here). The notion of preparation is inherently forward-looking. The addition of a sense of "beforehand" merely strengthens that sense of forward-looking action and thus, in this context, predestination.[270]

On the other hand, that strengthened sense of future orientation helps to signal that the preparation of which Paul speaks has the final state of glory in mind. That is likely why Paul uses the προ-compound verb προετοιμάζω in contrast to the use of καταρτίζω without a προ- prefix for preparation in v. 22, which we argued has present considerations in addition to future ones in view. Paul's word choice here subtly adds to the text's focus on the future eschatological blessedness of believers, a prominent theme in Paul (and the NT).

But the sense of "beforehand" naturally raises the question, "before what?" That question is answered by the prepositional phrase εἰς δόξαν (for glory). That is, God prepared the vessels of mercy for experience of his glory in all its fullness, the unadulterated and undiminished presence of God, and the infinite blessing wrapped up in it, all in their consummate form and consummately bestowed "on the day when God judges the secrets of men ... through Christ Jesus" (Rom. 2:16; see the discussion of the riches of God's glory in Section 4.2.d.8.b). To put it more simply, God prepared the vessels of mercy for experience of his glory and all its blessings in the age to come. And to put it more simply still, God prepared the vessels of mercy for Heaven.

προητοίμασεν being a προ-compound verb in the aorist active indicative with explicit indication of God as the agent who performs the action in 9:23.

[268] Otherwise, mere stylistic difference would be most likely.
[269] See Cranfield, *Romans*, 497; Jewett, *Romans*, 597–8; Dunn, *Romans*, 560–1; Black, *Romans*, 133.
[270] Jewett's (*Romans*, 597–8) appeal to the language of preparation of the Tabernacle/Temple in Wisd. 9:8 and Sir. 49:19, and to predestinarian language at Qumran, and to "Paul's repeated use of the prefix προ- to convey the prior decision of God in the earlier argument of Romans" (598) seems unnecessary in light of our comments above if it is meant to substantiate that Paul speaks of a form of predestination here. And it is curious if it is meant to substantiate that an absolute or unconditional predestination is in view. It is questionable whether any of the references he gives involve that. And even if some do, it is dubious to assume Paul shares the same view. Similar language does not necessarily mean the same outlook. What is needed is close attention to Paul's discourse and its actual background to determine what he means by the language he uses.

But to what does God's preparation of the vessels of mercy refer? How did he prepare them? Just as with the nature of God's preparation of the vessels of wrath for destruction in 9:22 (see Section 4.2.d.6), the Old Testament background of Paul's potter/clay metaphor in Rom. 9:21 suggests the best understanding of the nature of God's preparation of the vessels of mercy for glory here in 9:23. Jeremiah 18:9-10 in essence speaks of God preparing a people for good by slating them to be built up and planted. In light of that background, the primary sense of God's preparation of the vessels of mercy for glory is his slating of them for eschatological glory. That is similar to other theological phenomena in Romans that amount to God declaring or designating or assigning believers a salvific status or experience, New Covenant blessings such as foreknowledge (in the sense of prior acknowledgment of covenant partnership; 8:29; 11:2),[271] calling (in the sense of naming as God's own people; 1:1, 6-7; 4:17; 8:28, 30; 9:7, 12, 25-26),[272] predestination (8:29-30), and justification (1:16-17; 3–4 passim; 5:1).

In addition to this primary sense of preparation as consignment to eschatological blessing, it seems likely that the process of sanctification mentioned in Romans is also in view to some extent as an aspect of the preparation of the vessels of mercy for glory.[273] Romans 8.29 states that God predestined believers to be "conformed to the image of his son." This probably includes, at least in part, the sanctification process Paul spoke about earlier in the same chapter and in ch. 6—the leading of the Spirit in believers and the power he provides "to put to death the deeds of the flesh" (8:13-14; cf. 6:11-23), offer themselves to God and as slaves to righteousness (6:11-23; cf. 12:1-2), and to obey God from the heart (6:17). It likely also includes the Spirit's intercession on behalf of the saints (8:26-27), the transforming of the believer by renewal of the mind (12:1-2), and God's work of perseverance and encouragement in the believer (15:5; cf. 5:3-5 in light of the character transformation it says perseverance accomplishes).[274]

How would the process of sanctification prepare believers for glory? Its fostering of perseverance in faith facilitates the believer's arrival at final salvation since perseverance in faith is necessary for final salvation in Paul's theology.[275] Moreover, for Paul, it would seem that the process of sanctification prepares believers for glory by contributing to the degree of their experience of blessing in the age to come. At least, that might be inferred from Paul's indication that God "will render to each [person] according to his works" and that continuing sin stores up/increases divine wrath for the final judgment (Rom. 2:5-6; cf. 1 Cor. 3:5-15; 2 Cor. 4:16-18; 5:10).

---

[271] On foreknowledge as prior acknowledgment of covenant partnership, see below in this section.

[272] On the naming sense of calling, see Abasciano, *Romans 9.1-9*, 198–208, and the literature cited there, as well as discussion of the concept in our treatment of v. 24 below along with the related excursus.

[273] Witherington, *Romans*, 258–9, appears to think that the process of sanctification is the primary if not the only sense of the preparation in view, since that is the only sense he mentions.

[274] On God's role in the sanctification process in Romans, see especially all of Romans 6 and 8. Cf. 1 Cor. 1:8; 2 Cor. 3:18; 4:16-17; Gal. 5:16-26 (note the primary role of the Spirit intertwined with human action); Eph. 1:4-5 (note "holy and blameless"); 4:11-16; 5:18; Phil. 1:6, 9-11; 2:12-13 (esp. v. 13); Col. 1:9-14; 2 Thess. 1:11-12; 2:16-17; 2 Tim. 1:9, 14.

[275] See Rom. 8:13; 11:20-23; 1 Cor. 9:24-27; 10:1-13; 15:1-2; Gal. 1:6-9; 5:1-4; Col. 1:22-23; 1 Thess. 3:1-5; 1 Tim. 6:9-10; 2 Tim. 2:12.

Just as with the preparation of the vessels of wrath for destruction, Paul speaks about the preparation of the vessels of mercy for glory as something done in the past.[276] This is not to limit the preparation to the past in relation to those who are currently vessels of mercy. Rather, Paul likely speaks about it in the past (1) because the primary sense of preparation (discussed above) would be past for the vessels of mercy and (2) in order to present the preparation more concretely and starkly for the purpose of setting it forth most clearly.[277] When uttered in a context in which ongoing preparation would be expected, the use of the past tense would not rule out that ongoing preparation. It would not specifically refer to it. But it allows for reapplication to the present. As noted earlier, Paul undoubtedly considered the divine endurance of the vessels of wrath to be a continuing phenomenon, not only that God endured the vessels of wrath in the past (the focus of what he says in the text) but that he continues to endure them (application of the past phenomenon he describes to the present).[278] Application of the principle articulated in 9:22-23 to the present would naturally encompass the preparation of the vessels of mercy up to the present. If the process of sanctification is part of the preparation envisaged to some extent, then the sanctification experienced up to the present would be included in the preparation of the vessels of mercy for glory in application of 9:23 to the present.

That leads us to the question of when the preparation of the vessels of mercy for glory takes place. We have already seen that it takes place before the full bestowal of eschatological glory on the vessels of mercy (i.e., the church). But can we get more specific? To the degree that the process of sanctification is part of the preparation, it takes place during the lifetime of believers.

But what of the more primary sense of consignment to eschatological blessing? Given the corporate orientation of this passage and Paul's doctrine of union with Christ that has manifested previously in Romans (3:24; 6:11, 23; 8:1-2, 39; cf. 9:1; 12:5; 15:17; 16:3, 7, 9-10), Paul would most likely conceive of Christ's procuring of redemption in his death and resurrection as the fundamental point at which the New Covenant people (the vessels of mercy) were slated for glory. This accords with our earlier observation that the preparation of the vessels of mercy for glory is roughly equivalent to other theological phenomena mentioned in Romans, such as justification, that set believers apart for divine blessing.

Romans 3:24 indicates that justification takes place by grace and "through the redemption that is in Christ Jesus," which implies that justification itself is in Christ since redemption is in Christ and brings justification to the one who experiences it (1 Cor. 1:30; 2 Cor. 5:21; Gal. 2:17; Phil. 3:8-9). As 8:1 states, "There is now no condemnation for those in Christ Jesus."[279] Faith in Christ brings union with Abraham/Christ, and

---

[276] See Section 4.2.d.6.
[277] Otherwise, Paul's use of the past might be merely stylistic. He had to speak about the preparation in one way or another.
[278] See again Section 4.2.d.6.
[279] On justification being in Christ in Paul's thought, see, e.g., M. F. Bird, "Incorporated Righteousness: A Response to Recent Evangelical Discussion Concerning the Imputation of Christ's Righteousness in Justification," *JETS* 47 (June 2004), 253–75; J. Piper, *The Future of Justification: A Response to N.T. Wright* (Wheaton, IL: Crossway, 2007), 171–4.

that in turn brings the Holy Spirit and sonship/New Covenant membership, which in turn brings heirship of the covenant promises (Romans 4 and 8), making believers co-heirs with Christ. That is, believers share in Christ's blessings, including a future experience of his glory (8:17). Even the justification of believers is a sharing in the justification of Christ (4:25).[280] The significance of all of this is that the establishment of the New Covenant and Christ's procurement of all the blessings of God in his death and resurrection is likely to be regarded as the point at which the New Covenant people of God were slated for glory. Individual believers come to share in that consignment to glory upon becoming united to Christ through faith.

Given Paul's doctrine of corporate election, one might wonder if the slating of the church for glory should rather be placed at the election of Christ before the foundation of the world (Eph. 1:4). That is certainly possible.[281] But Paul has not mentioned anything about election in eternity past in Romans. One might take the reference to foreknowledge in 8:29 along these lines as is often done. But there is no specification as to the prior timing of the knowledge mentioned there. In the context of Romans, it seems more likely that it refers to God's prior acknowledgment of the church as his covenant partner in his acknowledgment of Israel as his covenant partner in that the church is the fulfillment of OT Israel (the option I find most likely), or to his acknowledgment of the church as his covenant partner in the Old Testament's promises of the New Covenant and the seed of Abraham (cf. Rom. 1:1-6; 4:9-25; 9:6-9, 24-33; 16:25-27).[282] This is a corporate concept and blessing that individual Christians come to share in upon incorporation into the covenant people.

4.2.d.9. The Relationship between the Purposes in Rom. 9:22-23

Paul expresses three purposes in Rom. 9:22-23 for God enduring the vessels of wrath with great patience:

1. to show his wrath
2. to make known his power
3. to make known the riches of his glory upon vessels of mercy

We have already discussed these purposes in our exegesis of 9:22-23, and something of their relations. But now that we have come to the end of v. 23, it seems helpful to draw

---

[280] On the justification of believers as a sharing in the justification of Christ in Romans, see G. K. Beale, *A New Testament Biblical Theology: The Unfolding of the Old Testament in the New* (Grand Rapids, MI: Baker Academic, 2011), 495-504 (and in Paul more generally, 492-505); M. F. Bird, "Justified by Christ's Resurrection: A Neglected Aspect of Paul's Doctrine of Justification," *SBET* 22.1 (Spring 2005), 72-91.

[281] On corporate election in relation to Eph. 1:4, see Abasciano, "Misconceptions," 66-72, and specifically in relation to the verse's reference to election before the foundation of the world, 69-70. The journal version of that article has some misprinting on p. 69; an accurate version may be found at http://evangelicalarminians.org/brian-abasciano-clearing-up-misconceptions-about-corporate-election/.

[282] On foreknowledge as prior acknowledgment of covenant partnership, see Abasciano, *Romans 9.1-9*, 62-3; "Misconceptions," 66.

together our conclusions to offer a summary of their relations and further reflection upon them.

We have seen that purpose 3 is the primary divine purpose for patience with the vessels of wrath. Purposes 1 and 2 are subordinate to purpose 3. Purpose 1 serves purpose 3 in two ways. First, the expression of God's wrath on those who do not believe in Christ is necessary to fulfill God's plan to bless the world, for the granting of covenant membership by faith rather than works or ethnicity opens up covenant membership, with its benefit of experience of the riches of the divine glory, to Gentiles.

Second, the contrast between the divine wrath and the divine mercy manifests the divine glory more fully.[283] Some interpreters seem to regard this as the only logical relationship between purposes 1 and 2 on the one hand and purpose 3 on the other, and indeed, even between God's patience with the vessels of wrath and purpose 3 as well. But that fails to take account of so much that our exegesis has found, including the necessity of wrath for God's plan to bless the world (mentioned above), the salvific aspect of God's power, the full sense of God showing or making known his wrath, power, or glory, the natural fit of God's patience leading to and allowing for repentance, and so on.

Moreover, wrath as a clarifying backdrop to the merciful display of God's glory is not fit to be the sole connection between God's purpose of displaying his wrath and his purpose of making known his glory upon vessels of mercy, nor between his patience with the vessels of wrath and his purpose of making known his glory upon vessels of mercy. The reasoning given by those who present it as the sole connection is less than convincing. As Daniel Fuller articulates it,

> How could God's mercy appear fully as His great mercy unless it was extended to people who were under His wrath and therefore could only ask for mercy? It would be impossible for them to share with God the delight He has in His mercy unless they saw clearly the awfulness of the almighty wrath from which His mercy delivers them. Thus to show the full range of His glory God prepares beforehand not only vessels of mercy but also vessels of wrath, in order that the riches of His glory in connection with the vessels of mercy might thereby become more clearly manifest.[284]

As Schreiner explains it, "The mercy of God would not be impressed on the consciousness of human beings apart from the exercise of God's wrath, just as one delights more richly in the warmth, beauty, and tenderness of spring after one has experienced the cold blast of winter."[285] In addition, this perspective also holds that God unconditionally creates individuals as vessels of mercy and vessels of wrath, unconditionally hardening the latter unto eternal condemnation. And as Schreiner states, "Verses 22-23 inform us why God made human beings whom he planned to punish: to exhibit the full extent of his wrath and power."[286]

---

[283] So Piper, *Justification*, 214–16, following Daniel Fuller; Schreiner, *Romans*, 493, 499–500.
[284] Cited by Piper, *Justification*, 215–16.
[285] Schreiner, *Romans*, 500.
[286] Ibid., 491.

There are numerous problems with this approach, only two of which we will address here.[287] First, the notion that God's desire to glorify himself moves him to create vessels of wrath whose wickedness he brings about so that he can pour out wrath on them in order to show forth the full range of his glory is incoherent. For the full range of God's glory includes justice. But making people do evil in order to punish them for doing evil appears to contradict the very essence of justice.[288] God's wrath can only glorify him if it is just wrath, imposed on people who deserve it.

Second, on the supposition of an omnipotent and omniscient God such as Paul believed in, it is doubtful that the exercise of God's wrath would be necessary to impress the mercy of God on the consciousness of human beings. It seems clear that the exercise of God's wrath would serve to do so, but unlikely that God would need it to do so. Surely an omnipotent and omniscient God could impress his mercy on the understanding of human beings without actually pouring out his wrath on certain sinners. That makes it hard to imagine that God would find it necessary (or desirable) to make people sinful so that he could punish some of them for the sin he irresistibly determined them to commit while having mercy on others of them, in order to show his mercy most fully. It could be that for Paul the only connection between God showing his wrath and making known the riches of his glory is that his wrath serves as a contrasting, and therefore, clarifying, backdrop to his mercy. However, the suggestion that such a contrasting backdrop is necessary does not succeed as support for the view. And it is contradicted by our exegesis.

Turning to purpose 2, we can say that it also serves purpose 3 in two ways that accord with two main aspects of the meaning of the making known of God's power in

---

[287] For an extensive treatment, see T. H. McCall, "I Believe in Divine Sovereignty," *TJ* 29/2 (Fall 2008), 205–26, esp. 215–26, which critiques John Piper's view on this and related matters. Piper responded with "I Believe in God's Self-Sufficiency: A Response to Thomas McCall," *TJ* 29/2 (Fall 2008), 227–34, and McCall replied compellingly with "Rejoinder."

[288] Schreiner, *Romans*, 495, appeals to the philosophical concept of compatibilism as expressing Paul's theology when discussing this issue in relation to Rom. 9:20-21. But that is a dead end in my judgment; see T. H. McCall, *An Invitation to Analytic Christian Theology* (Downers Grove, IL: IVP, 2015), 56–81; K. Timpe, *Free Will: Sourcehood and Its Alternatives*, 2nd ed. (London: Bloomsbury, 2013); cf. the two articles by McCall referenced in the immediately preceding note above. Some older treatments of the issue are still very helpful, addressing what is now called compatibilism as represented most notably by Jonathan Edwards; see D. D. Whedon, *The Freedom of the Will as a Basis of Human Responsibility and a Divine Government* (New York: Carlton and Lanahan, 1864); T. N. Ralston, *Elements of Divinity* (Louisville, KY: E. Stevenson, 1851), 239–65; R. Dunn, *A Discourse on the Freedom of the Will* (Dover: W.M. Burr, 1850). Piper, *Justification*, 216 n. 34, quotes Daniel Fuller addressing what many would find to be a fatal problem for (theological) compatibilism in holding that responsibility-rendering freedom consists in being able to do what one desires to do, yet that God is the one who determines what human desires are and thereby determines human actions. Fuller notes that the human conscience does not sense wrongdoing if one is physically kept from doing right, but does sense wrongdoing when one refuses to do right because of desiring something else. He then pinpoints the problem noted above and offers these comments: "Why conscience should act this way when motives are ultimately given and not chosen is a reflection of the fact that God is sovereign yet He is also glorious and righteous, so conscience accuses for failure to do right brought about by ill-advised motives. If God is God it could not be otherwise." In my opinion, that does not provide an answer to the problem posed by theological compatibilism, and if it is meant as an answer, it is shockingly question-begging. Its inclusion by Piper as "helpful in reflecting on the problem of human accountability" suggests that neither Piper nor Fuller has a good explanation for human accountability on the basis of compatibilism.

this context that we have observed. First, the making known of God's power involves the power of God in judgment/wrath. Thus, it serves purpose 3 in the same way that purpose 1 does (see the above discussion). Second, the making known of God's power in this context also involves the power of God in salvation. Thus, it serves purpose 3 in facilitating it. That is, covenantal election and salvation bring the vessels of mercy to experience the riches of God's glory. That is part of the benefit of New Covenant election and salvation.

Finally, it is worth restating the relationship between the main clause of 9:22-24, contained in 9:22 and expressing God's patience with the vessels of wrath, and the purpose clause of 9:23, expressing the ultimate purpose for God's patience. God endured the vessels of wrath with great patience in order to make known the riches of his glory upon vessels of mercy. But how does God's patience work toward the making known of the riches of his glory upon vessels of mercy? The most obvious and main way that God's patience with the vessels of wrath accomplishes his purpose of making known the riches of his glory upon vessels of mercy is by giving the vessels of wrath time and opportunity to repent and thereby become vessels of mercy.[289] Secondarily, God's patience with the vessels of wrath brings about the making known of the riches of God's glory in a similar fashion to one of the ways that purpose 1 helps to accomplish purpose 3, namely by allowing for the storing up of divine wrath against those who continue in sin and impenitence unto a greater display of God's justice and wrath, which in turn serves as a contrasting and clarifying backdrop to the divine mercy given to the vessels of mercy in the riches of the divine glory.

4.2.d.10. Rom. 9:24

4.2.d.10.a. Structure, Syntax, Phrasing, and Emphasis

Verse 24 (οὓς καὶ ἐκάλεσεν ἡμᾶς οὐ μόνον ἐξ Ἰουδαίων ἀλλὰ καὶ ἐξ ἐθνῶν) contains difficult syntax and phrasing, contributing to disagreement over whether v. 24 continues and finishes the sentence begun in vv. 22–23 or starts a new sentence that is completed by v. 25 and itself starts a new paragraph. The verse begins with a relative pronoun (οὓς), which would normally refer to something in the previous clause and be part of the same sentence. However, a relative pronoun in Greek can lack an antecedent and begin an independent sentence,[290] allowing for the possibility in the opinion of some scholars that v. 24 begins a new sentence with no antecedent for οὓς.[291] But v. 24 does

---

[289] See previous discussion of this point at various points in the present volume, esp. Sections 4.2.d.3.b and, most importantly, 4.2.d.7.

[290] Cranfield, *Romans*, 498, asserts that "the use of a relative pronoun, as in Latin, to connect an independent sentence to its predecessor is sometimes found in Greek." But the term "connect" is open to misunderstanding. It could give the impression that the relative pronoun still has some reference to the previous sentence. But the question is whether the relative pronoun beginning 9:24 has an antecedent in the previous clause or not. If so, then the sentence continues; if not, the relative pronoun starts a new sentence.

[291] So Moo, *Romans*, 630; Käsemann, *Romans*, 272-3 (seemingly); H. Schlier, *Der Römerbrief* (HTKNT; Freiburg: Herder, 1977), 302–3; Newman and Nida, *Handbook*, 189–90; Dunn, *Romans*, 569–70. Few translations take this approach. Moo, 629, translates, "[Whom] God has called us, not

not fit the conditions for when this might happen.²⁹² Moreover, clearly 9:24 identifies the vessels of mercy in 9:23.²⁹³ Given all of that, and that reference to the previous clause is more natural and straightforward, 9:24 most likely continues and finishes the sentence that begins in 9:22-23.

This leaves open two possibilities for construing v. 24 depending on whether οὓς is taken to refer directly to (1) σκεύη (vessels) in v. 23, in which case ἡμᾶς (us) in 9:24 is in apposition to οὓς (whom) in the same verse (yielding: "whom he indeed called—us—not only from Jews but also from Gentiles");²⁹⁴ or (2) ἡμᾶς (us) in 9:24, in which case ἡμᾶς is in apposition to σκεύη (vessels) in v. 23 (yielding: "us, whom he indeed called, not only from Jews, but also from Gentiles").²⁹⁵ Counting against οὓς referring directly to σκεύη is that the former differs in gender from the latter (οὓς is masculine and σκεύη is neuter) even though relative pronouns normally agree with the gender of their antecedent. However, it is not uncommon for relative pronouns to diverge from the rules of agreement,²⁹⁶ and the specific context here is ideal for the most common reason for a divergence—a *constructio ad sensum*.²⁹⁷ Paul puts the relative pronoun in the masculine because, despite the antecedent σκεύη being neuter, it metaphorically represents people, and the relative clause begun by οὓς identifies the people σκεύη ἐλέους represents.

Counting against οὓς referring directly to ἡμᾶς (us) in 9:24 is that it is unusual for the antecedent of a relative pronoun to come after the relative pronoun.²⁹⁸ Nevertheless, the antecedent can come after the relative pronoun and occasionally does.²⁹⁹ However, it is typically obvious when that occurs (there is no other reasonable antecedent), and in any case, it is much more natural for the relative pronoun to follow its antecedent even if diverging from its gender. Another problem for this option is that ἡμᾶς in 9:24 must be taken to be in apposition to σκεύη in 9:23 but is rather distant from it for apposition, which normally involves adjacency. Thus, the best reading is that οὓς in v. 24 refers directly to σκεύη in v. 23, and ἡμᾶς in v. 24 is in apposition to οὓς: "whom he indeed called—us—not only from Jews but also from Gentiles."

---

only from among Jews but also from among Gentiles," which is awkward and curiously leaves the καί that follows οὓς untranslated.

²⁹² Such conditions include the relative pronoun having an unstated demonstrative pronoun embedded within it (on which see BDAG, s.v. ὅς, 1b; Wallace, *Greek*, 339–40) or functioning as a demonstrative pronoun (on which see BDAG, s.v. ὅς, 2) or combined with a preposition for conjunctive force (on which, see ibid., 1k; Wallace, 342–3) or with ἄν/ἐάν (on which, see BDAG, s.v. ὅς, 1jα; s.v. I ἄν, b; BDF, § 380.1) or in poetry (on which, see Wallace, 340–2). It is telling that Moo, *Romans*, 631–2 n. 293, points to 1 Cor. 12:28 as "The closest Pauline syntactical parallel," for the relative pronoun functions as a demonstrative pronoun in that verse, which is used as an example of the phenomenon by BDAG, s.v. ὅς, 2b.

²⁹³ Cf. Cranfield, *Romans*, 498; Moo, *Romans*, 630.

²⁹⁴ So, e.g., Cranfield, *Romans*, 498; Schreiner, *Romans*, 503–4; Morris, *Romans*, 369; Black, *Romans*, 133–4; Jewett, *Romans*, 598 (though this is not reflected in his translation on 587).

²⁹⁵ So most English translations, though this is probably because it makes for the smoothest English; Barrett, *Romans*, 189; Fitzmyer, *Romans*, 572–3; Kruse, *Romans*, 388.

²⁹⁶ Wallace, *Greek*, 337.

²⁹⁷ On the *constructio ad sensum*, see ibid., 337–8; BDAG, s.v. ὅς, 1cβ (note esp. ג); BDF, § 296.

²⁹⁸ Cf. Moo, *Romans*, 630 n. 293.

²⁹⁹ See BDF, § 294.5; BDAG, s.v. ὅς, 1e.

No matter how the syntax and phrasing is construed, it is awkward. Yet as in 9:23, that is probably not accidental, but intentional (cf. Section 4.2.d.8.a). Dunn describes Paul's strategy well:

> The awkwardness of the phrasing is presumably deliberate and almost certainly meant that in being read aloud the words would have to be taken slowly and with emphasis, particularly on the awkward ἡμᾶς (cf. Black). We should envisage therefore that the careful reader (to the congregation) was intended to leave the incomplete vv 22–23 hanging, pause, catch fresh attention with the unexpected οὓς (following ἅ), and reinforce the impact with the identifying ἡμᾶς.[300]

The reason for Paul's heavy emphasis is that the point 9:24 makes (that God has called vessels of mercy not only from Jews but also from Gentiles) addresses the practical heart of the central issue Paul has been dealing with in Romans 9—God's right to call his people by faith rather than works or ancestry, resulting in the exclusion of unbelieving ethnic Jews from the covenant and its salvation, and the inclusion of believing Gentiles (cf. Section 4.2.d.2). The very phenomenon that called God's faithfulness into question and provoked Paul to mount such a detailed and sustained defense of God's righteousness as Romans 9–11 is expressed in 9:24 at its most offensive point—the inclusion of Gentiles against the backdrop of the exclusion of many Jews.[301]

It would not be the claim of the rejection of many Jews that would be especially offensive to Jews at the time Paul wrote Romans. Various Jewish groups in the first century made claims that excluded other Jews from true Israel. As Howard Clark Kee has stated,

> It is now evident that the major issue in Judaism from the time of the return of the Israelites from captivity in Babylon—especially in the two centuries before and after the birth of Jesus—was: What are the criteria for participation in the covenant people? This question was fiercely debated between the Jewish nationalists, the priests, and those Jews who had in some degree assimilated to Hellenistic culture,

---

[300] Dunn, *Romans*, 570, who has been followed by Moo, *Romans*, 630; and Jewett, *Romans*, 598. Moo regards this as supportive of taking v. 24 as starting a new sentence. But it is just as supportive of the other options since it serves to bring emphasis, which does not require a new sentence.

[301] On the extreme offensiveness of Gentiles being included among God's people as Gentiles, see Abasciano, *Romans 9.10-18*, 205–6, where I discuss Acts 22's report of Paul's mere mention of mission to the Gentiles driving a Jewish crowd into a murderous rage, and reference 1 Thess. 2:14-16, where Paul charges that the Jews "are not pleasing to God and [are] hostile to all people, hindering us from speaking to the Gentiles in order that they might be saved." Räisänen, "Analyse," 2905, points out that 9:24ff. gives the impression of being the climactic point of the chapter and that the inclusion of Gentiles is what needs justification; he notes that several commentators find the thrust of the passage here. However, he objects that it was not the inclusion of the Gentiles but the exclusion of most Jews that would call God's faithfulness into question. But I would counter that it was both points together that brought out the fullness of the problem and that it was in fact the inclusion of the Gentiles that was the most offensive point when the two were combined, the proverbial adding of insult to injury; see further below.

on the one hand, and dissident groups such as the Dead Sea community and the Pharisees, on the other.[302]

It does not seem to have been particularly offensive to Jews for fellow Jews to deny that Jewish ancestry was itself enough to guarantee membership in the covenant people. What seems to have been exceedingly offensive to many Jews, though, was any denial of a need to obey the Mosaic law or of the necessity of Jewish ethnicity, which were thoroughly intertwined. While it would not be surprising that some or even many Jews might be excluded from the covenant and its salvation, it would be unthinkable to many Jews for Jewish ethnicity to not be a requirement for membership in the covenant people of God. And for Gentiles to be welcomed in as Gentiles without observance of the Law while Law-observant Jews were rejected would be beyond unthinkable. The mention of the inclusion of Gentiles embodies the rejection of the Law and Jewish ethnicity as requirements for membership in the people of God in the most offensive way possible, placing the very ones marked by both lack of obedience to the Law and Jewish ethnicity into the covenant people of God while rejecting many Jews who kept the Law, when the Jewish people were the historic people of God to whom the covenant most naturally belonged[303] and they regarded the Gentiles as unclean (cf. e.g., Acts 10:1–28; n.b. 10:28).

Virtually all translations that translate the first καί of v. 24 translate it as a simple additive ("also").[304] This finds some support in Paul's similar, earlier, longer sequence in Rom. 8:29-30, which repeatedly uses the same relative pronoun (οὕς) and an additive καί, most notably at one point with predestination followed by God's call: οὓς δὲ προώρισεν, τούτους καὶ ἐκάλεσεν (and those whom he predestined, these he also called; 8:30).[305] But the parallel is not precise,[306] and the immediate context here of heavy emphasis with multiple emphasizing elements is more striking. Therefore, an intensive meaning for the first καί (indeed) of v. 24 seems more likely, yielding "whom he indeed called—us—not only from Jews but also from Gentiles."[307] By using καί, Paul is not particularly trying to highlight that God both prepared the vessels of mercy for glory *and also* called them,[308] but he is stressing that God called his people from

---

[302] H. C. Kee, *Knowing the Truth: A Sociological Approach to New Testament Interpretation* (Minneapolis, MN: Fortress, 1989), 5; cf. M. A. Elliott, *The Survivors of Israel: A Reconsideration of the Theology of Pre-Christian Judaism* (Grand Rapids, MI: Eerdmans, 2000).

[303] Provided that they remained faithful to God by believing in Christ. On the concept of the covenant most naturally belonging to ethnic Israel, see Abasciano, *Romans 9.1-9*, 89–146.

[304] Some translations leave it untranslated, such as the NET, ESV, KJV, RSV, and NRSV, though this seems unjustified.

[305] Cf. Moo, *Romans*, 631; Dunn, *Romans*, 570.

[306] Rom. 9:23-24 has ἃ προητοίμασεν εἰς δόξαν, οὓς καὶ ἐκάλεσεν (which he prepared beforehand for glory, whom he καί called).

[307] Though a decision between a simple additive meaning and an intensive meaning is difficult. On the intensive use of καί, see BDAG, s.v. 2.b.

[308] Though, of course, what he says does imply that, but that is not the purpose of the καί. As argued earlier, calling is part of the preparation mentioned in 9:23's προετοιμάζω. That point is consistent with either an additive or intensive καί, though more comfortable with the latter, and so mildly supportive of it over the former. The additive καί is still consistent with the point because Paul might very well indicate an action (preparation) that covers a broad category of other actions, and then add another action (calling) that falls under that broad category but which Paul wishes to specially highlight, though that might be a bit unusual. By way of illustration, it would be like

among the Gentiles as well as the Jews,[309] for the inclusion of the Gentiles represents the greatest challenge to God's right to choose who his people are, the right Paul has been defending from the beginning of Romans 9 in response to the greatest challenge to his gospel.

Further emphasis is given to the inclusion of Gentiles by the "not only/but also" (οὐ μόνον/ἀλλὰ καί) structure Paul uses in 9:24. God has called the vessels of mercy not only from Jews—that he would call Jews is an obvious given—but also from Gentiles, which was, as discussed above, shocking and offensive to Jewish sensibilities. The phrase "not only" (οὐ μόνον) de-emphasizes the calling of Jews in order to give greater emphasis to the calling of Gentiles, which is emphasized by the phrase "but also" (ἀλλὰ καί). The phrases "from Jews" (ἐξ Ἰουδαίων) and "from Gentiles" (ἐξ ἐθνῶν) use the preposition ἐκ with the genitive to indicate separation from a group.[310] It indicates that only some Jews and only some Gentiles have been included in God's people.[311] In this case, the separation is not total, as if Jewish vessels of mercy are no longer Jews or Gentile vessels of mercy are no longer Gentiles. Rather, the separation is with respect to being vessels of mercy. That is, the vessels of mercy are separate from the rest of the members of their respective ethnic groups, whether Jews or Gentiles, in that they are vessels of mercy while the rest of their ethnic groups are not vessels of mercy. Thus, the vessels of mercy, whom Paul identifies as "us" (i.e., Christians), were called from among two groups, the Jews and the Gentiles.[312] The covenant people of God, the seed of Abraham, Israel, now consists of both Jews and Gentiles who believe in Jesus (cf. 9:6-8; 11:15-24).

4.2.d.10.b. Naming the Covenant People

In saying that God called the vessels of mercy, Paul is saying that God named or designated them as his covenant people, who are heirs to the covenant promises. Some interpreters insist that Paul's use of καλέω (to call) here does not denote naming, but

---

saying that on a certain afternoon, John prepared for the party and also bought napkins (when buying napkins is part of preparing for the party). If this be thought too difficult, then the position that the preparation of 9:23 includes calling strongly supports the intensive usage here, and the additive usage here would argue strongly against calling as part of the preparation of 9:23.

[309] Cf. Moo, *Romans*, 631, who notes that "Paul's focus here is not on the antecedents of God's calling or on its nature, but on its scope."

[310] On this usage, see BDAG, s.v. ἐκ 1.b, which lists Rom. 9:24 as an example.

[311] Romans 9:27-29 will add indication that only a relatively small minority of Jews had been included in God's people; see Section 5.2 in Chapter 5 of this volume.

[312] Some might wish to argue that the selection of a remnant out of two larger groups demands individual election; so Schreiner, "Election," 99, though he focuses on Rom. 9:6-9 and 11:1-6; *Romans*, 471. See Abasciano, "Election," 360-1, for a direct response; 358-61 are quite relevant too. N.B.: This argument for individual election and against corporate election misunderstands the nature of corporate election (at least the strongest version of it) as if it excludes individuals completely from its scope. But it has individuals coming to share in the corporate election (which is focused first on the covenant head [Christ] and then the corporate body identified with him) through faith. I have explained this in detail in the works listed in note 149 above. E. Peterson, "Die Kirche aus Juden und Heiden," in E. Peterson, *Theologische Traktate* (Ausgewählte Schriften, 1; Würzburg: Echter, 1994), 141-74 (155), stresses that 9:24 shows Paul's approach to calling, election, hardening, and mercy in Romans 9 to be corporate rather than individual.

summoning.³¹³ However, this is quite unlikely. The verse surely picks up the idea of calling from 9:7, which refers to God's naming/identifying of the seed of Abraham (i.e., his covenant people),³¹⁴ a meaning that flows directly into reference to the concept in 9:12. Indeed, I have argued that the theological concept of calling in Paul and the New Testament refers to an effectual naming.³¹⁵

But an even more important consideration regarding the concept in 9:24 is that the term clearly means "to name" in 9:25-26, which use the double accusative and give biblical support for Paul's claim about calling in 9:24. As Cranfield acknowledges, "it is true that καλεῖν with a double accusative must mean 'call' in the sense of name, as Sanday and Headlam point out."³¹⁶ This virtually demands the sense of naming in 9.24. But surprisingly, this definitive point has been ignored by most interpreters, who facilely assume a summoning sense (presumably because of tradition). Even more surprising is that this definitive point has been ignored by interpreters who show awareness of divine naming as a possible meaning for Paul's calling language but insist on a meaning of summoning in 9:24 (and indeed universally in Paul).³¹⁷ With regard to 9:24, they are simply not reckoning with the evidence. That is also the case with the meaning of calling in Paul and its figurative/theological usage elsewhere in the New Testament.

Scholars like Schreiner and Moo in their commentaries have mostly asserted the idea of calling as an effectual summons rather than argued for it over against calling as an effectual naming. Their main arguments in their commentaries in favor of calling

---

³¹³ Schreiner, *Romans*, 503-5 (cf. 439); Moo, *Romans*, 631 (cf. 552); J. Hoglund, *Called by Triune Grace: Divine Rhetoric and the Effectual Call* (SCDS; Downers Grove, IL: IVP, 2016), 55-7.
³¹⁴ See Abasciano, *Romans 9.1-9*, 198-201.
³¹⁵ Ibid., 198-208.
³¹⁶ Cranfield, *Romans*, 500. Cranfield is quick to insist that the divine naming in 9:25-26 is effectual. On that basis he equates it with the more traditional construal of calling as an effectual summoning (or so it seems since he offers Rom. 8:30 for comparison as to the meaning, which he explains as effectually bringing about the response of the obedience of faith in the man to whom it is given [432]). But that does not follow, and it conflicts with the simple but critical observation that summoning and naming are different phenomena. There is nothing about naming being effectual that would suggest that it is equivalent to summoning. Indeed, its effectual character distinguishes it all the more from the traditional view of effectual calling/summoning. For that view holds that God's summons to faith necessarily creates faith in those to whom it is given (the elect). However, an effectual naming that makes people children of God comes in response to faith. In Paul's theology, sinners become children of God and members of the New Covenant by faith. This fits with divine naming effectually making them children of God. They believe, and God responds to their faith by naming them as his children, which in fact makes them his children. But effectual naming that makes sinners God's children does not fit comfortably with the idea of the naming creating the faith that then brings God to accept them as his children. The idea would have to be something like this: God names certain unbelievers as his children, and this naming causes them to believe, which only then actually effects their becoming God's children. But this would awkwardly have God naming them as his children when they are not his children, and then another step needing to be taken by them—faith—before they are actually made his children.
³¹⁷ See note 313 above. Hoglund, *Called*, 55-6, is an exception. See my assessment of his analysis in section 12 of Excursus 4.1. Cranfield's (*Romans*, 500) position that calling in 9:24 refers to summoning while acknowledging the naming sense in 9:25-26 yet not considering that the naming sense in 9:25-26 might indicate a naming sense in 9:24 is perplexing, and all the more so given that he does take the usage of καλεῖν in 9:25-26 as decisive on another matter. One might suspect that Cranfield does see 9:24 as referring to an effectual naming, but that does not seem to be the case; see note 316 above.

as an effectual summons have to do with it being effectual. Moo points out that Paul uses the language of calling to designate those who are Christians.[318] And Schreiner observes that Rom. 8:30 "fuses the called and justified together so that *all* those who are called receive the blessing of justification."[319] However, these points do not address whether calling is a summons versus naming, but merely support calling as effectual, which is wholly consistent with either effectual summoning or effectual naming.

Establishing calling in Paul's thought (or the thought of the New Testament) as effectual does nothing to address the question of whether it refers to summoning versus naming. It merely begs that question if offered as evidence for the summoning sense. Schreiner's reasoning in statements like the following assumes the summoning sense: "If all those who are called are also justified, then calling must be effectual and must create faith, for 'all' those who are called are justified, and justification cannot occur without faith (3:21-22, 28; 5:1)."[320] There is question over whether Rom. 8:30 really indicates that *all* who are called are justified.[321] But be that as it may, even if we grant that all who are called are justified and that calling is effectual, it does not at all follow that calling creates faith. If calling refers to effectual naming, then calling is based on faith in that God responds to human faith with effectually naming believers as his children, which in fact makes them his children, changing their very identity and status.[322]

Scholars such as Moo and Schreiner have failed to engage with the strong evidence I have presented for the naming sense of calling in Paul and the rest of the New Testament. In sum, that evidence is:[323] (1) The naming sense occurs far more often than the summoning sense in the main term for calling, the verb καλέω.[324] (2) The naming sense with the nuance of designation or appointment or identification fits instances of indication of appointment to an office or role or situation better than summoning. (3) The naming sense with the nuance of designation or identification similarly fits instances of the use of the concept as a designation for Christians and their life better than summoning. (4) Name/naming language and familial themes often occur in connection with the concept of calling. (5) Naming more simply and straightforwardly fits calling as an effectual act whereas summoning requires an additional, unstated assumption as part of the intended meaning; it requires adding the idea of positive response to the call so that "to call" means something like "to summon in a way that causes obedience to the summons," and calling, "the summons you heard and necessarily responded positively to," and called, "having been divinely summoned and

---

[318] Moo, *Romans*, 552 n. 1175.
[319] Schreiner, *Romans*, 439; emphasis original.
[320] Ibid.
[321] See Forlines, *Romans*, 239–40, for an alternative view from an individual election perspective, and from a corporate election perspective, B. J. Oropeza, *Paul and Apostasy: Eschatology, Perseverance and Falling Away in the Corinthian Congregation* (WUNT, 2.115; Tübingen: Mohr Siebeck, 2000), 206–10.
[322] Cf. note 316 above.
[323] For full discussion, see Abasciano, *Romans 9.1-9*, 198–208, though this summary goes beyond that discussion in some ways. N.B.: Not each of these points is strong (though some are), but together the points make a cumulative case, and some points are quite strong.
[324] All the uses of the noun κλῆσις and the adjective κλητός in the NT are debatable except for κλητός in Mt. 22:14, which clearly means "invited/summoned."

responded positively to the summons." (6) Calling terminology is widely recognized as technical terminology when referring to Christians, which has a consistent meaning, a point that takes on significance in combination with the next point. (7) We know that calling refers to naming in Rom. 9:25-26, but there is no indisputable usage of calling language as summoning anywhere in Paul. Moreover, the naming sense in 9:25-26 strongly argues for the naming sense in the terminology in the rest of the chapter, as it is all part of one theme of calling in the argument (not to mention that the Old Testament background of Rom. 9:7 strongly argues for the naming sense of the term there, where the concept is introduced in the argument of the chapter). Points 6 and 7 together argue for naming as the meaning of calling normally throughout Paul and the New Testament. Scholars like Schreiner and Moo think that calling refers to summoning everywhere in Paul. But given that it clearly refers to naming in Romans 9 (at the very least, certainly in 9:25-26, and almost certainly in the rest of the chapter), it is much more likely that it refers to naming everywhere in Paul.

Excursus 4.1: **Objections to Divine Calling as Divine Naming**

Jonathan Hoglund has provided a substantial critique of my understanding of divine calling as divine naming in Romans 9 and elsewhere.[325] But his critique is riddled with problems and is fatally flawed.

(1) He indicates that I contended that if I can establish a naming sense for calling in the five references to calling in Romans 9, then the traditional view of calling as an effectual summons to faith is eliminated. But that is not what I argued. I stated that the naming sense in Romans 9 calls for a reassessment of the concept of calling in the rest of the Pauline corpus and the New Testament as to whether naming might be in view rather than, as typically assumed, summoning. I then argued in detail for the naming sense in all the occurrences of the figurative/theological use of the term (i.e., when God is the subject of the calling action, Christians are the object, and the call is effectual).

The statement that Hoglund quotes from my argument—"the traditional notion of effectual calling would be eliminated, for it is based on the idea of a *summoning* which effectively creates the response of faith and obedience to the call"[326]—is immediately preceded in its original context by the words, "If this view be accepted," referring to the view I had just argued for at length, that all the figurative/theological calling language in the New Testament refers to naming. It could be that Hoglund has in mind my point that the terminology of calling in its figurative/theological usage is widely recognized as technical terminology and that this pushes for a relatively uniform meaning throughout the figurative use of the terminology,[327] though he does not mention it. One

---

[325] Hoglund, *Called*, 53–7. Again, my main treatment of calling in Romans 9 may be found in Abasciano, *Romans 9.1-9*, 198–208, though Hoglund cites pp. 196–207. He probably includes pp. 196–7 because they include key treatment of Rom. 9:8, which figures into his critique of my understanding of calling.

[326] Originally in Abasciano, *Romans 9.1-9*, 207, and quoted in Hoglund, *Called*, 53.

[327] See Abasciano, *Romans 9.1-9*, 203 n. 166; cf. p. 205. The terminology specifically in mind is the verb καλέω, the noun κλῆσις, and the adjective κλητός.

could reason that if the terminology is uniform in its usage, and if I establish a naming sense for the terminology in Romans 9, then that supports taking the terminology with the naming sense elsewhere. And that is indeed true, but I did not explicitly draw that point out in my argument. I wish I had. It is implicit in my argument. But even though a naming sense in Romans 9 would suggest a naming sense for figurative usage of the terminology elsewhere due to it being technical terminology, I would not present that as a definitive point conclusively proving the naming sense elsewhere. Nevertheless, it is a weighty point in favor of the naming sense as the figurative/theological meaning of the terminology that I now happily and explicitly affirm.

(2) Hoglund claims that I hold that calling/naming is about God stating that someone has become a Christian similar to N. T. Wright's conception of justification being the declaration that someone has become a Christian rather than being what makes someone a Christian.[328] But that is false. While Hoglund does quote me accurately from one of the spots where I provide a definition of calling as naming,[329] astonishingly, he misses that I emphasize that divine naming is creative and effectual, making the called God's children/the elect people.

(3) This points up a third and core error in Hoglund's appraisal that seems to underlie much of his critique of my position, namely, assuming that divine naming is not effectual but analytic/observational despite multiple explicit statements in my analysis that it is effectual.

(4) This assumption can be seen in Hoglund's erroneous description of my view of Rom. 9:8 and the children of promise.[330] As he describes it, "That the children of promise are 'considered to be offspring' (Rom 9:8) of Abraham is analytic. God does not change anything about these people but recognizes those who have faith as the true seed of Abraham."[331] This is not at all my view, and it is hard to see how Hoglund arrived at such an understanding given the explicit affirmation of the effectual character of divine naming throughout my treatment of calling in Romans 9 and the rest of the New Testament. It could be that he merely considered phrasing in my treatment such as "to reckon, regard, or identify those who believe in Christ as the true seed of Abraham"[332] apart from context, for such language could theoretically be used in a merely analytic way. But that would violate basic, essential principles of exegesis and scholarship.[333]

(5) There is another, related error in Hoglund's description of my view of Rom. 9:8 and the children of the promise: that in my view, "one is named a child of the promise because one has become a member of Abraham's family by faith, as in

---

[328] Hoglund, *Called*, 54; cf. N. T. Wright, *What Saint Paul Really Said: Was Paul of Tarsus the Real Founder of Christianity?* (Grand Rapids, MI: Eerdmans, 1997), 125, 132.
[329] Hoglund, *Called*, 53, citing Abasciano, *Romans 9.1-9*, 201.
[330] Hoglund, *Called*, 54.
[331] Ibid.
[332] Taken as an example from Abasciano, *Romans 9.1-9*, 198.
[333] Another possibility is that Hoglund mistakenly has me pegged as an advocate of the New Perspective on Paul (NPP) and is reading certain NPP views into my work and interpreting what I say through that lens. But I do not fundamentally hold to the NPP, though I believe it has brought many valuable insights to Pauline scholarship and seek to identify where my research supports the NPP to some degree and where it is at odds with it. Some readers could get the wrong impression from places I find support for certain aspects of the NPP. On my view of the NPP, see further, note 338 below.

Galatians 3:26-29."[334] This is not stated in my treatment of Rom. 9:8, including the page Hoglund cites. And it is not my view. In my view, Paul certainly held that one becomes a member of Abraham's family by faith as he teaches in Gal. 3:26-29. However, one is not named a child of the promise because one has become a member of Abraham's family, but divine naming, which is also by faith, makes one a member of Abraham's family. As an analogy, we could imagine that a formal adoption would be effected by a legal document naming the child involved as adopted to the adopting family.

Both naming and becoming a member of God's covenant people can be said to be by faith because faith ultimately leads to both of them. More specifically, God responds to a person's faith by naming the person as his child, making the person in fact his child. As I expressed it in the section critiqued by Hoglund, "those who have been called, those who belong to Christ, have been called by his name as his own people, so that they bear his name and have become his family."[335]

(6) Hoglund asserts that I understand the works of the law "as Jewish marks of covenant membership such as circumcision."[336] But that is false, and I do not see any indication of that view on the page of my work cited by Hoglund.[337] My actual position is that "the works of the Law" refers to what the Law requires. I do, however, hold that Jewish marks of covenant membership were often especially in view for Paul in his speaking of the works of the Law, though not exclusively in view.[338]

---

[334] Hoglund, *Called*, 54.
[335] Abasciano, *Romans 9.1-9*, 205. N.B.: The phrase "so that" in this quotation indicates result.
[336] Hoglund, *Called*. 54.
[337] He cites Abasciano, *Romans 9.1-9*, 201.
[338] For my view of "the works of the Law" and related matters in Paul, see ibid., 220–1; and especially, Abasciano, *Romans 9.10-18*, 226–7. It should be noted that my affirmation of the position of N. T. Wright and others that the language of justification in Paul refers to covenant membership (citing Wright, *Climax*, 148, 203, 214) was not meant to restrict the meaning of justification language to covenant membership or to endorse Wright's larger view of justification. I only meant to endorse the view as described in the references to Wright mentioned above, which record an earlier stage of Wright's view. I tried to give some indication of covenant membership as only part of the meaning of justification language in Paul by saying that "the vocabulary of human righteousness should be understood as *including* the notion of covenant membership" (Abasciano, *Romans 9.1-9*, 220; emphasis added). Similarly, when I wrote, "We have seen reason to believe that *while the vocabulary of God's righteousness is rich and multifaceted, to a significant degree* it should be understood covenantally as God's faithfulness to fulfill his promises," I tried to give some indication in the italicized words that covenant faithfulness is only a part of God's righteousness while emphasizing it is as an extremely important part (ibid.; emphasis added). As implied in ibid., 171–2, I regard the most fundamental meaning of God's righteousness to be God's faithfulness to his own person and character. But divine righteousness often has more specific meanings that are a manifestation of this broader meaning. In Romans 9, there is a more specific meaning in view, and that is God's faithfulness to his promises (to Israel). As for human righteousness, my view is that Paul regarded its most basic, essential meaning to be right standing/relationship with God. However, in the New Covenant, this is thoroughly tied up with covenant membership. If one is right with God, then one is a member of the New Covenant. If one is a member of the New Covenant, then one is right with God. Both blessings are contingent on faith. God responds to faith by naming believers as his own people, which makes them members of the New Covenant, and declaring them to be right with him (righteous), which makes them in fact right with him.

(7) Hoglund states, "Abasciano is correct that one of Paul's primary goals in Romans is to show that those who imitate Abraham's faith are his children (Rom 4:16-17), but calling speaks about God's way of bringing this family about."[339] This is worded as if divine naming does not speak about God's way of bringing Abraham's family about, but it surely does since it is effectual. This seems to be based on the false assumption that divine naming is not effectual.

(8) Regarding God's purpose connected to election[340] spoken of in Rom. 9:11, Hoglund claims, "Abasciano inserts his point about faith into this verse and argues that God's purpose in election is his decision to choose people not on the basis of works, but on the basis of faith," and he refers readers to Piper's argument against my view of calling being based on faith vis-à-vis Rom. 9:11-12.[341]

There are two substantial problems here. First, I do not argue "that God's purpose in election is his decision to choose people not on the basis of works, but on the basis of faith," and there is no indication of that position in the place in my book Hoglund cites.[342] Rather, I argue that God's purpose in election is to bless the world in Abraham[343] or, to put it more simply, to save the world.[344] God's decision to choose people by faith apart from works or ancestry comes in as God's means of accomplishing that purpose of election, to save the world.[345]

Second, Hoglund refers readers to Piper's argument but shows no awareness that the very section of my book that he references responds in detail to Piper's argument.[346] So Hoglund offers no rebuttal to my response to Piper's argument. There is even specific response to the part of Piper's argument that Hoglund singles out for special mention, presumably singled out because he finds it especially compelling.

(9) Hoglund asserts that I read "Romans 9:7-8 not as evidence for sovereign divine selection (on whatever and for whatever purpose), but as a general statement that through a promise—in Genesis, this is Isaac, and in the present, *faith*—God will name some people as members of Abraham's family."[347] In context, this appears to be a criticism. Assuming that, there are two problems here. First, I do not particularly deny that Rom. 9:7-8 provides evidence of sovereign divine selection. It does, but that is not its focus. Paul makes that point more directly in later verses. What Paul is doing in vv. 7-8 is summing up the meaning of his statement in 9:6b: the covenant descendants of Abraham who are heir to the covenant promises of God are not determined by physical descent, but only the children of the promise are regarded as the covenant people to

---

[339] Hoglund, *Called*, 54.
[340] Ibid., uses the translation "[God's] purpose of election," but this is not the best translation. "The purpose of God in election" or some other translation that conveys what most interpreters take as the basic meaning of the phrase—election as the means to accomplishing God's purpose—would be best in my judgment. For a detailed discussion of the phrase, see Abasciano, *Romans 9.10-18*, 46-50. My phrasing above is an attempt to describe the phrase neutrally.
[341] Hoglund, *Called*, 54-5.
[342] He cites Abasciano, *Romans 9.10-18*, 55.
[343] Ibid., 49-50.
[344] As I put it in ibid., 167 and 219.
[345] See ibid., 50-7, and most directly, 56-7.
[346] See ibid., 54-5 for my response to Piper.
[347] Hoglund, *Called*, 55.

whom the promises were made.³⁴⁸ This is a matter of exegesis, and Hoglund does not present any substantial exegesis of these verses. I refer the reader to my detailed exegesis of Rom. 9:7-8.³⁴⁹

Second, while it is true that Isaac was the promise in Genesis, faith is not the promise in the present. Paul teaches in Romans 4 that covenant membership/elect status/justification/heirship of God's blessings is the promise, and faith is the means through which the promise is obtained.

(10) Hoglund responds to my position that Rom. 9:8 indicates that covenant membership is by faith by claiming that this is not the point of the verse but that it evidences a naming that "is selective and based on God's sovereign word or promise."³⁵⁰ But that does not counter my view of calling. It is a major concession to it. It concedes that naming is in view. And my position agrees that it is a selective naming based on God's word/promise. But in the context of the epistle, and based on the meaning of "the children of the promise," God's selective naming based on his word/promise falls on those who believe.

This is a matter of exegesis. And the question of whether Rom. 9:8 indicates that covenant membership is by faith depends on the meaning of "the children of the promise" (τὰ τέκνα τῆς ἐπαγγελίας). I have provided a detailed discussion of the meaning of the phrase that concludes that faith in God's promise is part of what characterizes the children of promise,³⁵¹ but Hoglund has not shown any sign of grappling with my analysis. Nor does he provide any substantial discussion of the phrase in his critique.

Hoglund does appeal to 9:9 as demonstrating that covenant membership by faith is not the point of 9:8 because it reveals a promise that "is a miraculous divine word that ensures that Sarah will give birth to a son,"³⁵² from which he infers a naming that "is selective and based on God's sovereign word or promise."³⁵³ I have already pointed out that this is not inconsistent with 9:8 affirming covenant membership by faith or naming by faith. But it is telling that Hoglund identified that one aspect of the promise yet ignored other aspects that support faith as part of the picture. Just one example is that in Rom. 4:19-22 Paul highlights Abraham as believing God's promise of a son by Sarah and considers it justifying faith in fulfillment of Gen. 15:6, a faith that will justify and grant covenant membership to anyone who imitates it. My analysis of the phrase "the children of the promise" found it to be multifaceted with one important and prominent facet being faith in Christ.

---

³⁴⁸ Cf. the summary of Rom. 9:7-8 by Schreiner, *Romans*, 476, whose argument for calling as an effectual summoning Hoglund adopts: "Both verses 7 and 8 restate the main thesis of verse 6b: the saved offspring of Abraham are not merely the physical children of Abraham or the children of the flesh; they are the children of Isaac and the children of promise." While different than my summary in some respects, there is substantial similarity.
³⁴⁹ See Abasciano, *Romans 9.1-9*, 189–208.
³⁵⁰ Hoglund, *Called*, 55.
³⁵¹ See Abasciano, *Romans 9.1-9*, 196–8.
³⁵² Hoglund, *Called*, 55.
³⁵³ Ibid.

(11) Hoglund struggles in interpreting Romans 9 in relation to calling because he has to concede that naming is present. Speaking of Rom. 9:22-26, he concedes, "It is challenging to balance the different uses of calling in this text."[354] But I do not find it challenging at all. Naming accounts perfectly for every occurrence of the concept in Romans 9. I would suggest that it is only challenging for Hoglund because he is struggling against the clear meaning of naming in the text and to make calling mean summoning at least some of the time in the passage. He has already acknowledged that calling is naming in Rom. 9:7. So when Paul comes back to calling later in the passage, why would it not be naming?

(12) Hoglund says that naming is difficult for Rom. 9:24 and summoning is difficult for 9:25-26, and that accepting summoning in 9:24 makes 9:25-26 more difficult.[355] But naming is certain in 9:25-26 because it uses the double accusative and clearly speaks of designation: "As he also says in Hosea, 'I will call "Not My People," "My People," and "Not Loved," "Loved." And it will be, in the place where it was said to them, "You are not my people," there they will be called sons of the living God.'" But this, then, almost certainly means that calling in 9:24 is also naming because vv. 25-26 give biblical support for Paul's claim about calling in 9:24.

Hoglund gives two reasons for preferring summoning in 9:24. The first is the reference in 9:23 to the vessels of mercy having been prepared beforehand for glory.[356] He reasons that this "strongly pulls in favor of the similar construction in Romans 8:30, where 'predestined' and 'called' are related in sequence (cf. Gal 1:15). 'Summoned' here makes good sense of the dynamic between a prior setting apart and a historical divine address."[357] But it is not at all evident that these observations support summoning.

First, Hoglund assumes a summoning sense for calling in Rom. 8:30, but a naming sense fits Rom. 8:30 perfectly well. Similarly, a historical naming fits just as well with a prior setting apart.[358] Indeed, in Gal. 1:15, invoked by Hoglund, the naming sense (with a nuance of designation or appointment) fits with the prior setting apart even better than a summoning sense (or at least just as well). Paul is speaking about his appointment as an apostle there.[359] And at the risk of stating the obvious, a sense of appointment goes even better with Paul's appointment to apostleship than does a summoning to apostleship.

---

[354] Ibid.
[355] Ibid.
[356] Ibid., 55-6.
[357] Ibid., 56.
[358] Though the prior setting apart need not be thought to be nonhistorical or prehistorical. See Section 4.2.d.8.c concerning foreknowledge in Rom. 8:29.
[359] Even Hoglund's main exegetical source for his position on calling, Thomas Schreiner, takes Gal. 1:15 to be talking about Paul's appointment to be an Apostle (*Galatians* [ZECNT; Grand Rapids, MI: Zondervan, 2010], 101). This does not mean that Schreiner thinks that calling specifically refers to appointment there. But he agrees that the verse is about Paul's appointment to apostleship. Schreiner's treatment of Gal. 1:15 is actually a bit muddled because he assumes calling is a summons. He seems to equate Paul's calling with his appointment to apostleship. Yet he goes on to define Paul's calling as a summons.

Second, Hoglund is critiquing my argument that the figurative/theological use of calling always refers to divine naming. So pointing to an alleged summoning sense in Rom. 8:30 because of a similar sequence of thought is begging the question. Third, the immediate context of naming as the clear meaning of calling in 9:25-26 is more determinative than some similarity to a different section of the epistle.

The second reason Hoglund gives for favoring summoning over naming in 9:24 is that it lacks a double accusative.[360] But a double accusative is not *required* for the naming sense. Indeed, Rom. 9:7, which Hoglund concedes is a naming, lacks the double accusative. The double accusative certainly indicates naming, but lack of it does not argue for summoning over naming. This makes the naming sense of calling in Rom. 9:25-26 clear and obvious—both verses use the double accusative!

(13) Hoglund's argument for calling in 9:25 as summoning is extremely strained. He observes that "Paul replaces the LXX verb 'I will say' (ἐρῶ) in Hosea 2:25 with καλέσω: 'I will *call* "not my people," my people.'"[361] Hoglund sees this as Paul applying "God's declaration that he will restore his rejected people ... to Gentile Christians."[362] That is true, whether one sees it as a direct application or the application of a principle drawn from the passage. But that declaration is clearly phrased as a designation. Those designated "not my people" will be designated "my people," which indicates that those who were rejected will be accepted. This is so obvious because of the use of the double accusative—a definitive factor—and the descriptors ("not my people" vs. "my people") that it should go without saying. Moreover, if the original context in the LXX is important, as Hoglund implies, then the designating sense of calling is all the clearer since "Not My People" (οὐ λαῷ μου) in the original context actually functions as a name. Even Hoglund's own translation of the passage puts "not my people" in quotation marks to indicate it is a name or designation.[363]

Hoglund seems to contrast the concept of a declaration over against that of a naming/ designation. But a designation is a declaration. So that does not support a summons over designation. In fact, it supports naming over summoning. For a summoning is not so much a declaration as it is an invitation or perhaps a command. Perhaps it could be argued that either an invitation or a command is a form of declaration; one can declare an invitation or a command. But naming/designating is a more direct form of declaration; it asserts something. But at the very least, naming/designation is no less of a declaration than summoning. It seems like Hoglund is again falling prey to the false assumption that naming is not effectual. For he concludes that Paul's use of καλεῖν "underscores 'the effective character of the Lord's word that makes Not-my-people the Lord's people.'"[364] But in my view, God's designation is effective to make "Not my People" his own people.

---

[360] Hoglund, *Called*, 56.
[361] Ibid.
[362] Ibid.
[363] Ibid. Cf. the NETS translation, which indicates "not my people" is a name by capitalizing each word of the phrase.
[364] Ibid. Hoglund quotes Seifrid, "Romans," 647, here.

Hoglund argues that Paul in essence merges the two senses of summoning and naming/designation.[365] But he has not provided any substantial reason to think Paul has merged the two domains. The summoning aspect is simply not needed. Every instance of calling in Romans 9 makes perfect (and better) sense with the meaning of naming/designation. But not every instance works with summoning. The sense of designation is certain in 9:25-26, and virtually certain in 9:24 because of its connection to 9:25-26. The sense of designation is much more likely in 9:7 in light of the Old Testament background and its connection to 9:24-26. It is also more likely in 9:12 because of its connection to 9:7 and the otherwise uniform theme in the chapter.

(14) Assuming the blurry combination of designation and summoning in Rom. 9:24-26 (especially 9:25), Hoglund further claims that summoning can explain the designation aspect in a way that the designation aspect cannot explain the summoning aspect.[366] This seems to be an attempt to indicate that summoning is the more fundamental meaning (in the figurative/theological use of the terminology). I have just argued that the notion that Paul merges the designation and summoning domains is unjustified. But even if we grant the point, the contention that summoning accounts for the aspect of designation while the latter cannot account for the former does not hold up to scrutiny.

Hoglund's reasoning for this point is baffling. The basis for his assertion seems to be that divine summoning is "an event of divine discourse" but naming/designation is not.[367] But naming/designation actually is an event of divine discourse, and it is very puzzling that Hoglund assumes it is not. Naming someone is an intelligible act of speaking,[368] as is designating someone something. Divine naming or divine designating is God speaking, an act of divine discourse.

Hoglund does not do justice to my argumentation for calling as naming in Paul. He does not really consider the main points I have made or the various lines of evidence I have presented or my discussion of the various texts. Critically, he does not show awareness of a primary part of my position that undermines much of his critique, and that is that naming is effectual. He also seems to pigeonhole me as holding to the New Perspective on Paul, which I do not particularly hold (though I accept some of its claims as do most scholars), attributing some specific positions to me that I do not hold. The number and degree of problems in Hoglund's critique are shocking, leaving even greater confidence in the conclusion that Paul conceived of calling as a divine naming/designation/appointment.

****

Romans 9:24 recalls Paul's language from earlier in the chapter (9:7, 12), continuing the primary concern of the argument: God's right to name/call whom he chooses as his people, that is, to name his people by faith rather than works or ancestry.[369] This

---

[365] Hoglund, *Called*, 56.
[366] Ibid., 56–7.
[367] Ibid.
[368] Cf. Ibid., 45, where Hoglund seems to define "discourse" as "intelligible speech."
[369] Cf. Moo, *Romans*, 629, who sees Paul as returning to the theme of vv. 6–13, which concerns God's calling, and points out that Paul uses "the characteristic vocabulary of that earlier paragraph" in vv. 24–29. Unlike Moo, I do not take vv. 14–23 as an excursus, and I would not separate v. 23 from v. 24.

principle has both a positive and a negative side to it. Positively, God names those who believe in Christ as his children/covenant people. Negatively, God rejects those who do not believe in Christ from the covenant people.

Paul has been defending the righteousness of this call throughout the chapter, namely that it is faithful to his promises to Israel. Having given a substantial and complex defense of the principle in the previous verses, he now states the positive, practical result of the principle very specifically: from Jews and Gentiles God has called/named his covenant people/his children/the seed of Abraham. This practical result has been in view throughout the discourse, as we have argued throughout the exegesis of the chapter. But Paul has not stated it as explicitly as at this climactic, heavily stressed moment. It is not until he has given substantial and powerful defense of God's right to effect this result that he dares to articulate it with specificity and in such an offensive form.[370]

Paul's return to the language of calling here makes explicit what he has left only implicit in the argument of ch. 9 to this point: the identity of the true Israel referred to in 9:6 (i.e., the second occurrence of Ἰσραήλ in 9:6). Our exegesis of 9:6 took a nuanced view of the true Israel mentioned there, finding that Paul did not define the true Israel at that point in the argument, but left the definition implicit in light of what he had written in the epistle.[371] That definition, we concluded, is the church composed of Jews and Gentiles, who believe in Jesus Christ. Paul now makes that definition explicit by stating that God has called his people, the vessels of mercy, from both Jews and Gentiles.

I would submit that Paul did not expressly articulate that definition for a strategic rhetorical purpose, to delay direct articulation of the offensive idea in this section of the epistle until he had given substantial argumentation for God's right to choose whom he wants as his people, or to put it in the language of v. 24, to name whom he chooses as his people, specifically, to name his people from both Jews and Gentiles. This has been the point of Paul's discourse all along in Romans 9, and Paul would intend and expect the careful reader to see that. But leaving an offensive point implicit while presenting the case for the principle that would justify it, even if the audience is expected to grasp the unstated point/application or even if the point had been made explicitly in an earlier section of the discourse, can help in persuading the audience to accept the argument. Sometimes explicit, specific language can raise resistance to an argument when vaguer language will meet with a fairer hearing. In the following verses (25-29), Paul will give evidence from the Old Testament for this more specific claim that God not only has the right to name whomever he wants as his people, but that he has indeed named the Church of Jews and Gentiles as the seed of Abraham, heirs to the covenant promises.

---

[370] Keeping in mind that Paul's argument is framed as largely aimed at a Jewish point of view skeptical of his gospel. Cf. Section 4.2.b.3, and for a caveat on speaking about the "Jewish point of view" and the like, see Abasciano, *Romans 9.10-18*, 172-3 n. 89.

[371] The modern exegete also has the benefit of access to Paul's other NT epistles for help in determining his meaning in any Pauline text. That evidence supports our conclusion concerning the implicit meaning of the true Israel in Rom. 9:6. N.B.: To say that the meaning is implicit is to say that the meaning is really there and is discoverable; it is just not expressly or directly stated.

4.3. Summary/Conclusion

Due to the length of this chapter and its role as the central chapter in the book, presenting my exegesis of Rom. 9:19-24, I will provide a detailed summary of its findings in the concluding chapter of this investigation. Here, I will provide only a very basic, general summary/conclusion to the present chapter.

Romans 9:19-24 takes up the objection to vv. 14-18 that God would be unrighteous to judge Israel for their sin (of rejecting Christ) because God accomplishes his purpose through their sin, especially since his decision to name his people by faith apart from works or ancestry provoked their rebellion. Verses 19-24 support 9:14-18 (and its denial that God is unrighteous for choosing his people by faith apart from works or ancestry) with scriptural argumentation that highlights God's right to name whom he wants as his people and especially to judge Israel, in light of his identity as the sovereign Creator God and the elector of Israel, and in light of humanity's humble estate before him. After 9:19 articulates the objection, vv. 20-21 give the basic response (20a) and scriptural grounding (20b-21). Like the thought of clay challenging the potter's fashioning of it, it is ludicrous to suggest that God Almighty does not have the right to name whom he wants as his people and to bestow eschatological blessing upon them or to judge with eschatological condemnation those who rebel against his plan of salvation.

Verses 22-24 then interpret and apply vv. 20b-21. In so doing, they become more specific and give greater clarity, drawing the logical stress of Paul's rhetoric in the section (20b-24) in support of 20a and its rebuke of the objection raised in 9:19. Paul reveals that God has rightly endured those who will receive his eschatological wrath for three purposes: to show his wrath, to make known his power in judgment and salvation, and most primarily, to make known the riches of his glory upon vessels of mercy in the age to come. The first two purposes contribute to the third.

The passage comes to a climax in v. 24, where Paul indicates that God has named his people, who are the objects of his mercy that will enjoy the riches of his eschatological glory, from Gentiles as well as Jews. This comes as the climax because, in light of the exclusion of unbelieving Jews, the inclusion of Gentiles is the most offensive aspect of the gospel Paul defends in Romans 9. The logical weight of 9:20b-29 in support of 20a comes to rest here (vv. 25-29 furnish scriptural support for v. 24). Romans 9:19-29 supports 9:14-18 as the former refutes an objection to the argument of the latter. At the same time, by indicating more specifically what God has done in its argument for his right to do as he has done, 9:19-24 (particularly v. 24) actually draws the emphasis in the rhetorical flow of Paul's argument from 9:14 through 9:29 and joins 9:8 (covenant membership is only by faith) to form the main point of Rom. 9:6b-29 in support of 9:6a (the faithfulness of God to his promises to Israel). (See the concluding chapter of this work for the broader flow of Romans 9.)

5

Conclusion

This investigation picks up where my previous study of Rom. 9:10-18 left off, bringing our intertextual exegesis of Romans 9 to v. 24. I have provided summaries of my exegesis of the Old Testament background texts in Section 2.1.d (for Isa. 29:16), Section 2.2.e (for Isa. 45:9), and Section 2.3.b (for Jer. 18:6) in Chapter 2 along with some concluding observations on those texts in Section 2.4. A summary of our survey of interpretive traditions relating to the Old Testament potter/clay texts has been provided at the end of Chapter 3 in Section 3.11. Hence, there is no need to provide a summary of that material here; I would direct the reader to the aforementioned locations in this monograph for a summary of the findings of this investigation in Chapters 2–3. That leaves the need for a detailed summary of our exegesis of Rom. 9:19-24 conducted in Chapter 4. Due to the length of Chapter 4 and the space needed to summarize it adequately, we will provide the summary in this chapter (rather than adding to the length of Chapter 4) before giving some consideration to how the rest of Romans 9 after v. 24 impacts exegesis of 9:1-24. We will then consider the logical flow of Romans 9 and offer concluding reflections for this volume.

5.1. Conclusion Regarding Exegesis of Rom. 9:19-24

We compared the Greek text of Rom. 9:20-21 with the Greek and Hebrew texts of Isa. 29:16, Isa. 45:9, and Jer. 18:6. All three Old Testament texts have some level of verbal correspondence with Rom. 9:20b-21. Isaiah 29:16 shares the greatest level of verbal correspondence with Rom. 9:20-21, which gives an informal, exact quotation from the LXX of a portion of the Old Testament passage (μὴ ἐρεῖ τὸ πλάσμα τῷ πλάσαντι). But the verbal correspondences in each passage are enough to warrant investigation of their original contexts in order to assess whether there is also thematic correspondence and if the meaning of Paul's discourse has been shaped by any of these Old Testament texts. Our analysis suggests the following additional sourcing for Paul's wording in Rom. 9:20-21:

- From Isa. 29:16 only: με ἐποίησας in Rom. 9:20 and ἤ in Rom. 9:21 with the dual-question structure of Rom. 9:21 deriving from Isa. 29:16 and its use of the conjunction ἤ.

- From Isa. 29:16, and (especially) Jer. 18:6: οὐχ in Rom. 9:21 with the question of Rom. 9:21 partly and substantially framed from Jer. 18:6 (cf. also ἐξουσία in Rom. 9:21 and δύναμαι in Jer. 18:6).
- From Isa. 29:16, Isa. 45:9, and Jer. 18:6: ὁ κεραμεύς in Rom. 9:21 (especially from Jer. 18:6) and ὁ πηλός in Rom. 9:21.
- From Isa. 45:9 only: τί in Rom. 9:20b.
- From Jer. 18:6 only (or at least primarily): ποιῆσαι in Rom. 9:21.

Paul clearly quoted from the LXX of Isa. 29:16, though the part he quotes largely accords with the Hebrew of the MT. As for the relationship of the Septuagintal texts of Isa. 29:16, 45:9, and Jer. 18:6 to the Hebrew, the variations in the LXX texts from the Hebrew as represented by the MT carry relatively minimal impact with respect to the overall meaning of the verses. There does not appear to be any significant differences between the relevant Greek texts of the Old Testament as represented by the LXX and the relevant Hebrew texts of the Old Testament as represented by the MT to call for special attention to one or the other for considering potential alternatives in meaning that might have formed Paul's or his readers' understanding of the Old Testament background.

In Rom. 9:19, Paul employs the diatribe to bring up an objection to his argumentation in vv. 15–18 in support of v. 14's denial of unrighteousness in God: "You will say to me then, 'Why does he still find fault? For who has resisted his purpose?'" These questions are rhetorical, implying that God should not find fault, because no one has resisted his purpose. Arising especially from 9:18's assertion that God "hardens whom he desires," the fault mentioned by the objection concerns hard-heartedness in the form of stubborn rejection of Christ. Assuming that the hardening spoken of in 9:17-18 is irresistible/deterministic, many interpreters construe 9:19 to ask why God blames us for doing what he irresistibly caused us to do. But our exegesis of those verses found that their concept of hardening is not deterministic.

As most scholars recognize, Romans 9 resumes the brief discussion of Rom. 3:1-8. Thus, 9:19 is better understood as returning to the questions of 3:5 and 3:7, asking why God blames those whose sin demonstrates his righteousness and magnifies his glory. Romans 9 adds the element of God provoking ethnic Israel's hard-heartedness by making elect status conditional on faith in Christ apart from works or ancestry. The objection is that it would be unrighteous for God to find fault with those whose unrighteousness he provokes in this way and uses to manifest his righteousness and glory. In ch. 3, Paul answers the objection based on God's identity as the judge of the world and the basic point that God must judge. In 9:20-21, he deepens that response with the points that God is the Creator and human beings are his creation, and thus, judging is his prerogative, and challenging his judgment on sin is challenging the Creator/creature distinction.

The objection brought up in 9:19 is "laden with overtones of Job's heart-rending protests against the apparent injustice of God."[1] This is most likely a general allusion

---

[1] Wagner, *Heralds*, 56.

Conclusion 173

to Job's language rather than to any specific text in the book. The book of Job reveals Job's questioning of God's justice as totally preposterous and invalid. By coloring the objection to his gospel in 9:19 with accents of Job's ill-advised accusations against God, Paul colors it with an air of biblical authority as ludicrous and false.

The second question of 9:19 ("For who has resisted his purpose?") provides support for the implicit assertion of the first question that God should not blame those whose unrighteousness he makes accomplish his purpose of glorifying his righteousness, by underscoring that God's purpose is accomplished by their rebellion, and accomplished certainly. The rhetorical question implies with respect to the rejection of Christ by unbelieving ethnic Israel in Paul's day that no one has ever successfully resisted God's purpose of manifesting his power in judgment and salvation and proclaiming his name in all the earth, the purpose identified in 9:17.

The tone of Paul's response to the objection raised in 9:19 is one of stern rebuke, reflecting that the objection is insolent. The hypothetical objector arrogates to himself the right to pass judgment on God and would deny him the right to judge his own creation and do with them as he sees fit. Romans 9:20a is another rhetorical question (like those of v. 19). "Who are you, the one who answers back to God?" means "you should not answer back to God." In context, more fully and specifically it means that the objector should not dispute God's judgment upon unbelieving ethnic Israel when he glorifies himself and accomplishes his purpose through their rebellion. This is the main point of 9:19-24. Verse 19 evokes the point with its objection to Paul's argument. Verse 20a provides the basic response to the objection, in effect asserting that the objection is invalid. And the rest of the passage supports the point of 20a that v. 19's objection to God's judgment on unbelieving ethnic Israel is false.

Responding to the objection of 9:19, Paul quotes Isa. 29:16 in Rom. 9:20a ("Will the thing molded really say to the molder") and, rather than continuing with quotation of Isa. 29:16, completes the thought in the rest of v. 20 with continued allusion to Isa. 29:16 along with allusion to Isa. 45:9. The language in both Isaiah passages in their original contexts challenges the wisdom/appropriateness of God's treatment of his people, and this is mirrored in Rom. 9:20's "Why did you make me like this?" which implies that God was unrighteous in his treatment of ethnic Israel in Paul's day (see below for explanation of this alleged unrighteousness). More specifically, both passages from Isaiah concern rejection of God's chosen means of salvation for his people. The parallels to Romans 9 and Paul's argument as we have construed it are remarkable. They function as pointers to their original contexts.

Our exegesis of Romans 9 has found that Paul has been defending God's plan of salvation in the form of Paul's gospel of justification/salvation/election by faith apart from works or ancestry. The objection to Paul's gospel in Romans 9 is in essence an objection to God's plan of salvation and his right to judge from the viewpoint of unbelieving ethnic Israel, God's historic but rejected people. In response, Paul invokes Isa. 29:16 and 45:9, which concern God's people's objections to his plan of salvation. Just as, against the backdrop of God's people objecting to his plan of salvation, the broad section in which Isa. 29:16 appears (Isa. 28–33) has the purpose of urging trust in the Lord and in his chosen means of salvation rather than in some means of human making, so Rom. 9:20-21, against the backdrop of God's people objecting to his plan of salvation and in the context of Romans, has the purpose of urging trust in the Lord and in his chosen means of salvation, Jesus Christ and faith in him, rather than in some means established by human beings such as ancestry (9:6-13), works (9:12, 32), or their own righteousness (10:3).

Moreover, just as Isa. 29:16 issues a warning to those who would try to avoid the Lord's judgment on their disloyalty and rebellion against him, so Rom. 9:20-21 issues a rebuke of the one—represented by the interlocutor—who tries to avoid God's judgment on their unbelief, disloyalty, and rebellion against him in their rejection of Christ. And just as the warning of Isa. 29:16 is issued on the ground that God's blessing would fall upon the righteous and his judgment upon the wicked, so the rebuke of Rom. 9:20-21 is ultimately grounded on God's blessing for the righteous by faith in Christ and his judgment upon the unrighteous. Furthermore, just as the context of Isa. 29:16 prophesies the reversal of God's hardening judgment upon his people by the fulfillment of his word in the working of his salvation, so the context of Rom. 9:20-21 looks to the reversal of God's hardening judgment upon his people by the fulfillment of his word in the working of his salvation/the gospel.

The context of Isa. 45:9 also concerns Israel's rejection of God's plan of salvation. But it specifies the reason for Israel's objection to God's plan—opposition to his chosen means of salvation, specifically the man he chose as the deliverer, a Gentile king (Cyrus). Just as the Gentile ethnicity of God's choice of a Gentile savior (Cyrus) and all that it meant hardened Israel of Isaiah's day to God's plan of salvation and provoked their rejection of it, so God's choice of Jesus as savior, and faith in him apart from works or ancestry as the means of participation in God's salvation of his people, hardened Israel in Paul's day to God's plan of salvation (the gospel) and provoked their rejection of it. Moreover, just as one of the main purposes of YHWH's choice of Cyrus as the deliverer of his people was for the world to know that YHWH is the only true God, so one of the main purposes of God's choice of Jesus as the deliverer of his people was for the world to know the saving power and glory of God.

Furthermore, just as Israel's resistance to God's choice of a savior for his people in Isaiah's day was, in effect, resistance to God's plan for the salvation of the Gentiles, so Israel's resistance to Jesus as the savior of all in Paul's day was, in effect, resistance to God's plan for the salvation of the Gentiles. Finally, just as the purpose of Isa. 45:9 and the passage in which it is found (45:9-13) is to urge those who object to God's plan of salvation/choice of a deliverer to abandon their distrust of and opposition to God and his plan, and rather to trust in and embrace them, so the purpose of Rom. 9:20-21 is ostensibly to urge those who reject God's choice of a savior—Jesus—and God's plan of salvation by faith in him to abandon their distrust of and opposition to God and his plan and rather to trust in and embrace them. But the more fundamental and practical purpose was to encourage acceptance of Paul's teaching by his audience of Christians in Rome, who were not necessarily resistant to his teaching or to Jesus.

The question of 9:20b-c ("Will the thing molded really say to the molder, 'Why did you make me like this?'") is rhetorical and implies a negative answer—the thing molded will not and would not ask such a question of the molder. The idea that a pot would object to the way it was made is preposterous. Similarly, Paul's use of the metaphor portrays objecting to God's judgment on unbelieving ethnic Israel for its rejection of Christ as absurd; it turns the Creator/creature relationship on its head. This sort of overt sense is present in the Isaiah texts with respect to objecting to God's plan of salvation, and Paul's allusion to these texts underscores the point in Rom. 9:20. The metalepsis of Isa. 29:16 especially intimates that the objection being considered practically (1) denies God as Creator because it denies his basic right as Creator to judge his creatures; (2) has man sitting in judgment of God rather than God sitting in judgment of man because it seeks to avoid God's judgment and renders judgment on God's actions; (3) denies God as savior because it serves the rejection of his plan of salvation; (4) has man saving himself rather than being saved by God; and (5) has man possessing superior wisdom to God, because it serves the establishment of a human plan of salvation in place of God's plan.

The transumption of Isa. 45:9 mostly reinforces these meaning-effects. But it adds two nuances. First, since Isa. 45:9 uses the metaphor in reference to the rejection of God's choice of a savior (not just his chosen means of salvation more generally) and his plan for the salvation of the Gentiles, Paul's allusion to the verse contributes to the perception that his use of the metaphor has these same concerns in view vis-à-vis Jesus Christ and his gospel. Second, allusion to Isa. 45:9 adds to the sense of the absurdity of contending against God's judgment by 45:10 setting forth an additional metaphorical illustration, namely a child in the process of being born challenging its father or mother about its constitution.

While the rhetorical question of Rom. 9:20b-c ("Will the thing molded really say to the molder, 'Why did you make me like this?' ") makes the point that the creature should not challenge the Creator's plans for or treatment of the creature, 9:21 adds another rhetorical question making the same basic point from a different, supplementary angle: "Or does the potter not have the right over the clay to make from the same lump one a vessel unto honor and another unto dishonor?" (9:21). The question of 9:20b-c makes the point with respect to the right of the clay/creature—It is not right for the creature to dispute God's plans for or treatment of or judgment of the creature. The question of 9:21 makes the point with respect to the right of the potter/Creator—it *is* right for God to make from the same group a vessel unto honor and another vessel unto dishonor, and it is absurd to suggest otherwise as it would be to suggest a potter does not have the right to make what he pleases of the clay he uses. This draws the logical stress over 9:20b-c because it is more prominent and pointed due to being more specific and more in line with the focus on God in Romans 9, leading naturally into the following verses, which seem to pick up especially 9:21 for interpretation and explanation.

Paul alludes to Jer. 18:6 in Rom. 9:21. The thematic correspondence between the two verses in their contexts is perhaps even more remarkable than the thematic correspondence between Rom. 9:20 and Isa. 29:16 and 45:9, for Jer. 18:6 and its context answers the objection Paul is addressing even more directly than the passages from Isaiah, specifically addressing God's right to judge Israel. In response to a challenge to God's right to judge unbelieving Israel for its rejection of the gospel, Paul alludes in Rom. 9:21 to an OT passage that argues for God's right to judge Israel.

Just as Jer. 18:6 serves as part of the grounding for 18:1-12's call to Israel to turn from covenant unfaithfulness to submission to the Lord and his ways, so Paul's allusion to it serves as part of the grounding for his implicit call to turn from covenant unfaithfulness in the form of rejection of Christ and his gospel to submission to God's ways in Christ and the righteousness of his judgment upon unbelieving ethnic Israel. And just as Jeremiah called Israel to repent based on God's intention to destroy them for their evil rebellion and to spare them if they would repent, so the implicit appeal of Rom. 9:20-21 to repent of opposition to the gospel (in the form of objection to God's judgment on unbelieving Jews for their rejection of the gospel) is ultimately based in part on God's intention to bless those who believe in Christ and to judge those who reject Christ. Paul's more fundamental and practical purpose in all of this was again to encourage acceptance of his teaching by his audience of Christians in Rome, who were not necessarily resistant to his teaching or to Jesus or to God's judgment upon unbelieving ethnic Israel.

Further thematic contact between the contexts of Rom. 9:21 and Jer. 18:6 can be seen in the possibility of escaping God's judgment. As we saw in our exegesis of Rom. 9:18, the hardening of Romans 9–11 is reversible, and Paul holds out hope in Romans 11 that through his ministry hardened Jews would turn from their hard-heartedness and come to faith in Christ. Moreover, Paul alludes to multiple Old Testament passages in Romans 9 prior to v. 21 with the intertextual significance of God's purpose to embrace those whom he had rejected, including apostate Israel. The Jeremiah context heavily stresses the possibility of escaping God's judgment by repentance.

To the attentive reader, Paul's allusion to Jer. 18:6 conveys that unbelieving ethnic Israel need not finally end up under the judgment to which the interlocutor objects. This thematic connection confirms our detection of both the motif earlier in Romans 9 and Paul's allusion to Jer. 18:6 in Rom. 9:21. In light of the heavily conditional nature of the context of Jer. 18:6, Paul's allusion to the passage tinges his reply to the interlocutor's objection with a sense of conditionality (cf. the conditionality of 2 Tim. 2:20-21 and its use of the potter/clay metaphor). This adds an additional support for Paul's defense of God's righteousness in election, showing of mercy, and hardening. While the objection Paul is addressing is not focused on Jewish inability to avoid God's judgment, the point that they can avoid it weakens the interlocutor's charge in a supplementary way.

The intertextual undercurrent of conditionality emanating from Paul's allusion to Jer. 18:6 is related to another theme that comes into greater focus later in Paul's argument—Israel's responsibility, guilt, and wickedness in their unbelief (cf. Rom. 9:30–10:21). The context of Jer. 18:6 lays heavy stress on the wickedness and culpability of Israel since they could repent and be spared but stubbornly refused to repent. Paul's allusion subtly casts unbelieving ethnic Israel as both extremely wicked and fully responsible for their condemnation before God. That contributes to the vindication of God's judgment on them against the interlocutor's objection.

The passages from Isaiah and Jeremiah to which Paul alludes are corporately focused. Paul's concern is not the predestination of individuals to salvation or damnation but the defense of God's treatment of Israel, given the truth of his gospel of justification and election by faith. This includes defense of God's faithfulness to his covenant promises to Israel and the righteousness of God's judgment against unbelieving ethnic Israel on the supposition that his Jew-hardening gospel is true. It also comports with the conclusion that Paul operates with a primarily corporate concept of election in Romans 9–11.

Paul's use of Isa. 29:16 and Jer. 18:6 is in line with a pattern of Pauline interpretive practice that we have seen at work repeatedly in Romans 9—Paul's OT allusions frequently anticipate the next or otherwise later stage of his argument. In the case of his use of Isa. 29:16, Paul subliminally anticipates the theme of the reversal of hardening, which is a theme he will come to express explicitly later in Romans 9–11. In the case of his use of Jer. 18:6, Paul again anticipates the theme of the reversal of hardening and adds anticipation of the theme of the guilt and responsibility of Israel, which he takes up in Rom. 9:30ff. That such intertextual anticipation is a Pauline interpretive practice strengthens the probability of an allusion to Jer. 18:6 in Rom. 9:21 since the proposed allusion falls in line with that practice. And in properly circular fashion, seeing that practice in play in Rom. 9:21 further confirms that this is indeed a Pauline practice and that his use of Scripture was contextual and evocative of additional associations of unstated elements of the original contexts of his allusions.

The Old Testament background sheds light on Paul's conception of God as potter and the language of molding and making in 9:20-21. In all three Old Testament background texts, the language of molding and making primarily refers to God's shaping the situation of Israel, whether in the form of being subject to the conditions of his plan of salvation (the Isaiah texts) or consignment to judgment versus blessing (the Isaiah texts to some degree, but especially Jer. 18). Both forms of molding/making are probably in view in Romans 9, the condition for salvation in the New Covenant that hardened ethnic Israel and to which they objected (the objection Paul is responding to in Rom. 9), and especially God's judgment upon unbelieving Jews in rejecting them from the New Covenant and consigning them to eternal condemnation (a provisional consignment that becomes final if unbelief persists to the end) versus his saving mercy upon believing Gentiles.[2]

The Old Testament background suggests that the most appropriate translation of εἰς in the phrases εἰς τιμὴν and εἰς ἀτιμίαν in 9:21 is "unto," conveying the use of εἰς to indicate the result of an action. In the same verse, Paul's phrase "from the same lump" (ἐκ τοῦ αὐτοῦ φυράματος) is best taken as applying to humanity as a whole, the mass of humanity. As for the meaning of a vessel unto honor (εἰς τιμὴν) versus unto dishonor (εἰς ἀτιμίαν), it refers to eschatological, eternal destiny, that is, salvation versus damnation. More specifically, in line with the corporate orientation of Rom. 9:21, each vessel represents a group made from the mass of humanity, and God making one group unto honor refers to God embracing that group/people as his covenant partner and the bestowal of the covenant blessings wrapped up in that; it is the equivalent of covenant election and its blessings, including salvation. God making unto dishonor in

---

[2] The wording of most of this paragraph is drawn from my forthcoming essay "Romans 9, Election, and Calvinism." While that essay is based in part on the research and manuscript of this book, it was completed before the finalization of this book, enabling me to use some of what I wrote there for this summary.

9:21 means the judgment of eternal condemnation, which will fall upon those who do not have the New Covenant to save them from God's wrath against sin.

In 9:22-24, Paul interprets and applies the potter/clay metaphor of 9:20-21. From 9:20 on (until 9:29) Paul responds to an objection of his use of Exod. 9:16 (Rom. 9:19). After fundamentally refuting the objection with the Old Testament potter/clay metaphor in 9:20-21, Paul constructs his interpretation and application of the potter/clay metaphor in 9:22-24 on the pattern of Exod. 9:16/Rom. 9:17.

Verses 22-24 consist of a difficult, incomplete, conditional sentence with no expressed apodosis. The conjunctive particle δέ near the beginning of 9:22 denotes continuation and further thought development with a nuance of contrast between the unobjectionable point of 9:21 (God's right to save one group and condemn another according to his discretion) and the offensive idea that God has a right to call a people consisting of Gentiles as well as Jews his own covenant partner/heir of salvation and leave unbelieving Jews among the condemned. The point made by 9:22-24 is that God has the right to do all that is mentioned in the verses, which in context includes pouring out his eschatological wrath on the unbelieving (which applies especially in the context to unbelieving Jews) and giving the eschatological riches of his glory to believers, a group consisting of both Jews and Gentiles. Having proved the principle of Rom. 9:17-18 in vv. 20–21, Paul has, in 9:22-24, rephrased the principle in concrete terms related to the specific expression of it that met with the hypothetical interlocutor's objection, election based on faith rather than works or ancestry so that believing Gentiles and Jews are called children of God but unbelieving Jews are accursed.

The adverbial participle θέλων (desiring) in 9:22 is best taken as causal while the power God the Creator desires to show (i.e., express/exercise) is his supreme divine power and sovereignty as expressed in its exercise in both judgment and mercy/salvation. God's desire to show his wrath and make his power known amounts to purposes for his patient endurance of the vessels of wrath. On the pattern of God forestalling his final judgment on Pharaoh, allowing him to live (Rom. 9:17 quoting Exod. 9:16), Paul's reference to God enduring "with much patience vessels of wrath prepared for destruction" refers to God patiently tolerating the vessels of wrath by forestalling the pouring out of his wrath upon them in fatal judgment. They bear wrath even in the present to some extent, but God withholds the fullness of eschatological wrath for the final judgment. God's tolerance contributes to wrath being poured out on the vessels of wrath because, like Pharaoh, they build up wrath against themselves by their continuing sin and impenitence, wrath that will eventually come to full expression. But God's tolerance also contributes to the riches of God's glory being given to the vessels of mercy, because it gives opportunity for vessels of wrath to repent and become vessels of mercy.

The perfect participle κατηρτισμένα (prepared) in 9:22 is almost certainly passive and is best understood as having multiple implicit agents (one reason why Paul used the passive)—God and the vessels of wrath (unbelievers), though God's agency is more primary. The vessels of wrath prepare themselves for destruction by their sin and impenitence, which makes them increasingly fit for the destruction God will inflict on them in his wrath. And God prepares them for destruction by marking their wickedness and impenitence and storing up his wrath against them accordingly.

He also prepares them for destruction (at least the Jewish ones) by the offensive/hardening act of making faith in Christ apart from works or ancestry the exclusive basis of covenant membership. But in line with the Old Testament background from Jeremiah, the primary and most basic aspect of God preparing the vessels of wrath for destruction is God slating them for destruction, though they can repent and become vessels of mercy until the day of wrath finally comes. In line with Jeremiah 18 and Rom. 2:4-5, God desires most that people repent and be saved from his wrath rather than continue in their rebellion and perish, but he does desire to bring calamitous judgment upon them if they will not repent.

In various ways, the purpose clause of 9:23 receives emphasis, suggesting it to be God's chief purpose in his patient endurance of the vessels of wrath. That purpose is "to make known the riches of his glory upon vessels of mercy" by bestowing the riches of God's glory upon the vessels of mercy. The riches of God's glory refer to the abundant benefits that God's glory gives, experience of the fullness of all the goodness of the divine nature, the manifold perfections of God, and all the good the almighty God has promised to those who belong to him. The vessels of mercy are objects/recipients of God's mercy in the form of New Covenant membership and all that entails, including the riches of God's glory just mentioned, adoption/sonship, eschatological honor, immortality, eternal life, and experience of God's eschatological grace, love, kindness, forgiveness, redemption, and so on.

Paul indicates that God prepared the vessels of mercy beforehand for glory. The word for preparation used of the vessels of mercy (προετοιμάζω) is different than the word used for preparation of the vessels of wrath in v. 22 (καταρτίζω), most likely to match the difference of group and destiny between the two verses. The concept of preparation is inherently forward looking, but the use of the προ- prefix strengthens that sense of forward-looking action and thus a sense of divine predestination in the passage in the sense of God setting a particular destiny for the vessels of mercy. The strengthened sense of future orientation helps to signal that the preparation of which Paul speaks has the final state of glory in mind.

God prepared the vessels of mercy for experience of his glory and all its blessings in the age to come. The Old Testament background of Paul's potter/clay metaphor in 9:21 suggests that the primary sense of God's preparation of the vessels of mercy for glory in 9:23 is his slating of them for eschatological glory. In addition to this primary sense of preparation as consignment to eschatological blessing, it seems likely that the process of sanctification mentioned in Romans is also in view to some extent as an aspect of the preparation of the vessels of mercy for glory. Paul most likely conceived of Christ's procuring of redemption in his death and resurrection as the fundamental point at which the New Covenant people (the vessels of mercy) were slated for glory. Individual believers come to share in that consignment to glory upon becoming united to Christ through faith. To the degree that the process of sanctification is part of the preparation, the preparation of the vessels of mercy also takes place during the lifetime of believers, who are members of the New Covenant.

Paul expresses three purposes in Rom. 9:22-23 for God enduring the vessels of wrath with great patience: (1) to show his wrath; (2) to make known his power; and (3) to make known the riches of his glory upon vessels of mercy. Purpose 3 is the primary divine purpose for patience with the vessels of wrath, and purposes 1 and 2 are subordinate to it and serve it. The expression of God's wrath on those who do not believe in Christ is necessary to fulfill God's plan to bless the world, for the granting of covenant membership by faith rather than works or ethnicity opens up covenant membership, with its benefit of experience of the riches of the divine glory, to Gentiles. Moreover, the contrast between the divine wrath and the divine mercy manifests the divine glory more fully. Furthermore, the exercise of God's power in salvation fulfills purpose 3.

Verse 24 continues and finishes the sentence begun in vv. 22-23. The relative pronoun οὓς (whom) beginning 9:24 refers directly to σκεύη (vessels) in v. 23, and ἡμᾶς (us) in 9:24 is in apposition to οὓς (whom) in the same verse, yielding, "whom he indeed called—us—not only from Jews but also from Gentiles." As with 9:23, the awkward syntax of v. 24 intentionally brings emphasis in what Paul says. The awkwardness of the syntax in 9:24 is especially pronounced, bringing heavy emphasis to the verse. The reason for Paul's heavy emphasis on 9:24 is that the point it makes (that God has called vessels of mercy not only from Jews but also from Gentiles) addresses the practical heart of the central issue Paul has been dealing with in Romans 9—God's right to call his people by faith rather than works or ancestry, resulting in the exclusion of unbelieving ethnic Jews from the covenant and its salvation, and the inclusion of believing Gentiles. The very phenomenon that called God's faithfulness into question and provoked Paul to mount such a detailed and sustained defense of God's righteousness as Romans 9-11 is expressed in 9:24 at its most offensive point—the inclusion of Gentiles. Paul seems to have waited until v. 24 to make this point explicitly in his argument because of its offensiveness to a typical Jewish viewpoint.

The first καί of v. 24 is best taken as an intensive and translated as "indeed," adding to emphasis on what Paul says in the verse (God calling his people from among the Gentiles as well as the Jews). Further emphasis is given to the inclusion of Gentiles by the "not only/but also" (οὐ μόνον/ἀλλὰ καί) structure Paul uses in 9:24. The covenant people of God, the seed of Abraham, Israel, now consists of both Jews and Gentiles who believe in Jesus.

In saying that God called the vessels of mercy, Paul is saying that God (effectually) named or designated them as his covenant people, who are heirs to the covenant promises. The naming sense of the calling language in vv. 24-26 confirms the same sense to the language we found earlier in the chapter (9:7, 12) and normally in the rest of the New Testament. One way of succinctly describing the thrust of Romans 9 is that Paul has been defending his calling/naming of his people by faith as faithful to his promises to Israel. Having given a substantial and complex defense of the principle in the previous verses, Paul then states the positive, practical result of the principle very specifically: from Jews and Gentiles God has called/named his covenant people/his children/the seed of Abraham. Paul's return to the language of calling in 9:24 makes explicit what he left only implicit in the argument of ch. 9 to that point: the identity of the true Israel referred to in 9:6 (i.e., the second occurrence of Ἰσραήλ in 9:6). Romans 9:24 explicitly reveals that the true Israel is the Church composed of Jews and Gentiles, who believe in Jesus Christ.

5.2. Reflections on Rom. 9:25-33 in Relation to Our Exegesis of Rom. 9:1-24

Romans 9:25-29 gives evidence from the Old Testament for Paul's claim in 9:24 that God has named the Church of Jews and Gentiles as the seed of Abraham, heirs to the covenant promises. Verses 25-26 specifically support the inclusion of Gentiles, and vv. 27-29 specifically support the inclusion of Jews. The latter also indicate and support v. 24's implication that only some Jews are included in the covenant people of God.[3] Indeed, in this context, they seem to indicate that most Jews were excluded from God's New Covenant people.[4]

In addition to supporting the point of 9:24 (see our exegesis of the verse in Chapter 4 of this volume) and its expression of the central issue Paul addresses in Romans 9 (God's right to call his people by faith rather than works or ancestry, resulting in the exclusion of unbelieving ethnic Jews from the covenant and its salvation, and the inclusion of believing Gentiles) in support of God's faithfulness to his promises to Israel, these verses also add confirmation to what we have argued to be a major part of the occasion for Romans 9-11. And that is, that the vast majority of Jews had not received the fulfillment of God's promises to Israel even though the promises had been realized in the elect messianic community, the Church of Jews and Gentiles, consisting of many more Gentiles than Jews. This could be taken to suggest that God was unfaithful to his promises to Israel, making him unrighteous. It is this that posed the most compelling objection to Paul's gospel, moving him to defend that gospel in Romans 9-11 by arguing for God's faithfulness to his promises to Israel.

Romans 9:30-33 is best taken as a literary hinge which concludes 9:6-29 and introduces 10:1-21, but that is more closely connected to the former. Its subject matter belongs to both chapters logically, but rhetorically it belongs more to ch. 9, as indicated by the inferential question of 9:30 (Τί οὖν ἐροῦμεν;), the section's summarizing/concluding force in relation to what precedes, and what appears to be a significant break at 10:1.[5] Whether it goes more with ch. 9 or ch. 10, it is at least significantly

---

[3] That is part of the significance of v. 24 affirming that the Church has been named "from Jews" (ἐξ Ἰουδαίων), likely a genitive of separation.
[4] So e.g., Cranfield, *Romans*, 501-2; Schreiner, *Romans*, 496-7, 499-500.
[5] See further, esp. J. Lambrecht, "The Caesura between Romans 9:30-3 and 10:1-4," *NTS* 45 (1999), 141-7. In light of our focus on Paul's use of the OT, Lambrecht's observation that other subdivisions in Romans 9 are rounded off by OT quotations is especially noteworthy. Indeed, the broad midrashic structure of Romans 9-11 (on which, see Abasciano, "Romans 9:1-9," 95-7) also argues for the inclusion of 9:30-33 with what precedes. The clear majority of scholars take Rom. 9:30-33 with ch. 10. J.-N. Aletti, "L'argumentation paulinienne en Rm 9," *Bib* 68 (1987), 41-56 (42), claims that very few still regard 9:30-33 as part of 9:6-29 (as a conclusion). But A. Reichert, *Der Römerbrief als Gratwanderung: Eine Untersuchung zur Abfassungsproblematik* (FRLANT, 194; Göttingen: Vandenhoeck & Ruprecht, 2001), 168, is more cautious to state that grouping the verses with ch. 10 is the most common view. There are a number of scholars who favor 9:30-33 as more closely related to what precedes, such as Reichert, 168-9 (from a "pragmatisch-funktionaler Perspektive" and with simultaneous approval for the typical structure); N. A. Dahl, *Studies in Paul* (Minneapolis, MN: Augsburg, 1977), 143; Klappert, "Traktat," 76; F. Siegert, *Argumentation bei Paulus: gezeigt an Röm 9-11* (WUNT 34; Tübingen: Mohr Siebeck, 1985), 115-19; M. Theobald, "Kirche und Israel nach Röm 9-11," *Kairos* 29 (1987), 1-22 (12); *Die Römerbrief* (Erträge der Forschung, 294; Darmstadt: Wissenschaftliche Buchgesellschaft, 2000), 263-8; C. Plag, *Israels Wege*

related to ch. 9. The verses strongly confirm our exegesis of Rom. 9:1-24 as arguing for God's right to name his people by faith apart from works or ancestry rather than as arguing for God's right to choose his people unconditionally.

The section opens with an inferential question that clearly points back to Paul's argument in Romans 9 before v. 30: "What, therefore, shall we say?" The sense of this is, "What can be concluded from what I have said in the previous verses?" probably catching up all of Rom. 9:1-29 as in view, but especially vv. 24–29 as the representative climax of what God has the right to do and has indeed done (see again our exegesis of 9:24 in Chapter 4 of this volume).[6] What can be concluded from Rom. 9:1-29 is

> that Gentiles, those not pursuing righteousness, obtained righteousness, but the righteousness that is by faith; but Israel, pursuing a law of righteousness, did not attain to [that] law. Why? Because [they pursued it] not by faith but as by works. They stumbled over the stone of stumbling, just as it is written, "I am laying in Zion a stone of stumbling and a rock of offense, and the one who believes in him will not be put to shame."[7]

Paul sums up the implications of his argument in 9:1-29 to be that the Gentiles have attained the elect status of righteousness by faith while (ethnic) Israel failed to attain it because they pursued it by works rather than faith, echoing the language of 9:12.[8] This is exactly what our exegesis of Rom. 9:1-29 has contended to be going on in the passage in part. Paul has been arguing for God's right to do this very thing, grant New Covenant membership by faith apart from works or ancestry and exclude unbelieving Jews from the covenant. Romans 9:30-33 vindicates our reading of Rom. 9:1-24 over

---

zum Heil: Eine Untersuchung zu Römer 9 bis 11 (Stuttgart: Calwer, 1969), 13; Haacker, *Römer*, 198; R. Schmitt, *Gottesgerechtigkeit-Heilsgeschichte-Israel in der Theologie des Paulus* (Frankfurt: Lang, 1984), 265; W. Schmithals, *Der Römerbrief: Ein Kommentar* (Gütersloh: Gütersloher, 1988), 326; Ziesler, *Romans*, 234–5; H. Boers, *The Justification of the Gentiles* (Peabody, MA: Hendrickson, 1994), 135; Edwards, *Romans*, 229; A. Maillot, "Essai sur les citations vétérotestamentaires continues dans Romains 9 à 11, ou comment se servir de la Torah pour montrer que le 'Christ est la fin de la Torah,'" *ETR* 57 (1982/1), 55–73 (71–2) (seemingly); J. Radermakers and J.-P. Sonnet, "Israël et l'Eglise," *NRT* 107 (1985), 675–97 (678); S. Hillert, *Limited and Universal Salvation: A Text-Oriented and Hermeneutical Study of Two Perspectives in Paul* (ConBNT, 51; Stockholm: Almqvist & Wiksell International, 1999), 131; Lambrecht, "Caesura." D.J.-S. Chae, *Paul as Apostle to the Gentiles: His Apostolic Self-Awareness and Its Influence on the Soteriological Argument in Romans* (PBTM; Carlisle: Paternoster, 1997), 229 n. 65, opts for the typical structure but recognizes that 9:30-33 functions as a conclusion to what precedes and an introduction to what follows. W. Kraus, *Das Volk Gottes: Zur Grundlegung der Ekklesiologie bei Paulus* (Tübingen: Mohr Siebeck, 1996), 294 n. 145, also argues for 9:30-33 as a conclusion to what precedes and an introduction to what follows, though he also regards Rom. 9:30-33 as its own unit.

[6] Cf. Schreiner, *Romans*, 513–14; Moo, *Romans*, 636, 640.
[7] Rom. 9:30b-33.
[8] As I pointed out in Abasciano, *Romans 9:10-18*, 205 n. 199, Rom. 9:31 more specifically says that Israel did not attain the Law of Righteousness, but not attaining the Law of Righteousness implies not attaining the righteousness connected to it. Moreover, the contrasting parallel with Gentiles obtaining righteousness in 9:30 pushes concern for Israel's failure to obtain righteousness to the forefront along with the Law in 9:31-32. Interpreters regularly speak of these verses as indicating Israel's failure to obtain righteousness.

against interpreters who contend that the notion of faith is absent from the meaning of the passage.

One of the major questions of interpretation concerning Rom. 9:1-24 is whether Paul is arguing for unconditional election or for a certain kind of conditional election. I have argued based on the broader context of Romans and various indications in Romans 9 itself that Paul is defending election on the condition of faith. But it is understandable how two such different views of the text could be perceived by interpreters. Arguing for the right to elect unconditionally and for the right to elect on the condition one chooses would look very similar.[9] Applied to God and election, both would argue for God's right to do as he deems best in election.

But Rom. 9:30-33 provides confirmation that our exegesis has been on track. When Paul asks why unbelieving Jews have failed to attain righteousness, if Paul had been teaching unconditional election in Romans 9, we would expect him to answer something like, "because God did not choose Israel but hardened them." But if Paul had been teaching election conditional on faith, then we would expect him to answer something like, "because they did not believe"—and that is what he does in fact answer. Paul then goes on in 10:1-21 to continue to stress the responsibility and guilt of Israel for their unbelief and resulting cursed state.

Scholars who think Paul has unconditional election in mind in Romans 9 have not fully grappled with the significance of Rom. 9:30-33 for the question of the nature of election in the chapter. In particular, in conjunction with the observations made above, they fail to fully grapple with a critical point that they acknowledge, namely, that 9:30 indicates that Paul is summing up the thrust of Romans 9 or much of it.[10] Both Moo and Schreiner seem to reason that 9:1-29 establishes unconditional election, and therefore, 9:30ff. must give a complementary perspective that emphasizes human response and responsibility without specifying how they relate, though ultimately their relationship is inferred to be one of cause and effect, with unconditional election causing faith.[11] But this ignores that in 9:30-33, "Paul summarizes the state of affairs from 9:6b-29 and draws a conclusion,"[12] and that "the conclusions that can be drawn from the preceding verses, especially verses 24-29, are elucidated,"[13] and that Paul "takes up an issue raised by the main line of Paul's teaching in 9:6-13, 24-29,"[14] and that Paul "introduce[s] an implication of his teaching in 9:6b-29 (and esp. vv. 24-29)."[15] As even Moo and Schreiner recognize, what Paul says in 9:30-33 is drawn from 9:6b-29 (I would say 9:1-29). But what Paul says in 9:30-33 has to do with faith as the basis of the elect status of righteousness/inclusion in the people of God. Yet that is the very thing that their

---

[9] Cf. Shellrude, "Freedom," who compellingly and consistently takes language in Rom. 9:6-29 conditionally when interpreters who argue for unconditional election in the passage take it unconditionally. The difference in construal is often very slight, but the import for how Paul is applying the statements results in vastly different theological conclusions.
[10] See note 6 in this chapter.
[11] See Moo, *Romans*, 636-7, 641 (including note 327); Schreiner, *Romans*, 510-11, 514.
[12] Schreiner, *Romans*, 513.
[13] Ibid., 514.
[14] Moo, *Romans*, 636.
[15] Ibid., 640.

unconditional election view is at pains to deny in 9:6b-29[16] and the very thing that the conditional election view argues is present in the passage.

I take all of 9:30-33 as drawn from 9:1-29. But one could argue that only the content of vv. 30-31 are drawn from 9:1-29 or 9:6b-29 and that Paul then adds a new thought in vv. 32-33, that is, unbelief as the explanation for Israel failing to attain righteousness. More specifically, it might be argued that the only point that Paul draws from 9:6b-29 is "God's calling of Gentiles and of only some Jews,"[17] or "that God has elected many gentiles unto salvation while choosing only a remnant of Jews,"[18] or that, "Gentiles, once 'not a people,' are now entering into the people of God; Israel, blessed and given so many privileges, is failing to act on her privileges and experience salvation in Christ."[19] But this could not be correct, for Paul includes faith in his basic description of the situation in 9:30. Moreover, even if faith were not referred to in 9:30, Paul still answers the question he raises in a way expected by the conditional election view and not expected by the unconditional election view (see that point made above).

Furthermore, Moo's and Schreiner's descriptions of what Paul draws from 9:6b-29 would seem to associate Paul's language of righteousness with election unto salvation (Schreiner), calling (Moo), and "entering into the people of God" (Moo) so closely that it can stand in for those phenomena. But if we apply Paul's question to those phenomena, asking why God has chosen only a remnant of Jews for salvation, or why God has not called many Jews, or why Israel has not been included in the people of God, Paul's answer is, "Because [they pursued it] not by faith but as by works" (9:32). It could be argued that righteousness can stand in for those phenomena because they cause a person to believe and attain righteousness, and so righteousness implies them. But that causal relationship has to be assumed. It is not the straightforward reading of the text. I have argued that faith is part of the conceptual framework of Rom. 9:1-29. But even apart from that, it seems clear that Paul is observing that God has chosen Gentiles and some Jews (calling/naming is a way of talking about election, as most scholars recognize) using the language of righteousness—Moo's and Schreiner's language seems to reflect this—and asks, "Why?" His answer is: faith versus unbelief.

Romans 9:30-33 supports another key aspect of our exegesis of Romans 9, the construal of Paul's conception of the hardening of unbelieving ethnic Israel. I have argued that what hardened ethnic Israel to the gospel was its principle of election by faith in Christ apart from works or ancestry, which was exceedingly offensive to Jewish sensibilities. In Rom. 9:32-33, part of Paul's explanation of why Israel failed to attain the elect status of righteousness is that they were offended at Christ. This connects to the idea of failing to attain righteousness because of unbelief. Israel did not believe in Christ because they were offended at him and faith in him as the condition for the elect status of righteousness.

---

[16] See, e.g., ibid., 603-4, 607-8, 618; Schreiner, *Romans*, 480, 494.
[17] Moo, *Romans*, 640.
[18] Schreiner, *Romans*, 514.
[19] Moo, *Romans*, 636. It is actually hard to tell exactly how much of Rom. 9:30-33 Moo and Schreiner think Paul draws from 9:6b-29. They especially highlight what I have quoted in this paragraph. But I offer these comments in case it were to be claimed that limiting the reference to 9:6b-29 like this would rebut my line of argument here.

5.3. The Logical Flow of Romans 9

Now that our exegesis of Rom. 9:1-24 is concluded, it would be helpful to outline the logical flow of Romans 9.[20] Romans 9:1-5 introduces the basis of the problem Paul addresses in the rest of Romans 9–11, that the vast majority of Jews (ethnic Israel as a whole but not every Jew) was separated from Christ and therefore cut off from the New Covenant and its fulfillment of God's promises to Israel and devoted to destruction under the eschatological wrath of God. At the same time, the promises have come to fulfillment for the New Covenant people of God, the Church of Jews and Gentiles, which is made up of mostly Gentiles. All of this raises the most compelling objection to Paul's gospel, that, if it is true, it would mean God has been unfaithful to his promises to Israel.

In response, Paul contends, on the assumption that his gospel is true, that God has been faithful to his promises to Israel (9:6a), which is the thesis statement for all of Romans 9–11. Romans 9:6b-9 specifically ground this programmatic statement. More specifically, 9:6b ("not all who are from Israel are Israel") provides what also turns out to be a programmatic statement, which Paul fleshes out over much of the rest of chs. 9–11, indicating that not all ethnic Israelites are part of the true Israel, to whom the covenant promises were actually made. Romans 9:8 ("it is not the children of the flesh who are children of God, but the children of the promise are regarded as seed") interprets Paul's quotation of Gen. 21:12 in 9:7b and sums up and explains all of 9:6b-7, becoming Paul's practical main point in support of 9:6a. That point is that God does not (nor did he ever) name or regard mere physical descendants of Abraham ("children of the flesh") as heir to the covenant promises, but he regards those who believe the promises ("children of the promise") as the true heir to them (i.e., the true Israel). That is, as it pertains to the present time of eschatological fulfillment, all and only those who believe in Christ are named or regarded as God's covenant people to whom the promises were made. Finally, 9:9 supports Paul's interpretation of Gen. 21:12 in 9:8 by quotation of Gen. 18:10, 14, showing that Isaac and the covenantal descendants of Abraham represented by him would be named/identified through promise rather than ancestry. Thus, Paul's response to the charge against God's faithfulness through 9:9 is that God never guaranteed enjoyment of the promises to ethnic Israel, but only to spiritual Israel, which means, in the context of Romans, all and only those who believe in Christ. Romans 9:8 most clearly articulates the main point in support of 9:6a, and the rest of the chapter ultimately supports it.

Romans 9:10-13 add to the support Paul adduced from Gen. 18:10, 14 for the contention of Rom. 9:8 that only those who believe in Christ are the covenant seed of Abraham/rightful heirs of the covenant promises by furnishing an even stronger example than the Sarah/Isaac/Ishmael example given in 9:7, the example of Rebekah, Jacob, and Esau from Genesis 25. Paul argues from Gen. 25:23 that God intended that

---

[20] For a fuller treatment of the logical flow of Rom. 9:1-24 specifically, one could add the summary of my exegesis of Rom. 9:19-24 above in Section 5.1 of this chapter to my summary of the argument of Rom. 9:1-18 in Section 4.2.a in Chapter 4 of this volume and consider them together. This summary is meant to provide a more concise delineation of the logical flow of thought in Romans 9.

the fulfillment of his purpose to bless the world would proceed on the basis of his sovereign right to name whomever he wants as his covenant people rather than on the basis of human works or ancestry. This purpose statement (found in 9:11c-12b) is the main point of vv. 10–13 and serves as the essence of 10–13's support of the principle enunciated in 9:8 that only those who believe in Christ are rightful covenant heirs.

Romans 9:14-18 then supports vv. 10–13 (and so ultimately 9:8) by addressing the same basic objection but reworded in response to the sharpened statement of sovereign divine election in the quotation of Mal. 1:2-3. This allows Paul to add further scriptural argumentation and to broaden his argument. The objection is that God choosing his people without regard to works or ancestry would make him unrighteous through violation of his covenant promises to Israel. Paul vehemently denies that God is unrighteous (v. 14) and supports his assertion with two quotations of Scripture, Exod. 33:19b (Rom. 9:15) and Exod. 9:16 (Rom. 9:17).

Romans 9:15-16 take up the positive side of election. Verse 16 presents Paul's inference from and interpretation of Exod. 33:19b ("I will have mercy on whomever I have mercy, and I will have compassion on whomever I have compassion"; quoted in Rom. 9:15): the bestowal of mercy that is the election of God's covenant people is (rightly) at the discretion of the mercy-bestowing God, as are any stipulations he chooses to lay down for the bestowing of his mercy. Romans 9:17 ("for this very purpose I raised you up, that I might show my power in you and that my name might be proclaimed in all the earth") gives further scriptural support for God's righteousness in sovereign election with special reference to its negative side—covenantal rejection and hardening.

Paul puts forth Pharaoh as a type of hardened, unbelieving, and rejected ethnic Israel. Just as God hardened Pharaoh to bring about the renewed election of his people and to advance his plan for fulfilling the climactic covenant promise of blessing all the nations in Abraham, so he has hardened unbelieving ethnic Israel in the time of covenant fulfillment to accomplish the same purposes. Far from violating God's covenant promises to Israel, the hardening and rejection of ethnic Israel actually contribute to fulfilling them. The hardening of Pharaoh in Exodus is nondeterministic, and in harmony with that, Paul's invocation of hardening in Rom. 9:17-18 has specific reference to God making ethnic Israel of his day unyielding to the claims of the gospel message by means of God's sovereign act of making elect status conditional on faith in Christ apart from works or ancestry. This cause of hardening—election by faith—is the very means for opening salvation up to the Gentiles while providing salvation for the Jews as well. Romans 9:18 ("So therefore, he [rightly] has mercy on whom he desires, and he [rightly] hardens whom he desires") sums up vv. 15–17 and their support for v. 14's denial of the unrighteousness of God in election by faith apart from works or ancestry.

Romans 9:19-24 takes up an objection to v. 18 (God rightly shows mercy and hardens as he wills) in its representation of the argument of vv. 15–17 in support of v. 14 (God is righteous in electing by faith rather than works or ancestry), and thus takes up an objection to all of vv. 14–18, the main point of which is v. 14. The objection is that God would be unrighteous to judge Israel for their sin (of rejecting Christ) because God accomplishes his purpose of making known his power and name through their sin, especially since his decision to name his people by faith apart from works or ancestry provoked their rebellion. Verses 19–24 support 9:14-18 (and its denial that God is unrighteous for choosing his people by faith apart from works or ancestry) with scriptural argumentation that highlights God's right to name whom he wants as his people and especially to judge Israel, in light of his identity as the sovereign Creator God and the elector of Israel, and in light of humanity's humble estate before him. After 9:19 articulates the objection, verses 20–21 give the basic response (9:20a) and scriptural grounding (9:20b-21). Like the thought of clay challenging the potter's fashioning of it, it is ludicrous to suggest that God Almighty does not have the right to name whom he wants as his people and to bestow eschatological blessing upon them or to judge with eschatological condemnation those who rebel against his plan of salvation.

Verses 22–24 then interpret and apply vv. 20b–21. In so doing, they become more specific and give greater clarity, drawing the logical stress of Paul's rhetoric in 9:20b-24. Paul reveals that God has endured those who will receive his eschatological wrath for three purposes: to show his wrath, to make known his power in judgment and salvation, and most primarily, to make known the riches of his glory upon vessels of mercy in the age to come. The first two purposes contribute to the third.

The passage comes to a climax in v. 24, where Paul indicates that God has named his people, who are the objects of his mercy that will enjoy the riches of his eschatological glory, from Gentiles as well as Jews. This comes as the climax because, in light of the exclusion of unbelieving Jews, the inclusion of Gentiles is the most offensive aspect of the gospel Paul defends in Romans 9. The logical weight of 9:20b-29 comes to rest here; vv. 25–29 furnish scriptural support for v. 24.

The logical role of 9:19-29 is complex. It supports 9:14-18 as it refutes an objection to the argument of the latter, making 9:19-29 subordinate to 9:14-18. At the same time, by indicating more specifically what God has done in its argument for God's right to do as he has done, 9:19-24 actually draws the emphasis in the rhetorical flow of Paul's argument from 9:14 through 9:29.

Formally, 9:24 and all of 9:20b-24 logically support 9:20a's rebuke of 9:19's objection to v. 18. But as the climax of 9:19-24, we can take 9:24 as representative of the point of the section: God has the right to exclude Jews who reject Christ from the New Covenant and its blessings, and he has in fact named his covenant people from believing Gentiles as well as believing Jews. On the one hand, by answering an objection to v. 18 (God rightly shows mercy and hardens as he wills), which sums up support for v. 14, v. 24 supports v. 14 and its insistence that God is righteous in electing by faith rather than works or ancestry. Verse 14 itself defends the affirmation of election by faith apart from works or ancestry in vv. 11c–12b, which in turn supports the affirmation of v. 8 that only those who believe in Christ are the covenant seed of Abraham/rightful heirs of the covenant promises, which in turn supports v. 6a's affirmation of God's faithfulness to his covenant promises to Israel.

On the other hand, 9:24 adds to 9:8's affirmation that only those who believe in Christ are the covenant seed of Abraham by specifying the implications of its principle: God has indeed named his people from Jews and Gentiles. Verses 27–29 add an implication already indicated in 9:1-5, but now with scriptural support, namely that only a relatively small minority of Jews had been named as part of God's New Covenant people (in the context of Paul's argument, that would be because only a relatively small minority of Jews had believed in Christ). Thus, 9:24 joins with 9:8 in conveying Paul's main point in support of 9:6a and its affirmation of God's faithfulness to his promises to Israel. That point is that God only regards those who believe in Christ as the true Israel (his covenant people/the seed of Abraham), who alone receives the fulfillment of the covenant promises and blessings (salvation), and he has in fact named his covenant people from Gentiles as well as (a relatively small number of) Jews. Romans 9:30-33 provides a conclusion to the chapter that confirms Paul has been talking about election by faith apart works while also introducing the next major section of the argument, in which he stresses the responsibility and guilt of Israel for their unbelief and resulting cursed state.

5.4. Concluding Reflections

My exegesis of Rom. 9:19-24 has confirmed the conclusions set forth in my first two volumes, both the general thrust of my exegesis of 9:1-18 and, by and large, the specific, overarching conclusions set out in the first book's final chapter. Therefore, I would direct readers to those specific conclusions for the conclusions of the present work, bolstered now by further research and exegesis. However, there are some points that call for revision or clarification.

First, in my original conclusions, I claimed that justification results in calling/naming.[21] However, I revised that claim in my monograph on Rom. 9:10-18 to viewing the two concepts as closely related, touching on the same reality, with calling logically prior, though minimally so.[22] Calling in Paul refers to the naming of a people as God's own (i.e., his son/covenant partner), while justification refers to the declaration of his people's right relationship with him. Both are contingent on faith. Second, my affirmation in my original conclusions that justification language in Paul refers to covenant membership perhaps warrants clarification,[23] and that has been provided in note 338 of Chapter 4 of this volume.

Third, it should be noted that, in my original conclusions, I suggested implications that my exegesis of Rom. 9:1-9 had for other texts in Romans 9–11. Here, I would note that the two succeeding volumes, including the present one, treat some of those texts in depth and should be consulted as updating my original conclusions for those texts as the much fuller treatment. The texts or textual elements receiving detailed attention in a succeeding volume are Rom. 9:11, in particular, the phrase ἡ κατ' ἐκλογὴν πρόθεσις τοῦ θεοῦ,[24] the issue of individual versus corporate election in 9:10-13,[25] and Rom.

---

[21] Abasciano, *Romans 9.1-9*, 219.
[22] Abasciano, *Romans 9.10-18*, 55 n. 86.
[23] See Abasciano, *Romans 9.1-9*, 220.
[24] Cf. ibid., 223; and Abasciano, *Romans 9.10-18*, 46–50.
[25] Cf. Abasciano, *Romans 9.1-9*, 222; and Abasciano, *Romans 9.10-18*, 58–62; see also Section 1.1.d.3 in Chapter 1 of this volume.

9:15.[26] Finally, in my original conclusions, I listed Isa. 64:8 among potter/clay texts that Paul alluded to. But a closer look at that text brought me to conclude that Paul does not allude to it in Rom. 9:20-21.[27]

Amid my original conclusions, I expressed the conviction that further intertextual study of Romans 9–11 would confirm our view of the contextual character of Paul's *Schriftgebrauch* and the profound influence of Scripture upon his theology and proclamation in general and his argument in Romans 9–11 in particular.[28] My second volume with its exegesis of Rom. 9:10-18 did just that. And now this third volume with its exegesis of 9:19-24 has further confirmed the findings of the first two volumes on this point. This strengthens our conviction that intertextual exegesis of the rest of Romans 9–11 and elsewhere in Paul would further confirm our findings to date and be of great benefit.

Just as with my first two volumes, of the various contributions this study makes to current scholarship, the most significant is perhaps its exegesis of the specific text under consideration (Rom. 9:19-24) and its implications for understanding the rest of Romans 9, all based upon an analysis of Paul's use of the Old Testament in its sociocultural milieu. Its other contributions are founded on this rigorously exegetical approach, whether judgments about Paul's use of Scripture or identifying the content of his theology. Our exegesis of Rom. 9:19-24 confirms that Romans 9 is largely about the identity of the true people of God and God's right to name whom he wants as his covenant people (i.e., as Israel) in defense of God's faithfulness to his promises to Israel (9:6a) vis-à-vis his naming of the Church of Jews and Gentiles as his covenant people and his exclusion of unbelieving Jews from the covenant and its blessings (including salvation). Rom. 9:19-24 fits into this formulation by supporting a corporate and conditional election and arguing for God's right to elect by faith and especially to judge Israel for their rejection of Christ despite God provoking their rebellion with an offensive means of salvation and using their sin to glorify himself, and by specifying that God has indeed named his people from Gentiles as well as Jews.

---

[26] Cf. Abasciano, *Romans 9.1-9*, 222–3; and Abasciano, *Romans 9.10-18*, 174–84.
[27] Cf. Abasciano, *Romans 9.1-9*, 234 n. 43; and note 1 in Chapter 2 of the present volume.
[28] Abasciano, *Romans 9.1-9*, 235.

Bibliography

Abasciano, B. J., "Clearing Up Misconceptions about Corporate Election," *ATJ* 41 (2009), 59–90.
Abasciano, B. J., "Corporate Election in Romans 9: A Reply to Thomas Schreiner," *JETS* 49/2 (June 2006), 351–71.
Abasciano, B. J., "Corporate Election Misrepresented in the Pillar Commentary on Romans by Colin G. Kruse," August 31, 2012, http://evangelicalarminians.org/brian-abasciano-corporate-election-misrepresented-in-the-pillar-commentary-on-romans-by-colin-g-kruse/.
Abasciano, B. J., "Diamonds in the Rough: A Reply to Christopher Stanley Concerning the Reader Competency of Paul's Original Audiences," *NovT* 49 (2007), 153–83.
Abasciano, B. J., "Does Regeneration Precede Faith? The Use of 1 John 5:1 as a Proof Text," *EQ* 84.4 (2012), 307–22.
Abasciano, B. J., "Paul's Use of the Old Testament in Romans 9:1-9: An Intertextual and Theological Exegesis," PhD thesis, University of Aberdeen, 2004.
Abasciano, B. J., "Romans 9, Election, and Calvinism," in D. L. Allen and S. W. Lemke (eds.), *Calvinism: A Biblical-Theological Critique*; Nashville, TN: B&H, 2022.
Abasciano, B. J., *Paul's Use of the Old Testament in Romans 9.1-9: An Intertextual and Theological Exegesis*, JSNTSup/LNTS, 301; London: T&T Clark, 2005.
Abasciano, B. J., *Paul's Use of the Old Testament in Romans 9.10-18: An Intertextual and Theological Exegesis*, JSNTSup/LNTS, 317; London: T&T Clark, 2011.
Achtemeier, P. J., *Romans*, IBC; Atlanta, GA: John Knox, 1985.
Aletti, J. N., "L'argumentation paulinienne en Rm 9," *Bib* 68 (1987), 41–56.
Aletti, J. N., *God's Justice in Romans: Keys for Interpreting the Epistle to the Romans*, trans. P. M. Meyer, SB, 37; Rome: Gregorian and Biblical Press, 2010.
Alexander, J. A., *Commentary on the Prophecies of Isaiah*, 2 vols. in 1; Grand Rapids, MI: Zondervan, 1975.
Alexander, R. H., "יָד," TWOT, 1.362–64.
Alexander, T. D., *Exodus*, AOTC, 2; Downers Grove, IL: IVP, 2017.
Allen, L. C., "Jeremiah: Book of," *DOTP*, 423–41.
Allen, L. C., *Jeremiah: A Commentary*, OTL; Louisville, KY: Westminster John Knox, 2008.
Allen, L. C., *Psalms 101–150*, WBC 21; Waco, TX: Word, 1983.
Balogh, C., "Blind People, Blind God: The Composition of Isaiah 29.15-24," *ZAW* 121 (2009), 48–69.
Baltzer, K., *Deutero-Isaiah: A Commentary on Isaiah 40–55*, trans. M. Kohl, Hermeneia; Minneapolis, MN: Fortress, 2001.
Barrett, C. K., "Romans 9.30–10.21: Fall and Responsibility of Israel," in L. de Lorenzi (ed.), *Die Israelfrage nach Röm 9–11*, Monographische Reihe von "Benedictina" Biblisch-ökumenische Abteilung, 3; Rome: Abtei von St Paul vor den Mauern, 1977, 99–121.
Barrett, C. K., *A Commentary on the Epistle to the Romans*, 2nd ed., BNTC; London: A & C Black, 1991.

Beale, G. K., "Did Jesus and His Followers Preach the Right Doctrine from the Wrong Texts?," in G. K. Beale (ed.), *The Right Doctrine from the Wrong Texts? Essays on the Use of the Old Testament in the New*; Grand Rapids, MI: Baker Academic, 1994, 387-404.

Beale, G. K., *A New Testament Biblical Theology: The Unfolding of the Old Testament in the New*; Grand Rapids, MI: Baker Academic, 2011.

Beale, G. K., and D. A. Carson (eds.), *Commentary on the New Testament Use of the Old Testament*; Grand Rapids, MI: Baker Academic, 2007.

Belli, F., *Argumentation and Use of Scripture in Romans 9-11*, AnBib, 183; Roma: Gregorian and Biblical Press, 2010.

Bence, C. L., *Romans: A Bible Commentary in the Wesleyan Tradition*; Indianapolis, IN: WPH, 1996.

Bengel, J. A., *Gnomon of the New Testament*, 3rd ed.; Edinburgh: T&T Clark, 1860.

Beuken, W. A. M., "Isa 29.15-24: Perversion Reverted," in F. C. Martinez, A. Hilhorst, and C. J. Labuschagne (eds.), *The Scriptures and the Scrolls: Studies in Honour of A.S. van der Woude on the Occasion of His 65th Birthday*; Leiden: Brill, 1992, 43-64.

Beuken, W. A. M., *Isaiah II: Chapters 28-39*, trans. B. Doyle, HCOT; Leuven: Peeters, 2000.

Bird, M. F., "Incorporated Righteousness: A Response to Recent Evangelical Discussion Concerning the Imputation of Christ's Righteousness in Justification," *JETS* 47/2 (2004), 253-75.

Bird, M. F., "Justified by Christ's Resurrection: A Neglected Aspect of Paul's Doctrine of Justification," *SBET* 22.1 (Spring 2005), 72-91.

Black, M., *Romans*, NCB; London: Marshall Morgan and Scott, 1973.

Boers, H., *The Justification of the Gentiles*; Peabody, MA: Hendrickson, 1994.

Bray, G. (ed.), *Ancient Christian Commentary on Scripture: New Testament, VI: Romans*, ACCSNT, 6; Downers Grove, IL: IVP, 1998.

Brenton, L. C. L., *The Septuagint with Apocrypha*; London: Samuel Bagster, 1851.

Brooke, G. J., "Review of Abasciano, Brian J., *Paul's Use of the Old Testament in Romans 9.10-18: An Intertextual and Theological Exegesis*," *JSOT* 37.5 (Book List 2013), 207.

Bruce, F. F., *The Epistle to the Romans*, TNTC, 6; Grand Rapids, MI: Eerdmans, 1963.

Brueggemann, W., *Isaiah 40-66*, WBCo; Louisville, KY: Westminster John Knox, 1998.

Büchsel, F., "ἀποκρίνω, ἀνταποκρίνομαι," *TDNT*, 3.944-45.

Bullinger, E. W., *Figures of Speech Used in the Bible: Explained and Illustrated*; Grand Rapids, MI: Baker, 1968.

Bumgardner, C. J., "Paul's Letters to Timothy and Titus: A Literature Review (2009-2015)," *STR* 7.2 (Winter 2016), 77-116.

Burnett, G. W., *Paul and the Salvation of the Individual*, BIS, 57; Leiden: Brill, 2001.

Byrne, B., *Romans*, Sacra Pagina, 6; Collegeville, MN: Liturgical, 1996.

Calvin, J., *Jeremiah and Lamentations*, CCC; Wheaton, IL: Crossway, 2000.

Campbell, D. A., *The Deliverance of God: An Apocalyptic Rereading of Justification in Paul*; Grand Rapids, MI: Eerdmans, 2009.

Carroll, R. P., *The Book of Jeremiah: A Commentary*, OTL; London: SCM, 1986.

Carson, D. A. (ed.), *The Perfect Storm: Critical Discussion of the Semantics of the Greek Perfect Tense under Aspect Theory*, SBG, 21; New York: Peter Lang, 2021.

Chae, D. J.-S., *Paul as Apostle to the Gentiles: His Apostolic Self-Awareness and Its Influence on the Soteriological Argument in Romans*, PBTM; Carlisle: Paternoster, 1997.

Charles, R. H., *The Book of Jubilees or the Little Genesis*; London: Adam and Charles Black, 1902.

Childs, B. S., *Isaiah*, OTL; Louisville, KY: Westminster John Knox, 2001.

Chilton, B. D., "Rabbinic Literature: The Targumim," *DNTB*, 902–9.
Chilton, B. D., *The Isaiah Targum: Introduction, Translation, Apparatus, and Notes*, TAB, 11; Wilmington: M. Glazier, 1987.
Chisholm, R. B., Jr., "Divine Hardening in the Old Testament," *Bsac* 153 (Oct.–Dec. 1996), 410–34.
Chrysostom, J., "The Homilies of St. John Chrysostom, Archbishop of Constantinople, on the Epistle of St. Paul the Apostle to the Romans," in P. Schaff (ed.), *Nicene and Post-Nicene Fathers, Vol. 11: Chrysostom on the Acts of the Apostles and the Epistle to the Romans*, First Series; Peabody, MA: Hendrickson, 1995, 329–564.
Ciampa, R. E., and B. S. Rosner, *The First Letter to the Corinthians*, PNTC; Grand Rapids, MI: Eerdmans, 2010.
Clements, R. E., *Isaiah 1–39*, NCBC; Grand Rapids, MI: Eerdmans, 1980.
Coppes, L. J., "עָנָה," *TWOT*, 2.682–84.
Corley, J., *Sirach*, NCBCOT, 21; Collegeville, MN: Liturgical, 2013.
Cottrell, J., *Romans*, II, CPNIVC; Joplin: College Press, 1998.
Craigie, P., P. H. Kelley, and J. F. Drinkard, Jr., *Jeremiah 1–25*, WBC, 26; Waco, TX: Word, 1991.
Cranfield, C. E. B., *A Critical and Exegetical Commentary on the Epistle to the Romans*, ICC, 2 vols.; Edinburgh: T&T Clark, 1975–9.
Dahl, N. A., *Studies in Paul*; Minneapolis, MA: Augsburg, 1977.
Davies, P. R., "Potter, Prophet and People: Jeremiah 18 as Parable," *HAR* 11 (1987), 23–33.
deClaissé-Walford, N., R. A. Jacobson, and B. L. Tanner, *The Book of Psalms*, NICOT; Grand Rapids, MI: Eerdmans, 2014.
Delitzsch, F., *Isaiah*, trans. J. Martin, Commentary on the Old Testament, 7, 2 vols. in 1, repr.; Grand Rapids, MI: Eerdmans, 1973.
Delling, G., "καταρτίζω," *TDNT*, 1.476.
Dempster, S., "Canons on the Right and Canons on the Left: Finding a Resolution in the Canon Debate," *JETS* 52.1 (March 2009), 47–77.
deSilva, D. A., "Wisdom of Solomon," *DLP*, 1268–76.
Dodd, C. H., *According to the Scriptures: The Substructure of New Testament Theology*; London: Nisbet, 1952.
Dodd, C. H., *The Epistle of Paul to the Romans*; London: Collins/Fontana, 1959.
du Toit, A. P., "Review of R. M. Thorsteinsson, *Paul's Interlocutor in Romans 2: Function and Identity in the Context of Ancient Epistolography*," *Neot* 38.1 (2004), 152–4.
Dunn, J. D. G., *Romans*, WBC, 38, 2 vols.; Dallas, TX: Word, 1988.
Dunn, R., *A Discourse on the Freedom of the Will*; Dover: W.M. Burr, 1850.
Durham, J. I., *Exodus*, WBC, 3; Waco, TX: Word, 1987.
Eaton, J., *The Psalms: A Historical and Spiritual Commentary with an Introduction and New Translation*; New York: Continuum, 2005.
Edwards, J. R., *Romans*, NIBCNT; Peabody, MA: Hendrickson, 1992.
Ellingworth, P., "Translation and Exegesis: A Case Study (Rom 9,22ff.)," *Bib* 59 (1978), 396–402.
Elliott, M. A., *The Survivors of Israel: A Reconsideration of the Theology of Pre-Christian Judaism*; Grand Rapids, MI: Eerdmans, 2000.
Enns, P., "Wisdom of Solomon," *DOTWPW*, 885–91.
Esler, P., "Review of *If You Call Yourself a Jew: Reappraising Paul's Letter to the Romans*," *RBL*, May 2017, https://www.sblcentral.org/home/bookDetails/10048.
Fanning, B. F., *Verbal Aspect in New Testament Greek*; Oxford: Clarendon, 1990.

Fitzmyer, J. A., *Romans: A New Translation with Introduction and Commentary*, AB, 33; New York: Doubleday, 1993.
Forlines, F. L., *Romans*, RHBC; Nashville, TN: Randall House, 1987.
Forster, R. T., and V. P. Marston, *God's Strategy in Human History*, 2nd ed.; Eugene, OR: Wipf and Stock, 2000.
Fretheim, T. E., "The Repentance of God: A Study of Jeremiah 18:7-10," *HAR* 11 (1987), 81-92.
Fretheim, T. E., *Jeremiah*, SHBC; Macon: Smyth & Helwys, 2002.
García Martínez, F., and E. J. C. Tigchelaar, *The Dead Sea Scrolls Study Edition*, 2 vols.; Leiden: Brill, 1997-8.
Gaston, L., "Israel's Enemies in Pauline Theology," in L. Gaston, *Paul and the Torah*; Vancouver: University of British Columbia Press, 1987, 80-99.
Gerstenberger, E., "ענה," *TDOT*, 10.230-52.
Gifford, E. H., *Epistle of St. Paul to the Romans*; London: John Murray, 1886.
Godet, F., *Commentary on St. Paul's Epistle to the Romans*, trans. A. Cusin and T. W. Chambers; New York: Funk & Wagnalls, 1883.
Goering, G. S., "Election and Knowledge in the Wisdom of Solomon," in G. G. Xeravits and J. Zsengellér (eds.), *Studies in the Book of Wisdom*, JSJSup, 142; Leiden: Brill, 2010, 163-82.
Goldingay, J., and D. Payne, *Isaiah 40-55: A Critical and Exegetical Commentary, Volume 2*, ICC; London: T&T Clark, 2006.
Goldingay, J., *Isaiah*, NIBCOT, 13; Peabody, MA: Hendrickson, 2001.
Goldingay, J., *Volume 3, Psalms 90-150*, BCOTWP; Grand Rapids, MI: Baker Academic, 2008.
Good, E. M., *Irony in the Old Testament*; Philadelphia, PA: Westminster, 1965.
Goodrich, J. K., "Review of *Paul's Use of the Old Testament in Romans 9.10-18: An Intertextual and Theological Exegesis*," *RSR* 38.1 (March 2012), 21.
Greathouse, W. M., and G. Lyons, *Romans 9-16: A Commentary in the Wesleyan Tradition*, NBBC; Kansas City, MI: Beacon Hill, 2008.
Grindheim, S., *The Crux of Election*, WUNT, 2.202; Tübingen: Mohr Siebeck, 2005.
Haacker, K., *Der Briefe des Paulus an die Römer*, THKNT, 6; Leipzig: Evangelische Verlagsanstalt, 1999.
Hanson, A. T., "Vessels of Wrath or Instruments of Wrath? Romans IX.22-3," *JTS* 32 (1981), 433-43.
Hanson, P. D. *Isaiah 40-66*, IBC; Louisville, KY: Westminster John Knox, 1995.
Harrington, D. J., "Pseudo-Philo: A New Translation and Introduction," *OTP*, 2.297-377.
Hartley, D. E., *The Wisdom Background and Parabolic Implications of Isaiah 6:9-10 in the Synoptics*, Studies in Biblical Literature, 100; New York: Lang, 2006.
Hay, D. M., "Philo's Anthropology, the Spiritual Regimen of the Therapeutae, and a Possible Connection with Corinth," in R. Deines and K.-W. Niebuhr (eds.), *Philo und das Neue Testament: Wechselseitige Wahrnehmungen I. Internationales Symposium Zum Corpus Judaeo- hellenisticum. 1.-4. Eisenach/Jena, Mai 2003*, WUNT, 172; Tübingen: Mohr Siebeck, 2004, 127-42.
Hays, R. B., *Echoes of Scripture in the Letters of Paul*; New Haven, CT: Yale University Press, 1989.
Hill, A. E., *Malachi: A New Translation with Introduction and Commentary*, AB, 25D; New York: Doubleday, 1998.
Hillert, S., *Limited and Universal Salvation: A Text-Oriented and Hermeneutical Study of Two Perspectives in Paul*, ConBNT, 51; Stockholm: Almqvist & Wiksell, 1999.

Hodge, C., *Commentary on the Epistle to the Romans*, rev. ed.; Grand Rapids, MI: Eerdmans, 1886.

Hoehner, H., *Ephesians*; Grand Rapids, MI: Baker, 2002.

Hoglund, J., *Called by Triune Grace: Divine Rhetoric and the Effectual Call*, SCDS; Downers Grove, IL: IVP, 2016.

Holland, T., *Romans: The Divine Marriage: A Biblical-Theological Commentary*; Eugene, OR: Pickwick, 2011.

Hollander, H. W., and M. de Jonge, *The Testaments of the Twelve Patriarchs: A Commentary*, SVTP; Leiden: Brill, 1985.

Hübner, H., *Gottes Ich und Israel: Zum Schriftgebrauch des Paulus in Römer 9–11*; Göttingen: Vandenhoeck & Ruprecht, 1984.

Huey, F. B., *Jeremiah, Lamentations*, NAC, 16; Nashville, TN: Broadman, 1993.

Jacobson, H., *A Commentary on Pseudo-Philo's Liber Antiquitatum Biblicarum with Latin Text and English Translation*, 2 vols.; Leiden: Brill, 1996.

Jewett, R., *Romans: A Commentary*, Hermeneia; Minneapolis, MA: Fortress, 2007.

Johnson, A. F., *Romans*, EvBC; Chicago: Moody Bible Institute, 2000.

Johnson, E. E., *The Function of Apocalyptic and Wisdom Traditions in Romans 9–11*, SBLDS, 109; Atlanta, GA: Scholars, 1989.

Johnson, L. T., *Reading Romans: A Literary and Theological Commentary*; New York: Crossword, 1997.

Johnson, M. D., "Life of Adam and Eve: A New Translation and Introduction," *OTP*, 2.249–95.

Joüon, P., and T. Muraoka, *A Grammar of Biblical Hebrew*, repr. with corrections, SB 14/1–14/2, 2 vols.; Rome: Editrice Pontificio Istituto Biblico, [1991] 1993.

Kaiser, O., *Isaiah 13–39: A Commentary*, trans. R. A. Wilson, OTL; Philadelphia, PA: Westminster, 1974.

Kaminsky, J. S., "The Sins of the Fathers: A Theological Investigation of the Biblical Tension between Corporate and Individualized Retribution," *Judaism* 46.3 (1997), 319–32.

Kaminsky, J. S., *Corporate Responsibility in the Hebrew Bible*; Sheffield: JSOT, 1995.

Käsemann, E., *Commentary on Romans*, trans. G. W. Bromiley; Grand Rapids, MI: Eerdmans, 1980.

Keck, L. E., *Romans*, ANTC; Nashville, TN: Abingdon, 2005.

Kee, H. C., "Testaments of the Twelve Patriarchs: A New Translation and Introduction," *OTP*, 1.775–828.

Kee, H. C., *Knowing the Truth: A Sociological Approach to New Testament Interpretation*; Minneapolis, MN: Fortress, 1989.

Keener, C. S., *Romans*, NCCS, 6; Eugene, OR: Cascade, 2009.

Kidner, D., *Psalms 73–150: A Commentary on Books III-V of the Psalms*, TOTC 14b; London: IVP, 1975.

Kim, S., "Does Romans 9 Teach Corporate Election? Revisiting Brian Abasciano's Understanding of Romans 9:6-13," 「한국개혁신학」 67 (2020), 237–66.

Klappert, B., "Traktat für Israel (Römer 9–11)," in M. Stöhr (ed.), *Jüdische Existenz und die Erneuerung der christlichen Theologie*; Munich: Kaiser, 1981, 58–137.

Klawans, J., *Josephus and the Theologies of Ancient Judaism*; Oxford: Oxford University Press, 2012.

Knight, G. A. F., *Deutero-Isaiah: A Theological Commentary on Isaiah 40–55*; Nashville, TN: Abingdon, 1965.

Koch, D.-A., *Die Schrift als Zeuge des Evangeliums: Untersuchungen zur Verwendung und zum Verständnis der Schrift bei Paulus*, BHT, 69; Tübingen: Mohr Siebeck, 1986.
Koole, J. L., *Isaiah, Part 3, Volume I: Isaiah 40–48*, trans. A. P. Runia, HCOT; Kampen: Kok Pharos, 1997.
Kraus, W., *Das Volk Gottes: Zur Grundlegung der Ekklesiologie bei Paulus*; Tübingen: Mohr Siebeck, 1996.
Kruse, C. G., "Review of Brian J. Abasciano, *Paul's Use of the Old Testament in Romans 9.10-18: An Intertextual and Theological Exegesis*," *CBQ* 76 (2014), 341–2.
Kruse, C. G., *Paul's Letter to the Romans*, PNTC; Grand Rapids, MI: Eerdmans, 2012.
Kugel, J. L., *Traditions of the Bible: A Guide to the Bible as It Was at the Start of the Common Era*; Cambridge, MA: Harvard University Press, 1998.
Laato, A., *The Servant of YHWH and Cyrus: A Reinterpretation of the Exilic Messianic Programme in Isaiah 40–55*, CBOT, 35; Stockholm: Almqvist & Wiksell, 1992.
Lambrecht, J., "The Caesura between Romans 9:30-3 and 10:1-4," *NTS* 45 (1999), 141–7.
Leenhardt, F. J., *The Epistle to the Romans: A Commentary*; London: Lutterworth, 1961.
Leonard, J. M., "Review of *Paul's Use of the Old Testament in Romans 9.10-18: An Intertextual and Theological Exegesis*," *JETS* 55.4 (December 2012), 869–71.
Linebaugh, J. A., *God, Grace, and Righteousness in Wisdom of Solomon and Paul's Letter to the Romans: Texts in Conversation*, NovTSup, 152; Leiden: Brill, 2013.
Longenecker, R. N., *The Epistle to the Romans: A Commentary on the Greek Text*, NIGTC; Grand Rapids, MI: Eerdmans, 2016.
Longman III, T., *Psalms: An Introduction and Commentary*, TOTC, 15–16; Downers Grove, IL: IVP Academic, 2014.
Luz, U., *Das Geschichtsverständnis des Paulus*, BevT, 49; Munich: Kaiser, 1968.
Lyonnet, S. "De doctrina praedestinationis et reprobationis in Rom 9," in S. Lyonnet, *Etudes sur l'Epître aux Romains*, AnBib, 120; Rome: Editrice Pontificio Istituto Biblico, 1989, 274–97.
Maillot, A., "Essai sur les citations vétérotestamentaires continues dans Romains 9 à 11, ou comment se servir de la Torah pour montrer que le 'Christ est la fin de la Torah,'" *ETR* 57 (1982/1), 55–73.
Marshall, I. H., with Philip H. Towner, *A Critical and Exegetical Commentary on the Pastoral Epistles*, rev. ed., ICC; Edinburgh: T&T Clark, 1999.
Mayer, B., *Unter Gottes Heilsratschluss: Prädestinationsaussagen bei Paulus*; Würzburg: Echter, 1974.
McCall, T. H., "I Believe in Divine Sovereignty," *TJ* 29/2 (Fall 2008), 205–26.
McCall, T. H., "We Believe in God's Sovereign Goodness: A Rejoinder to John Piper," *TJ* 29/2 (Fall 2008), 235–46.
McCall, T. H., *An Invitation to Analytic Christian Theology*; Downers Grove, IL: IVP, 2015.
McGlynn, M., *Divine Judgment and Divine Benevolence in the Book of Wisdom*, WUNT, 2.139; Tübingen: Mohr Siebeck, 2001.
McNamara, M., *Targum and New Testament: Collected Essays*, WUNT, 279; Tübingen: Mohr Siebeck, 2011.
Merklein, H., "πλοῦτος," *EDNT*, 3.114–17.
Moo, D. J., *The Epistle to the Romans*, 2nd ed., NICNT; Grand Rapids, MI: Eerdmans, 2018, ProQuest Ebook Central.
Moody, D., "Commentary on Romans," in C. Allen (ed.), *The Broadman Bible Commentary, Vol. 10*, BBC, 10; Nashville, TN: Broadman, 1970.

Morison, J., *Exposition of the Ninth Chapter of the Epistle to the Romans: A New Edition, Re-written, to Which Is Added an Exposition of the Tenth Chapter*; London: Hodder and Stoughton, 1888.
Morris, L., *The Epistle to the Romans*; Grand Rapids, MI: Eerdmans, 1988.
Motyer, J. A., *The Prophecy of Isaiah: An Introduction and Commentary*; Downers Grove, IL: IVP, 1993.
Mounce, R. H., *Romans*, NAC, 27; Nashville, TN: Broadman & Holman, 1995.
Mounce, W. D., *Pastoral Epistles*, WBC, 46; Nashville, TN: Nelson, 2000.
Moyise, S., "Review of B. J. Abasciano, *Paul's Use of the Old Testament in Romans 9:1-9: An Intertextual and Theological Exegesis*," RBL, October 2006, https://www.sblcentral.org/home/bookDetails/5248.
Moyise, S., "Review of B. J. Abasciano, *Paul's Use of the Old Testament in Romans 9:10-18: An Intertextual and Theological Exegesis*," RBL, April 2012, https://www.sblcentral.org/home/bookDetails/8334.
Müller, C., *Gottes Gerechtigkeit und Gottes Volk: Eine Untersuchung zu Römer 9-11*, FRLANT, 86; Göttingen: Vandenhoeck & Ruprecht, 1964.
Müller, D., "βούλομαι," *NIDNTT*, 3.1015-18.
Munck, J., *Christ and Israel: An Interpretation of Romans 9-11*; Philadelphia, PA: Fortress, 1967.
Murray, J., *The Epistle to the Romans*, NICNT, 2 vols. in 1; Grand Rapids, MI: Eerdmans, 1959-65.
Naidoff, B. D., "The Two-fold structure of Isaiah 45:9-13," VT 31.2 (1981), 180-5.
Newman, B. M., and E. A. Nida, *A Handbook on Paul's Letter to the Romans*, UBSHS; New York: UBS, 1973.
Nygren, A., *Commentary on Romans*; Philadelphia, PA: Muhlenberg, 1949.
O'Brien, P. T., *The Letter to the Ephesians*, PNTC; Grand Rapids, MI: Eerdmans, 1999.
O'Neill, J. C., *Paul's Letter to the Romans*; Harmondsworth: Penguin, 1975.
Oepke, A., "ἀπώλεια," *TDNT*, 1.396-97.
Oropeza, B. J., "Is the Jew in Romans 2:17 Really a Gentile? Second Thoughts on a Recent Interpretation," *Academia Letters* 444 (2021), https://doi.org/10.20935/AL444.
Oropeza, B. J., *Paul and Apostasy: Eschatology, Perseverance and Falling Away in the Corinthian Congregation*, WUNT, 2.115; Tübingen: Mohr Siebeck, 2000.
Osborne, G. R., *Romans*, IVPNTC; Downer's Grove, Il: InterVarsity Press, 2004.
Oswalt, J. N., *The Book of Isaiah*, NICOT, 2 vols.; Grand Rapids, MI: Eerdmans, [1986] 1998.
Pate, C. M., *Romans*, TTCS; Grand Rapids, MI: Baker, 2013.
Paul, S. M., *Isaiah 40-66: Translation and Commentary*, ECC; Grand Rapids, MI: Eerdmans, 2012.
Peterson, E., "Die Kirche aus Juden und Heiden," in E. Peterson, *Theologische Traktate* Ausgewählte Schriften, 1; Würzburg: Echter, 1994, 141-74.
Phua, M., "Sirach, Book Of," *DOTWPW*, 720-8.
Piper, J., "Are There Two Wills in God?" in T. R. Schreiner and B. A. Ware (eds.), *Still Sovereign: Contemporary Perspectives on Election, Foreknowledge, and Grace*; Grand Rapids, MI: Baker, 2000, 107-31.
Piper, J., "I Believe in God's Self-Sufficiency: A Response to Thomas McCall," TJ 29/2 (Fall 2008), 227-34.
Piper, J., *Desiring God*, rev. and exp.; Sisters: Multnomah, 2003.
Piper, J., *The Future of Justification: A Response to N.T. Wright*; Wheaton, IL: Crossway, 2007.

Piper, J., *The Justification of God: An Exegetical and Theological Study of Romans 9:1–23*, 2nd ed.; Grand Rapids, MI: Baker, 1993.

Plag, C., *Israels Wege zum Heil: Eine Untersuchung zu Römer 9 bis 11*; Stuttgart: Calwer, 1969.

Plumptre, E. H., "The Potter and the Clay: Jer. xviii. 1-10; Rom. ix. 19-24," *Expos* 1.4 (1876), 469–80.

Radermakers, J., and J.-P. Sonnet, "Israël et l'Eglise," *NRT* 107 (1985), 675–97.

Räisänen, H., "Römer 9-11: Analyse eines geistigen Ringens," *ANRW* 2.25.4 (1987), 2891–939.

Ralston, T. N., *Elements of Divinity*; Louisville, KY: E. Stevenson, 1851.

Reasoner, V., *A Fundamental Wesleyan Commentary on Romans*; Evansville, IN: FWB, 2002.

Reichert, A., *Der Römerbrief als Gratwanderung: Eine Untersuchung zur Abfassungsproblematik*, FRLANT, 194; Göttingen: Vandenhoeck & Ruprecht, 2001.

Rendtorff, R., *The Problem of the Process of Transmission in the Pentateuch*, trans. J. J. Scullion; Sheffield, UK: JSOT, 1977.

Rijksbaron, A., *The Syntax and the Semantics of the Verb in Classical Greek: An Introduction*, 3rd ed.; Chicago: University of Chicago, 2002.

Robertson, A. T., *A Grammar of the Greek New Testament in the Light of Historical Research*, 3rd ed.; London: Hodder & Stoughton, 1919.

Robertson, A. T., *Word Pictures in the New Testament*; Nashville, TN: Broadman, [1932–3] 1960, https://www.studylight.org/commentaries/eng/rwp.html.

Rodríguez, R., *If You Call Yourself a Jew: Reappraising Paul's Letter to the Romans*, Eugene, OR: Cascade, 2014.

Ryken, P. G., *Jeremiah and Lamentations: From Sorrow to Hope*, Preaching the Word; Wheaton, IL: Crossway, 2001.

Sanday, W., and A. C. Headlam, *A Critical and Exegetical Commentary on the Epistle to the Romans*, 10th ed., ICC; New York: Charles Scribner's, 1905.

Schlier, H., *Der Römerbrief*, HTKNT; Freiburg: Herder, 1977.

Schmithals, W., *Der Römerbrief: Ein Kommentar*; Gütersloh: Gütersloher, 1988.

Schmitt, R., *Gottesgerechtigkeit-Heilsgeschichte-Israel in der Theologie des Paulus*; Frankfurt: Lang, 1984.

Schreiner, T. R., "Corporate and Individual Election in Romans 9: A Response to Brian Abasciano," *JETS* 49/2 (June 2006), 373–86.

Schreiner, T. R., "Does Romans 9 Teach Individual Election unto Salvation? Some Exegetical and Theological Reflections," *JETS* 36 (1993), 25–40.

Schreiner, T. R., "Review of Brian J. Abasciano, *Paul's Use of the Old Testament in Romans 9.10–18: An Intertextual and Theological Exegesis*," *Themelios* 38.3 (November 2013), 450–3.

Schreiner, T. R., *Galatians*, ZECNT; Grand Rapids, MI: Zondervan, 2010.

Schreiner, T. R., *Romans*, 2nd ed., BECNT, 6; Grand Rapids, MI: Baker, 2018, ProQuest Ebook Central.

Schrenk, G., "βούλημα," *TDNT*, 1.636-37.

Seifrid, M. A., "Romans," in Beale and Carson (eds.), *Commentary*, 607–94.

Seybold, K., "הָפַךְ," *TDOT*, 3.423-27.

Sharp, C. J., *Irony and Meaning in the Hebrew Bible*, ISBL; Bloomington: Indiana University, 2009.

Shellrude, G., "The Freedom of God in Mercy and Judgment: A Libertarian Reading of Romans 9:6-29," *EQ* 81.4 (2009), 306–18.

Sherwood, A., "Paul's Use of the Old Testament in Romans 9:6-29: God's Judgment upon Israel's Idolatry," MCS thesis, Regent College, 2007.
Sherwood, A., *Romans: A Structural, Thematic, and Exegetical Commentary*; Bellingham: Lexham, 2020.
Sherwood, A., *The Word of God Has Not Failed: Paul's Use of the Old Testament in Romans 9*, SSBL; Bellingham: Lexham, 2015, ProQuest Ebook Central.
Shum, S.-L., *Paul's Use of Isaiah in Romans: A Comparative Study of Paul's Letter to the Romans and the Sybilline and Qumran Sectarian Texts*, WUNT, 2.156; Tübingen: Mohr Siebeck, 2002.
Siegert, F., *Argumentation bei Paulus: gezeigt an Röm 9-11*, WUNT 34; Tübingen: Mohr Siebeck, 1985.
Silva, Moisés, *Biblical Words and Their Meaning: An Introduction to Lexical Semantics*, rev. and exp., Grand Rapids, MI: Zondervan Academic, 2010.
Skehan, P. W., and A. A. Di Lella, *The Wisdom of Ben Sira*, AB, 39; New York: Doubleday, 1987.
Smith, G. V., *Isaiah*, NAC, 15A-B, 2 vols.; Nashville, TN: B&H, [2007] 2009.
Smith, R. L., *Micah–Malachi*, WBC, 32; Waco, TX: Word, 1984.
Smyth, H. W., *Greek Grammar for Colleges*; New York: American Book, 1920.
Snaith, J. G., *Ecclesiasticus*, CBCNEB; Cambridge: Cambridge University Press, 1974.
Stählin, G., "The Wrath of Man and the Wrath of God in the NT," *TDNT*, 5.419-47.
Stanley, C. D. "Paul's 'Use' of Scripture: Why the Audience Matters," in S. E. Porter and C. D. Stanley (eds.), *As It Is Written: Studying Paul's Use of Scripture*, SBLSymS, 50; Atlanta, GA: SBL, 2008, 125-55.
Stanley, C. D. "The Social Environment of 'Free' Biblical Quotations in the New Testament," in C. A. Evans and J. A. Sanders, *Early Christian Interpretation of the Scriptures of Israel: Investigations and Proposals*, JSNTSup, 148, SSEJC, 5; Sheffield: SAP, 1997, 18-27.
Sterling, G. E., "Different Traditions or Emphases? The Image of God in Philo's *De Opificio Mundi*," in G. A. Anderson, R. A. Clements, and D. Satran (eds.), *New Approaches to the Study of Biblical Interpretation in Judaism of the Second Temple Period and in Early Christianity*, STDJ, 106; Leiden: Brill, 2013, 41-56.
Stott, J. R. W., *The Message of Romans: God's Good News for the World*, BST, 106; Downers Grove, IL: IVP, 1994.
Strauss, J. D., "God's Promise and Universal History: The Theology of Romans 9," in C. H. Pinnock (ed.), *Grace Unlimited*; Minneapolis, MN: Bethany, 1975, 190-208.
Stuhlmacher, P., *Paul's Letter to the Romans: A Commentary*, trans. S. J. Hafemann; Louisville, KY: Westminster John Knox, 1994.
Sweeney, M. A., *Isaiah 1–39 with an Introduction to Prophetic Literature*, FOTL, 16; Grand Rapids, MI: Eerdmans, 1996.
Theobald, M., "Kirche und Israel nach Röm 9-11," *Kairos* 29 (1987), 1-22.
Theobald, M., *Die Römerbrief*, Erträge der Forschung, 294; Darmstadt: Wissenschaftliche Buchgesellschaft, 2000.
Thielman, F. S., "Ephesians," in Beale and Carson (eds.), *Commentary*, 813-33.
Thompson, J. A., *The Book of Jeremiah*, NICOT; Grand Rapids, MI: Eerdmans, 1980.
Thornhill, A. C., "To the Jew First: A Socio-historical and Biblical-Theological Analysis of the Pauline Teaching of 'Election' in Light of Second Temple Jewish Patterns of Thought," PhD thesis, Liberty University, 2013.
Thornhill, A. C., *The Chosen People: Election, Paul, and Second Temple Judaism*; Downers Grove, IL: IVP, 2015.

Thorsteinsson, R. M., *Paul's Interlocutor in Romans 2: Function and Identity in the Context of Ancient Epistolography*, ConBNT, 40; Stockholm: Almqvist & Wiksell, 2003.
Timpe. K., *Free Will: Sourcehood and Its Alternatives*, 2nd ed.; London: Bloomsbury, 2013.
Tobin, T. H., *Paul's Rhetoric in Its Contexts: The Argument of Romans*; Peabody, MA: Hendrickson, 2004.
Toffelmire, C. M., "Form Criticism," DOTP, 257–71.
Towner, P. H., *The Letters to Timothy and Titus*, NICNT; Grand Rapids, MI: Eerdmans, 2006.
Verhoef, P. A., *The Books of Haggai and Malachi*, NICOT; Grand Rapids, MI: Eerdmans, 1987.
Waaler, E., "Book Review: *Paul's Use of the Old Testament in Romans 9.10-18: An Intertextual and Theological Analysis*," BTB 44.2 (2014), 115–16.
Wagner, J. R., *Heralds of the Good News: Isaiah and Paul "in Concert" in the Letter to the Romans*, NovTSup, 101; Leiden: Brill, 2002.
Wagner, J. R., "'Who Has Believed Our Message?': Paul and Isaiah 'in Concert' in the Letter to the Romans," PhD thesis, Duke University, 1999.
Wallace, D. B., *Greek Grammar beyond the Basics: An Exegetical Syntax of the New Testament*; Grand Rapids, MI: Zondervan, 1996.
Wallace, D. R., *Election of the Lesser Son: Paul's Lament-Midrash in Romans 9–11*; Minneapolis, MN: Fortress, 2014.
Waltke, B. K., and M. O'Connor, *An Introduction to Biblical Hebrew Syntax*; Winona Lake, IN: Eisenbrauns, 1990.
Watts, J. D. W., *Isaiah*, WBC, 24–25, 2 vols.; Waco, TX: Word, [1985] 1987.
Watts, R. E., "Consolation or Confrontation? Isaiah 40–55 and the Delay of the New Exodus," TynBul 41.1 (1990), 31–59.
Weber, C. P., "הוֹי," TWOT, 1.212.
Weiser, A., *The Psalms: A Commentary*, trans. H. Hartwell, OTL; Philadelphia, PA: Westminster, 1962.
Wenham, G. J., *Genesis 16–50*, WBC, 2; Dallas: Word, 1994.
Westermann, C., *Isaiah 40–66: A Commentary*, trans. D. M. G. Stalker; London: SCM, 1969.
Whedon, D. D., *The Freedom of the Will as a Basis of Human Responsibility and a Divine Government*; New York: Carlton and Lanahan, 1864.
Whitley, C. F., "Deutero-Isaiah's Interpretation of Ṣedeq," VT 22.4 (1972), 469–75.
Whybray, R. N., *Isaiah 40–66*, NCBC; London: Marshall, Morgan & Scott, 1975.
Wildberger, H., *A Continental Commentary: Isaiah 28–39*, trans. T. H. Trapp; Minneapolis, MN: Fortress, 2002.
Williams, R. J., *Hebrew Syntax: An Outline*, 2nd ed.; Toronto: University of Toronto, 1976.
Williamson, H. G. M., "Isaiah: Book of," DOTP, 364–78.
Wintermute, O. S., "Jubilees: A New Translation and Introduction," OTP, 2.35–142.
Witherington III, B., with D. Hyatt, *Paul's Letter to the Romans: A Socio-rhetorical Commentary*; Grand Rapids, MI: Eerdmans, 2004.
Wong, G. C. I., "Make Their Ears Dull: Irony in Isaiah 6:9-10," TTJ 16 (2008), 24–34.
Wright, C. J. H., *The Message of Jeremiah*, SBT; Downers Grove, IL: IVP, 2014.
Wright, N. T., "Romans and the Theology of Paul," in D. M. Hay and E. E. Johnson (eds.), *Pauline Theology III: Romans*; Minneapolis, MN: Fortress, 1995, 30–67.
Wright, N. T., "Romans," in L. E. Keck (ed.), *The New Interpreter's Bible*, X, NIB, 10; Nashville, TN: Abingdon, 2002, 393–770.

Wright, N. T., *The Climax of the Covenant: Christ and the Law in Pauline Theology*; Edinburgh: T&T Clark, 1991.
Wright, N. T., *What Saint Paul Really Said: Was Paul of Tarsus the Real Founder of Christianity?*; Grand Rapids, MI: Eerdmans, 1997.
Young, E. J., *The Book of Isaiah*, 3 vols.; Grand Rapids, MI: Eerdmans, 1965–72.
Ziesler, J., *Paul's Letter to the Romans*, TPINTC; Philadelphia, PA: TPI, 1989.

Index of References

OLD TESTAMENT

Genesis
1:2	66
3	39
4:25	12
5:1	65
7:4	124
12:1	42
12:12	124
13:16	12
15:3	12
15:5	12
15:6	164
17:5	13
17:19	12
17:19-21	12
18:10	11, 75, 185
18:14	11, 75, 185
19:16	29
21:12	11–15, 20, 75, 185
21:12b	11–12, 15
21:12-13	12
22:18	42
25	75, 185
25:19-34	10
25:23	10, 15–17, 76, 185
35:10	13

Exodus
1–15	10
6:6	124
9:16	10, 77–8, 123–4, 127, 131, 136, 140, 143, 178, 186
15:7	124
20:12	38
21:15	38
21:17	38
32–34	78, 143
32:32	20, 74, 107
33:18-19	143
33:19	8, 124
33:19b	76, 186
34:5-7	8
34:6-7	8

Leviticus
26:37	85

Numbers
20:9	34

Deuteronomy
3:13	13
7:24	85
9:2	85
9:4-5	19
11:25	85
22:6	13

Joshua
1:5	85
7:13	85
23:9	85

Judges
2:14	85
9:15	27

1 Samuel
14:12	126

2 Samuel
7:21	126

1 Kings
5:3	27
8:53	126

2 Kings
14:9	27
19:23	27

2 Chronicles

20:6	85
20:12	85

Job

9:12	84, 91
9:19	84
10:8-9	23
10:9	84
30:19	84
33:6	84
33:9-10	84
35:2	84, 90
38:2-3	84
38:3	84
40:1-2	84
40:2	84
40:3-5	84
40:4b-5	84
41:2-3	85
42:1-6	84
42:6	84

Psalms

2:9	57
29:5	27
37:35	27
68:18	3
72:8-11	42
76:7	85
77:14	126
90:12	126
92:13	27
98:2	126
104:16	27
106:8	126
115:1 (LXX)	3–4
115:2 (LXX)	4
116:10	3
119:60	29

Proverbs

22:29	66

Isaiah

1–39	36
1:2-4	38
1:21-31	33
1:27-28	33
2:13	28
3	31–2
3:1-4	31
3:9	85, 133
6:9-10	30
6:10	30
7	24
7–39	35
8:5-8	35
9	31–2
9:1-6	35
9:2-7 (Eng.)	35
9:14-16	31
10:5-34	27–8
10:19	28
10:25	27
10:33-34	28
10:34	28
13–39	24
14:7	13
14:8	28
14:20	13–14
22:11	98
27:11	98
28–32	24
28–33	23–4, 33, 92–3, 173
28–35	24, 26
28–39	24, 34
28:1	23
29	31, 39, 102
29:1	23
29:1-8	29, 32
29:1-14	28
29:5-7	32
29:9	28–30
29:9-14	28, 32, 65
29:10	30–1, 91, 94
29:10-12	32
29:11	32
29:11-12	32
29:13	30, 32
29:14	32, 97
29:15	23, 25–7, 32–4, 48, 65–6
29:15-16	23–5, 34, 37
29:15-24	23–4, 34, 37, 40, 92
29:16	22–3, 25–7, 34, 48, 51, 58, 62–7, 69–74, 91–4, 96–9, 101, 106–10, 171–5, 177
29:16b	72

29:16c	107	45:11	39, 42
29:16e	107	45:11-13	36
29:17	27-8, 35, 65	45:11b	39
29:17-18	65	45:12	40, 43, 97
29:17-21	25, 27, 35	45:12-13	39-40, 43
29:17-24	25, 35	45:13	40
29:18	28-9, 32-5	45:14	36, 65
29:18-19	33	45:14-25	42
29:18-21	28, 32-3, 35	45:18	98
29:19	33-5	45:20-25	36
29:20-21	33-5	56:7	13-14
29:22	33	60:13	27-8
29:22-24	25, 33	64:8	23, 64, 106, 189
29:23	34		
29:23-24	34	*Jeremiah*	
29:24	33-4	1	43
30:1	23	1-24	43
30:1-5	35	1-25	43
30:9	38	2-24	43
30:9-33	35	2:17	133
31:1	23	2:19	133
33	24	2:35	45
33:1	24	4:18	133
33:9	28	5:3	133
34-35	24	5:19	45
35:2	28	6:28	133
36-37	32	9:12-16	45
37:24	28	12:14-17	45
40-48	35-6, 93	16.10-13	45
40-55	35-6, 41	16:16-21	45
40-66	36-7	16:21	126
41:1-44:22	36	17:5-11	45
41:23-47:15	36	18	44, 49, 106, 123, 177, 179
41:25	23	18-20	43
43:1	98	18:1-4	44, 48
44:2	98	18:1-6	105
45	42, 99, 106	18:1-12	43-4, 48, 101-2, 113, 175
45:1	40	18:4a	44
45:6	37, 42, 93	18:4b	44
45:9	22-3, 35, 38, 42-3, 48, 51, 58, 62-5, 67, 69-73, 91-9, 101, 106-10, 171-5	18:5-11	108-9
		18:5-12	44, 48
		18:6	22-3, 43, 45, 48, 51, 53-5, 64-7, 69-73, 91-2, 94, 100-3, 105-10, 116, 171-2, 175-7
45:9-10	36-40		
45:9-11	43		
45:9-13	35-6, 42, 93, 96, 174		
45:9a	37-8	18:6a	44, 48, 72
45:9b	37-8	18:6b	44, 48
45:9c	72, 92	18:7	135
45:10	38, 97, 175	18:7-10	45, 110

18:7-11	45, 101	*Malachi*	
18:8	54–5, 135	1:2-3	2, 10, 17, 76, 186
18:9-10	148	1:2-3a	10
18:11	46, 135	1:2-5	10
18:12	46–7	1:2b-3a	17
18:14	27–8	3:15	85
22:6	28		
22:23	28	APOCRYPHA	
25	43		
26–51	43	*Judith*	
27:1-11	45	11:18	85
27:24	85		
31:27-30	45	*1 Maccabees*	
52	43	8:1-4	136
		8:4	136
Ezekiel			
17:3	27	*2 Maccabees*	
18:23	103, 123, 138	6:12-14	136
18:30-32	123		
18:31-32	138	*Sirach*	
18:33	103	15:11-20	52–3
31	28	27:5	51
33:11	123, 139	33:7-13	107
		33:7-15	51
Daniel		33:10-13	53, 107
2:22	66	33:10-15	53
10:13	85	33:11	53
		33:11-13	52
Hosea		33:12	52–3
2:25	166	33:12cd	52
14:1	85	33:13	51–4, 107
		33:14-15	53
Amos		38:29-30	51
8:11-12	31	46:7	85
		49:19	147
Obadiah			
1:7		*Wisdom of Solomon*	
		9:8	147
Micah		11:3	85
2:7-8	85	11:23	106
3:5-7	31	12	107
		12:3-22	106
Nahum		12:12	84, 107
1:4	28	15	59
		15:1-13	60
Zechariah		15:7	59–62, 67, 71–3, 106–8
11:1-3	28	15:8	60–1
		15:11	60
		15:17	60

Index of References

NEW TESTAMENT

Matthew
22:14	159

Mark
8:38	116

Luke
6:40	131
7:30	85
9:26	116

John
12:47-49	55
17:22	144

Acts
10:1-28	156
10:28	156
14:17	139
17:26f	139
22	155

Romans
1-8	74
1:1	148
1:1-6	150
1:6-7	146, 148
1:16	78, 126, 146
1:16-17	148
1:16-4:25	83
1:18	127, 129
1:18-23	139
2	83
2-3	80-1
2:1-29	6
2:1-3:20	80
2:4	123, 125, 132, 136, 139-40, 142-3
2:4-5	132, 139, 144, 179
2:5	125, 127, 132-3, 135
2:5-6	148
2:5-16	129
2:7	115, 125, 143-4
2:7-10	115, 144
2:8	125, 127
2:10	115, 125, 143-4
2:15	139
2:16	147
2:17	83
2:17-29	81
3	82, 88, 172
3-4	138, 146, 148
3:1-2	81
3:1-4	80
3:1-8	6, 80, 90, 172
3:3	81
3:4	82
3:4-5	81
3:4-7	81
3:5	80-2, 89, 127, 172
3:5-6	82
3:6	80, 82, 129
3:7	80-2, 89, 172
3:8	82
3:9-20	6
3:21-22	146, 159
3:23	143
3:24	146, 149
3:28	159
4	146, 150, 164
4:9-25	150
4:13-25	146
4:15	127
4:16-17	163
4:16-18	146
4:17	148
4:19-22	164
4:25	150
5:1	148, 159
5:1-2	146
5:2	125, 143
5:5	146
5:9	125, 127, 129
5:9-10	146
5:10-11	146
5:21	146
6	82, 148
6:5	146
6:11	146, 149
6:11-23	148
6:13	146
6:17	148
6:22-23	146
6:23	146, 149
8	74-5, 146, 148, 150
8:1	146, 149

8:1-2	149	9:6	20-1, 81, 168, 180
8:13	148	9:6-8	126, 157
8:13-14	148	9:6-9	115, 150, 157
8:14	139	9:6-13	94, 146, 167, 174, 183
8:14-23	146	9:6-15	81
8:15-23	146	9:6-16	146
8:17	143, 146, 150	9:6-18	6-7
8:18	125, 143	9:6-24	117
8:21	125	9:6-29	62, 73, 181, 183
8:24	146	9:6a	75, 78, 169, 185, 187-9
8:26-27	148	9:6b	163-4, 185
8:28	146, 148	9:6b-7	75, 185
8:29	148, 150, 165	9:6b-9	75, 185
8:29-30	148, 156, 158	9:6b-29	169, 183-4
8:30	5, 143-4, 146, 148, 156, 159, 165-6	9:7	14, 75, 148, 158, 160, 164-7, 180, 185
8:39	149	9:7-8	163-4
9	1, 3, 6-8, 11, 20-2, 56, 58, 60, 62, 65-6, 71, 77, 80-1, 83, 85, 87-8, 90-1, 93-5, 98, 100, 102, 105, 109-17, 120, 126, 139-40, 143-4, 155, 157, 160-2, 165, 167-9, 171-3, 177, 180-3, 185, 187, 189	9:7-9	11, 94, 102
		9:7a	75
		9:7b	11, 15, 75, 185
		9:8	7, 75-6, 78, 126, 160-2, 164, 169, 185-8
		9:8-9	146
		9:9	75. 164, 185
		9:10-13	5, 15, 17, 75-6, 185-6, 188
9-11	23, 54, 66, 69, 71, 74-5, 80, 83, 93-5, 100, 102, 105-7, 109, 114-15, 117, 142, 146, 155, 176-7, 180-2, 185, 188-9	9:10-18	1-2, 5, 8-11, 17, 20-1, 64, 74, 78-81, 83, 94-6, 102, 113, 117, 123, 126, 133-4, 140, 143-4, 155, 162-3, 168, 171, 182, 188-9
		9:11	6, 163, 188-9
9-16	80	9:11-12	163
9:1	149	9:11c-12b	75-6, 78, 186-7
9:1-3	74, 115	9:12	76, 94, 148, 158, 167, 174, 180, 182
9:1-5	74-5, 185, 187		
9:1-9	1, 3, 8, 20-1, 23, 30, 53, 62, 64, 70, 74, 80, 85, 95, 107, 113, 117, 124, 143-4, 148, 150, 156, 158, 160-2, 164, 181, 188-9	9:12-13	94, 102
		9:13	17, 94, 102, 126
		9:14	76, 78, 80, 169, 172, 186-7
		9:14-18	76-9, 83-4, 89, 125, 169, 186-7
9:1-13	11, 20, 81	9:14-23	140, 167
9:1-18	74, 85, 114, 185, 188	9:14-29	103
9:1-24	171, 181-3, 185	9:15	76, 87, 94, 102, 124, 143, 186, 189
9:1-29	80, 182-4		
9:1-11:36	83	9:15-16	76-7, 81, 146
9:3	20, 74, 85, 94, 102, 107	9:15-17	78, 186
9:3-5	81	9:15-18	78, 172
9:3-9	126	9:16	6, 76, 81
9:4	146		
9:4-5	74, 143		

Index of References

9:17	77, 86-7, 123-4, 126-7, 131, 136, 140, 143, 173, 178, 186	9:22-24	117-19, 124, 153, 169, 178, 187
		9:22-26	165
9:17-18	77, 79-81, 85, 94, 102, 143, 172, 178, 186	9:23	1, 104, 115, 118, 121-5, 128, 131-3, 135-7, 141-2, 145-50, 153-7, 165, 167, 179-80
9:18	2, 78, 81, 87, 94-5, 102, 112, 120-1, 123, 131-2, 134, 140, 172, 176, 186-7	9:23-24	118, 156
9:19	74, 78-84, 86-7, 89-91, 107, 116, 120, 169, 172-3, 178, 187	9:23-26	94, 102
		9:23b	143
		9:24	1, 5, 21-2, 118-20, 148, 153-8, 165-9, 171, 180-2, 187-8
9:19-20	107		
9:19-21	84, 106-7, 111		
9:19-24	1, 21-2, 69, 74, 87, 90, 169, 171-3, 185-7	9:24-26	167, 180
		9:24ff.	155
9:19-29	23, 78, 169, 187-9	9:24-29	167, 182-3
9:19a	87-8	9:24-33	150
9:19b	79, 84, 87-8	9:25	118, 153, 166-7
9:19b-21	171	9:25-26	146, 148, 158, 160, 165-7, 181
9:20	62, 70-1, 73, 84, 91-2, 96, 98-9, 102, 107, 109-10, 171, 173, 175, 178, 187	9:25-29	141, 168-9, 181, 187
		9:25-33	181
9:20-21	23, 51, 53-4, 62, 65, 69-71, 74, 80, 82, 89, 91, 93-4, 96, 98, 101-3, 106-9, 113, 115-17, 119-20, 135, 169, 171-4, 176-8	9:26	146
		9:27-29	157, 181, 187
		9:28	94, 102, 146
		9:29	169, 178, 187
		9:30	94, 102, 118, 181-4
9:20a	89-91, 120, 169, 173, 187, 189	9:30-31	183-4
		9:30ff.	177
9:20b	61, 70, 96, 100, 108, 172	9:30-33	7, 146, 181-4, 188
9:20b-c	92, 96, 100, 174-5	9:30-10:21	105, 176
9:20b-21	54, 61, 70, 72, 91, 169, 187	9:30b-33	182
9:20b-24	169, 187	9:31	182
9:20b-29	169, 187	9:31-32	182
9:20c	92, 96	9:31-33	94, 102
9:21	59-62, 71-3, 91-2, 94, 100-2, 104-5, 107-8, 110-11, 113-16, 119-20, 125, 127, 129, 135, 137-8, 145, 148, 171-2, 175-9	9:32	94, 109, 174, 184
		9:32-33	184
		9:33	94, 102, 115-16
		10	83, 146, 181
		10:1	116, 146, 181
9:21-24	85	10:1-4	181
9:22	94, 102, 115, 118-23, 125-9, 131-6, 141-2, 145-8, 153, 178-9	10:1-21	181, 183
		10:3	94, 174
		10:8-13	146
9:22-23	113, 115, 118-19, 123-5, 128, 132, 134-5, 137, 139-44, 149-51, 153-5, 179-80	10:9-13	94, 102
		10:11	115-16
		11	94, 102-3, 145-6, 176
9:22ff.	119	11:1-6	157
		11:2	148

11:4-7	94, 102	12:2	139
11:5	146	12:28	154
11:7	95	13:11	146
11:7-10	94, 102	14:36-38	90
11:8	91, 94	15:1-2	148
11:11	144, 146	15:18	125
11:12	142, 144	15:41	125
11:13-14	78		
11:15	146	*2 Corinthians*	
11:15-24	157	2:15	125
11:17-24	146	3:18	144, 148
11:19-20	94, 102	4:3	125
11:20-22	94, 102	4:13	3
11:20-23	148	4:16-17	148
11:22	146	4:16-18	148
11:22-23	94, 102	4:17	125
11:25	95	5:10	148
11:30-31	2	5:21	149
11:32	136	9:5	131
11:33	142	13	90
12:1-2	148		
12:5	149	*Galatians*	
12:19	127	1–2	90
13:2	85	1:6-9	148
13:4-5	127	2:17	149
15:3-5	148	3:26-29	162
15:5	148	5:1-4	148
15:17	149	5:16-26	148
16:3	149	5:18	139
16:7	149		
16:9-10	149	*Ephesians*	
16:25-27	150	1:4	144, 150
		1:4-5	148
1 Corinthians		1:5	144
1:8	148	1:7	142, 144
1:10	131	1:15	165
1:18	125	1:18	125, 142
1:19	125	2:1-5	137
1:23-31	5	2:3	136–7
1:26a	5	2:4	137
1:30	149	2:4-7	144
2:7	125	2:6	144
3:5-15	148	2:7	137, 142, 144–5
8:11	125	2:10	137
9:24-27	148	3:8	142
10:1-13	148	3:16	142, 144
10:9	125	4:8	3
10:10	125	4:11-16	148
11:19	104	5:6	125

5:18	148	2:20	104–5, 112
		2:20-21	103–4, 112, 176
Philippians		2:21	103–5
1:6	148	3:6	139
1:9-11	148	4:11	139
1:28	125		
2:12-13	148	*Hebrews*	
2:13	148	2:10	139
3:8-9	149	10:5	131
3:19	125	11:3	131
3:21	125		
4:19	142, 144	*James*	
		4:7	85
Colossians			
1:9-14	148	*1 John*	
1:22-23	148	5:1	88
1:27	125, 142		
2:2	142	PSEUDEPIGRAPHA	
3:4	125		
3:6	125	*4 Ezra*	
		7:72-74	136
1 Thessalonians			
1:10	125	*Joseph and Aseneth*	
2:12	125	8:11	62
2:14-16	155	15:4	62
2:16	129		
3:1-5	148	*Jubilees*	
4:14	139	5:12-13	55
5:9	125	5:15	55
		5:17	55
2 Thessalonians			
1:11-12	148	*Liber Antiquitatum Biblicarum*	
2:3	125	53	63
2:10	125	53:13	62–3, 66
2:14	125		
2:16-17	148	*Life of Adam and Eve*	
		27:2	64
1 Timothy			
6:9	125	*3 Maccabees*	
6:9-10	148	2:6	126
2 Timothy		*Psalms of Solomon*	
1:9	148	17:23	57
1:14	148		
2:10	125	*Sibylline Oracles*	
2:12	148	11:198	62
2:14-18	103, 105		
2:18	105	*Testament of Naphtali*	
2:19	105	2	56

2:2-10	56	18:10-12	58
2:5	56	19:3	57
2:6-8	57	19:6	58
2:9	57	19:7	58
2:9-10	57	19:8	58
		19:10	58
		20:15	58

PHILO
Leg. All.
		20:19-21	58
1:31	63	20:22	58
		20:24-32	57

Migr. Abr.
		20:26-35	59, 66
1:3	63	20:27-28	58
		22:11	57

Op. Mund.
		22:13	58
1:134-135	63	22:18	57
1:134-37	63	23:12	57
1:135	63		

1QIsa^a
45:9	37

Plant.
1:44	63

1QS
11:20	58
11:21-22	58
11:22	57–8, 66

Quaest. in Gen.
1:4	63
2:56	63

4Q386
frg. 1 col. III.1-2 57

Rer. Div. Her.
1:58	63

4Q511
frg. 28	58
frgs. 28-29, line 4	57

Spec. Leg.
3:58	63

TARGUMS

QUMRAN

Pseudo-Jonathan

1QH^a
9:7-8	58
9:10	58

Isaiah
29:10	65
9:19-20	58	29:16	64–5, 67, 109
9:19-26	58	29:16a	64
9:21-23	57	45:9	64–5
9:25-26	58, 66	45:9a	65
11:17	58	45:14	65
11:21-22	58		
11:23-25	57	Jeremiah	
11:34-35	58		
12:28	58	18:6	64
12:29	57	18:6b	64
12:30-31	58	18:12	64
18:3-7	57		

BABYLONIAN TALMUD

Berakot
5:1   66

Sukkah
5:4   66

TALMD YERUSHALMI
Berakot
9:3   66

TOSEFTA
Baba Qamma
7:2   66

MIDRASH

Genesis Rabbah
1:6   66
2:3   66
24:1   65
72:6   66

Exodus Rabbah
14:2   66

Leviticus Rabbah
27:1   65

Numbers Rabbah
1:1   66
2:10   66
9:1   66
9:45   66

Pesiqta de Rab Kahana
9:1   66

Song of Songs Rabbah
1:1   66

EARLY CHRISTIAN WRITINGS

Chrysostom

Homilies on Romans
9:22   130

Origen

Commentary on the Epistle to the Romans
9:21   106–7

Index of Modern Authors

Abasciano, B. J. 1-10, 16-18, 20-1, 23, 30, 53, 62, 64, 70, 78-81, 83, 87, 94-6, 102, 110, 113, 116-17, 123-4, 126, 134-5, 140, 143-4, 148, 150, 155-64, 168, 177, 181-2, 188-9
Achtemeier, P. J. 112, 114
Aletti, J.-N. 80, 181
Alexander, J. A. 29, 31-2
Alexander, R. H. 38
Alexander, T. D. 8, 80
Allen, C. 106
Allen, D. L. 81
Allen, L. C. 4, 43-4, 47, 73
Anderson, A. A. 4
Anderson, G. A. 63
Archer Jr., G. A. xiv, 25, 33, 38, 191, 193, 200
Arndt, W. F. xi, 85, 89-90, 100-1, 111-12, 125, 130-1, 134, 142, 145, 154, 156-7

Balogh, C. 23-5, 27
Balz, H. xii, 142, 196
Baltzer, K. 36, 41
Barrett, C. K. 105-7, 117, 118, 141, 154
Bauer, W. xi, 85, 89-90, 100-1, 111-12, 125, 130-1, 134, 142, 145, 154, 156-7
Baumgartner, W. xii, 25-6, 30, 47
Beale, G. K. 3, 95, 106, 150
Belli, F. 106-7
Bence, C. L. 106-7
Bengel, J. A. 130
Beuken, W. A. M. 23-5, 27-9, 31-4
Bird, M. F. 149-50
Black, M. 107, 139, 147, 154-5
Blass, F. xi, 87, 89, 118, 128-9, 139, 154
Boda, M. J. xii, 43, 73, 191, 200
Boers, H. 182
Botterweck, G. J. xiv, 26, 33, 194, 198
Bray, G. 106
Brenton, L. C. L. 135

Briggs, C. A. xi, 38, 41, 47
Bromiley, G. W. xiv, 86, 101, 118, 130, 133, 193, 197-9, 129
Brooke, G. J. 21
Brown II, A. P. 34
Brown, C. xiii, 86, 197
Brown, F. xi, 38, 41, 47
Brown, M. L. 34
Bruce, F. F. 106
Brueggeman, W. 36-7, 41-2, 46
Büchsel, F. 90
Bullinger, E. W. 29
Bumgardner, C. J. 104
Burnett, G. W. 18-19
Butler, T. C. xii, 29
Byrne, B. 80, 84, 106-7, 112, 130

Calvin, J. 45
Campbell, D. A. 62, 107
Carrol, R. P. 45
Carson, D. A. 3, 87, 106
Chae, D. J.-S. 182
Charles, R. H. 55
Charlesworth, J. H. xiii, 54-7, 62, 64, 195, 200
Childs, B. S. 23-5
Chilton, B. D. 64
Chisholm Jr., R. B. 30
Ciampa, R. E. 88
Clements, R. A. 63
Clements, R. E. 28-9
Coppes, L. J. 33
Corley, J. 52-3
Cottrell, J. 83, 85-6, 98, 106, 111-12, 130
Cowley, A. E. xii, 29, 41
Craigie, P. C. 43-4, 47, 73
Cranfield, C. E. B. 79, 82, 86-91, 106-7, 112, 117-18, 119, 122, 128, 130-2, 139, 141, 147, 153-4, 158, 181

Dahl, N. A. 181
Danker, F. W. xi, 85, 89–90, 100–1, 111–12, 125, 130–1, 134, 142, 145, 154, 156–7
Davies, P. R. 44–5
Debrunner, A. xi, 87, 89, 118, 128–9, 139, 154
deClaissé-Walford, N. 4
Deines, R. 63
Delitzsch, F. 26, 29
Delling, G. 130
Dempster, S. 54
deSilva, D. A. 107
Di Lella, A. A. 52–4
Dodd, C. H. 79, 95
Drinkard Jr., J. F. 43–4, 47, 73
Driver, G. R. 4
Driver, S. R. xi, 38, 41, 47
Du Toit, A. P. 83
Dunn, J. D. G. 83–4, 86, 88, 91, 101, 106–7, 111–15, 118–19, 121–2, 128–9, 131, 133, 141, 143, 147, 153, 155–6
Dunn, R. 152
Durham, J. I. 10

Eaton, J. 4
Edwards, J. 152
Edwards, J. R. 80, 182
Ellingworth, P. 119
Elliott, M. A. 156
Enns, P. xii, 60
Esler, P. 83
Evans, C. A. xi, 3, 64, 193

Fanning, B. F. 87, 130
Fitzmyer, J. A. 80, 88, 91, 112, 118, 130, 154
Foerster, W. 101
Forlines, F. L. 85–6, 106–7, 159
Forster, R. T. 85, 106–7, 111–12
Fredriksen, P. 83
Fretheim, T. E. 43–5
Friberg, B. xi, 84, 120, 125, 130, 142
Friberg, T. xi, 84, 120, 125, 130, 142
Friedrich, G. xiv, 86, 101, 118, 130, 133, 193, 197–9
Fuller, D. 151–2
Funk, R. W. xi, 87, 89, 118, 128–9, 139, 154

García Martínez, F. 57–9
Gaston, L. 141

Gerstenberger, E. 33
Gesenius, W. xii, 29, 41
Gifford, E. H. 113–14
Gingrich, F. W. xi, 85, 89–90, 100–1, 111–12, 125, 130–1, 134, 142, 145, 154, 156–7
Godet, F. 82, 86, 104, 106, 111, 118, 121, 128, 130, 144
Goering, G. S. 61
Goldingay, J. 4, 29, 35–7, 39, 41
Good, E. M. 29–30
Goodrich, J. K. 20
Greathouse, W. M. 80, 107
Grindheim, S. 53

Haacker, K. 80, 182
Hafemann, S. J. 80
Hanson, A. T. 128, 145
Hanson, P. D. 36–7
Harrington, D. J. 62
Harris, R. L. xiv, 25, 33, 38, 191, 193, 200
Hartley, D. E. 30
Hay, D. M. 63, 114
Hays, R. B. 9, 102–3, 105–7, 109–10, 113
Headlam, A. C. 62, 87–8, 107, 112, 119, 128, 130
Hilhorst, A. 23
Hill, A. E. 10
Hillert, S. 182
Hodge, C. 107, 117–18, 128–9, 139
Hoehner, H. 137
Hofmann, J. C. K. von 86
Hoglund, J. 158, 160–7
Holladay, W. L. xi, 26, 47
Holland, T. 80, 106–7, 112
Hollander, H. W. 56
Hollenbach, B. 29–30
Hübner, H. 69
Huey, F. B. 43, 47
Hyatt, D. 106

Jacobson, H. 63
Jacobson, R. A. 4
Jewett, R. 79, 83–92, 101, 107, 112, 121, 128–9, 131, 133, 141, 147, 154–5
Johnson, A. F. 106
Johnson, E. E. 54, 107, 114
Johnson, L. T. 84, 91
Johnson, M. D. 64

Jones, H. S. xii, 90
Jonge, M. de 56
Joüon, P. 34, 41

Kaiser, O. 24-6, 29
Kaminisky, J. S. 17-19
Käsemann, E. 129, 153
Kautzsch, E. xii, 29, 41
Keck, L. E. 54, 80, 107
Kee, H. C. 56, 155-6
Keener, C. S. 80, 106-7
Kelley, P. H. 43-4, 47, 73
Kidner, D. 4
Kim, S. 11-20
Kittel, G. xiv, 86, 101, 118, 130, 133, 193, 197-9
Klappert, B. 106-7, 181
Klawans, J. 52
Knight, G. A. F. 41
Koch, D.-A. 73, 107
Koehler, L. xii, 25-6, 30, 47
Kohl, M. 36
Koole, J. L. 36-7, 39
Kraus, W. 182
Kruse, C. G. 9, 54, 79, 105-7, 113, 130, 139, 154
Kugel, J. L. 56

Laato, A. 36
Labuschagne, C. J. 23
Lambrecht, J. 181-2
Leenhardt, F. J. 106, 112, 130-1
Lemke, S. W. 81
Lenski, R. C. H. 130
Leonard, J. M. 9
Liddell, H. G. xii, 90
Linebaugh, J. A. 60
Longenecker, R. N. 83, 89, 92. 105-6
Longman III, T. xii, 4, 60
Lorenzi, L. de 105
Louw, J. E. xii, 84, 90
Luz, U. 80, 121
Lyonnet, S. 104, 106-7
Lyons, G. 80, 107

Maillot, A. 182
Marshall, I. H. 104, 112
Martin, J. 26
Marston, V. P. 85, 106-7, 111-12

Martinez, F. C. 23
Mayer, B. 107, 117
McCall, T. H. 140, 152
McConville, J. G. xii, 43, 73, 191, 200
McGlynn, M. 60
McNamara, M. 64
Merklein, H. 142
Meyer, P. M. 80
Miller, N. F. xi, 84, 120, 125, 130, 142
Moo, D. J. 73, 79-80, 82-3, 87-9, 91, 94, 106, 111-12, 118-19, 125, 128-30, 137, 139, 141-2, 144, 153-60, 167, 182-4
Moody, D. 106, 112
Morison, J. 83
Morris, L. 86, 91, 98, 107, 112, 117, 122, 128, 130-1, 139, 141, 154
Motyer, J. A. 24, 31, 37, 39, 41-2
Moule, C. F. D. 139
Mounce, R. H. 106, 130
Mounce, W. D. 104, 112
Moyise, S. 1-3, 9-10, 20
Müller, C. 117
Müller, D. 86
Müller, K. 130
Munck, J. 80, 106, 112-13, 128, 145
Muraoka, T. 34, 41
Murray, J. 106, 117-18, 128, 139

Naidoff, B. D. 36
Newman, B. M. 142, 145, 153
Nida, E. A. xii, 84, 90, 142, 145, 153
Niebuhr, K.-W. 63
Nygren, A. 118

O'Brien, P. T. 137
O'Connor, M. 41
Oepke, A. 133
O'Neil, J. C. 106
Oropeza, B. J. 83, 159
Osborne, G. 106-7, 111-12, 139
Oswalt, J. N. 24-30, 34-42, 98, 108

Pate, C. M. 106
Paul, S. M. 36-7, 41-2
Payne, D. 35-7, 39, 41
Peterson, E. 157
Phua, M. 54
Pinnock, C. H. 106

Piper, J. 6, 52–3, 59–61, 79, 82, 85–6, 88, 91, 94, 97, 104–6, 108, 112–14, 116, 118, 122, 124, 129–30, 132–4, 136, 139–41, 143, 149, 151–2, 163
Plag, C. 181
Plumptre, E. H. 106–7
Porter, S. E. xi, 3, 64, 193
Prat, F. 130

Radermakers, J. 182
Räisänen, H. 79–80, 155
Ralston, T. N. 152
Reasoner, V. 106–7
Reichert, A. 181
Rendtorff, R. 12
Richardson, M. E. J. xii, 25–6, 30, 47
Rijksbaron, A. 87, 130–1
Ringgren, H. xiv, 26, 33, 194, 198
Robertson, A. T. 86–7, 129–30
Robinson, H. W. 20
Rodríguez, R. 83, 85
Rosner, B. S. 88
Runia, A. P. 36
Ryken, P. G. 45

Sanday, W. 62, 86–8, 107, 112, 119, 128, 130
Sanders, J. A. 3
Satran, D. 63
Schaff, P. 130
Schlier, H. 153
Schmithals, W. 182
Schmitt, R. 182
Schneider, G. xii, 142, 196
Schreiner, T. R. 5–8, 11, 79–80, 82, 86, 88, 91, 104, 106, 112–13, 115–16, 118, 125, 130, 132–3, 137–8, 140, 151, 154, 157–9, 164–5, 181–4
Schrenk, G. 86
Scott, R. xii, 90
Seifrid, M. A. 106, 130, 166
Seitz, C. R. 36
Seybold, K. 26
Sharp, C. J. 29
Shellrude, G. 112–13, 183
Sherwood, A. 60, 73, 80, 108–9
Shum, S.-L. 23, 69, 91, 106–7
Siegert, F. 181
Silva, M. xiii, 88, 142

Skehan, P. W. 52–4
Skinner, J. 14
Smith. G. V. 24–7, 29, 31–2, 35–9, 41–2, 73
Smith, R. L. 10
Smyth, H. W. 90
Snaith, J. G. 52–3
Sonnet, J.-P. 182
Stählin. G. 118
Stalker, D. M. G. 36
Stanley, C. D. 3–5
Stenschke, C. 80
Sterling, G. E. 63
Stöhr, M. 106
Strauss, J. D. 106, 130
Stuhlmacher, P. 80, 106–7
Sweeney, M. A. 36

Tanner, B. L. 4
Theobald, M. 181
Thielman, F. S. 3
Thiessen, M. 83
Thompson, J. A. 43, 73
Thornhill, A. C. 52–3, 56, 61, 117
Thorsteinsson, R. M. 83
Tigchelaar, E. J. C. 57–9
Timpe, K. 152
Tobin, T. H. 91, 106
Toffelmire, C. M. 44
Towner, P. H. 104
Trapp, T. H. 34

Verhoef, P. A. 10

Waaler, E. 8–11
Wagner, J. R. 23, 52–3, 57–8, 61, 64–5, 69, 73, 80, 84, 92, 106–7, 172
Wallace, D. B. 15, 87, 90, 128–31, 134, 139, 142, 144, 154
Wallace, D. R. 80, 105–7
Waltke, B. K. xiv, 25, 33, 38, 41, 191, 193, 200
Ware, B. A. 140
Watts, J. D. W. 24
Watts, R. E. 36
Weber, C. P. 25
Weiser, A. 4
Wenham, G. J. 10, 12
Westermann, C. 36–7
Whedon, D. D. 152

Whitley, C. F. 41
Whybray, R. N. 36–7, 41
Wildberger, H. 34
Wilk, F. 80
Williams, R. J. 13–14
Williamson, H. G. M. 73
Wilson, J. L. 29
Wintermute, O. S. 55
Witherington III, B. 106–7, 113, 136, 139, 148
Wong, G. C. I. 29–30
Woude, A. S. van der 23

Wright, C. J. H. 43–4, 46
Wright, N. T. 80, 114, 123, 128, 130, 161–2
Wright, R. B. 57

Xeravits, G. G. 61

Young, E. J. 27, 29, 31–2, 37, 39–41, 98

Zerwick, M. 87
Zetterholm, M. 83
Ziesler, J. 106–7, 182
Zsengellér, J. 61

www.ingramcontent.com/pod-product-compliance
Lightning Source LLC
Chambersburg PA
CBHW062219300426
44115CB00012BA/2132